Strategic Styles

Strategic Styles
Coping in the Inner City

Janet K. Mancini

Foreword by George W. Goethals

University Press of New England

Hanover, New Hampshire and London, England
1980

University Press of New England

Sponsoring Institutions:
Brandeis University
Clark University
Dartmouth College
University of New Hampshire
University of Rhode Island
Tufts University
University of Vermont

Library of Congress Catalog Card Number 79-56773
International Standard Book Number 0-87451-179-8
Printed in the United States of America
Library of Congress Cataloging in Publication data
will be found on the last printed page of this book.

For my children,
Mark and Kyra

Contents

Foreword

In writing this foreword, let me provide some background so that Janet Mancini's work can be placed not only in the general human context—as I'm sure she would want it to be—but also in the context of the social sciences.

The study of lives, broadly construed, goes back to ancient times. The crisp writings of Plutarch, Suetonius, and other scholars of the golden ages of Greece and Rome attest to the human interest in the unfolding of individual lives. The *Confessions* of Saint Augustine and of Jean Jacques Rousseau show the power that autobiography can bring to the same subject. I am emphasizing that this book comes out of a tradition that has a long past, but it is to be found within a framework that has a short history: that is, the attempt, using case materials or the study of individual lives, to illuminate general trends in personality. Probably the classic in this domain is Burton and Harris's *Clinical Studies of the Personality*. Probably the most masterful in terms of scholarly precision is Robert White's several editions of *Lives in Progress*. I myself, on a more limited scale, have tried to use case materials to explore key issues in the development of the adolescent. I am speaking here of my own work, *Experiencing Youth*, which obviously owes a debt to Robert White, since it was dedicated to him.

Mancini's work thus stands in two traditions, human interest and behavior science. She has presented us with a number of individuals who are unusual, and in being unusual, mark her book—in my estimation—as important and different from the other works I have cited. Without in any way demeaning previous research, the author of this book has worked with a long-neglected segment of society, namely inner-city youth, who form a subculture—and an important one—in our society at large. Each case that she presents fulfills the criterion of what a good case should be: that is, a personification of a particular style of character which goes beyond idiosyncratic boundaries. Thus each of her cases is about an individual, but that person in turn represents something on a larger scale.

Mancini's book, however, takes another major step forward from the works I have mentioned previously. She devotes a great deal of her thinking to the *context* in which these interpersonal orientations develop, as well as to the interpersonal orientations themselves. Her study is therefore a remarkable blend of interdisciplinary thinking, drawing from the best there is in clinical observation and sociological analysis. She has written, and written well, about a most interesting and significant part of our population—one that will be a critical factor in our future—and about a lifestyle of which all too few of us are informed. I believe this book gives not just what any good book should, a step forward in our knowledge and orientation as social scientists; the author's careful methodological treatment serves also as a guide for future research.

George W. Goethals

Cambridge, Mass.
October, 1980

What social science is properly about
is the human variety,
which consists of all the social worlds
in which men have lived,
are living, and might live.
   — C. WRIGHT MILLS

Preface

Heidegger once said that meditative thinking is in need of more care than any other craft. The need is particularly great when the thinking is about human lives.

The five case studies that form the heart of this book represent one person's attempt to make theoretical sense out of the day-to-day lives of five young boys, and ultimately those of their families. When first interviewed, the boys were growing up in the Roxbury of the late 1960's amid racial and political confusion and crushing poverty. Undoubtedly many different types of analysis could be applied to the study of their lives. Portraits could be drawn from other interpretive palettes. No one could ever do their lives justice, however, or completely tap the richness and complexity of their unique realities. It is for this reason that I have relied as much as possible on their own words to tell their fascinating stories.

In order to focus conceptually on the interpersonal orientations—"strategic styles"—created by each boy to cope with his social world, I have deliberately ignored other types of analysis. As Allport has warned us, we must not "forget what we have chosen to ignore." The political and social class pressures on the lives of those who participated in our study remain critical issues, as does the impact of growing up black in a society that even a decade later persists in engaging in a multiplicity of racist and discriminatory practices.

My emphasis is on the interpersonal world of the five boys. I have attempted perhaps an unforgiving task: trying to find patterns (styles) of interaction among individuals whose complexity threatens always to defy categorization. People are not easy to understand. It is perilous to pigeonhole them, and the danger lies in losing sight of the integrity of each person *as* a person. It is nonetheless as compelling a truth that those who work with adolescents and their families eventually find themselves noticing patterns and types of behavior among the ways in which real people think, feel, act. I have found it useful to speak of such patterns in terms of each boy's strategic style, his distinctive ways of coping with his social environment. It must be emphasized that this is not the only way to view the boys; there is much more to say about them which must remain outside the scope of this book.

Harry Stack Sullivan believed that in spite of individual differences, people are really much more similar than different from one another. He was drawing our attention to the fundamental humanity in which we all participate, regardless of social station, personality, sex, race, beliefs, and so on. In writing these portraits I hope to accomplish two things: to show first that sharing the same social environment with others does not wipe out individual differences; and to show how from those differences we can discern patterns of social interaction that are shared by others in different contexts. We are each of us unique, down to our voices and our fingerprints; we are each of us products of human interaction and therefore in important ways the same.

There is another sense in which care of meditative thinking can be interpreted. As virtually anyone who has written a book must realize, it is in no way written alone. A book, too, is the product of a social context. To write acknowledgments after a ten-year incubation period of research and writing is no easy task. For offering me the opportunity to work in an exciting research project, I am indebted to the Harvard University program, Pathways to Identity (funded by the Office of Education and the Ford Foundation), and especially to Robert A. Rosenthal, whose assistance in formulating the concept of strategic styles was invaluable, and who later served as a critical and insightful outside reader for the dissertation version; and to Bernard E. Bruce, who read with sensitivity much of the original draft.

For creating an atmosphere in which both mind and spirit can grow, I am continually grateful to the Department of Sociology at Brandeis, especially to professors Kurt H. Wolff, Gordon A. Fellman, Morris S. Schwartz, and Irving K. Zola. The first three served as my dissertation committee, making the process humane and the product immeasurably better. Its strengths derive largely from their challenging supervision; its weaknesses, of course, are mine.

I am deeply appreciative of the conscientious typing skills of Mrs. Gerry Ingegneri of Rhode Island College, who prepared the manuscript through several revisions. Her dedication to the project has matched my own. I wish to thank also the Department of Sociology at RIC for facilitating a manageable teaching schedule for me at various phases in the book's career, as well as the staff at Adams Library and the RIC Audiovisual Department for their unrelenting assistance.

David Horne, formerly Director and Editor of the University Press of New England, has been both supportive and constructive in his efforts to bring the manuscript into the light of day. I am deeply grateful to him for his assistance.

The greatest debt is to my children and my friends, whose love and support have sustained me beyond measure. This book is dedicated to them, to my parents, Clifford and Kathleen Ramey, and to Kurt Wolff.

J.K.M.

Providence, R.I.
February, 1980

Strategic Styles

[It is in families] that children
are born and brought to adulthood;
that women and men love and hate;
that major interpersonal
and intrapersonal conflicts
are generated and stilled;
and that men, women and children
struggle with the demands
from the changing world
outside their doors.
—LILLIAN RUBIN

1. Strategic Styles
Individual Responses to Social Reality

Five Portraits from the Cityscape

There are five young men growing up in the heart of the Roxbury section of Boston, Massachusetts. Let's call them Keith, Ernie, Leroy, Dave, and Hank. They have much in common: they are adolescents; they are black males; they are living in poverty and need. They are trying to learn how to be individuals, and men, in the social and physical decay of an inner-city environment.

But the similarities end there, overshadowed by the differences in how they feel about themselves, how they relate to others, how others see them, and how they are answering the question all adolescents must begin to face: "Who am I?"

While the process of forming an identity reaches a particularly crucial phase during adolescence for any person, the challenge the *black* adolescent faces is doubly hazardous. Not only must he cope with the strains classically associated with the transitional role of adolescent, but he must also cope with the simultaneous marginality of being black.[1]

This book is not designed to explicate group-wide responses to oppression and marginality—which all black people in our society share to some extent, regardless of their social station. Instead, I hope to explore meaningful variations within the group, holding constant such factors as age, sex, residence, income level, and social class.

The portraits that follow attest to the richness and range of interpersonal "styles" composed and played by young black males within the context of an inner-city subculture. Although they share demographic characteristics, we find critical differences among the boys in *how* they relate to that cityscape, and to the people who form the fabric of their daily lives.

All the boys live in poverty, but poverty alone has not made Leroy a "troublemaker," Ernie a "withdrawn kid," or Dave a "con artist." Though we may find higher rates of social disorganization in inner-city areas, integrity, conventional values, and emotional and social stability are by no means foreign, as will be evidenced by Keith the "conformist" and Hank the "together guy."

By holding constant such macroscopic forces as race and socioeconomic status, we can take a closer microscopic look at the interaction patterns between each boy and his family, friends, classmates, and teachers. We can examine in detail the coping styles that arise out of each boy's interpersonal world, peopled as it is by others who, by virtue of time, propinquity, and special roles, have become significant to them.[2]

For instance, as we meet each youth through interviews with him and the members of his family, we detect almost immediately the impact of being black in a racially oppressive society, and of being poor in a society that is ranked as one of the world's most affluent. Fathers who find frustration in the realm of work, whose training and education have doomed them to unemployment or underemployment, are linked with mothers who bypassed school in order to bear and raise babies who came too early, and with too little money to support them. Men and women whose creative energies and potential remain untapped face a constant struggle to cope with a lack of financial and social resources. In one way or another these pressures affect each family in the study. Yet just as remarkable as their similarities along these lines, is the fact that each family, and ultimately each boy, has learned to cope differently with the external pressures of their daily existence, and the internal pressures of their own personalities.

My purpose in developing the concept of strategic styles is not to discover groupwide responses to oppression and marginality or to view blacks as a monolithic and homogeneous group. On the contrary, I will systematically analyze *differences* in interpersonal orientations through the concept of "strategic style," which is seen to represent a connective link between each boy and his sociocultural world.

Conceptually, the book is grounded in symbolic interactionism. It focuses on family interaction patterns as an instance of "small group" process, and is intended to contribute to the growing body of literature supporting the new emphasis on clinical sociology. Before discussing the research design of Pathways to Identity,[3] which produced the data from which the portraits are drawn, we examine briefly each of these theoretical contexts—symbolic interactionism and clinical sociology.

Meaning and Strategic Styles

The symbolic interactionist perspective searches for connections between individual psychology and social structure through the investigation of how people interact with each other. Shibutani summarizes the interactionist perspective in explaining human behavior: "symptoms, defenses, character structure and personality can be seen as terms describing the individual's *typical* interactions which occur in response to a particular interpersonal context."[4] These "typical interactions" are what I designate strategic styles: the pattern of Ernie's hiding under a car when police chase him, or escaping to his room when his parents are angry, or retreating into the fantasy world of glue-sniffing to escape friction can be interpreted as his "typical" way of responding to significant others.

Shibutani insists that these patterns are not the result of instincts, drives, or other internal dynamics. They represent "products of communication" spun out of the individual's efforts to adjust to others with whom he regularly interacts.[5] Ernie was not born a "withdrawn kid." He learned, through interaction with others, to rely on withdrawal as his primary strategic style.

I write the portraits from an interactionist point of view in order to discover both the nature of the patterns and their etiology. For example, I am not concerned so much with a boy's achievement level in school, or whether he likes the subject matter. My focus is on how he relates to his teachers, his principal, his friends and classmates—and how he interprets their behavior, how he defines their interaction with him, how he portrays it to his family and to the interviewer. That is to say, I am concerned with the *meaning* these encounters have for him, and, consequently, how he shapes his behavior to provide the most satisfactory outcome for himself in interaction with others.

Symbolic interactionism rests on the basic assumption that meaning is not inherent in social interaction—it must be "negotiated" by the participants in a given situation. "Strategic style" is the characteristic way the individual handles himself, others, and his physical/cultural world, based on the meaning he has come to attach to himself and others—through his interactions with those others.[6] Strategic style is regularized or patterned, but at the same time in flux. It is the person's way of constructing a "more compact personal environment,"[7] and indicates that he takes into account the attitudes and meanings communicated by others as well as his own.[8] Thus the concept of strategic style throws into relief the articulation of societal forces and individual constitution as mediated through interpersonal interaction and exemplified by differences in interpersonal orientation.

The idea that human behavior is based on the intermeshing of self and other views is not new. It was explored carefully by Mead,[9] and implies that people not only *react* to messages from others, but, through a process of redefinition and being able to view one's self as a social unit, also *act*, create, are autonomous. Otherwise, we would all be instant replays of our parents and their parents and their parents before them. This assumption is directly related to why I have chosen the term strategic to modify style. I assume that interpretation, thought, and negotiation of meaning are intimately related to how a person copes with others. This is perhaps best exemplified by the audience segregation each boy practices to some extent.[10] Hank, with some others—for example his friends—relies on particular ways of behaving which he would define as inappropriate or ineffective with other audiences, say his mother. As Laing says, "People have identities. But they may also change quite remarkably as they become different others-to-others."[11]

To study the individual, then, we must study him in relation to others. We cannot comprehend Keith's conformist, obedient, strategic style, for instance, until we explore the messages to obey and conform and do well that permeate Keith's existence. As he interprets each encounter with others, he defines its significance for him, and the consequences of a range of behaviors open to his choice. As Laing points out, he may not only act differently for different others, but also experience and define himself differently. This is all deeply entwined with a person's sense of identity.

Yet life is not a series of disconnected, freshly defined encounters, determined by the others with whom a boy is interacting. By using the term style, I am suggesting that a person constructs a typical way of dealing with others which is characteristic of him, even though it may embody variations appropriate to specific audiences. One important finding that emerged from analysis of the Pathways data is that each boy operates within a primary style, but usually has a secondary style which is used for occasions on which the primary style does not function well or is inappropriate. For example, when Leroy employs toughness in a battle with his brothers, he is using his "troublemaker" style; when the battle becomes too vicious and threatens to end in serious physical harm, he suddenly breaks into his secondary style of "withdrawn kid"—retreating into the tightly defended privacy of his own room, runs into the streets to drain his explosive energy, sinks into the oblivion of his fourteen-hour hibernatory sleeps, or watches television alone.

The word style is derived from the Latin "stylus," meaning an instrument sharpened at one end to cut into wax, with the other end blunt for erasing mistakes. In this sense we can see primary and secondary styles functioning in tandem for each person, balancing and supporting each other. I shall examine this notion in greater detail in the portraits.

The self, according to interaction theory, has a career or history which makes it possible for a person to handle situations on the basis of how he handled similar situations in the past—as long as that way led to a satisfactory outcome, or he has no better way, or chooses to take an old way because he wishes to hurt himself. As Blumer notes, "there is always some connection and continuity with what went on before." [12] This continuity is vital to Erikson's definition of identity:

Ego identity then, in its subjective aspect, is the awareness of the fact that there is a self-sameness and continuity to the ego's synthesizing methods, the *style of one's individuality*, and that this style coincides with the sameness and continuity of one's meaning for significant others in the immediate community. [13]

A reflection of this "self-sameness and continuity" of which Erikson speaks can be found in each boy's strategic style.

Thus the theoretical focus of the present book is on the existence of patterns in the lines of action that are available to and/or constructed by the individual:

Fundamentally, action on the part of a human being consists of taking account of various things that he notes and forging a line of conduct on the basis of how he interprets them. The things taken into account cover such matters as his wishes and wants, his objectives, the available means for their achievement, the actions and anticipated actions of others, his image of himself, and the likely result of a given line of action. [14]

Finally, as Blumer notes in his criticism of the structural-functional perspective, much sociology leaves us with social action falling into one of two categories: "conformity, marked by adherence to the structure, and deviance, marked by departure from it." [15] Following Mead, he sees a person as having the capacity for much more than mere responses to the dictates of structure. In developing the concept of strategic style, I will elaborate on the other types of response which fall outside the range of sheer conformity or deviance. I will also specify more clearly what is involved in the process of conformity in discussing the portrait of Keith.

I have taken a nonpsychoanalytic and nonintrapsychic point of view in this study of identity-formation, not only because there are many works which approach the explanation of individual behavior from an internal point of view, but because the sociological perspective has not often enough been applied to this area of analysis. [16]

My bias is clearly toward interactional explanations of causality. We can argue that Hank is a "together guy" because his mother sends him messages encouraging his competence; I feel it is equally important to recognize that Hank's acting competently in turn feeds back into his mother's perception of Hank, and consequently her messages to him. Emphasis on circular causality, rather than linear, and on the context of interpersonal action rather than the internal dynamics of the person leads me to place the portraits in the theoretical framework of family interaction process. Each boy is studied as part of an *interaction matrix* comprised of family, friends, teachers, etc. How loyalties, conflicts, broken promises, expectations, and the vagaries of intimate living are handled constitute the heart of each portrait.

Family Interaction Process. The "Crucible of Identity" [17]

Many studies have tried to weigh the relative power of various socializing agents—home, school, peers, church, the media—in the formation of personal identity. When I began to write, I did not intend to study family interaction, nor was I convinced that the family would be the most salient factor in the genesis of each boy's strategic style. It is clear that peers and school have potentially enormous influence on the child, especially during adolescence. In the portraits I will address the relative "valence" or explanatory power of each of these influences. Yet it appears to me that the family is in fact the most critical influence in the lives of each of the five boys analyzed here. [18]

We can view the family first as a small group, subject to the principles of internal dynamics peculiar to all small groups. Issues such as the location of power, leadership, decision-making, division of labor, coalitions, trust, solidarity, conflict, and so forth can be discussed.

If we view the family as a *special* instance of small groups, with its own peculiar characteristics, we highlight one of its primary roles: the procreation, protection, and socialization of newcomers into our society. It is in the family (or its substitutes) that the individual learns to be a person and a social animal. The family as a small group not only teaches its young the norms, skills, values, beliefs, and traditions of the society, it also develops its own culture, including myths, norms, and values. Jackson has found in his research into family constellations that rules of interaction evolve—which may or may not be compatible with society's broader norms—which keep their members in line with accepted standards of behavior.[19] Mishler and Waxler also discovered norms in their studies of the families of schizophrenic patients:

There is evidence . . . in the interfamily differences and the lack of intra-familial differences, for the presence of differential family norms or standards for expressing feelings. The parents are the prime 'carriers' of the norm and the differences between them are most clearly seen in comparisons that involve interaction with the patient son.[20]

The family also develops values which are instrumental in enforcing the familial norms. Strategic styles, then, can be viewed as patterns of interaction with others which evolve initially through contact with the family, deriving from its particular patterns, norms, myths, values, and personalities, and later extend to other interpersonal situations.

Recent trends in psychiatry, psychology, and psychotherapy have stressed the centrality of interaction patterns within the family as the most appropriate and fruitful focus for research into emotional disorder and for therapeutic intervention.[21] Sociology has also played a valuable role in helping to elucidate patterns of family interaction which can be translated into therapeutic guidelines.[22] By focusing on the process instead of the content of interaction, we can identify the typical constructive and destructive processes that make a family tick. Jackson points out that "only when we attend to *transactions between* individuals as primary data" can we shift conceptually from study of the person as a psychological entity to the person as a social entity.[23] That a boy is disagreeing with his father over money or sex or clothes is no more important than that he is disagreeing. Strategic styles are manifestations of the *process* patterns established by the boy with his significant others.

Instead of operating as though psychology and sociology could in practice be rigorously (or legitimately) differentiated, we can explain a person's relationship to society better through synthesis and integration of theory—with the goal of understanding people as people, not as isolated psyches tangled in their internal webs, or social robots caught in the morass of structural positions. We are neither beasts, nor gods, as Aristotle once argued, but social animals. As Haley says: "The problem is no longer how to characterize and classify . . . individuals; it is how to describe and classify the habitual patterns of responsive behavior exchanged by intimates."[24] We can apply such a synthetic approach by studying the formation of identity in Hank, Dave, Ernie, Leroy, and Keith in terms of their relationships with their significant others.[25]

Translating Knowledge into Action

When Mishler and Waxler published their seminal *Interaction in Families* in 1964, they hoped the work would be seen as a "bridge between clinical-psychiatric and academic social science traditions," and that it would stimulate further application of methods and concepts from sociology and social psychology to clinical problems.[26] It is my hope that this study will serve as another span in that bridge, for which Louis Wirth laid the original cornerstone. It is almost fifty years since Wirth coined the term "clinical sociology."[27] He argued in 1931 that the insights of sociology should be put to work in solving the social problems found in any setting where people come together in groups or members of groups. Over the years, sociologists have served as consultants in organizational settings, working primarily in a human relations or social policy framework. But only since the late 1960's have we seriously begun to prepare the ground conceptually for effective clinical intervention from a sociological point of view.[28]

Recently Glassner and Freedman have distilled the work in this tradition, defining clinical sociology as the use of "a variety of critically applied practices which attempt sociological diagnosis and treatment of groups and group members in communities."[29] They claim that "diagnoses and therapies derived exclusively from psychology are logically incorrect, have historically been inadequate, and ignore the sociological nature of persons' problems. Persons' experiences as individuals are formed and structured by groups."[30] Several sociological methodologies are particularly suited to understanding groups in interactional networks or systems—participant observation, in-depth cluster interviewing, and interaction process analysis.[31] Clinical sociology attempts to "understand and treat the problems of the *group as a whole*,"[32] which is what these methodologies are most sensitive to. As with good psychotherapy, the authors feel that clinical sociology is as much art as science. In addition to the application of empirically tested and theoretically sound principles and concepts, clinical sociology requires insight and the capacity to integrate disparate threads of information and relate them to feelings and behaviors.

The assumptions underlying this strategy are that human behavior never occurs out of the contextual meaning derived from interaction with others, and that how we behave becomes patterned, ritualized, repetitive.[33] Therefore, social science can evolve theories and principles of social interaction which can be applied to problems of living in groups. For instance, in his study of attachment, Bowlby states that interactional patterns between mother-baby couples probably stabilize within the first year of the relationship, and persist throughout childhood. The pattern develops because it is adaptive for both parties, which in itself is a strong press toward its perpetuation. As Bowlby points out, these patterns may be positive or negative for one or both members of the couple; if they should change, concomitant change in the behavioral organization of both would be necessary.[34]

The portraits of Keith, Ernie, Leroy, Dave, and Hank show how these interactional patterns are born out of the crucible of the family, how they are reinforced and rewarded, how alternatives to them are either absent or thwarted, and how they extend into other relationships as the boys develop networks beyond the family.

Glassner and Freedman say that sociological methods can be used by clinical sociologists in a three-step process of diagnosis: (1) describing the problem, (2) addressing the problem with theoretical insights, and (3) locating research support for these theories.[35] It is my hope that the strategic styles typology and the focal-cluster method through which the Pathways data were gathered will serve as useful diagnostic tools, and will provide therapeutic principles for clinical intervention.

By making an entire network of family members aware of their styles, helping them practice alternatives, providing immediate positive reinforcement for breaking destructive processes, and providing frequent opportunities for growth and change, the clinician could enable a family to reduce the negative impact of certain styles or style combinations, if not eliminate them altogether. An important part of such an approach would be to help families learn to diagnose their own strategic styles and to recognize their manifestations. In this way, problems of damaged self-esteem, low self-concept, negative identity, power seeking, and affiliational deprivations can be alleviated.

Research Design and Procedures

The portraits in this book utilize data from Pathways to Identity, a longitudinal research project which since 1966 has conducted intensive interviews with 61 black adolescent males who (at least initially) lived in Roxbury.[36] A brief description of the project follows.

Many studies, particularly those which compare blacks to whites, of necessity treat both as relatively homogeneous groups.[37] Others, which compare blacks to one another on isolated variables such as father-absence, dropping out of school, or delinquency, focus on narrowly defined factors that do not form a global picture of black identity.[38] Classic and contemporary case studies of blacks living in particular cultural contexts, and novelistic or autobiographical accounts of black identity, offer valuable insights into the dynamics of identity formation.[39] Generally, however, they do not attempt to systematize data by holding class, income, age, and sex constant, by virtue of their nature.

Pathways to Identity is geared to providing systematic data from a specified population that can be used to develop broad theoretical frameworks. Pathways has concentrated on the experience of young black males as they live through the formative years of adolescence, a period of expanding personal and racial awareness during which potential roles for the present and future are tested, rejected, altered, and sometimes adopted. The project, through interviews with each boy and his family, friends, and teachers, is trying to determine why some boys from the same sociocultural background take pathways which lead to jail, addiction, even premature deaths, while others take roads which lead them to the good life, as they call it—success in school, work, and family.

Pathways began in 1966 with a pilot study in the Roxbury community to formulate questions and research approaches for the longitudinal study, which to date has completed three rounds of interviews, ending in 1973. Further interviews are contemplated.

In 1967 the research sample of subjects was selected. Because of the centrality of school during adolescence (and legally required attendance at this age level), a local junior high school (the "Du-Bois"), which serves a relatively homogeneous (black and poor) population, was chosen for study. The school's enrollment of 605 students was approximately 98 percent black; most of the students lived within eight or ten blocks of the school. The sample consisted of all boys from this group who met the following criteria:

a. Family income close to or below the nationally defined poverty level of income (at the time from $3200 to $4000 annually, depending on the number of children);

b. Residence and education in a Northern urban center from at least second grade on;

c. Willingness of all family members to participate in the study over time.

Of 98 poverty-level families screened by the project, 63 were found to meet the residency and low-income criteria (some families had additional income provided by a second worker); of those, two refused to participate.

Pathways utilized the focal-cluster method of data-gathering, which studies each subject (referred to as "focal boy" or "focal child") through examination of his relationships with the significant others in his life—from both his point of view and theirs. Each focal child and his significant others form a "focal cluster." [40] Interviews were conducted by same-sex, same-race interviewers (all members of the community) with the focal boy, his parents (whether living with him or not), closest sibling, best friend, favorite and least favorite teachers, and any other persons mentioned as significant by the focal boy in the course of his interviews.

All Pathways interviews were tape-recorded and followed a schedule of open-ended questions. Interviewers were encouraged to pursue confusing or potentially enlightening responses. Each participant was informed at the beginning of the interview session that his or her identity would be protected; a pause button was indicated for the participant's use if desired (it was rarely used, and only by teachers). Interviews with focal boys ranged in length from a total of six to fourteen hours; reference individual interviews averaged a total of six hours each. All focal child interviews were conducted at the project's Roxbury office. Others were interviewed there, at the Cambridge office, or in their own homes, according to their preference. All subjects were paid nominal sums for their participation in the project.[41]

Although the project was not initially oriented to the symbolic interactionist perspective, it happens that interview questions served to elicit information along lines compatible with it: "the process of everyday interactions, particularly the outcomes of interpersonal bargaining and communication; and the process of socialization, especially the acquisition of culture and the determinants of self concepts."[42]

Each boy was asked, among other things: his reactions to everyday occurrences; to describe himself and his relationships with others; how he would like to change; his hopes and expectations regarding future school, occupation, and family; and basic background information. At the end of each section—Family, Peer, Work, Race, Self-Concept, School, and Neighborhood/House/Travel—the subject was asked to tell a story about each of a series of projective pictures appropriate to that section.

It may be helpful to elaborate briefly on a few questions which elicited some of the most intriguing data for the concept of strategic style, and are referred to frequently in the text:

• *The brainwash question* (Self-Concept, 4)—If somebody was trying to brainwash you in order to change you as much as possible from what you are now, what about yourself would you fight hardest to keep the same?

• *The spy question* (Self-Concept, 16)—Let's pretend you wanted to disappear from the scene for a while, but you had to get someone to take your place so that no one would know you were gone. You have to teach him, like with a spy, how to act like you so that no one would know the difference . . .

How would you tell him to act around home? With your friends? At school? (etc.)

Both of these questions are designed to evoke images symbolic of the boy's core identity; similarly, two key questions tend to pinpoint a boy's racial consciousness and identification:

- *The pill question* (Race, 14)—If there was an injection or a pill you could take that would make you white, what would you do? Why? *Explore.*

- *The magic button question* (Race, 15)—If you could press a button and by magic it would turn everyone in America into Negroes (or whatever term subject uses), would you do it? Why? *Explore.*

All the boys were also given IQ tests, Draw-A-Man tests, the Internal-External Control Questionnaire (version of the Rotter scale),[43] and Ladder tests to detect social aspirations and expectations.

Reference individuals were asked, in turn, to characterize their relationships with the focal boy, and to evaluate his performance in roles and activities of which they were aware. In many cases their questions were parallel to those asked of the boys. Complete interview schedules for focal boys, parents, and peers (Time I) may be found in Appendixes A and B.

Developing a Typology of Strategic Styles

In sifting through transcripts of the first round of interviews, it became obvious that the strategic style each boy uses in getting what he wants out of life is as important as the specific pathway taken. Interviewer discussions about the boys were peppered with references to one being a "tough guy," another "slick," another "withdrawn." These terms were also employed frequently by the boys when referring to themselves and to each other. Even without the benefit of face-to-face contact experienced by the interviewers, transcribers and other staff found they could designate a boy's strategic style—simply by listening to his tapes—with surprisingly high agreement with the interviewer's assessment.

The concept of strategic style was born, then, out of the vernacular current in the late 1960's in Roxbury; the terms are retained here to preserve the sense of everyday life within that context. Each style contains two subtypes, reflecting the extremes we found within the main categories:

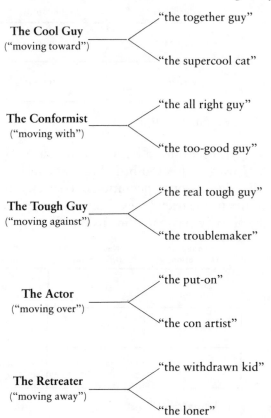

The Cool Guy
("moving toward")
- "the together guy"
- "the supercool cat"

The Conformist
("moving with")
- "the all right guy"
- "the too-good guy"

The Tough Guy
("moving against")
- "the real tough guy"
- "the troublemaker"

The Actor
("moving over")
- "the put-on"
- "the con artist"

The Retreater
("moving away")
- "the withdrawn kid"
- "the loner"

Each style is defined more specifically in introducing the portraits in Chapters 2 through 6.

In order to systematize the concept, I related the styles to two basic dimensions: the extent of each boy's relatedness or affiliation with others, and the nature of his power relationships with others.[44] Each of the strategic styles is seen as a solution to the dilemma of *power over* versus *affiliation with* others.[45]

The styles are tools with which the individual shapes and structures interaction with others in terms of controlling them (or allowing them to control him) and satisfying his needs for affection, approval, intimacy, status, and so forth. Thus the strategic styles are the product of two variables—activity-passivity on the one hand, and friendliness-hostility on the other:

	Friendliness	Hostility
Activity	approach	attack
Passivity	alignment	retreat

FIGURE 1: Power/Affiliation (I)

This typology is useful for a basic categorization of interaction possibilities. However, it is too broad in its inclusiveness and too narrow in the dimensional definitions. I specify it further by adding neutrality to the friendliness-hostility dimension, and over-activity to the activity-passivity dimension. This yields:

	Friendliness (Attraction)	Neutrality (Insulation)	Hostility (Antipathy)
Overactivity (Dominance)	smother/ exhibit	control	attach
Activity	approach	compete	rebel
Passivity (Submission)	align	avoid/ tolerate	retreat

FIGURE 2: Power/Affiliation (II)

Terms such as "dominance" and "submission" imply not merely a simple interaction mode, but also something about what a person "gets out of" interaction with others. Following Leary,[45] and incorporating Barker and Wright's "action modes," I refer to the friendliness-hostility dimension as *affiliation*, and the activity-passivity dimension as *power*.[46] With further elaboration of parallel concepts, the strategic styles emerge as basic orientations toward others as shown in Figure 3.

The strategic styles discussed in this book happened to be pulled out of analysis of data regarding young, black males. My suspicion is that similar studies of females, or whites, or other age groups would uncover similar styles—although the vernacular terms used to describe them might vary. The dimensions of power and affiliation are central to the interpersonal behavior of any person. Each

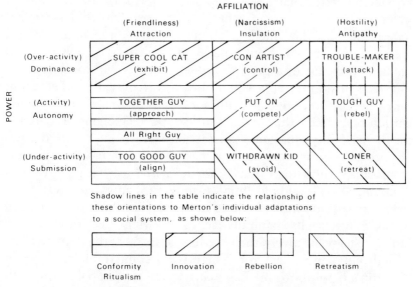

FIGURE 3: Power/Affiliation (III): Basic Interpersonal Orientations

of us, regardless of social station, must cope with pressures from others that compete with pressures from our own self-image, aspirations, dreams, needs. Each of us must also cope with the delicate balance between dominance and affiliation, in terms of our own propensities and those of others.

Merton's "modes of individual adaptation" to the "culture-bearing society" echo some of these same concerns. They are defined in terms of acceptance or rejection of cultural norms and goals, and speak to the individual's way of going about achieving those goals:

a. conformity (societal goals, societal means)
b. innovation (societal goals, own means)
c. ritualism (own goals, societal means)
d. retreatism (abdication of goals and means)
e. rebellion (own goals, own means)[47]

These adaptations contain strong implications for a person's position on both power and affiliation dimensions, and will be discussed in the cases in order to shed light on each boy's strategic style.

Merton states that these adaptations speak to the individual's relationship to society in general. I propose that they occur between the individual and small units as well—for example, family, peer groups, school. Conformity can be defined as adherence to goals and means of a peer group—or parents—or local community. Ritualism may appear not only in the context of a Pentagon-like bureaucracy, but also within a ritual- and rule-bound family structure in which the child has little hope of changing his parents, or their rigidity, but gains satisfaction from being a "good boy." To bring Merton's terminology into my perspective, we can view conformity and ritualism as "moving with" others; retreatism as "moving away"; and rebellion as "moving against." Innovation, in which means are individualized in the service of attaining societal goals, is essentially manipulative, or "moving over" others. They are parallel respectively, then, to the Conformist, the Retreater, the Tough Guy, and the Actor. There is no comparable category in Merton's typology to my Cool Guy style, who, in balancing both affiliation and power, is seen as "moving toward" others.

The styles can also be related to Lee Rainwater's "strategies for living" and "strategies for survival." Keith's Conformist style, for example, is heavily oriented toward the strategies for living—the "good life" and "career success." To some extent the Cool Guy also searches for the good life. Rainwater's strategies for survival—the "expressive life style," the "depressive life style," and the "violent strategy"—are linked with the Actor, the Retreater, and the Tough Guy, respectively.[48] Finally, the strategic styles can be analyzed in terms of their degree of stability, flexibility, security, spontaneity, and sincerity, following Goffman.[49] These connections are shown in Figure 4.

After precise definitions of each style were developed, based on global assessment of the interaction patterns of all 61 boys, each subject was reexamined and assigned a primary—and, if appropriate, secondary—style.

Analysis of Data: Five Portraits

For the portraits I have selected five 7th grade boys who are of similar age (12–14), who clearly show a primary and secondary style, and whose transcripts were complete for the entire set of

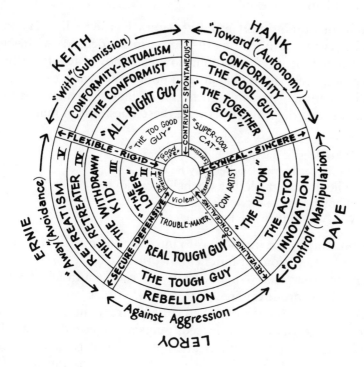

RINGS:

V — Merton's Individual
Adaptations
IV — Strategic Styles

III — Type I
II — Type II
I — Rainwater's Strategies

SPOKES:

Adapted from Goffman

NOTE: The order in which the portraits are presented throughout the book follows the "wheel" above, moving counterclockwise from Keith the Conformist around to Hank the Cool Guy; conformity and retreatism are "under-active" on the power dimension; tough and actor styles are "over-active" on the power dimension; the cool guy has balanced power with affiliation to achieve "autonomy."

FIGURE 4: Strategic Styles in Relation to Other Concepts

significant others interviewed at Times I (1967 +), II (1970 +), and III (1973 +). In reading the transcripts I focused on questions that elicited information about how each boy reacts to ordinary situations, such as bringing home a poor report card, experiencing conflict between parents and peers, or making a new friend. In general I read the transcripts with these questions in mind:

a. Who does the boy say he is?
b. Who does he say he would like to be?
c. Who does he think others say he is?
d. Who does he think they would like him to be?
e. Who do they think he is?
f. Who would they like him to be?

The portraits are written so as to integrate the boy's point of view with the perceptions of him held by others.

The interpersonal dynamics between each youth and his reference others are examined carefully in order to discern how discrepancies in self/other perceptions are managed, and how each strategic style is reinforced, punished, ignored, changed, or fixed. The analysis includes attempts to identify causal factors working to produce each style, as well as the consequences of the styles for those who live with them.[50]

Because of the length of transcripts and the complexity of each focal cluster, most analysis of the cases will be reserved until the fourth section of each chapter, in order to allow the descriptive strength of the data to stand intact. In the analysis sections I will discuss the family matrix, critical messages from others, the impact of role models, the boy's alternatives, other issues pertinent to the genesis of the strategic style, and its relation to the concepts from Merton, Rainwater, and Goffman mentioned earlier ("analytical dimensions").

All of the quotations from focal or reference interviews are identified as to their source either through context or parentheses (e.g., Mother); to identify them by interview section or page number would be distracting and serve no useful purpose. The method of inspection was used to glean pertinent information from each cluster of interviews, utilizing passages regardless of the actual question that evoked them. For this reason not all boys will be discussed in terms of exactly the same set of questions (with the exception of the core questions mentioned above).

Limits of the Study

The hazards of classifying human behavior are many. Three stand out in the present endeavor. One is that no individual responds as consistently in everyday life as the term strategic style would imply. I am proposing that if one observed a boy's behavior over time, he would notice not perfect consistency but a pattern of interpersonal orientation. The styles are not intended to reflect reality precisely, nor am I suggesting that a person's behavior is always clearly within the bounds of one style or another. Even Keith, the Conformist par excellence, at times rebels against his parents' demands. Ernie, whose world is restricted against pain and rejection, reaches out in later adolescence to establish intimacy with a young girl.

In light of this, I try in the portraits to be as accurate as possible in reporting inconsistent or contradictory behavior: the "troublemaker" who treats his sister with tenderness; the Actor who relinquishes his conning behavior in order to achieve closeness with a special girl. Yet, as with any ideal-typological construct, certain segments of reality are subordinated to other more obvious or accessible segments.

Secondly, the strategic styles designated here are not intended to be exhaustive. They should remain basically the same across subcultures, but specific subtypes would change. In a hippie community the "too-good guy" might be called "straight." Furthermore, the types were derived from data regarding males; it is probable that other types might be designated for females, if for no other reason than that the basic qualities traditionally deemed normative for conformity—motherliness, nurturance, sensitivity—have been different for females.

In addition, the concept was generated from data obtained from a small number of cases (61). Although the case study method is used, it is possible that larger numbers of cases from other inner-city areas (or from a different era), might yield more and/or different styles. Thus we can generalize from these data only to other groups of low-income, Northern, inner-city black males living in comparable circumstances.

Another problem is of particular import for a symbolic interactionist framework. Are my classifications (tough, withdrawn, conforming, etc.) the salient ones for the subjects themselves? Although they use these terms, there is no proof that I use them in the same way they do, or for the same behavior. In addition, my analysis exists on one plane only—the *reported behavior* of each boy, and its *reported meaning* for him. Any attempt to detect or evaluate underlying meaning is fraught with the risk of misinterpretation, since my frame of reference is not identical with the boys'.

As Laing points out, an "interview is itself not a naturally occurring family situation."[51] Our description is limited, then, by the ability of the person interviewed to articulate his or her behavior and feelings. For the withdrawn kid, for example, who relies on "I don't know" so often, we are kept ignorant of his true responses. Also, because interview data are retrospective, they suffer from inconsistencies and misinterpretation which are impossible to check out. However, since the questions are designed to create a picture of family interaction, that limitation does not hamstring us completely. In addition, there is ample evidence from clinical case reports (cf. Laing and Jackson) that because of the overwhelming power of family myths, disordered conduct, and mystification of feelings, family members often deal in inconsistencies and misinterpretations in front of the interviewer in joint sessions—and even if they are pointed out, they are often not acknowledged by the family.[52]

The question of "Who am I?" is an on-going one which represents a dynamic and sometimes disturbing aspect of our lives. The portraits are "slice of life" insights into how five young boys try to answer that question. The nature of the answer, and the boy's strategic styles, may shift as he grows closer to manhood. Are the styles we see in early adolescence the same ones we will find later in the boy's life? In order to tackle this question of possible change over time, I completed the analysis of Time I data and wrote the portraits which appear in Chapters 2–6 prior to reading transcripts from Times II or III. Chapter 7 explores the extent to which early styles become crystallized. It is my hope that funding will be available for further interviewing of the Pathways youths—at least once a decade—so that we can see whether and how their adolescent strategic styles change.

Toward a Synthetic View of Identity

As should be clear by now, the process of identity formation is seen in a dual perspective: the individual's perception of who he is and who he would like to be—and the perceptions of others in his life. Strategic style incorporates both perspectives in an effort to explicate the nature of identity formation.

The concept sheds light on a phenomenon which has often been noted—namely, individuals appear to act, consciously or unconsciously, on the basis of their ideal image of who they want to be, and their notion of what others want them to be. The availability of data from all members of a boy's reference group enables us to perceive more clearly the intersection of these two forces. In addition, strategic style explicitly recognizes the common observation that individuals in the same role do not necessarily carry it out in the same way. On the contrary, strategic styles cut across roles.

Ernie is a "withdrawn kid" in his roles of son, brother, friend, student. Both Leroy and Keith are sons, but for Leroy, expression of affection is accomplished through wrestling, fighting, punching his father around—for Keith it is achieved through doing favors for his father and being a "good boy." His style is also apparent in the way a boy deals with various situations. Leroy propels an encounter in the dead of night into murder. Ernie would undoubtedly have run for his life before the situation could have become a conversation, let alone an intense physical confrontation.

A final word before turning to the portraits. Strategic style is the way a person deals with the definitions prevailing in the cultures most salient to him. It includes the way in which he defines situations in his own right, and by the information about himself he expresses or "gives off."[53] It includes values, attitudes, assumptions, and feelings about self and others, as they are expressed in a composite behavioral pattern: It is a characteristic personal adaptation to, and management of, the conflict between self and others, internal and external pressures.

Yet, as we see in the portraits, each boy's complexity and uniqueness are as impressive as the underlying thread of a strategic style.

. . . he's the kind of a kid
that has a wonderful personality;
he's the type of a kid
that will do anything that he can for you . . .
he gets along nicely with people,
he makes friends easily . . .
—GRANDFATHER

. . . he's thoughtful and he's meek
and he's humble.
—MOTHER

2. The Conformist *Keith Sutton*

Moving With. The All Right Guy and the Too-Good Guy

The Conformist accepts the basic terms of social situations as others define them; he does not attempt to change, reject, or manipulate people or rules for his own end. Or if he does, he follows prescribed means of manipulation, i.e., institutionalized or otherwise acceptable "deviance." His motivational impetus in social relationships is the need for acceptance; he operates within the confines of culturally defined (conventional) norms and goals.

In ideal-typological terms, the true conformist is an individual who perfectly meets the expectations of others concerning his roles. Obviously, this purity is not translated into everyday life. In fact, we know that minor let-downs or slip-ups are not only tolerated but expected in someone who is nevertheless generally considered a conformist.

What we *are* observing in the "all right guy" (as exemplified in the case study of Keith Sutton) is an overwhelming tendency to *attempt* to meet those role expectations. In many cases unsuccessful attempts to meet expectations may be accepted as conformity because of the *intent* to meet them. For example, Keith plays the role of student to his family's specifications. Yet even when he does not succeed in obtaining precisely defined objectives (for example, he brings home the grade of B or C instead of an A), he is nonetheless respected for having met their role expectations by virtue of his show of hard work and good study habits—an A for effort.

The all right guy is concerned with the way others see him, and tends to take his cues from them. He is not as uptight as the "too-good guy," however, and would not earn labels such as "sissy" or "goodie-goodie." He may engage in small infractions that are not risky or that are more or less acceptable, but assiduously avoids any serious trouble. He selects a peer group whose values and behaviors are in keeping with his own conformist style, and joins in the prevailing mood when he is with them. He does passing work in school, may have a girl friend, may smoke or drink, but will not get into trouble because of it. He is not "cool," nor does he show much street savvy.

The too-good guy,[1] on the other hand, is not likely to engage in any such activities as drinking, smoking, fighting, petty thievery, and so forth. He does not challenge authority (even that of older children) and is often very sensitive about himself. He is likely to be more immature and less self-confident than the all right guy. In the Pathways sample, the too-good guys tended to spend much of their free time playing, whereas some of the all right guys held part-time jobs in addition. Although the all right guy is basically oriented toward his parents' value system, the too-good guy is an extremely conservative and faithful carrier of his parents' values; he is therefore less able to tolerate ambiguity in his friends (and will perhaps therefore be less intimate in his peer relationships than boys with other styles).[2]

The conformist style is the only one of the five strategic styles which derives its energy from legitimate means focused on system-wide goals. In Merton's terminology, "conformity represents adaptation in which both ends and norms are positively evaluated and relatively balanced."[3] For Keith and his family certain goals are paramount and defined as achievable through certain acceptable means. Thus the motivations of "striving for acceptance" and "avoidance of guilt" are understood to operate within conventional value systems.

The person who seems to exhibit a persistently conformist interpersonal behavior vis-à-vis his peer group but is rebellious toward parents or teachers will not for our purposes be considered as having a conformist style. Moving with the peer group, unless accompanied by a tendency to go along with parents, teachers, siblings, and so forth, does not indicate (at least for the adolescent) a conformist style. Theoretically it is possible for a youth to exhibit a conforming style toward all significant persons in his life, all of whom happen to have a deviant or nonconventional value system and behavior pattern—from the point of view of the mainstream. No one in the Pathways sample happened to be in that situation.

The Conformist must be distinguished from a chameleon-like person. A few boys in Pathways have the capacity to slip in and out of styles for the benefit of different audiences (subsets of reference figures). These youths are adept at creating audience-specific styles—"too-good guy" for parents, "real tough guy" for peers, "troublemaker" for teachers, "con artist" with the girls—without seeming to have an overriding or dominant style. Rather than viewing them as conforming to the discrete expectations of various audiences, it is more useful to consider them as manipulative and thus having an affinity with the Actor style.

To summarize, to the extent that the focal child generally attempts to mold his behavior to meet the expectations others hold for him, he is considered to have a conformist strategic style. If he only appears to be conforming to the others' expectations, but in fact is secretly deviating from them, he is not considered to be the Conformist; the Conformist's self-characterizations as well as the characterizations of him by others must agree.

Naturally, if he misperceives others' expectations, he will not meet them (except by chance) and is not, from an interpersonal point of view, a conformist. This would represent a case of faulty communication and imperfect socialization. To the extent that the focal child meets the expectations of others only *incidentally* as an expression of his own inner needs and goals, he is not considered to be the Conformist.

A focal child is categorized as the Conformist if he:

(a) accepts his parents' basic value system;

(b) internalizes his parents' goals, values, wishes;

(c) strives for acceptance through submitting to their definition of the situation;

(d) makes little attempt to change that definition (only occasionally to hide his inability to fit it);

(e) wants what they want and wants to get it the way they would want him to, and desires their approval.

Since Keith Sutton fits the above description, he will provide case material for the Conformist portrait (all right guy).

Self-Characterization. "Just act nice . . ."

In the Time I interviews (age 13), Keith Sutton aspires to the "good life," and seems to live in a world which is mainly "nice"— filled with "nice" people, "nice" houses, "nice" times. His experiences to date have been relatively positive, even to the point of suggesting naiveté and shelteredness, which might be considered extraordinary for a boy who is growing up in Roxbury. He has been blind since birth in his left eye, a handicap he has apparently dealt with in a positive way.

Keith stresses such values as getting a good education and job, being kind, and staying out of trouble. He wants to be an "electronic" (even though it would entail long, hard hours). Keith says his mother would like him to be a preacher; his grandfather has suggested a mathematician which, indeed, is Keith's second job choice. In describing one of the men in a Work Picture, Keith says the man probably has a "modern life" like himself, a "regular life like any other person would have." His accounts of his family and peer life verify this image.

Keith's attitude toward his family is warm. He speaks with affection and respect for all the family members, and obviously relishes their expressions of love and praise for him. His stories in response to Family Pictures are full of warm days and the family going on picnics in the park. Of one picture in which a family is sitting on a mattress, apparently being evicted, he remarks that the father is "thinking about keeping the babies warm." Another elicits: "He really likes it . . . it's so nice and warm out and they've taken advantage for it may not be warm for another four or five days again."[4]

His father, who sometimes gets up at 5:30 A.M. to go to work, takes Keith to "different places . . . when he has time off." Sometimes Mr. Sutton goes out late at night to get Keith a sandwich. Keith, in turn, will hang his father's clothes up for him and shine his shoes on those early mornings. His relationships with his mother, grandfather, brother Frank (age 21), and sister Molly (age 3) seem to follow the same lines: you do favors for me and I will do favors for you and we'll all be one big happy family.[5] This attitude ("The way I react to people") carries over into his peer and school life as well.

Keith is reluctant to say which of his family members he cares for the most: "I think for all of them . . . because they're nice to me." He says he gets along with everybody just about the same. When he was younger they all loved him: they "used to buy me candy and lollipops, and I got toys . . . they used to give me parties." He was punished occasionally for minor "mischief," sometimes by a spanking, but most often by being locked in his room. When asked how he is punished by his parents now, he says he is not, because he does not get into "jams" anymore. Responsibility is impressed on Keith. He says he is admonished to stay out of trouble ("Well, I haven't gotten in serious trouble so far"), and would have to pay out of his own pocket for anything like a broken window. His family, he says, want him to be a "good person . . . don't go out in the street and get into trouble."

His 21-year-old brother Frank (with whom he was sharing a room at Time I) is "all right—he gives me money." When he and Frank argue, it is usually over clothes. The fight is resolved by both of them leaving ("He usually goes somewhere else, and I go outside sometimes"). He retreats from conflicts with his parents also, rather than fighting or trying to reach a compromise. Compared to the other 33 boys in the seventh-grade sample, Keith's relationship with his siblings seems typical (fighting and getting on each other's nerves), although somewhat more harmonious than most. Furthermore, Keith seems not to initiate the conflicts as often as many of the others boys do.

Keith's peer group supports his interest in school work. At Time I the group consists of one significant person, Alfie (14), and three peripheral figures (Rick, 13, Herman, 12, and Chuck, 13). His friends (especially Alfie) basically reflect the same values Keith espouses and apparently lives by. They constitute a rather loosely structured group whose members would stand up for each other if called upon. Herman is an influential, key peer, so might be considered leader, according to Keith. He denies conflict in the group, and emphasizes compromise and democratic cooperation as the prime modes of interaction. When there is a disagreement, Keith says they usually do not talk to each other for a while (an hour, a day); again, the withdrawal and cooling off, rather than open confrontation or fighting it out. When asked about rules, Keith emphasizes two: no trouble and no stealing.

Interviewer: "Suppose one of the guys would steal something?"
Keith: "They wouldn't be with us no more."

During the Peer Picture responses, and in sharp contrast to his more direct accounts of his peer life, Keith touches on such themes as a thief trying to make people think he is innocent, a boy thinking of beating up someone, and another "stealing and trying to kill somebody." Most significantly, he makes reference to one boy "turning against his friends"; and, again, "They look like they're about ready to beat up somebody, and I don't know, one might turn against all the rest of them. . . ." In a scenario where he says some boys were stealing and one is happy that "he got what he want," he adds: "I think he's thinking about when he get the stuff, all the other boys jump him and take it away from him." He portrays adults as solving fights, or calling the police on youth who are in the act of being deviant. He obviously depends on adult authority to solve problems, and also perhaps to protect him. Though Keith is willing to obey the rules, he seems unsure that others will. At the end of the Peer Picture session he asks that a window be opened.

Competing with time spent with his friends is the time Keith dedicates to school work. He is very firmly and positively oriented toward school, and has confidence at Time I in his ability to do well: "I'm getting good marks . . . just keep on working like I usually am."

Indicative of Keith's conformist style in school is his role as milk and/or supply monitor for five out of six grade school years. (In contrast to Leroy's case, being monitor is for Keith a reward for conformity rather than a school's admission of defeat.) He relates that all through his school years he has "had no trouble with none of my teachers." His favorite teacher in grade school gave him small change for running errands and took the students on trips ("he liked me"). In the seventh grade his favorite teacher "would let us get away with some things." While Keith is prepared to conform to the school rules (and even help implement them), it is clear that he also appreciates flexibility and leniency.

This attitude is reflected in Keith's answer to the question of how he would deal with a "boy in hot water": he would "treat him a little better than the others so that he would do a little more . . . ah, ah, bit more work." He identifies more with the "boy who is doing well" because "he has more manners."

It is interesting that Keith's general view of school and his performance is that school is fine, the teachers are good, and *he* is the one who must strive harder to make his mark. His racial identity at age 13 is hardly militant, as exemplified by his blaming the school's problems on "mixing kids . . . colored people are just taking advantage of them" (white students). Similarly, if other students do not fare well, he sees this as their fault, not the teachers':

I think some of the kids don't like some of their teachers . . . they give them bad marks and they do a little work and they think they're supposed to give them good marks for that . . . it's just some of the kids over there. I would take the kids that are going to play around if they don't want to do their work, take them out of there, go someplace else.

As with family and peers, Keith views school as rightfully dominated by the authority figures whom he accepts at face value and to whose demands he expects himself and others to bend. The administration, he thinks, is doing a good job, "the best they can." He has never played hookey. (Keith's identification with authority seems almost complete when he tells the interviewer that his favorite comic book is about a "good guy who is covered with a lot of steel and has different kind of rays . . . he works for the Police Department.")

Keith adheres to his family's definition of school as the stepping stone to the "good life": school is "okay . . . a place where you can learn something. You need your education. You have to go all the way if you want one." He plans to attend college and feels he can do anything he makes his mind up to.

At Time I he describes his experiences with two jobs—paper boy and helper in a local grocery store. His account of the first job is positive: he made money, had no conflict with the white boss, and quit because he could not handle the route early in the mornings before boarding the bus for his suburban school (he has been in this program since the beginning of the eighth grade). The job at the store cut into his peer group and school work time, but is valued for the experience it gives him. In the Work Picture responses, Keith speaks of men "obeying orders," planning, carrying out directions, and so forth. But it is in the Self-Concept section of the interview that we see most clearly his conformist style. His style is tempered throughout by a pull toward autonomy, and by a relatively high self-concept and sense of internal control, which may later in life allow him to become more "together" than conformist in style. For example, Keith says he is good at mathematics, basketball, fixing televisions, and driving a car—because "I know a lot about it" or "I studied it a lot." (Keith was one of only three seventh-grade boys who named as many as five different skills that they were better at than the average boy their age.) The things he is not so good at (soccer, riding roller coasters alone, being in high places) he does not care about because he does not have to do them. When asked how he would like to be different, Keith replies: "I'd like to stay the same way as I am." If someone were trying to brainwash him, he would fight hardest to keep his "attitude . . . the way you talk to people . . . the way you act to people . . . react to them." He feels that his parents and best friend also would not have him change; nor does he perceive any conflict between how his parents and his peers want him to be.

Keith says he would not want to change places with anyone he knows with the possible exception of his brother (mainly because his brother has finished high school, has a good job, and is making money!); he would not change families if he had the chance.

In response to the "spy" question at Time I (below, page 255), Keith says he would tell the boy to "act just like I do—behave." He mentions taking the garbage downstairs when he comes home from school, washing the dishes, and mopping the floor. He would have to act "nice and all that" toward family members, teachers, and peers: "the same way toward everyone." Symbolic of Keith's positive attitude toward school is his insistence that the spy would not need to know how he acts in school since he "would probably be back by then—I wouldn't stay that long." When the interviewer presses him on how the spy would have to act toward Keith's teachers, he replies, "The same way toward everyone—just act nice."

The only point in the Time I interviews that Keith directly shows other than a passive-conformist style is in the Racial Awareness section. He says that if some white children called a black child "nigger" (and if the child knew what it meant), the child would probably "give them an argument . . . and probably would think about beating them up." Even here, however, he states it in terms of thinking about, rather than actually committing, an aggressive act. His general responses in this section reveal a fairly strong identification and satisfaction with being "Negro," as he calls himself, along with a tendency to prefer analyzing situations and events in terms of individual rather than in black-white terms.

For example, his reaction to hearing about a black leader being killed (presumably by a white person) is: "I would feel it would be between them two . . . and they probably . . . had an argument or something like that about whose race was better." He thinks that a local minister who was killed during a civil rights conflict in the South "shouldn't have gone over there . . . he knew it was rough." Then, "I felt kind of funny about it . . . he was a nice teacher." (Just as Keith would have had the minister avoid danger, he, too, would rather go to jail than to Vietnam, not for ideological reasons but because it is "dangerous over there.")

Keith's responses to the Race Pictures again recall the theme of fighting which adults break up. He also expresses a great deal of balance and sensitivity to the needs of others throughout his stories. His responses to the Racial Awareness schedule in general are much more soft-pedaled and filled with a sense of accepting one's fate than are those of his parents, grandfather, or brother.

Although he feels that "whites are just as bad as they say colored people are," Keith's response to hearing about a riot would be to wonder what was causing it, and to "feel kind of bad because they're just making a bad name for the race unless, let's say, that the white people had started something." As for interracial contact, he does not like dating, but approves of less intimate levels of social interaction. Keith would refuse to take a pill to make him white—"I'm satisfied with my own race." Nor would he push a "magic button" to make everybody the same race—"I think people are satisfied with the race they have. Not everybody can have the same color."

One disadvantage Keith sees in being black is that blacks do work for white people which white people should be able to do for themselves (presumably housecleaning, which his mother does). In overall racial awareness (knowledge of black people and organizations), he is above average. He feels America is changing for blacks, and by the time he grows up, he hopes "they won't be no more fighting and people will be able to get along with each other."

Characterizations by Others. "He just go like everybody . . ."

Winding its way throughout all of the Sutton family interviews is the stress laid on working and learning and being kind. It is evident that Keith is being guided along a carefully mapped route that has engaged his parents and grandparents and siblings before him.

His grandfather says that Keith's parents are very much interested in his future, "in seeing him get the type of an education that he's qualified to get." For this they will make sacrifices, "they'll do most anything that they can to help him along." Keith's father, he says, is a "fine fellow" who will do anything that he can for others; his mother is "the type of girl that . . . thinks an awful lot of her children" and is concerned about their future.

Keith's father says Keith takes after his grandfather and his mother; both sides of the family are "good people" and easygoing, "so he just go like everybody." Specifically, Mr. Sutton thinks Keith imitates him in fishing and eating, and follows his mother in his interest in church activities. Mrs. Sutton concurs: "he's well trained and he knows God . . . and he believes in the Ten Commandments. . . ."

The "easy-going" quality comes from him, declares Mr. Sutton:

I mean he'll want something and go without it before he'll ask for it likely . . . that's one part . . . like me; because I let people sometime just walk all over me till I get so tired and can't take no more; I just hold it inside, and when I do let go, I let it all go at once.

Keith tends also to let others "walk all over" him—in subtle ways, perhaps—but is not given to his father's angry outbursts. Rather, Keith apparently deals with angry and resentful feelings about the demands placed on him through a combination of passive resistance, procrastination, and occasional tears. As Mrs. Sutton comments in describing him as being thoughtful and sensitive, "He'll slow up one minute, and the next minute he's doing you a favor—that's the way I am." When he does not obey her requests, Mrs. Sutton scolds Keith, and "then he'll do it," but possibly with tears of frustration.

Mrs. Sutton says Keith is not like his father: "My husband is not as compassionate as he is . . . my husband doesn't show his feelings, and Keith does." It is positive feelings to which Mrs. Sutton refers. Both Keith and his father emphasize that Keith rarely shows anger in an open way. When he is angry with his grandfather, for example, he is unlikely to say anything. His grandfather says, "He may talk back to me, give me word for word once in a while, but it's seldom . . . he has utmost respect for me." Mrs. Sutton claims that when Keith is angry with her, he "sulks" and talks under his breath: "I say, what are you saying, and he says I'm not saying nothing . . . he mumbles out the door." His father maintains that Keith has never become angry with him, but adds that he notices the change in Keith when he is unhappy and will question him:

and maybe he might not tell you, but if you keep after him . . . then if you keep aggravating him by the reaction, you can get it yourself about what's wrong . . . but, I don't care how hurt he are, he never seem to show it you know.

When asked how he and his son get along, Mr. Sutton responds, "good, very good." He remarks that his own family of orientation was similar to Keith's, and that he held the same middle position Keith does, between an older brother and younger sister whom he watched frequently. Mr. Sutton characterizes Keith as a "pretty smart" baby who walked early, and who has always been "good to get along with." "He's always agreeable. He'll agree with you if you're right or wrong . . . I'll just say he's extremely good." He adds that Keith would "give you the shirt off his back . . . if he got a nickel, you can have half of that."

Part of this cooperative and helpful nature stems, Mrs. Sutton suggests, from the loving atmosphere in his family: "We're very devoted to each other . . . very close." When he goes into his bedroom after dinner to watch television, Keith and his little sister sometimes "pile right up on the bed" beside their father and watch with him. He enjoys this contact with his children, adding that the only time that Keith gets on his "nerves" is when he is trying to watch television and the children make too much noise. Even then, if he tells them to stop, they do. Mrs. Sutton says that the most important people to Keith are "his mother and father." Keith worries about them if they are sick, and "knows that if things doesn't go right we become unhappy, so he tries to make us happy."

Mrs. Sutton characterizes Keith as a "mischievous baby . . . he was always doing one thing after another." Now he is not so mischievous; "he's more grown up and talks more intelligently than he did before." She feels that she and Keith get along well:

Whenever I tell him, like if he says that he doesn't want to do a thing, and I show him I think that he should, he doesn't argue, he goes right on and does it. . . . He feels that whatever I say . . . is for the best and he accepts it as right so he does them.

Mr. Sutton feels that Keith is closest to his mother: "Naturally a child holds onto his mother mostly." Frank, who during the later stages of Time I interviewing was living out of his parents' house, claims that Keith is a "mama's boy" because he follows her proscriptions so closely: "He comes up to my house, and I'll say take a drink Keith, but he won't touch it . . . I've never seen him smoke neither. He might; maybe he won't do it because he figure I might get mad and tell my mother." He adds that before Molly was born, Keith was allowed to "get away" with misbehavior; now, he says, their mother is easy on the "baby" and is "tightening up on Keith . . . to try to get the whininess out of him, that baby out of him." Frank says that Keith does not like the fact that his sister can do things for which he would "get knocked off the side of the head— he doesn't like that at all. He's always throwing it in my mother's face."

Keith likes a lot of attention, says Frank, and knows how to get what he wants: "He's mature in one way, and he's immature in another way; like he'll cry and whimper for a whole lot of stuff, but he knows what he generally can get from you and what he can't get." This can be seen in the way Keith gets "his share" of money:

he doesn't really get allowance, he just hits you every day so to speak . . . Keith gets up early in the morning, he'll sell papers, he'll shine shoes; like if I give Keith a dollar, he's willing to work for it if I ask him to . . . he just gathers about $10 during the week easy by just doing me and everybody in the house.

Frank feels that Keith is not as dependable and cooperative as his parents have described him to be. He will do housework if "he's in the corner where he knows he has to do it," but will slip out of the house if he sees a chance to avoid helping. He likes Keith's quality of doing things for others, but would want to change the fact that Keith "lets people walk over him, you can stomp all over Keith." He describes Keith as "sensitive" and "weak—I don't think he'll ever be a roughneck or anything. I would make him meaner, I would make him more like me. . . . he's not evil, that guy ain't." Keith is like his mother; Frank is like his father.

Although Frank alludes to Keith's being "sneaky—you never know what Keith is going to do"—he captures his personality in these words: "he lets everything go the way it has to go . . . he gets along good with everybody . . . he always wants to learn . . . and he'll do anything for anybody—that's the type of person he is." This characterization is echoed by other family members. His relationship with his little sister especially is full of love and caring, according to Keith's grandfather:

Keith has taken a lot of pains with her . . . from the time that she came home from the hospital, until this present date, Keith is very attentive to her. He'll do anything for her . . . even give her a bath.

Yet Keith's conformist style, which comes out in both passive acceptance and more active helpfulness, is precarious. All of his family agree that Keith is highly sensitive, perhaps because of the pressure on him to be "good" and "nice." This is shown in Keith's reaction to doing something which brings adult disapproval: "He becomes very upset very easily . . . and at that time it isn't a good idea to penalize him too much . . . because when he gets upset he starts to cry, and he just goes, well, he just goes to pieces" (Grandfather). Grandfather hints that Keith's propensity for getting "upset easily" is often the result of his own doing. "He come in and get to fussing with the baby" over television—"times like that when he's irritable it seems as though he do things just deliberately to cause confusion among them so that upsets me a lot."

His mother adds that when Keith is sick, he is irritable and "goes straight to bed and cries if anyone says anything to him."

Frank summarizes well the unique combination of maturity, sensitivity, and naïveté that others in the family sense about Keith:

Keith is pretty mature for his age . . . he amazes me sometimes the way he does things . . . usually kids think foolish. He thinks foolish, you know, he got his simple acting ways . . . but at times he can really get serious and talk about stuff that you know, that I could even talk to you about . . . that's the way he is, but other than that he's bashful.

Keith's reaction to a "bad" report card is another example of his sensitivity. His grandfather says Keith will "do the best he can to solve" problems with his schoolwork: "In fact, he knows he have to do it . . . if he doesn't want to hear his mother." Recently, however, his report card from the suburban school, where he seemed to be hopelessly far behind, was so poor that Keith could not bring himself to show his mother until a guidance counselor from school called wondering why it had not been returned. Says his grandfather:

He knew his mother would get upset about it, and she would scold him about it, and . . . he can't take it . . . that's why I told her she have to be careful with him . . . because, you never know just what he'll do, you know. You take a kid, and if he becomes unduly upset, he's just liable to . . . quit.

Frank verifies the intensity of this pressure from Mrs. Sutton, both on himself and on Keith:

I said I was going to quit school one day—kidding—and she told me if I got too big for her to beat, she'd spit in my face . . . She's nothing like she was when I was small. My mother used to be pretty stern, but she's wicked now . . . She got well-informed now, you know [presumably about schools], and she's hell to be truthful about it.

Some of this pressure also stems from the fact that Keith is compared by Mrs. Sutton to her father in terms of his "ability to get ahead." She and the other adults in Keith's family believe he has the capacity to do well. College is viewed by them as the pathway to a better life, particularly because it is likely to lead to intellectual rather than manual labor. Mrs. Sutton expresses this: "Digging ditches! I mean you can get yourself a typewriter or something and sit down and make a good week's salary, use your brains for a change, right?"

The Suttons feel that Keith is capable of finishing high school and even college, but place no pressure on him to follow a particular career line—"that would be left entirely up to him." The emphasis is clearly on working to one's potential.

Moving out of the immediate environment of the family, Keith takes with him into his peer and school life not only this pressure toward achievement, but also a bent toward respect for authority (often in terms of unquestioning obedience) and tolerance for others. For example, while Mrs. Sutton thinks that Keith is probably brighter than his older brother, she emphasizes Keith's way of relating to others as being equally important: "He's more alert . . . Keith is going to surpass him . . . because my oldest one, he doesn't like to take orders and Keith does, he'll listen." Although Keith is high on determination, he is perceived by his teachers as a "very nice child" who has "respect for the others."

The DuBois was the scene of disturbances during Keith's attendance there (small fires, demonstrations, suspensions, and so forth, all with racial overtones). Mrs. Sutton says she has not discussed the trouble with Keith; she suspects he hesitates to interfere: "Keith is afraid because one thing about it is that if you voice your opinion, then they'll be ready to beat you up so the best thing to do is mind your own business and go on." None of the family likes the school; Keith himself did not want to go there, but could not attend another school because they were all overenrolled. By the time of her first interview, Mrs. Sutton had arranged for Keith to be bused to a suburban Boston school for the rest of his secondary education. She is of the opinion that suburban schools are better: "I think they learn more, and you come in contact with different people, people who are trying to get ahead and make something of themselves." Echoing the Coleman report, she theorizes, "birds of a feather flock together . . . and if you be around a person, sometimes, you know, a child has a great influence over another child."[7]

Keith's parents feel that much of the "trouble" at the DuBois is a direct result of the lack of training and discipline by parents. They drum into Keith's head not only admonishments to achieve well, but also the notion that even if one cannot learn, he can obey:

You do not go to school to teach the teacher, because she knows; if she didn't she wouldn't be there. You can obey if nothing more . . . you can get A in conduct if nothing else. . . . that's one thing about it, you can be obedient.

[Mother]

She continues (confirming, incidentally, what many social scientists have discovered regarding how teachers grade their students): "you know, regardless of who you are, if the teachers find that you want to learn, and that you're obedient, naturally they'll pay attention to you, and it makes a difference."[8] Keith's grandfather feels that one problem at the DuBois is a lack of understanding by the teachers of "colored kids"—"they deal with them in a condescending manner . . . they feel moreover that here's a child you don't expect too much from him anyway; he's incapable because of the fact that he's colored. . . ."[9] He says of Keith and school: "He's not the type of a kid that will give a teacher a lot of trouble . . . when they tell him to do anything, he does it." Keith's docility is contrasted with the "terrible" behavior of other students, which his parents and grandfather feel is at the bottom of the school's difficulties.

It is indicative of Keith's style that, although he disliked the DuBois and "didn't care too much for the way they taught," he nonetheless "went along with it." In fact, as his grandfather notes, because there were so many children there who did not want to work, Keith was considered a "goof" for taking school seriously. Mr. Sutton adds that Keith has done much of the learning on his own in spite of the "bad environment" at the DuBois. He feels that his son is too school-oriented in a sense: "He tried to take up too devilish much at one time . . . he wants to learn it all as he goes along." He claims that Keith works hard in and out of school, "He just don't seem to let up."

Clearly Keith receives a substantial amount of encouragement and support regarding his education. Mr. Sutton makes it clear that Keith receives more "guidance" than actual help with his homework. He claims that Mrs. Sutton and the grandfather "give him an idea, and then he can go for himself." This responsibility and opportunity for making his own way in life is shown in Keith's response to failing the Classical High School test by only three points: "He didn't want to blame anyone, he just felt bad because he didn't pass, and when I asked him his reason for not passing, he said he just didn't know the work. It was new to him."[10]

Mrs. Sutton feels that Keith is a "little on the timid side," and at the time of her interview is not sure how Keith will fare in the suburban school. She views his timidity optimistically, however, because he "doesn't pick a fight, he minds his own business." Frank openly refers to Keith's ease in fitting into a white suburban school as a result of his conformist style and moderate racial views. He says that Keith would be able to handle the situation and adds, "I'm glad I wasn't my brother because I couldn't have did it, I couldn't have mixed with whities." (Yet Frank, in spite of his racial views, which are probably the most radical in the family, has developed extremely positive and nondocile relationships with the white people in the insurance company where he is employed.)

Keith's best friend, Alfie, feels that Keith gains an advantage through going to the suburban school: "He sees the way most of these kids act, and I think he's getting advanced to see it." He claims that Keith "likes being a Negro." His grandfather says that Keith is becoming more aware of race, especially since entering junior high school, but does not think that "color means so much to Keith" because he has had so many good friends who happened to be white:

I just tell Keith, don't think about the fact that you are a Negro; just try to prepare himself to compete with anybody irrespective of who they are or what color they may be. The color of a man's skin certainly doesn't give him any monopoly on education.

Mr. Sutton's influence on Keith's racial identity is profound. He says there is no sense in wishing he were white—he cannot "wipe" his color off. While Mr. Sutton is proud to be black, he is relatively low in racial awareness; he did not understand the concept of "black power," for example. Mr. Sutton believes that Keith has always known the meaning of "nigger," although he has never heard his son use that term or "Negro": "I guess he always, he seem to know it. In fact he could see the difference in some of his friends that he was playing with, but they get along perfectly." What Mr. Sutton lacks in racial awareness, Mrs. Sutton and Keith's grandfather make up for in their knowledge of civil rights organizations and black leaders. Both are integrationalists who believe there are good and bad people in both races. Mrs. Sutton, who says, "I don't go too much for color anyway . . . I'm not prejudiced at all," feels that schools should have a mixture of teachers (as does Keith, who insists on judging a person by his talent rather than his race). Predictably, she does not like the Black Muslims, for in her opinion they represent violence and view white people as "devils"—yet she is angry and well-informed in her discussion of the black person's place in America: "You can't take no back seat, you always got to know a little more because there's one mark that they have against us anyway—our face is dark."

Keith and his friends, Alfie, Herbie, and Chip, usually can be found playing basketball in the back yard, football in the school yard, or baseball in a nearby field. They also spend quite a bit of time in Keith's house (Mr. Sutton remarks, "We can never get lonely where I live . . . we have too much company"). Keith's parents do not have many rules about where he can go or what he can do, except to stay out of trouble and be home before dark. They generally know his whereabouts.

His parents agree that Keith's friends are all "pretty nice boys" who do not exhibit any "bad" behavior. Mrs. Sutton says Alfie is "well mannered, he isn't rowdy, and I don't think he has any bad habits." Asked if Keith ever swears, Mr. Sutton replies: "No. I never heard nobody on the street mention anything about it. People come up and say 'yours is a nice boy' . . . as a matter of fact they said that of both of my sons." He adds that one advantage Keith has over most boys his age is "manners for one thing . . . I'm talking about this misbehavior in the street and their disrespect for people around here."

The Suttons compare Keith's "good" and "quiet" behavior in his peer life with the "rowdies" who race their cars through the streets. Mr. Sutton says he does not feel safe walking outside at night. Both parents agree that there is nothing "wrong" with Roxbury—"it's just the people in it . . . people are people regardless of where you go." (Mrs. Sutton says that she, like so many others, would like to move out to Mattapan or a similar area: "You can hear the crickets out there—this way you don't hear no crickets." She complains that her house has rats and roaches.) Mr. Sutton does not interact socially with his neighbors, but expects them to cooperate by chastising Keith if they see him misbehaving:

> I can't raise no children by myself. . . . I say don't wait till you get to me. I say chastise him for it, if he give you any back talk, just let me know and I'll get that straightened out myself. I wanted respect. And so far I haven't had no trouble with them. . . . It's nice when people speak well of your son, not that they are better than anybody else, but you know, we really try.

Typically, Keith likes a white man on their street who teaches him typewriting, but does not like an older man who drinks heavily: "Keith don't care for all that loud talking and drinking and carrying on." In any case, Keith's heavy orientation toward school devours his time and diminishes the possible influence of any contradictory nonschool value system the street might offer.

Alfie has known Keith for about five years. He considers the basis of their relationship the fact that their parents know each other and get along well, and that they live next door to each other. He corroborates Keith's view that their group has no real leader. They do not make formal rules, but Alfie feels that one understanding is that he and Keith would never hurt each other. In spite of this closeness, Alfie appears to be caught between two distinctly different styles within his small peer group—Keith the Conformist on the one hand, and Herbie and Chip who are flirting with an openly Tough Guy style, on the other. Alfie claims that Herbie sometimes wants him to tell Keith that they do not want him "hanging around" with them because he is too small "or something like that." A careful reading of Alfie's transcript suggests that Herman's rejection of Keith is due to the latter's naïveté and reluctance to participate in some of the more deviant activities in which Herbie is peripherally involved. Alfie reaffirms his loyalty to Keith: "You know, we couldn't be enemies to each other. . . . I don't think we could split up because we just that kind of group, and I just couldn't tell him I didn't want to go around with him."

Alfie plays a balancing act, then, which finds him spending proportionately more time with Herbie and Chip because of Keith's "conformist" activities. Yet, he aligns himself squarely on Keith's side in terms of values and ideals, and refuses to exclude Keith from the peer group: "because me and Keith are just like that . . . whatever I know he knows it, we just that good friends." Alfie says that other boys like Keith, although he admits that Chip is somewhat cool to Keith because he is envious of Keith's success in school. Chip is "always trying to fight him, and I try to tell him, there ain't no way . . . he could prove anything by fighting."

In any case, Alfie and Keith dislike fighting. Alfie speaks of a boy across the street who was knifed and killed the previous year: "I don't fight no one with a knife; I wouldn't fight anyway." Mr. Sutton confirms that Keith "don't like to fight," to the point of letting bigger youth push him around too much. Brother Frank has had to go out and speak to one boy who was picking on Keith. "Once they find out that he's not the fighting type, they don't bother him any more." Alfie notes:

When we were going to school, there was a bunch of kids that . . . want to fight all the time, but we never did bother with them. They come and pull out knives, but if you ask them to fight fair, they'll put it in their pocket and when you come right at them they'll snatch it right out so I said let's go on home and mind our own business.

Keith and his friends, then, do not smoke, drink, swear, steal, or get into gang fights. In an ironic way, some of this conformity to parental values can also be seen as willingness *not* to conform to often self-destructive subcultural values. For example, Keith's grandfather makes a point several times in his interview that he and Keith's parents try to teach all the children to "dare to stand alone." It is not enough to tell a child not to do something; he believes you must also give them reasons why:

I tell them if you smoke and drink, it's easy to do that to conform . . . You don't have to conform. Dare to stand alone. If other kids drink, other kids smoke, its detrimental to their being . . . you don't have to do it . . . you never break a law, you run up against a law, and the law breaks you, whether that be a moral law or whatever.

Alfie feels that he and Keith are very much alike. Grandfather concurs, saying that Alfie is a "nice kid" with whom Keith has a lot in common. Mr. Sutton attests to a caring relationship between Alfie and Keith when he speaks of his son: "He got all his friends, I mean they give him the greatest respect. Sometime I get so tired at night, you'd think he was a girl so many of his boy friends come to the house, and they sit down there with him, you know." Alfie says that he trusts Keith most of all the friends he has; that Keith is the most generous; and that of all his friends, Keith likes Alfie the most in return. They share common interests (sports and school) and a penchant toward obedience.

In spite of their obviously intimate relationship, Alfie hints that Keith in a way lets him down, mainly by forgetting to bring his basketball home from school when he knows his friends will want to play with it Saturday mornings:

It seem like every time we ask him, he forgets it. I don't know if he's try-ing to let us down or not because he doesn't go with us, he could go if he wanted to, but he rather . . . he stays around and try to make a little extra money.

However, on the occasion of a fire in Alfie's house, Keith was the only one who invited him to stay overnight with him. And when Alfie had to visit the dentist, Keith encouraged him, telling him the novocaine was not so painful. Alfie appreciated Keith's ac-companying him, but adds, "I ran out, I couldn't stand it, I left Keith sitting down in there."

Keith's relationship to Alfie is typified in how they handle con-flict between them. When they disagree, says Alfie:

We usually go around asking other people or mostly if we have a argu-ment about some sport or something, he'll call down at the *Boston Globe* or something . . . but if we have a personal problem, we'll go and ask his mother or someone like that.

In this case, Keith's typical appeal to authority is evident. Alfie and Frank agree that Keith generally relies on adults to solve his inter-personal conflicts, but that he occasionally toys with aggressive behavior himself. Frank says that sometimes Keith will "act tough" in front of his peers by punching him in the back or "saying some-thing smart to me."

Alfie believes that, of all their friends, he and Keith will be the most successful in life: "because we're the ones . . . that seem to be trying, and we're talking about going ahead in life." He thinks he and Keith will also be the happiest because they will have good jobs and earn money. Alfie, who would like to be an engineer, says he has heard Keith aspire to be a lawyer.

The family maintains a "hands off" attitude toward Keith's work future. Mr. Sutton migrated to Boston from Georgia at age 16, went to work in a factory, then was employed as a skilled laborer in the food industry until the plant was shut down 16 years later. After a short period in construction, he became a skilled worker in a machine shop. Regarding his hopes for Keith's future, Mr. Sutton says: "I'd like for him to live a good decent life . . . a respectable life . . . that's something that's a pretty good ways off, but if he live the life that his mother and I try to teach him, he can't go too far wrong." He hopes Keith at age 40 will not be doing the kind of work he is doing: "I hope he'll be able to accomplish something where he can sit back and work with his brains, and take it easy—not get out there and do back-breaking work like I'm doing."

By the time Mr. Sutton is interviewed, Keith has landed a job at the nearby corner store. Mr. Sutton thinks it is fine that Keith is working, partly because it will help him later. Grandfather agrees:

I consider it a great experience. He had to learn how to use the cash register, he learns to wait on customers, and any time a colored kid can get that experience, I consider it a good thing . . . especially when you have no choice but to work your own way through school.

Furthermore, Mr. Sutton is pleased with the way Keith spends his money—soda and cupcakes for himself, gifts for the family: "he'd buy me something, if it was nothing but a pair of socks, gifts like that. He don't forget no special occasion like a birthday or Father's Day. . . ." He adds that Keith would share some of his money with Molly, and treats his friends occasionally. "In fact I feel so proud I want to let him know all the time. I just don't want to let him know all the time how I feel, and I keep telling him he can do better." Mrs. Sutton disagrees, saying, "if you just don't pin him down, he will spend all that money on junk." Both parents acknowledge that Keith does not spend his money on clothes—"he doesn't care how he looks" just as long as the clothes are clean. Mrs. Sutton says Keith is "meek and humble" in addition to being nonmaterialistic, and would make a good preacher or doctor. This reflects her own avocation as "missionary" in her church. For his future she hopes that "someday he will own his own home, and I hope he'd be a good father and train his children, and be living the good life in front of them, and in teaching them."

It is important that the only changes Keith's family would like to see in him reflect more growth in the same direction in which he is moving. Grandfather would have him develop more motivation for the things he wants to do in life. His philosophy, which he tries to impress on Keith is: "Do yourself justice. Every day do the very best that you can." Mrs. Sutton views Keith as a quiet, well-mannered child (not a rowdy type); she does not want him to change at all: "I would like for Keith to stay just the way he is because to me I think he's a good child . . . he'll grow up to be quite a young man if he doesn't change because he's very compassionate, and he's very thoughtful. . . ." Her advice to Keith combines conformity to mainstream values (and parental values in this case) with a propulsion toward "being your own man" and definite autonomy:

Be something . . . to make something out of your life, to try to be yourself, to try to progress, to try to elevate yourself in life. Don't try to be what you're not . . . and stay out of trouble, you know, don't go with a crowd even though they may call you chicken, just be yourself.

Mr. Sutton would not want Keith to change either: "I wouldn't like him to change, to tell you the truth. I might want him to better himself a little bit more, if he could be better than he is. . . ." His philosophy of life reveals a strength and stubborn autonomy which may serve well as a role model for personal growth and independence, rather than striving for praise and approval of others and playing by their rules. Says Mr. Sutton:

Life is worth living. Life is what you make it, too. You can make it miserable for yourself and you can make a decent life too . . . I didn't beg nobody for nothing. I go and eat just what I want, and I didn't sleep in a doorway.

His reaction to the Pathways project? "Well, it sure makes you take more interest in your child when you're sure that someone else is thinking about him besides you."

Analysis of the Conformist Style

Keith at Time I can be characterized as moving with the others in his life. Analysis of his focal cluster reveals an overwhelmingly consistent conformist strategic style. In some respects Keith is more the "too-good guy" than the "all right guy," although the thrust appears to be toward the latter. For him the critical dilemma of adolescence is to develop a sense of self which is not exclusively in response to the demands and expectations of others. Issues of independence and autonomy are central to his developing identity.

Earlier we defined the "too-good guy" as clinging to means even after goals have been discarded or have become relatively less important. To some extent Keith fits this definition. For example, he does his homework quickly and at the last minute, in order to please his parents—more, it seems than to please himself. The key element in Keith's style is that even if doing well in school were to diminish as a goal (whether imposed or internalized), pleasing his parents would not. Above all we see Keith struggling to find a place of his own in the world that will meet with the approval of his significant others.

There is plenty of evidence in the preceding pages that the adults in Keith's life (especially his mother) are exceedingly demanding in their expectations of him. It is clear that he strives to meet these expectations and goes to pieces when he fails to do so. He feels deeply rewarded when he manages to make these others happy, and equally guilty when he does not.

The external pressures to which Keith is subjected are wrapped up in parental expectations. His internal pressures focus on wanting to play with his friends and, generally, to be free. Keith plays a delicate balancing game between these two sets of pressures. That Alfie sees Keith as his best and most trustworthy friend indicates that Keith is successful in his peer relationships; that his family thinks so highly of him indicates a relatively successful family role. Before we analyze in depth the critical messages from others and Keith's reactions to them, it is necessary to place his family's values into perspective.

The Family Matrix.   For the society as a whole, conformity is the modal adaptation. As Rainwater points out, however, for members of the black "slum culture," the conformist style is "exceedingly vulnerable to the threats of unemployment or a less than adequate pay check, on the one hand, and the seduction and violence of the slum world around them, on the other." [12] The case study of Keith reveals that as a Conformist he risks being considered a "square" by those for whom the conventional mainstream values are less salient.

Placing the conformist style in a subcultural context, we may best interpret it in its relationship to the "lower class value stretch." [13] Although a family like Keith's may hold certain communal or subcultural values, its members also—like most, if not all, ghetto residents—hold or subscribe to certain cultural or mainstream values, some of which may be conflicting or contradictory. The Suttons have opted for the latter, and exert great effort to avoid slipping into the negative or conflicting subcultural values. They socialize their children into mainstream values, leaving no stone unturned (work, education, religion, stable family, dreamed-of suburban residence, the "good life" and so forth).

Rainwater speaks of "strategies for living" (the good life and career success) in which the central concerns involve "efforts to get along with others and not to rock the boat, a comfortable familism grounded on a stable work career for husbands in which they perform adequately at the modest jobs that enable them to be good providers." [14] Keith's family fits this picture, and the future life they are pushing Keith toward looks very similar. Given the environment in which the Suttons are living, this strategy must be seen as vulnerable, but also (from our data, and the data of other social scientists) as viable even for the most poverty-stricken families. The Suttons remind us that the conformist style is an option in terms of at least goals and values and strivings, if not in terms of actual success in gaining the rewards the larger system holds out for all. The high value placed on education is in itself a mainstream value which, if pursued, leads to self-discipline and an ethic of self-improvement which are also normatively prescriptive from the point of view of the dominant cultural framework. As we can see with the Suttons, this is a familial style handed down through several generations on both sides of Keith's heritage.

The Suttons are perhaps an extreme case of this family type, especially Mrs. Sutton, who represents a rigidly moral position and demands from all her children extremely high levels of obedience to conventional morality and to elevated standards of achievement. She apparently feels that the least bit of slacking off might lead to embracement of (for her) a deviant style of life—and thus she pressures her children to toe a very straight and clearly drawn mark indeed. That she has managed to do this in the face of those distracting and seductive forces Rainwater speaks of (including residence in the heart of Roxbury and severe strains stemming from the illness of husband and father, with her husband's resulting lack of work for long periods) may be a partial explanation of why she has become even stricter over the years, and why, at the time of first interviewing, Keith was more the "too-good guy" than the "all right guy" in some ways.

At the heart of the socialization process for this familial pattern is acceptance by others of feelings and behaviors that "fit" the appropriate mold, and rejection of or punishment for "negative" feelings such as anger or disagreement with cherished values, or for disobedience. Thus the critical influence in the formation of Keith's conformist strategic style is twofold: the clearly conformist expectations held by others toward him, and the discipline which those others utilize to bring Keith into line with those expectations. Let us examine in greater detail the shaping of conformity.

Critical Messages from Others.   Keith's family expects him to be obedient, hardworking, respectful of authority, school and work oriented, honest, kind, God-fearing, and even-tempered. For the most part, Keith is all of these. How do these messages get translated into behavior? Frank emphasizes the centrality of right and wrong in their upbringing: "Both ways—you get rewarded and you get punished, that's it."

Praise is abundant for Keith. When he brings home a good report card (which is almost always during the first seven years of school), his mother "says it's nice, keep up the good work." Father and grandfather echo her praise. Mrs. Sutton likes Keith to wash clothes and clean the house while she is working (cleaning house for white suburban families). When Keith complies, she rewards him by taking him places, buying him things, or giving him money. Her authority, like her husband's, is well tempered, with openly expressed affection:

If he brings home a good report card I hug him and kiss him, tell him that I'm happy . . . I promise him I'll buy him something that he wants, or I'll put my arms around him and tell him how proud of him I am.

In discussing punishment and rules, Mrs. Sutton indicates that she sees a child's energy as a natural phenomenon whose absence means that something is wrong with the child. She feels that children are never more trouble than they are worth, but also believes that it is crucial to "train" and teach a child from the early years as to what is right and wrong. If you show love when they are small, she says, "they won't want for it":

I believe in showing my children that I love them and respect them . . . when I tell them something it's for their own good, and I explain to them that if I didn't care, then I wouldn't care what happens to them . . . but I try to let them know that I love them, and regardless of what happens, I would want them to come and tell me, and talk it over with me regardless of whether it's bad or whether it's good.

Symbolic of this discipline/affection approach to child-rearing is Mrs. Sutton's belief that a parent can give in to a child's wishes some but not all of the time. If you do not give them enough of the material objects they desire, they might go out and steal; if you give them all, they will be spoiled. Money plays a central and catalytic role in Keith's relationship with other family members as well. He "gets" money from his father, grandfather, and brother. He evidently receives no regular allowance, but feels that he has enough to spend. (Brother Frank and grandfather confirm that Keith manages to wangle quite a bit of money out of them.) It is apparent that Keith uses money as a concrete symbol of adult love and acceptance; in turn, he frequently uses the money not only to reward himself, but also to show love and affection toward others. What is seen by Frank as a not so subtle "con" game might better be termed "bargaining"—"I'll be good but you must pay for it." This is typified by his willingness to do equally concrete work for the money: ironing a shirt, cleaning a room, running an errand.

Mrs. Sutton speaks of negative sanctions. If Keith forgets to take out the garbage, she reminds him and "he starts crying you know, and he'll start sobbing and says that I'm making him do too much." She will then scold him, stressing that he must not talk to his mother that way, and that if he does it again, she will spank him. Sometimes she makes him stay in the house or takes privileges away from him ("the things that he likes"). It is clear that not only refusal to contribute to the family responsibilities is punished, but also nonconformity to standards regarding interpersonal behavior.

Both parents emphasize verbal rather than physical discipline. Mr. Sutton feels their "training" of Keith has been successful:

He knows right from wrong . . . he try to do the right thing most of the time. If he think it's wrong, I don't think he will do it—I never had to scold that child. In fact I think I spanked him once in his life . . . but he never needed it . . . never had to even put him on punishment or anything . . . just a good kid.

From his father's point of view, a presentation of alternatives will usually suffice to persuade Keith to conform to his parents' wishes:

Well, if he wants to go some place, and you tell him he can't go, he won't cry or give you no argument or back talk or anything . . . if he can't go to the movie, he'll ask can he go play with some of his cousins.

Mrs. Sutton is confident that her ultimate authority will sway Keith when gentle reasoning and persuasion do not work: "He sulks . . . he thinks it over, and he finds that I'm going to win anyway, so he's just sorry for himself, but he sulks because he wants to do what he wants to do." If Keith can make a good case for his request, Mrs. Sutton says she will give in.

Keith's parents differ somewhat in their views on how discipline is handled with Keith. Mrs. Sutton apparently spends more time with the children than her husband does, and consequently is more involved in the discipline. Furthermore, everyone in Keith's family mentions at one time or another in the interviewing that Mrs. Sutton makes most of the decisions in the house, including financial. Mrs. Sutton acknowledges this:

He goes along with me, whatever I say . . . my husband is the type that . . . would scold the one minute and the next minute he's trying to reason why he did it. He's on the soft side; he scolds them . . . then he's trying to pet them and tell them he's sorry and all that, and that is wrong.

Keith's brother adds another dimension to the parental image. He says that Keith "is more or less scared" of his father, something which comes across in neither Keith's interview, nor his father's. Frank states his case persuasively: "My brother, he doesn't want to get knocked in the head no more than once so he won't do it." Nonetheless, it seems that the general way of disciplining Keith is through consistent firmness and reasoning with him, as well as through appealing to Keith's sense of guilt and responsibility. This last factor is important in understanding Keith's proclivity for obeying and conforming to his parents' expectations.

It is not insignificant that one quality others would like Keith to change is his forgetfulness and his lack of sustained motivation. They also speak of his "whininess." Perhaps in his effort to please others Keith "overloads" and eventually finds ways (consciously or unconsciously) to avoid meeting their expectations: he forgets his basketball on the way to meeting Alfie; he slips out of the house before being collared for some chore; he turns in sloppy homework; he teases his little sister; he loses interest in projects defined as "good for him."

Part and parcel of his patently conformist style, then, is an element of resistance to it. In the midst of "striving for acceptance" and "avoidance of guilt," Keith feels overtaxed in his efforts to please everyone, so he loafs or hangs back, feels guilty, is scolded, ultimately meets the demand. His occasional tears can thus be seen as an expression both of his guilt in not complying in the first place, and perhaps his anger at being placed in such a tightly laced corset of rules and expectations.

The Impact of Role Models.   Keith is obviously carrying on a family tradition of placing a high value on education, coupled with hard work and commitment to excellence. As Mr. Sutton remarks, alluding to the fact that both he and his wife did well in school, Frank and Keith have "both sides of us that they do take from." Of Keith's voluntary attendance at summer school, he adds, "Of course it costs . . . to send him to school, but it's worth it, it keep him out of the streets, you know." [15]

Of all the adults he knows, Keith says he feels closest to his father—"we play around and go different places." He feels that he "takes after" his father, but wants to grow up to be like his mother, especially to have her "attitude" and to be "nice to people." Keith points to one reflection of his own cooperativeness when asked how he is like his mother: "She does different things for me; when I ask her she doesn't all the time say no." He thinks that he acts and speaks like his mother. The family members all concur that grandfather has been of great importance in Keith's schooling. Frank mentions that once "you start studying," one becomes close to grandfather. Indeed, Keith would also like to be like his grandfather, who originally planned to become a doctor, spent three years at Howard University, then succumbed to a long and painful series of operations and finally amputation of one leg. He worked, when he was able, as a chef in a fish restaurant. For Keith, his grandfather possibly represents the strongest impetus toward getting a good education. He helps Keith with his homework and tells him to "keep it up."

Frank mentions that Keith takes him as a positive role model, perhaps because Frank watched him often during their younger years. ("As a matter of fact I minded Keith half my life if you want to get down to it.") Whatever Frank likes, Keith likes. They share a common interest in sports and music, mainly through Frank's lead: "He loves the Miracles [a black singing group] now just because I love them . . . plain everything I like he likes."

Frank also serves to reinforce the support Keith receives from his parents and his grandfather regarding school success. Frank admires Keith for his perseverance in school, and is convinced that Keith will "turn out to be something." He admits that the strain might be too much for Keith, but feels certain that his younger brother will not "collapse." If he needs help or becomes discouraged, Frank says he will "have enough sense to help him out then": "My brother knows he always got me with him so . . . as a matter of fact I think he's going to do better than me, twice as good as me. As a matter of fact I know he is." Since Keith looks up to Frank for his ability to hold a white-collar job and command a good income, these supportive attitudes are all the more salient for Keith.

Finally, Keith receives support for his role of "good student" from his friend Alfie, who also places a high value on staying in school and doing well. As mentioned earlier, Alfie is a bit more street-wise than Keith and appears to serve as a buffer between Keith and the tougher, more deviant styles of their other friends. Thus Keith's choice of best friend provides him with another prototype of the kind of youth his parents want him to be—"good," "nice," school oriented, and on the right side of the law.

Keith is unusual in the Pathways sample in having three positive male role models: father, grandfather, brother. Many boys have none, or at best one. His mother's strength is balanced nicely by the positive male models he can look toward. In addition to images of conformity and responsibility, Keith also finds nurturance and gentleness in all of his role models, both male and female. Keith's adult models stand for fairly rigid standards, which occasionally lead him to a sense of failure or guilt. I think it is critical to Keith's growth that Alfie and Frank offer not only compassion and loyalty, but also models of flexibility for those moments when adhering to adult standards seems to require superhuman effort.

Other Issues. Two other issues are central to understanding Keith's strategic style: his blindness in one eye, and his experience in suburban schools.

The question must be raised as to how much impact partial blindness has had on the cultivation of Keith's conformist style. Frank says that Keith never admits that his eye bothers him in any way, yet sometimes he notices him rubbing it when watching television or reading. He feels that Keith does not let it hamper his ability to play sports with his friends. In fact, he thinks Keith is a better basketball player than his friends: "He got a good eye. And that's amazing. Maybe that one eye makes him aim more accurately or something, but he shoots better than they do." The blindness may be a source of strength and determination, then, but it is also a source of sensitivity. Frank says that Keith deals with his handicap so well that Frank on at least one occasion misjudged his brother's sensitivity about it:

One day he was messing around, messing around, bothering me about something. . . . and I turned around and I said, "you blind little sucker, get out of my hair"—and it really hurt him, you know, and I didn't think nothing of it . . . and he be crying all over the place.

Keith may feel comfortable in playing sports, but he assiduously avoids street fighting. Obviously his parents teach him not to fight—but is the blindness another factor that keeps him out of "trouble?" Frank claims that Keith has never seen him fight, but assumes that his older brother could "whip" anybody. Frank's peer group is the exact opposite of Keith's—"my friends like to fight, you know, at the drop of a hat—so he looks up to me and all my friends anyway." If it were not for the handicap, perhaps Keith would look to Frank more as a model for fighting than as his "protector." Frank expresses his own protective feelings toward Keith: "I'd never let him fight, I wouldn't care who it is or where, if I was there, I would never let him . . . never. And there ain't nobody going to be hurting him either."

The other factor which stands to make a difference in Keith's future life is both a consequence of his conformity and a reinforcement of it. Because Keith was always a docile, hard-working, good student, he was a natural to be chosen (at his mother's request) for participation in a busing program from their impoverished Roxbury neighborhood school to a school in middle-class, white suburbia. His mother feels that Keith is not only brighter but more cooperative and less militant than Frank. Consequently, she is convinced that he will do well in the suburban setting. Although he is overwhelmed by the work as of the eighth grade (end of Time I interviews), Keith nonetheless presses on in his effort to "make the grade"—Mrs. Sutton's predictions seem to be coming true. If Keith successfully completes high school in this program, that in turn will propel him further toward the mainstream "good life" from which his parents' values stem in the first place.

Keith's Alternatives. In order to answer the question whether Keith has real alternatives to the conformist style he seems embedded in, we must explore the extent to which his parents' goals are his goals. This is a difficult question; there seem to be three major possibilities:

(1) he has internalized their goals;

(2) he acts as though their goals are his, but in fact his true goal is to please his parents;

(3) he happens to hold the same goals his parents do, but independently of them.

The third possibility would seem highly unlikely given what we know about the value systems of the significant others in his life, and given theories of role-taking and identification among children. Of the two remaining possibilities, my analysis is that both are in operation.

That is to say, many of the parental values have in fact become meaningful to Keith in and of themselves, initially through imitation and trying to please others, and later through his own reasoning and insight. The crux of the conformist style is that even when the content of the goals loses salience for Keith, he nonetheless continues to work toward them in a kind of ritual observance of conformity, in the service of meeting the still vital secondary goal of gaining parental approval.

It is conceivable that with increasing years and relatively more experience outside the parental umbrella, Keith will move from a fundamentally conformist to a fundamentally "together" strategic style. For along with the pressures to obey and succeed and achieve and be "good," we have also heard messages of "dare to stand alone" and admonishments for Keith to be himself. One indication that these messages have registered is Keith's reported willingness to take responsibility for his failing the Classical High School exam; another is his choice of work rather than play activities after school, which presumably serve to make him more independent financially. Although it is difficult to imagine Keith moving out of a conformist style completely, it is possible that he will find the room to replace striving for acceptance and avoidance of guilt with independence and autonomy.

A not so pleasant alternative—hinted by parents and brother alike and suggested by Keith's own behavior (e.g., his withholding an unsatisfactory report card from his parents)—is that Keith will undergo what Sullivan calls a "malevolent transformation." This involves the child's finding that his expression of the need for tenderness (and understanding) from his family habitually brings anxiety or pain. He thus adopts the "basic malevolent attitude" that he is living among enemies.[16] Whether Keith develops along these lines or toward further autonomy—or remains stuck in his conformist style—only time will tell. It is obvious from the emphasis placed on school by Keith and his family that his experiences in the realm of school and work will play an important role in influencing the nature of Keith's adult strategic style.

Analytical Dimensions.   On the basis of characterizations by self and others, we can see that Keith is clearly at the positive end of the affiliation dimension (as shown in the Basic Interpersonal Orientation Table, above, page 17). He is attracted toward other people in a friendly rather than a hostile way. He is capable of establishing warm interpersonal relationships. His motivational impetus, in large part, is a wish to please those whom he loves and who love him in return. He is intent on being close to and accepted by others, rather than using, destroying, injuring, or leaving them.

Yet it is also clear that Keith responds to the people and situations in his life largely on the basis of how others define his responses *for* him.[17] Along the power dimension it seems reasonable to place him closer to the submissive rather than the dominant end of the continuum. Keith moves *with* others in his day-to-day interactions, allowing them (all too often) to supply him with values, goals, attitudes, and a moral outlook. He lacks the self-knowledge, the insight, and the reserve to define situations for himself; to do so would be to threaten the balance of love and acceptance he receives from significant others—or to incur their wrath, or his own guilt.

For these reasons I propose that Keith operates from a slightly defensive (and therefore slightly insecure) stance. He may improvise on the script of his style, but only within certain conventional and parentally approved lines. Although I feel that he may develop more security and strength with age, at Time I he is still caught in a defensive position.

Furthermore, Keith plays his style with a certain amount of contrivance. He postures, pretends, tries to get away without being perfectly good and obedient. His "sneakiness" indicates that he is, in a literal sense, often playing the role of "good little boy," and not entirely believing in it. Yet we could hardly call this cynicism, as Goffman intends the term. The pain of guilt and the agony of remorse that greet his *failing* to meet parental expectations seem real enough.

Conclusion

My interpretation, then, is that Keith's conformist style—as overwhelmingly consistent as it may appear to be—is stretched and pulled to allow Keith some breathing space. He shows some deviance when he is frustrated in attempting to achieve his goals. This minor nonconformity is to be expected, even though the pressures in his immediate environment are largely toward conformist behavior. An airtight conformist style might, in fact, indicate a form of social, if not mental, illness.

Kovar defines autonomy as a "temporary withdrawal from others . . . that helps to reinforce one as a separate and distinct personality in personal relations."[18] Although Keith is fundamentally a conformist, the little ways in which he resists being defined by others and their expectations of him can be viewed as movement toward autonomy. Ruth Shonle Cavan's treatment of conformity is useful here. She offers a continuum of *degrees* of conformity: Under-conforming contraculture, extreme underconformity, minor underconformity, normal conformity, minor overconformity, extreme overconformity, overconforming contraculture.[19] Using this scheme, Keith might be seen as oscillating between "minor underconformity" and "minor overconformity" at Time I. If he moves toward a "together guy" style, he will find more satisfactory ways to balance the demands placed on him by others and the press toward autonomy and independence he is only beginning to experience at age 13.

Undoubtedly the conformist child is a delight—on the surface —for both teacher and parent. Yet, the teacher who finds a conformist student—docile, passive, obedient, responsive to rules, etc.—may do well to look past the cooperative demeanor to the child's unspoken needs. Precisely because this type of youth causes no disruption in the classroom, he is likely to be overlooked. He needs to be given opportunities to develop his own opinion on issues being discussed in the classroom, should be rewarded for expressions of initiative or individualism, and should be encouraged to find activities that interest him for their own sake.

Because this type of child is so tightly strapped into meeting the expectations of authority figures, both parent and teacher must be sensitive to the power of their words of praise or punishment.

They need to provide plenty of room for the child to develop a sense of self *independent* of their approval. As we have seen with Keith, it is a struggle for him to be himself without feeling guilty or frustrated. Yet, if he is to develop to his fullest potential, his capacity for self-love, for self-direction, and for creativity must be carefully nourished. The very people upon whom he is most likely to depend for his sense of well-being are the people who must nudge him toward increasing autonomy and independence as he moves through adolescence.

Keith's attempts to establish gratifying human relationships have by and large been rewarded by those around him. Through embodying both acceptable goals and normative means, Keith seems assured of achieving his dream of material and social status. Not all of the Pathways youths fit so neatly into mainstream patterns, however.

For some, like Ernie, the attempt to "fit in" is met with rejection, failure, and tribulation. Conformity offers no entrée to peace of mind, since attempts are met too often with failure. For this kind of person, it becomes emotionally more expedient to withdraw—both physically and psychically—from all but the most necessary social contacts. As we follow the case of Ernie, we discover the powerful statement reflected in the isolation and renunciation of his retreatist strategic style.

Then next there's Ernie,
he's my twin; he's 15. He's shy.
When he's with people he knows, he's far different.
He's kind of reserved with other people,
strangers and things.
—SISTER

3. The Retreater *Ernie Hayes*

Moving Away. The Withdrawn Kid and the Loner

The Retreater may be seen as a person who finds it necessary and/or desirable to involve as little of himself as possible in social situations. His primary motivational impetus is the avoidance of real contact (physical, emotion, or social) with others.

In Rainwater's scheme, the Retreater is within the range of the "depressive" strategy in which "goals are increasingly constricted to the bare necessities of survival."[1] The range, intensity, and frequency of social relationships are decreased in this style. Similarly, Merton's retreatism as a type of adaptation is a "failure to evaluate anything highly enough to extend effort toward either realization of a goal or observance of the norms, whether called torpor, cynicism, disenchantment, or what not."[2]

In this chapter I will focus on the boy who, for whatever reasons, tends to withdraw from or avoid social interaction with most or all members of his reference cluster. The logical extreme of this style is the "loner" or hermit, who essentially removes himself from society. Partly because of age, there are no boys in the

Pathways sample who could justifiably be put into the loner category, although two or three who have been characterized as "withdrawn kids" at times border on being total isolates.[3]

The "withdrawn kid" often engages in solitary activities, such as watching television or reading, more by preference than by happenstance. He may have one or two friends, but his contact with them is arbitrary and likely to be more accidental than sought after. He is relatively controlled, but may be forceful at times or display occasional outbursts of anger—especially when he is fending off intimacy or invasion of his privacy. He is thought of by others as shy, quiet, reserved, or even sad.

He may try to avoid contacts with others because he is unsure of himself; or he may feel pressure from everyone around him, in which case his withdrawal is a way of not giving in (a kind of passive resistance); or he may feel a genuine antipathy toward others based on what he perceives as negative and nonrewarding contact in the past and/or present. He may do passing work in school, and may in fact excel and gain the reputation of "egg-head" or "brain"—or he may find school another arena of interpersonal contact to be eliminated as soon as possible. The withdrawn kid may value the "quiet" label others attach to him.

In terms of the affiliation dimension, the withdrawn kid and the loner are quite clearly at the less involved end of the continuum, by virtue of either restriction of affiliational objects or low intensity of affiliation when it does exist. The retreater is obviously not a dominating person (although he may be relatively independent of others), and therefore is most appropriately placed at the submissive end of the power dimension. He does not seek to exert power or influence over others, except perchance to defend his right to remain withdrawn or in his own "world."

The deviance of the Retreater depends on the degree to which he rejects full participation in his social world. The hermit is the ultimate example of retreatism. He is usually seen as eccentric, but harmless enough not be to incarcerated. Becoming insane might be considered an equally ultimate form of retreatism. However, an important distinction can be made between the hermit who is ostensibly still "in control"—from his own and society's point of view—and the mental patient who is presumably "out of control." (The use of drugs and incarceration can be seen as attempts to bring the mental patient back under control.) Parsons refers to this process as "isolation and insulation" of deviant behavior from those who do not yet exhibit it. Therapy, especially in a mental hospital setting, is seen as an effort to bring the patient's behavior back into the normative realm, at least enough so that he can be eased back into society, thereby ending isolation. The line at which the need for isolation/insulation is felt varies from culture to culture. Because the hermit is self-isolating—and is presumably still in control of himself and still in touch with reality—his retreatism is less threatening to the social order than a mentally ill person who tries to maintain normal social contacts.[4]

Abuse of drugs and alcohol are also typically viewed as forms of retreatism, in that they tend to create barriers that mitigate the impact of interpersonal relationships. (Suicide, of course, is the ultimate withdrawal.) In Ernie's case, retreatism takes many forms, including glue-sniffing, which transports him away from other people into a world populated by only one person: Ernie. As he moves through adolescence, he exchanges glue for wine with virtually the same effect.

As discussed in the chapter on Keith, a certain amount of aloneness and separation from others is essential to the development of autonomy and independence. All of us, especially if we are to be considered healthy and mature, need to be alone on occasion. Many of the boys in the Pathways study described occasions on which they dealt with an unpleasant situation simply by removing themselves from it—going to their bedrooms, turning on loud music, going out for a walk. In order for this to be seen as a strategic style, however, withdrawal must be the *typical* response to interpersonal situations.

For Ernie the retreatist response becomes an engulfing style, filtering into every corner of his life, characterizing his everyday manner of dealing with people and situations and, it seems, even himself.

Self-Characterization. "This is the story about a lonely boy."

Although spoken in response to a projective picture at the end of his interview, these words form part of an unwittingly precise description of Ernie himself:

This is the story about a lonely boy who lives in a dirty Negro neighborhood and is lonely, and he has nobody to play with. And he's wishing that . . . he sees these three people . . . and he's wishing that they'd come over and play with him . . . he wishes that more people would come so he could play with them. . . .

Woven relentlessly through Ernie's self-portrait are the threads of loneliness, fear, self-doubt, rejection, panic. One gets the feeling from reading Ernie's Time I transcripts (13 years of age) that he lives in a world he cannot and will not trust, where people are potentially dangerous and harmful, in which Ernie has not yet found a sense of value of himself.

He says he is small for his age. In his descriptions of others in his family, his parents and siblings alike are pictured in terms of beatings and other forms of physical violence against which Ernie's protection is to hide or to hit back. He doesn't know his parents' ages, but he does know their strength:

I. And tell me a little bit about your mother.
E. Well she always hits the wrong person. [He describes this.]

I. Ok, let's move on to your father.
E. Well, he always hits us hard, like he's cruel to us . . . he always punches us.

His siblings are described in terms of not being there or of hitting. Abby, 18, is "never home" and during the early interviews is in prison for riding in a stolen car and purse-snatching. Candy, 16, is "always quiet most of the time." Two years later she is the only one of the Hayes children to have graduated from high school; five out of the six high-school-age siblings have dropped out by then, including Ernie. Teddy, 15, is always "in the bag" (sniffing glue) and "always hits everybody." Ernie adds, "then comes me . . . I'm always hitting my sister." He is referring to his twin sister, Donna, whom he describes as "always trying to fight with my . . . no she's always . . . she's kind of quiet, she starts yelling at my sister, and then they start fighting." Ernie and Donna seem to share a quiet nature knit with a propensity to hit their siblings early in an encounter as a form of getting the enemy before they get you.

Elly, 12, "always tries to start fights, she thinks she can beat everybody." Ten-year-old Silvia, he says, is "always yelling, she's never quiet. Every time we do something she starts yelling, and

that's all." Didi, at six, is "always squealing . . . she always squeals
so my mother never hits her, and she keeps squealing, and when
she gets mad, she pulls something down." Finally, there is the
"baby" (one year old), and "he's always fussy." It is interesting
that those whom Ernie likes are described in terms of the absence
of yelling and hitting. His Uncle Larry "never hollers or nothing,"
and his Aunt Hattie "yells at me and makes me mad, but I like her
because she always makes up for that, and she lets us have what
we want."

Thus Ernie is ensconced in a familial setting that is at once hostile and confusing. Much of the warmth and positive quality of life
in this large family which comes through in the parental interviews is conspicuously absent from Ernie's. When he is asked who
in the family he is most like, he says his mother, because "I guess
everybody else bothers me. . . ." He thinks he gets along with his
mother and father better than his siblings do. He gets along better
with his mother because "all the other ones, they yell more, they
try to start trouble." He does, but less than they do. And he gets
along better with his father for the same reason: his father beats
the girls and Teddy more because Teddy is "always bad . . . he's
always hitting everybody." In other words, Ernie is the least aggressive and is favored by his parents for that reason, not, in his
view, because he is someone special in a positive sense.

Ernie appears to operate within a predominant style of withdrawn kid and a secondary style of troublemaker.[5] Underlying
both is a sense of anger, hurt, rejection, or fear of rejection. Although he describes himself as less aggressive than his siblings, it is
clear that he does his share of starting fights in the family. When
asked how his siblings would have him change, he responds, "I
think stop hitting them because I always hit them."

Yet, as mentioned earlier, most of the Pathways subjects show a
dual theme of sibling fighting and docility vis-à-vis parents—it is
Ernie's avoidance of interaction and withdrawal in other areas of
his life which confirms his characterization as "withdrawn kid."
Even within the family, the withdrawn style is evident. In describing his reaction to his mother's attempts to hit him, he says,
"When I go hit somebody else I run from her, and she just stands
there." Again, when asked what he would do if his sister came up
and hit him, he replies, "I wouldn't say nothing, I'd just turn
around. . . ."

There is, furthermore, a sense of injustice that Ernie picks up in his family. (And in the school section he complains bitterly of a teacher who punishes the entire class for one child's misbehavior.) The Christmas Day before his first interview was filled with the smack of favoritism from Ernie's perspective: he received only three presents compared to the five each of his siblings received—"and they weren't good either . . . I just kept yelling that everybody else got more presents than me!" Some colored markers he gave away to his little sister; a "crazy helicopter" he left alone until it "got torn up." Ernie's feeling of rejection and lack of parental love rings poignantly through his description of that day. The one thing he really wanted, a chemistry set, was not under the tree, although in his perception, "everybody got what they wanted." He says he is "always" taking spices out of the house and mixing them together, but "I guess my mother didn't know that I wanted it."

The sense of injustice involves punishment in the family as well as the reward system. Ernie claims that if he "taps" his sister Elly, she will say he punched her and *he* will be "whacked." Similarly, when Teddy has been sniffing glue, he hits Ernie. Ernie accepts this as being out of Teddy's control: "He don't know what he's doing." When Ernie is angry with his mother, he mumbles—"and then she hits me, she just hits me more." With his father, he does not show anger. "If I get mad with him, I don't say nothing because he'll turn around and whack me." Much of his withdrawal is in reaction precisely to being hit by someone—or in anticipation of it. If Ernie gets into serious trouble, such as being caught sniffing glue by his father, he hides under the bed or in the yard under an abandoned car.

Ernie's description of a "typical day" reflects his interpersonal orientation in stark terms. On days when everyone is home (holidays, weekends), he and Teddy sleep in until noon then go up to the third floor attic and sniff glue for the rest of the day. On school days, Ernie "hooks" (often leaving by the front door only to return through the back door and sneak up to the attic to sniff glue). When asked how often he and Teddy sniff, he responds, "Every time we have a chance, probably three times a week."

Teddy is withdrawn also, and like Ernie swings between retreating from family members and lashing out at them. Teddy apparently is the only family member whom Ernie perceives as being interested in him or to whom he can talk. Ernie does not know where any of his classmates live, and appears to spend time only erratically with his small and rather ill-defined peer group. Most of his time is spent in the yard, in the attic, or in his room by the radiator pipes where it is warm.

Ernie says his parents never go to school to see about his progress (his mother does not like to go and his father must work); he asks his mother for help with homework, but she shunts him off to one of his sisters, "because she don't know that stuff." His father threatens to send him away for sniffing glue. When he is sick, he stays in bed, eats, or goes to sleep. Escape, then, is the byword of Ernie's life, reflected in the family as a whole in the story he tells about his parents asking whether the children would rather eat at home or go out: "Everybody says go because they want to get out of the house."

Ernie hints at the quality of his home life in his projective picture responses, which are filled with tales of rejection, and insufficient love, food, and money. In one picture of a young boy standing close to an older boy, he says they feel "unhappy" and the younger boy is afraid: he is holding on to his "older brother . . . so nothing will happen to him." Before the picture was taken, he says, they were "probably just riding around and decided to go away." This is parallel to his real-life relationship with Teddy: glue-sniffing in the attic is their means of "going away"—when asked in the school section how he feels when they hook school and sniff glue, he replies, "scared."

Another picture shown him—of a family at the dinner table (which most subjects interpret as a positive family situation)—Ernie says reminds him of the fact that his father usually dishes out their meals: "I guess he doesn't want us to take too much, or if my mother gave us, she would give us a lot." This sense of parental withholding combined with feelings of sadness and fear pervade his stories. In response to a picture of a mother and children sitting on a bare mattress in a rather meager apartment, Ernie says:

Everybody is worried about their father, and they probably don't have enough money to support them on, and they might have to send someone away to the orphanage. The landlord probably told them that they're going to have to move out and they probably said that they have to wait until their father comes home . . . they feel unhappy . . . they might . . . not have any place to go because they have too many children, and their father probably has a poor job, and the brother's probably wanted by the police.

This last sentence is a fairly accurate description of Ernie's real-life family. With eight children, the Hayeses find it difficult to make ends meet on the father's paltry and irregular wages. They live on a street where at Time I five houses had already been torn down—a sign that the neighborhood is rapidly deteriorating. Ernie's oldest brother, Abby, has been in trouble with the police for car theft, among other things.

Themes of parental rejection and lack of involvement are carried over into Ernie's fantasies about his own future family and occupation. He wants four children and would want them to go to church, "so they won't be home." He would tell his children "not to steal, not swear, and stay in school" in order to get a good job. For sniffing glue he would "whack" them, tear up the bag, and send them to bed without supper. He wants a "happy life"—"I'll probably be a scientist and make stuff"—but admits that he is not doing well now in school in preparation for that life, since he does not attend regularly.

In addition, Ernie does not know how to go about becoming a chemist; obviously his parents do not support him in this regard. The only person to whom he has spoken about it is the woman upstairs who "just says don't blow up the house." His second choice is fireman. The first thing he remembers wanting to be is a school teacher. When asked (a few questions later) what job he would *not* like to have, Ernie replies: "a school teacher—the kids might beat me up." He also would not want to be a driving teacher (another previously held aspiration) because the "car might crash." His fear and vagueness regarding the world of work are epitomized by the following interchange:

I. Have you ever tried to get a job?
E. I think so, but I forget what.

I. If you could have a wish to become anything in the world . . . what would it be?
E. A millionaire. (So softly that the interviewer must ask him to repeat three times.)

I. But that's not a job.
E. I know it.

I. What kind of job would you want?
E. I'd like to be a chemist.

I. Um hum. Why would you want to be a chemist?
E. Because I like to mix stuff.

I. Do you think you could ever become a chemist?
E. Nope.

I. How come?
E. I guess I'd be too lazy to study.

Ernie does not know what his mother would like him to be—only what she would *not* like him to be: a television repairman (an activity he singles out as being most enjoyable with his father, and one of the jobs his father has held). Thus in one breath, his sole point of identification with his father, in terms of both current activity and occupational role model, is negatively defined.

Ernie's peer group reflects to some extent his own approach to life. His friends seem really to be Teddy's; since he is close to Teddy, he hangs out with Will, 11, and Paul, 12, occasionally and almost by default. They are "just a bunch of guys" who have no real leader, and whose major activity is sniffing glue. Teddy, Will, and Paul also "go stealing cars," but Ernie stays home when they do. He believes they will all drop out of school by age 16; Paul has already done so. The only thing that keeps Ernie in school is his father. Those who remain hook so often that they are virtually out of school. Teddy had a job, but quit because "he didn't like to go there." He thinks Teddy will be a cleaning man when he does leave school for good, but will not be good at it because "he doesn't really like to do anything." Wally will be "stealing cars" at age 25; only for Paul does he predict a stable job/family situation (working on an oil truck, as he does at Time I). The constricted goals and absent or illegitimate means appear to be typical for the peer group as a whole.

Ernie says Paul is his best friend, but he trusts Teddy the most. His answers to questions regarding smoking, drinking, fighting, or "fooling around with girls" is a consistent "they do, but I don't." He went to a party once: "I didn't do anything, I was just standing there . . . I don't know how to dance." And, as with Ernie's work aspiration, his peers are negatively defined by parents: they think his friends are "pests" and "all right for sniffing glue."

As for girls, Ernie feels they are "too big" for him, but says in perhaps two years he would start dating. When the interviewer asks what he would do with a girl, he responds, "probably just kiss her." The interviewer presses with, "suppose she starts getting fresh?" Ernie replies: "I'd find a broom, and I'd send her out . . ." If she persisted, he would "kick her out . . . I guess because I'm bashful sometimes . . . I wouldn't like to hang around with girls." It appears that Ernie, at 13, wants the closeness a relationship with a girl might offer, yet is willing to use force to protect his privacy and to avoid being very intimate with another person.

School is no escape from home. Ernie views it as a hostile place where "they are always fighting" and which offers him little or nothing of value. He does not raise his hand, does not read, does not participate in school activities, does not complete his homework. There is nothing he would like to have available at the DuBois that is not already there. Ernie chose to go to the DuBois because it was closest to his home. He wants to attend Trade for high school because his brother Abby did; he has no idea what courses are offered there. When asked outright how he feels about school, he says "I don't know" (his first response to most questions, symptomatic in itself of his resisting, withdrawing style). He does not like the DuBois, where he is known as the "Wolfman" because of his long hair, and where he feels victimized by students who start trouble and try to take his money.

School has been a negative experience from the outset. Ernie recalls this memory of first grade:

I. What's the first thing you remember?
E. Just when I ran out.

I. Tell me the story.
E. They have a yard, but there was no gates on it, and it had a big wall around it, and I walked in, and I ran out, but my mother brought me back.

I. Why did you run out?
E. I don't know. [He says he liked the teacher.] I guess because I didn't have nobody to play with.

Part of Ernie's absence from school, I feel, stems from negative experiences with the subject matter itself. Ernie did well until he entered the DuBois (an experience not uncommon among the other subjects). At Time I, he does not like math because "it's too hard . . . I don't know how to change the fractions, I never learned how to do it." That frustration is added to by what he perceives as favoritism on the part of some teachers. For example, in history the boys talk, so the teacher "goes over and starts talking to the girls, and she don't talk to the boys."

Ernie claims not to know what teachers think of him, or whether they perceive him accurately. He liked best a teacher who told them "the right things" and gives the students advice. His least favorite teacher "was always yelling at us." He thinks he gets "bad marks" (lower than he could get) because he "never did anything they told us to do," and is absent so often. When asked if his grades show how well he is actually doing in school, Ernie "forgets" the question. He then admits that he does not try to do the work, but could learn the material if he wanted to. Similarly, he does not know the names of his teachers: "I don't pay attention."

Caught between his withdrawn and tough styles, Ernie resists telling the interviewer whether he feels more like the boy who is doing well or like the "boy in hot water" who is always starting trouble. Under pressure, he finally says the latter: "I guess I always like to start trouble, but not with anybody in the class, just my family" (an excellent example of audience segregation, showing how two styles can be utilized to handle two very different situations). Yet part of Ernie's difficulty with school is that it does not allow him to escape:

I. Think about it. What are you thinking about?
E. Just that I don't like it . . .

I. Why?
E. Because I can't smell my glue.

Ernie has one of the lowest racial awareness scores in the sample. Whether because of time or of Ernie's flat responses to the racial section, the interviewer asks him at one point if he wants to stop. Ernie's reply: "I don't care." His most frequent response to questions regarding black leaders and groups is "I don't know." He does not know what he thinks about being a "Negro," as he calls himself; he "guesses" that he is as good as white children, and he "guesses" in the next breath that white children are better than he is. He would not take a pill to make himself white, nor would he push a button to make all whites black—his lack of trust of others shines starkly through his responses: "I guess that then they [whites] might still start trouble on us, and we'll think that they're Negroes." Furthermore, in a series of questions designed to measure willingness to have social contact with whites, Ernie responds negatively to every level, giving the reason, "they might beat me up." Finally, the interviewer asks if Ernie would go to a white boy's house to watch television, a one-to-one situation to which most subjects respond positively:

E. I don't think so . . .
I. Why?
E. Because he might beat me up.
I. Supposing he was a friend of yours?
E. I probably still wouldn't go even if it was a colored person.
I. Why?
E. I guess because I might leave too late, and then I would have to go home by myself.
I. How come you're afraid everybody is going to beat you up?
E. I don't know.

He adds that some of the boys in his room at school have tried to beat him up; as for going to a party, he would not, even if it were all his own race, and even if they would not beat him up: "they probably have to dance or something."

This leads us to the section on Ernie's self-concept. Not only can he not dance, which he sees as good reason to restrict his social life, but he insists that there is *nothing* he can do better than the average boy his age. After much probing by the interviewer, Ernie tentatively says he is better at fishing, then narrows that down to "I think just casting, but not fishing." He also, under duress, says he is better than most boys at collecting TV guides (one per week). He claims he is worse at everything else, and would like to be better in everything, especially art. Yet in order to become better in art, he would have to pay attention: "I keep forgetting; today I forgot that we had two periods of art."

If he were being brainwashed, Ernie would fight hardest to keep his attitude toward his family:

> *E.* Oh, I guess hitting my sisters back.
> *I.* What else?
> *E.* That's all; oh, and not liking my family.
> *I.* You don't like your family at all?
> *E.* Yeah. I don't want them to change that.

As for personal change, he says his family would want him to stop hitting siblings, hooking, and sniffing glue—the very activities in Ernie's life which provide protection from others and from his fears.

Ernie has difficulty with the spy question. His lack of a clear self-image is reflected in his protest, "I wouldn't know what to tell him." He goes on to say:

> I would tell him to always hit my sisters, because my mother might think I'm sick or something, and I just be bashful in school, and do what my mother and father tell me . . . at school come in late . . . and be lazy in the morning and always go upstairs in my house . . . [with friends] oh, in school because no one come over to my house except for in the morning . . . be friendly with them.

He would tell the spy how to mix "stuff" in a container when his father is not home, and, when encouraged by the interviewer, how to sniff glue. Around the girls at school, the spy should not say anything—"if a girl says hello to him, just wave."

Ernie's story is indeed about a lonely boy.

Characterizations by Others. "He's really very quiet."[6]

The significant others in Ernie's life agree that he has always been very quiet. Mrs. Hayes expresses this most succinctly in response to a question regarding her view of Ernie's future: "What do I expect him to be doing? Oh, I don't know, it's hard to say that. I have a hard child to answer questions for because he's been so quiet . . . all the time. It's even hard to even *try* to think." She notes that Ernie has always been withdrawn, compared to her other seven children, and has stayed in the house or in the yard most of the time. She describes the others getting together to play, and Ernie hanging back. Mr. Hayes sketches a powerful vignette which confirms Ernie's quietness:

He's rather quiet. He could sit alone and work by himself, where the others usually get in a little group, or at least two of them . . . they want someone else there, too; whereas he will do things by himself . . . he doesn't tumble and jump, I've got a couple that like to tumble, and jump around—but he *can* do it, like when they go sledding; or jump, he can jump as good as the rest—but he doesn't do it for fun.

Although Mr. Hayes sees Ernie's quietness partly as an asset ("he doesn't argue at the drop of a pin," he takes responsibility to carry out projects such as baking a chicken all by himself), it is clear that he recognizes Ernie's tendency to withdraw from others. Mr. Hayes describes himself as being just like Ernie when he was a child and a young man, as illustrated by this story about how he acted when he first met his wife:

So like my son, Ernest, again I was quiet; I would sit off in the corner maybe, build something with matchsticks; and we walk up to the bus, and I seemed to have talked a little more or something. And she asked me if I wanted a stick of gum, which I never chewed gum, always would say no . . . I took her gum. And later on we went to Franklin Park, and it got a little chilly. I asked her if she wanted my coat, and from then it just seemed, uh, we were sort of natural together . . . and she's very quiet too.

Ernie's similarity to his father is traced through Mr. Hayes's description of how he is different from other people he knows: "I don't talk, I don't smoke, I don't drink, I can't dance, I don't care for nightclubs or parties or sitting around talking to people, and I like to be alone . . . I'd be a dead man at a party." Says Mrs. Hayes, who thinks Ernie is like her in being quiet and shy: "He's as quiet, I mean really very quiet, and where the others will dance, sing, like put on plays together, he is never in this . . . I don't believe I've ever heard him sing. I've never seen him dance."

Ernie is also like his father, says Mr. Hayes, in that "he doesn't want to be bothered by too many people," and he wants "to do things exact, slow, but do it right . . . maybe lazy." He sees no differences between them. Like Ernie at age 13, Mr. Hayes as an adult spends his time between home and work. When asked what his friends might like him to change about himself, he replies, "This word friends maybe throws me because I don't . . . I don't have any, say, *friends*." Mrs. Hayes claims in her first interview that Ernie has "no playmates . . . nobody comes to the house, and he doesn't go to anybody's house." His friends, she adds, are really Teddy's. She thinks his "shyness" and his dislike of fighting put him at a disadvantage when it comes to making friends.

By his own report, we know that Ernie hits his siblings—how does he otherwise handle his anger? His parents say that he goes to his room and closes the door. When his father is asked what happens when Ernie seems unhappy about something, he replies: "It's hard to tell. He's rather quiet, and he may be unhappy and be sitting down watching television or, when he goes to bed . . . but he doesn't make any outward sign of it, you know, like a lot of hollering . . . he doesn't complain too much."

Of course, simply being quiet and liking to be alone does not necessarily take on the implication of avoiding or rejecting others as a style. We see with Ernie, however, that part of his "moving away" activities—building models, doing puzzles, even wanting to be a chemist—are constructed more out of fear than an autonomous need for privacy. For example, Mrs. Hayes says that Ernie was held back in fifth grade because he was "immature"—Donna says that he failed because he never raised his hand. Ernie resists reaching out, or putting effort into things which could be considered means to the goals to which he pays lip service. Mrs. Hayes says her son does not bring books home to study, and does not seem to try to do well in school (although she feels certain, as he does, that he could finish high school and college if he put his mind to it):

right now he should be using his mind and studying and reading, and facing these problems in school . . . He's not doing it now, his mind is being dulled, you know . . . and how can he use it when he gets a little older? And he doesn't read except Batman and Superman. But like I say, right now he's in this doldrums, like, and his mind is numb.

Mrs. Hayes agrees with Ernie's conviction that he is not particularly good at anything (she says the same thing of herself). A low score on the Internal-External Control Questionnaire tends to confirm their view of Ernie. Mr. Hayes, however, feels Ernie is basically self-sufficient around the house and takes care of his own needs—traits he views as positive signs of independence and responsibility. Donna mentions that he is good at carpentry, a skill never suggested by Ernie in his own interviews.

We can gain some insight into Ernie's moving away from others in the fact that he spends more time with his baby brother Terry than do any of his other siblings. His parents and Donna agree that Ernie actually gets along best with Terry—the youngest and least threatening member of the family—"he'll play best with the baby." Peter says that Ernie "don't mind what little kids he plays with, but he don't like them to kid around too much." Thus his withdrawn style seems more a lack of confidence than free choice.

Mrs. Hayes does not care what Ernie will do as an adult as long as he is happy. She adds the broad aspiration that he will go to college so he can have a "better life," but her hopes for Ernie are no more specific and individualized than that. To another question—"what do you think he'll be doing at age 40?"—she replies, "Don't ask me, I won't be here then."

Mr. Hayes agrees that it would not "matter too much" what kind of work Ernie does, as long as it is clean, "not too hard," and "pays pretty good." He predicts that his son might get into printing or "something with his hands." Acknowledgment of Ernie's dream of being a chemist is conspicuously absent. Only Donna says she believes in Ernie's dreams: "We call him Destructo 'cause he's always, you know, doing things like ink blots and vinegar . . . salt and pepper and acid, soap." Donna believes Ernie will eventually go to college and become a chemist; her optimism for Ernie is matched by her own hopes of becoming a writer, though she, too, has disaffiliated herself from school.

As for Ernie's past, it is perceived as dimly as his nebulous future. Mrs. Hayes cannot remember whether as a baby Ernie was fussy, happy, bright, or dull: "Oh, I really don't know, it's been so long ago, and then I had the two of them, it's kind of hard to . . . remember that . . . I don't know whether he cried more or she did, or what . . . I really don't remember." Lest time be considered the villain here, it must be pointed out that even in the present, Ernie's wants and activities are unclear to the Hayeses. Mrs. Hayes cannot remember how Ernie is doing in school, or what subjects he is interested in. She keeps a chart on all her children's grades, but remembers only the grades of those who are doing well—all of them females. In first describing her children, Mrs. Hayes characterizes the twins (born when she was a 34-year-old mother of three) as being "like night and day"—Donna is smart, "willing to learn," and reads a lot; Ernie is "quite shy." (According to Donna, she and Ernie are not as different as their mother thinks. Donna was sniffing glue, apparently undetected, at the same time Ernie was, and they both hooked school. She claims that they are very close to each other, as illustrated by her story about their parents playing a "game" of asking if they could only have four children in the family, which three others would each child pick: "The first one I always pick is Ernie. I don't know, just because he's my twin, I guess.")

Mrs. Hayes cannot say whether Ernie is smart—she feels he has not found anything interesting enough to motivate him toward school work. Furthermore, when asked about Ernie's size, health, and athletic ability, Mrs. Hayes says:

I really don't know. I guess he's okay because, you know, they played ping pong the other night, he was playing, he was pretty good . . . I don't remember him playing outside . . . I really don't know if he's good or not, you know, compared with the others, I don't remember.

Mr. Hayes remarks that one of his sons, either Ernie or Teddy, missed one month of school at the beginning of the year; he could not remember which son it was. Although in general he is more sensitive to and aware of Ernie as an individual, he hints that working overtime has kept him from having detailed knowledge of his children's lives.

What *is* clear to both parents is that Ernie is changing. At age 13 he is beginning to be "fresh" and disobedient (hooking, sniffing glue, riding in stolen cars). When Mrs. Hayes is first interviewed, she comments: "He is changing, where he used to be quiet and sort of shy . . . he seems fresh, because he won't go to school like I tell him to . . . I don't know if that's for the good or not because a couple of times I've smelled glue on him." A few months later, Mr. Hayes is deeply concerned with this behavior. Comments by his sister and best friend a year and a half later indicate that Ernie's retreatist, shy, quiet style has not changed at all: the disobedience stems from his desperate attempts to retreat from school; the glue-sniffing appears to be a way to gain some relief from his frustrating home life. As Donna explains, "Glue makes you feel like you could do anything right?"[7]

Symptomatic of his withdrawing style is Ernie's chronic truancy.

School is at once unrewarding and frightening, a place where Ernie's natural shyness and small size place him at a distinct disadvantage—so much so, that he is willing to tolerate beatings at home in order to stay away from school. This stymies his mother, who feels that if his father would beat him each time he hooked, he would attend school regularly. She says that when he leaves in the morning with the other children, only to return a few minutes later, she pushes him back outside and locks the door. But when he rings again a few minutes later, she will let him in. "And I just work him in with whatever I'm doing . . . like you know I make him help." Since he is home, she has him help with housework, letting him fit into her day, thereby legitimizing his retreat from school. Once in the home environment, frequent forays into the attic provide a suitable retreat from the confusion and fighting there.

By the time of Donna's interview, both she and Ernie are no longer attending school with any regularity; he has been transferred to the Godvin (disciplinary school) for truancy. Their hooking is a painful issue for their parents. From Donna's comments it is apparent that at this point the Hayeses have given up: "They don't talk to me any more about school, 'cause they figure if they keep on talking, you know, I still ain't gonna go, so why talk?" Apparently school, which both Ernie and Donna find boring, becomes intolerable for Ernie after an incident in which some boys try to take his lunch money away from him. He skirts this in his interview, but his mother says that he has attended school only three days since the incident. Why does one incident have such an impact on Ernie? Mrs. Hayes suggests that until about age 13, Ernie had not gone out of his house (except to go to school), and had not "really matured . . . I think maybe now he's coming out of that, and he doesn't know how to act so that's why he just stays home from school."

While the Hayeses interpret their son's behavior as "quiet," Donna states that Ernie is "shy, but when he's with people he knows, he's far different. He's kind of reserved with other people, strangers and things." His friend Peter concurs, giving us some insight into the Ernie of fifteen years of age. He notes that in their three-man gang (Ernie, Peter, and the latter's brother Stanley), Ernie is second in command; he is trustworthy, and outwardly obeys their rules against smoking, drinking, swearing. Here he is respected, counted on, liked. Yet, it is indicative of his style that the name chosen for their gang, the Black Panthers, they interpret to mean "something like a teddy bear." Their major activity is building models together—two or three a week. Time not spent with Peter is drunk away with Teddy in their third floor retreat. The pattern of withdrawal seems immutable.

Analysis of the Retreatist Style

In many ways Ernie is an invisible person amidst this brood of squabbling children and anxious parents. His primary strategic style of withdrawn kid is a response to rejection and serves, in turn, to render him even more invisible. His withdrawing style means that he reveals little of himself to others. Their subsequent vagueness about him feeds right back into his muddy self-image, thus perpetuating a cycle which operates to reinforce a withdrawn style.

Insofar as Ernie utilizes the troublemaker style as a secondary coping mechanism, I submit that it serves the same purpose as withdrawing, and stems from the same sources: fear, frustration, lack of confidence, a low sense of fate control, and a lack of viable alternatives. He appears to have fallen victim to what Erikson calls "identity foreclosure"—a "premature interruption in the adolescent task of identity formation which can appear negatively, as the sense of inferiority, the feeling that one will never be any good"— or it can appear positively, as with Keith, who fixes on being "the good little worker" or the "teacher's pet."[8] Hauser has found in his study of black youths that the primary type of identity foreclosure is the negative one, usually a product of a pervasive sense of inferiority and mediocrity, degradation, and deprivation.[9] For Ernie, who experiences all of these, a retreatist style means seeking out havens for the mind and the body.

Ernie's "withdrawn kid" style seems to be linked to a relatively low self-concept and lack of self-esteem. His identity seems to be negative, one in which "the individual's identity configuration is prematurely fixed on the repudiated, the personally scorned, and rejected identifications and roles."[10] (As we shall find in the case of

Leroy, who can also be seen as having a negative identity, retreatism can be used to support a "tough" style.)

Although Hauser follows Erikson's classical psychoanalytical reasoning, whereby the negative identity arises from failure to resolve the initiative versus guilt conflict ("a self-restriction which keeps an individual from living up to his inner capacities or to the powers of his imagination and feeling"),[11] an interpersonal explanation can just as well suffice. The young male may resort to a flat, unidimensional strategic style—relatively safe but prematurely crystallized—when he fails to develop a set of relevant and practicable skills and competencies through lack of positive experiences with others, and/or lack of appropriately positive models, and/or lack of support from significant others. Ernie suffers from all of these lacks.

As Erikson so crucially points out, even this choice is an expression of "mastery" of sorts: "such vindictive choices of negative identity represent of course a desperate attempt at regaining some mastery in a situation in which the available positive identity elements cancel each other out."[12] He points out further that this choice, although paralytic and impoverished, provides some relief for the "ambiguity and conflicts inherent in multiple identifications."[13] It also involves an element of self-hatred (clearly for both Ernie and Leroy) which itself becomes part and parcel of the strategic style: "the choice of a self-defeating role often remains the only acceptable form of initiative . . . this in the form of a complete denial of ambition as the only possible way of totally avoiding guilt."[14]

Along similar lines, the authors of *Life Styles in the Black Ghetto* comment on the "passive stoic" and "defeated" styles as common responses to oppression and restricted opportunities.[15] The "defeated" are bound up in escapism and retreat into drugs, alcohol, and schizophrenia. The escape is an effort to deal with feelings of "helplessness and defeat." I would add in Ernie's case "anger"—with the emotional impoverishment and sense of isolation and injustice he experiences within his family constellation. McCord finds that addicts begin using drugs at an early age—"drugs serve to reduce intolerable anxiety." Alcoholics come from a background of general stress, erratic satisfaction of dependency needs, inadequate male models, and a façade of self-reliant manhood in childhood. He adds that adolescents who use drugs heavily are usually from broken or "openly hostile" homes.[16] All of these factors apply to Ernie's situation, contributing first to his glue-sniffing and later to his heavy reliance on wine.

The sociological addition to the psychoanalytical interpretation of retreatism (offered above) is that the retreatist style serves to protect and defend a beleaguered and unsupported individual—it provides him with a legitimate style which is usually accepted, if not fully admired, by his community of others. How and why did this become the most profitable style for Ernie?

The Family Matrix. The critical factor in the generation of Ernie's retreatist style is the size of his family and how his parents define that size. Ernie finds himself in the middle of an assemblage of children who require time and attention beyond what the Hayeses can afford to give—economically *or* emotionally. Mrs. Hayes wistfully confides at the end of her interview that if she had her life to live over again, she would not have so many children, and would somehow force herself to complete high school. Donna's story about their parents asking them to choose siblings if four were to leave is symbolically more than "just a game." It suggests that Mrs. Hayes is not completely successful in hiding her wishes from her children.

Furthermore, when the family goes out to dinner, there are so many of them that they have to take some children one week and the others the next week—perfectly rational in light of the family's brutally low income. Yet one can imagine Ernie's feelings when it is not his turn. Mrs. Hayes says he is unhappy when his parents go out without any of the children: "He looks kind of beat when he goes back from the car to the house, but we don't take anybody with us then, you know."

Mrs. Hayes feels that part of her inability to remember details about her children's lives is that she has so many. She handles this by not thinking about them, and by going away for a weekend to her sister's:

I believe in life there's all kinds of problems that can come up. And with as many kids as I have, I figure, well nothing is going to surprise me . . .

and I also feel that if I could sit down and think about it, I could go nuts thinking about the things that could happen to the kids.

The strain takes its toll on both parents. Her husband, she says, will try to get her to go to a movie with him, "or sometimes he'll just walk out . . . he won't say anything, he'll just—'well, I'll see you later'—and gets a chance to catch his breath."

Mr. Hayes spends only a few minutes each day with Ernie . . . he feels his time must be spread around. His response to a question about the most recent happy day he spent with Ernie is: "The trouble with that question is there's usually three or four of us around at the same time." He mentions that Ernie might have his family as an "advantage" over other boys his age—"but then you might say maybe too crowded for him . . . maybe some other boy with one or two in the family, uh, may have more advantages." He adds that Ernie seems to have a hard time finding "a place" in his family.

One cannot but wonder if this was an issue for Mr. Hayes and his wife as well, and at least one factor in the generation of their own withdrawn styles. Mrs. Hayes came from a family of thirteen children. Mr. Hayes was one of seven. His parents divorced when he was five or six years old. He and two sisters lived with his mother; the other four boys went to live with their father. Five years later his father died and the family was reunited. The price for Mr. Hayes of having a smaller family was loss of contact with his father and four brothers. He does not remember his father at all.

It is interesting that little evidence emerges for conflict between Mr. and Mrs. Hayes. Their relationship appears to be fairly solid. The lines of demarcation are between the children and their parents, although there is some hint of favoritism between mother and daughters. Fundamental to the family interaction is a parental sense of being buried under a myriad of demands and responsibilities, and a sense for the children of not receiving enough of anything—food, love, attention, time shared with parents, presents. This mutual sense of deprivation breeds both the desire to leave and the desire to strike out.

Critical Messages from Others.   The quietness/violence pattern

Ernie's parents engage in is complicated by their emotional coldness. While they both appear to be responsible people who care for and about their children, much of what they subject their children to is rejection in one form or another. This is amplified by their lack of intimate, direct, and warmly expressed affection:

> *I.* How is affection generally shown in your family?
> *Mrs. H.* Affection?
> *I.* Um hum.
> *Mrs. H.* Oh, I really don't know, I don't know whether they understand it or not; but I don't kiss them too often, once in a while if I'm going away . . .

She goes on to explain that she tells her children that taking them places and hitting them when they do something wrong is her way of showing affection. Mr. Hayes speaks of talking and playing with his children, but admits that "then again, I don't show too much affection for them . . . we don't kiss."

Rejection is both subtle and open in the Hayes family. Subtle, in Mrs. Hayes's feeling that none of her children acts like her or her husband, except Candy—"that's why I don't understand them." Or when Donna runs away one night, cannot find her cousin's house, and returns, only to find that her parents had not missed her. Or in Donna's story of an imaginary smaller family. Openly, the rejection comes, for example, in their threats to send their children to discipline school or jail if they misbehave. The threats are not idle: with their parents' blessing, Teddy, Ernie, Donna, and Eileen follow Abby's footsteps to the Youth Service Board for two weeks each. (Ernie does not mention this.) Mrs. Hayes says Teddy was also sent by the court to the state mental hospital nearby for ten days observation. Donna was eventually placed under psychiatric care; after two sessions the doctor asked for the whole family to come in. Most of them refused. Mr. Hayes deals with Donna's hooking school by warning her that she will go to jail. When she and Ernie come in late, she says, he threatens to "break our behinds."

The message from parents is painfully clear: a child does not understand or need affection except insofar as it might be expressed through discipline (hitting) or material symbols. Ernie's normal reactions of anger are thwarted by parental force whose magnitude he cannot hope to match. His quiet, avoiding responses are rewarded simply because they stop the hitting sooner than fighting back would. The only choices seem to be hitting or leaving, hitting or being sent away.

Lennard and Bernstein have found that the major difference between the schizophrenic and control families they studied is the mother's behavior. Mothers whose sons are schizophrenic tend not to confirm the child's presentation of self; tend to mystify the child's feelings through "mind-raping" ("oh, he doesn't understand affection . . ."); show less intrusive behavior (autonomy and initiative); and negatively reward autonomy and initiative in their sons—or ignore it.[17] Ernie is not schizophrenic at Time I, but the family interaction pattern which ignores his needs for affection as well as his interest in establishing competency (the chemistry, for example) seems fertile ground for the development of schizophrenic behavior.

Because Ernie restricts his interactions with others outside the family through hooking school and failing to weave an extensive peer network, messages from others that might define Ernie as a real person who counts are woefully absent.

The Impact of Role Models.   Another crucial factor in the generation of Ernie's withdrawn style is transmission of its basic elements through role models, both parental and sibling. His parents both describe themselves as extremely quiet people, but admit to impatience and "hollering" too much. They combine the same withdrawn/tough style that Ernie has evolved. They believe in firm discipline, as suggested earlier, which includes hitting their children with a hose or stick. Mrs. Hayes's solution to a child's misbehavior is either to ignore him or hit him. Apparently Ernie uses the same tactics:

> *I.* What are some of the things Ernie gets punished for?
> *Mrs. H.* Hitting one of the smaller kids, you know, infant . . . they don't argue really; well, one may be sitting in front of the television, and he wants to sit in front of him . . . and he'll hit them, you know, instead of try to sit beside them or maybe tricking them into moving or something.
> *I.* How do you usually punish him?
> *Mrs. H.* Oh, I usually hit him . . . with whatever is around.

About Ernie's truancy, for example, she says: "I think if his father really beat him . . . about three times in a row would straighten him out." Mrs. Hayes often witnesses the violation, tells her husband when he arrives home, and pushes him to add to her beatings (she is too weak to hit him hard)—a solution which Mr. Hayes apparently finds distasteful, but accedes to in order to keep the peace. Thus Ernie gets punished twice for many things. "He probably gets scolded or hollered at by both of us," admits Mr. Hayes. He says Ernie reacts by shrugging it off, and "like I mean he'll stand there quietly, say yeah, I shouldn't have done it . . . like that."

Obviously Ernie learns to hit from his parents, and copies their model in dealing with his own frustrations. The modeling goes further than this, however. Ernie seems to be following in his father's footsteps. Mr. Hayes is apparently a very bright man, having scored extremely high on every test he ever took in job training programs. He would like to have been an auto mechanic but has had to wend his way from one low-paying job to another, funneled by discrimination, poor education, and bad luck into manufacturing television parts—not his first job choice by any means. His father's frustration in seeing Ernie destroy himself is matched by his own inability to offer a crystal-clear example of ability focused on constructive activity that is rewarded and rewarding. When asked what his father wants him to be, Ernie says Mr. Hayes wants him to stop sniffing glue and to be "good," or he "won't learn anything." By hooking school and sniffing glue (which he knows destroys brain cells), Ernie is setting himself up for failure in the realm of schooling and occupation. It is highly unlikely that his pathway will lead him to his first job choice—chemist—any more than his father's did.

Typically, Ernie can think of no one he wants to grow up to be like. As with work and peers, much of his identity is spelled out in negative terms: he does *not* want to be like two other Pathways focal boys. Why? Because they steal cars and sniff glue. At one point in the interview when he is asked how he is like his father, he claims not to know. But he adds: "Well, I'm always helping him . . . and he doesn't hardly hit me, but he hits everybody else. . . . Oh, I always like to work on TVs and stuff, and he be TV repairing." He says he feels closest to his father, of all the men he knows, but later in the interview he says he loves his mother most, "cause I don't like nobody else." The interviewer asks him if he does not like his father, to which Ernie responds, "Not that much."

Yet when asked who in his family loves him the most now, Ernie (who first replies "no one") says, "They're always arguing, they're always arguing; I'd probably say my father."

As for models available to Ernie among his siblings, Abby stands out. He has been in all the major detention centers and training schools for boys in the Boston area, for truancy, stealing cars, fighting. He is a fighter, and obviously has an impact on Ernie, perhaps as a negative role model, as his mother suggests: "Once in a while if he gets a letter from his older brother [in jail], he'll cry . . . he wrote back to his brother, and he says your letter made me cry, so that was how I knew that he did cry." Brother Teddy has been his comrade in "escape" and offers the model of aggressive, fighting, yelling behavior as well. Donna and Eileen have at least been companions, if not examples, in retreating into the fumes that make one feel on top of the world.

Finally, the influence of his older brothers and sisters follows him uninvited into the school system, where Donna says the Hayes children have a reputation as difficult students and truants. The teachers see each of them not as individuals, she claims, but as "another Hayes."

Even at school, then, his identity is defined for Ernie by someone else—not in response to who *he* is as an individual, but on the basis of his being one of eight children. No one seems to be ready to take Ernie on his own terms, with the possible exception of Donna and Teddy, who are fellow travelers on the same flight.

Other Issues.   In Ernie's case it seems two other dimensions contribute to his inability to forge a clear, positive, and solid sense of identity. One is his twinship; the other is sniffing glue.

As suggested in the previous sections, Ernie has difficulty in being seen as *Ernie*. This is true in the family and at school. Not only is he one of eight, he is one of a set of twins. It is no small matter that Mrs. Hayes cannot remember what Ernie was like when he was a baby or a young child. Her vagueness in defining him is reflected in Ernie's own vagueness in defining himself. The hours of interviews laced with "I don't know" and "I don't remember" are eloquent testimony to the difficulty Ernie has in seeing himself as a unique individual, with needs and ideas, feelings and aspirations, apart from others. That Donna and Teddy (the two closest siblings both in age and personality) are also his partners in escape muddies the singularity of his person even further.

Ernie's greatest potential probably lies in his mind. His IQ score of 128 was the highest among the 61 Pathways subjects. At Time I Ernie does not seem to care that sniffing glue reportedly destroys brain cells. Although he pays lip service to mainstream goals of obtaining a good education and job, living in a house in the suburbs, etc., Ernie seems painfully aware that he is not following the path to achieve those goals. Merton's description of retreatism as a "restriction of goals and means" certainly seems to apply to Ernie at Time I. That his parents also negatively define his aspirations, even laughingly dismiss them, makes their attainment even less likely.

Ernie switches to wine by age 14, but there is no indication that he does so in order to avoid brain damage. It simply is more convenient, and his increasing age makes it more readily accessible to him than glue. By the time of Donna's interview (Ernie is going on 15), Teddy and Ernie are living in the third floor attic which has been converted into a small apartment for them. Donna describes Mr. Hayes going up to the attic to beat the boys for drinking wine. Nothing has changed.

This brings us to a larger question. Would a boy with his intellectual potential have become bored and frightened by school in Newton, in Belmont, in Lexington? How much damage and destruction to Ernie have occurred because of the fact that school, for him, could not serve as a counterbalance to his beleaguered and destructive home life? In smaller classes, with better-trained teachers and a less disruptive classroom atmosphere, could Ernie have become more of a person to outweigh the nonperson he appears to be at home? There is no certain answer, except for Ernie's own—he leaves the one place that could have enabled him to make his dream come true. Without officially giving up his goals, he in fear and distrust relinquishes the means.

Ernie's Alternatives.   Ernie, as far as we know, has no role model who offers an alternative either to withdrawal or violence as mechanisms for coping with interpersonal relationships. It is questionable whether the introduction into his life at this point of alternative models would make any real difference to him, since the other models have such emotional significance for him historically.

Nor does he receive rewards for developing initiative, autonomy, independence, or a positive self-image. His life is written in the tears of rejection and denial of him as a viable person. The one place where he might have found an opportunity to thrive and grow on his own—school—treats him as "another Hayes." He seems to have no means for handling his fear, his anger, his frustration than the double strategic styles of withdrawal and violence discussed in this portrait. For him there is no other escape from pain.

Analytical Dimensions. Running through Ernie's interview is a profound sense of confusion, worthlessness, fear, antipathy toward others, hesitation in reaching out to others. In terms of affiliation he is toward the negative end of the continuum; his expression of affection is restricted by his need to stay safely away from others. His capacity for emotional openness and warmth has been stunted by rejection and existential insecurity.

As Bowlby points out in his work on attachment between mother and child, the "anxious, insecure child may appear to be more strongly attached to his mother than does the happy, secure child who seems to take her more for granted." [18] Ernie's tears at being left behind when his parents go out may be seen less as a sign of strong attachment than of a child clinging to his mother out of deep insecurity. Nowhere in his interview does he indicate that he can or does take his parents' love "for granted."

Bowlby also cites studies which show that withdrawal from parental figures in times of pain or fatigue is characteristic of both autistic children and children who have become detached as "a result of long deprivation of maternal care." [19] That Ernie seeks comfort in his room and sleep when he is sick offers evidence of this detachment.

In terms of power, Ernie is much closer to submission and passivity than to dominance or autonomy. He sees others as controlling him, not vice versa. He controls others only in terms of the distance he keeps from them as part of his protective, retreatist, strategic style.

Ernie's style necessarily involves a great deal of concealing. He prefers to take as little risk as possible in his dealings with others. He hides himself, physically and emotionally, from the actual or anticipated hostility of others. In sniffing glue he masks his feelings from his own perception as well, dulling the impact of his environment (and his negative self-feelings), propelling him into a world of the mind where he can feel safe and at ease.

His style also requires a certain amount of contrivance. He sneaks in the back door in order to "escape" to the attic. He assiduously avoids social situations—especially those which involve social "dangers," such as dancing or talking. To say, however, that he must take pains to move away from social interaction, is not to suggest that his orientation is in any way cynical. I suspect that Ernie believes in and relies on his tendency to withdraw. The need to move away is impelling in its motivational force. He does not withdraw as a move in a game, to fool others. The basic insecurity of his situation—and his negative and weak self-concept—*demand* that he run and hide. He is operating from a defensive position of unremitting intensity. There is very little room for Ernie to take a chance, extend himself, try something new, reach out in love, demand what is his. In this sense, then, his style is also comparatively rigid. Except for occasional fighting with siblings—again, a self-protective, defensive device—Ernie's impulse is to move away from others, as quickly and completely as possible. Drugs assist him in his flight, taking him away from the pain inside as well.

Conclusion

It seems clear that the school is Ernie's best chance for escaping his family. Yet his truancy was accepted by a school system which (in the late 60's) was being criticized for operating a differential and unequal system in the inner city.

Many children are quiet in the classroom. Not all of them are withdrawn kids—on the playground, at home, in the hallways, they may "run, and jump, and play." For Ernie to have been found, a teacher or administrator must have been able to detect that for him, being quiet—or absent—is an expression of something deeper than adolescent shyness. Unfortunately for Ernie, no one did.

Many children are truant from school because they do not have the capacity to do well with relative ease, and consequently have more affinity to the street. This is not the case with Ernie. He could and should have been selected out—on the basis of his tested IQ if nothing else—for special attention, challenging work, interest in *his* growth as a student and as a person. We know that many "gifted" children, both white and nonwhite, have fallen between the cracks of classrooms in cities and suburbs alike. We are now more attuned pedagogically, and in terms of how we spend our school budgets, to identifying such children and attempting to meet their special needs. Perhaps if Ernie had become engaged constructively in this sphere, the devastation of his home life would not have been so complete.

The important point is that not only would a *mind* not be wasted, but that provision of optional messages, models, and ways of being might also have allowed this child to shift from a withdrawing style to a less painful one grounded in self-respect and confidence instead of fear and rejection.

Ernie's protection from the world lies chiefly in his ability to withdraw from it as much as possible. Underlying that retreatism is a secondary style of "tough guy"—also used in self-protection. These are his only tools for survival. As we have seen, they are pre-eminently self-destructive.

The portrait of Leroy Duncan illustrates the reversal of these two styles, with dramatically different consequences. For Leroy, protection comes not merely in retreat, but in the use of physical force to establish his identity, fulfill his needs, and express his personality. Punctuated as it is by long periods of sleep and television-watching—a form of human hibernation—Leroy's turbulent tough guy style is buttressed by his retreatism, rather than the other way around. But for Leroy, as with Ernie, his strategic style creates as many problems as it solves.

Well, the thing about Leroy,
there's always one in your family;
he's very stubborn . . . he's hardheaded,
I would say . . . he just kinda tough.

— MOTHER

4. The Tough Guy *Leroy Duncan*

Moving Against. The Real Tough Guy and the Troublemaker

The Tough Guy moves against people, relying on force or the threat of force to get what he wants out of interpersonal situations. The Tough Guy fits into Rainwater's "violent strategy . . . in which you force others to give you what you need once you fail to win it by verbal and other means."[1]

In its least extreme form we find the "real tough guy" or rebel, who strongly supports his independence and autonomy, to the point of using physical force, if necessary, to maintain his identity or to further a cause. The real tough guy may be a secondary style supporting a primary style of together guy (like Hank in Chapter 6), or it may stand alone. The real tough guy, attempting to define social situations in terms that will force others to yield to him, may seek to change normatively prescribed goals and means. He may be engaged in revolutionary or radical political activities. This style, more than that of the troublemaker, is in keeping with Merton's "rebellion," which "presupposes alienation from 'reigning goals and standards' and expenditure of effort to 'bring into being a new . . . greatly modified social structure.'"[2] The real tough guy is seen to be operating from a relatively secure and confident position; he enters risky and dangerous situations only when he must from a goal-oriented standpoint, rather than for fun.

On the other hand, the troublemaker seeks conflict and confrontation with others in a violent and aggressive manner, often for no apparent reason. He attempts to dominate and control others in ways destructive for them and often for himself. Attempting to achieve his definition of the situation through force or the threat of it, he may not seek a concomitant change in goals or means. His aggression is often off target, nonideological in intent, and likely to be considered by the society as,a whole as deviant or illegal rather than revolutionary. Delinquent behavior, including vandalism, falls into this category of interpersonal orientation. The motivational impetus behind the troublemaker style is to wield power (as a primary rather than secondary gain). The troublemaker operates from a relatively insecure and unvalidated position; his behavior is likely to bring retaliation, rejection, or incarceration, all of which feed into the frustration that plays a large role in the genesis of the style in the first place.

The boys for whom troublemaker was the primary strategic style at Time I were chronically in trouble at home, in school, and with the law. Indeed, trouble and excitement are the crucial themes of the troublemaker style. The search for change, freedom, action, risk, excitement is paramount. The troublemaker generally lacks support at home and is frustrated by school, but is usually enmeshed in a tightly knit peer group that provides an outlet for dangerous and impulsive behavior. He seems to get caught frequently, and to swing between periods of high-energy, high-risk activity (forays) and periods of listlessness, apathy, and extensive sleep (almost hibernation). Much of his behavior occurs on impulse ("I just felt like it") or because one of his peers initiated it. Because of his use of force, the troublemaker is high on the dominant end of the power dimension; yet, ironically, his style may emerge from a sense of powerlessness, defeat, helplessness. As McCord et al. point out, paralleling the "troublemaker" style:

The ghetto also spawns another type of person—"the rebel without a cause": Frustrated and goalless, the rebel, like the exploiter, usually takes his vengeance out upon his own people. He does so, however, in a violent fashion without any pretense of staying within the boundaries of the law.[3]

It is difficult to place the Tough Guy on the affiliation dimension. On the surface he appears to be closer to the negative end—antipathetic and disaffiliated. Although this may be true, it must be borne in mind that the rebel, in the course of working against the system he despises, is ultimately working toward what he is convinced will be its good. And the troublemaker, in the course of fighting and attacking those around him, may, in the long run, be expressing his desire for them to love and care for him. The hallmark of the Tough Guy is his use of force, either by choice or by necessity, as the salient means of dealing with interpersonal situations. Insofar as the troublemaker uses "any behavior whose goal is the destruction, injury, frustration, embarrassment, discomfiture, or annoyance of another person or group,"[4] we can say that he is using aggression as the significant aspect of his style. In the portrait of Leroy Duncan we find a young man for whom aggression is both the enemy and the instrument for survival.

Self-Characterization. "I get all mad . . . and wanna fight."

The troublemaker style permeates Leroy's life. It ranges from teasing his siblings to taunting teachers and school principals, from throwing a knife at his brother to throwing a gun at a cop. Leroy fights his way through life, caught in a whirlwind of anger, cursing, hitting, running. His score on the Internal-External Sense of Control Questionnaire indicates that he feels overwhelmed by forces outside himself. For him the fighting is not the pursuit of some elusive influence over others, or self-expression—it is the pursuit of survival, of that modicum of control that affords him some semblance of identity, however weak and however negative.

From the very first words of his interview, Leroy describes his family and friends in terms of situations that spiral upward to a violent climax, accelerating from threat, to counterthreat, attack, to counterattack. Often, the victor is not clear, although the expression of hostility is. The spiral frequently ends with one or both parties backing off, for to pursue the matter might end in too explicit an act, thus ending the relationship—which Leroy is careful not to do. His own phrases catch the quality of the spiral, as he describes each member of his family:

My father . . . uh, he's all right, once in a while; but . . . sometimes when I be truant from school . . . he starts, uh, punchin' on me, and . . . I get mad, and so, I got mad and started . . . uh, cursin' at him a little. So, he just, uh, grabbed me, and put me in the room and started talkin' to me— yellin' and everything. So I started . . . gettin' mad again, but I didn't say anything to him. So I just sat there on the, uh, bed. So he just got up and left out the room. . . . My mother . . . once in a while, she's like him, too, but, she's okay. . . . she give me breaks . . . she starts yellin' at me, like my father does, but she don't hit on me. . . . So, I started uh, yellin back at her, so she got mad, and . . . called the cops on me one day . . . so, they told me to go outside, and take a walk, so I can cool off.

Confrontations with his parents generally dissipate to a strained silence; occasionally, as in the example above, they end only when one of them leaves the scene, or his parents call the police. With his siblings, however, the spiral continues further, and Leroy has more opportunity to pursue his anger:

Now, uh, my brother Bart he's 16 years old; once in a while me and him . . . get in fights. Like before when he started gettin' on me about his coat, I accidentally ripped it on the fence; so he started gettin' mad at me, so I lost my temper, and . . . punched him in the chest, so me and him started rumblin' all over the house, so one of his friends tried to break it up, so I pushed him and ran in the kitchen, and I got, uh, a knife and a broom [chuckle], so, uh . . . he told me what am I gonna do with that; I told him—you butt in again, you find out. So I got mad at him, I, uh, raised the broomstick, and, uh, swung at him and hit him in the neck. He started comin' at me, and I . . . raised the knife up; then he stopped.

His brother Benny, 14, is described by Leroy in the same fight-ing terms. From this passage, we can see that Leroy not only re-sponds to challenges, but makes them also:

Sometimes he starts to . . . mess around with me . . . So 'fore I started, you know, pushin' on him, and twistin' his arm and everything, so he [chuckle] ranned outside, got a brick, and a couple of friends [chuckle]— like they was gonna do something—they came up, he told me—mess with me now, you scared? So I went over to him and I . . . grabbed him in the headlock, and I threw him over my back. So his friends just stood there, lookin' at him . . . I was waitin' for them to try somethin', so I could knock them down too. So he got mad, he . . . picked up the brick from the floor . . . he threw it at me, and hit me in my ankle, so I grabbed him and I threw him against the wall . . . and I went back over to him, and I put my knee on his chest, and I was tellin' him to say he's sorry . . . 'cause he's always messin' around with me. So he said it, so I let him up.

Youngest brother Stevie, 5, gets on Leroy's "nerves." Leroy slaps him; Stevie retaliates by throwing things and cursing at Leroy. More distant relatives, such as aunts and uncles, are portrayed as people who are "all right" but hit or throw things when they are angry with Leroy. For example, his favorite uncle threw a coffee table at Leroy and his friend Duke, then chased them through their apartment building with a pair of garden shears; the boys hid in the basement for two hours, until the uncle went home. The family constellation is interlaced with violent incidents such as these, making it clear that Leroy's troublemaker style is one of defense as well as attack.

Trouble—getting into it and getting out of it—is a parallel theme of Leroy's existence. When asked what kind of things his parents did when he was younger to show they cared for him, Leroy recalls that they got him "outa things." For example, when he breaks some windows at age 9, he runs home and tells his parents; when "the man" (police officer) comes to their apartment and accuses Leroy, his parents claim that Leroy could not have done it, since he has been in the house all day. On another occasion, a neighborhood woman sees Leroy and Duke take a radio from the glove compartment of a car. When she tells his parents, Leroy denies that he stole the radio. Mr. Duncan placates the woman, sends Duke home, and later tells Leroy that he should not do it again: "you wouldn't like me to call the cops on you, would you." The next day Leroy and Duke sell the radio to a local youth.

Sometimes the charges are trumped up, he claims, as when a woman in the subway station accuses Leroy of trying to steal her pocketbook. She calls the police, who interrogate him and talk to his mother. When asked how he felt about the woman's accusation, he responds: "Feelin' kinda bad, I wanted to hit her, or [chuckle] something like that . . . but I woulda got in more trouble." He has been to court several times by age 14, has served one

month at the juvenile detention center, and later follows his brother Benny to the boy's training school outside Boston. Although he
is falsely accused from time to time, Leroy admits that most of the
accusations, sentencing, and punishment have been deserved.

In fact, compared to his companion in trouble and best friend,
Duke,[5] Leroy is surprisingly realistic and frank about his part
in initiating and carrying out the activities that get them into trouble. Frequently it is Duke who makes the suggestion, but Leroy
is quick to accept. For instance, one summer day the two boys
lack cash for going to the beach. Duke says, "How about a
pocketbook?" Leroy suggests they go downtown to a department
store where he knows a cashier who keeps her purse behind the
counter:

I said, instead of snatchin' a pocketbook, get a bag, we can walk out with
one. So he got a bag . . . so he said, hold the bag open. So I started
lookin' around, no one was lookin'. So he went behind the counter, and
he threw it. I caught it in the bag and folded it up. So I gave him the bag,
we walked out.

They leave the store, find a secluded telephone booth, empty
the contents of the purse, and go to the beach with their fifty-
dollar find, leaving the purse behind. Another trip to the beach is
similarly financed. The boys are in a subway station (a popular
hangout):

There was this lady down there, so I said, Duke, I wanna get the pocketbook; okay, he said, where we gonna run at. I said, you should know,
where do we always run? So . . . I snuck up behind the lady first, I
grabbed it. She started yelling and everything, so we ran right under the
trolley tunnel . . . we started runnin', the trolley started comin' . . . so we
ducked in one of those big holes in the wall . . . so when the trolley go by,
we run, right out the tunnel . . . take all the money out . . . and go home.

They split the $160 and go to the beach the next day.

The regularity of such endeavors is equaled by the apparent
magnetism an "easy mark" holds for Leroy and Duke. Walking by
the Prudential Center, the two hear money jingling in the pockets
of two teenaged boys:

So Duke said, Hey Leroy, you ain't just gonna let 'em pass by, are you? I
said no, I can't do that [chuckle].

They push the boys into a doorway and tell them, "hand over the money, or we'll . . . beat your butts in." The boys comply; Leroy and Duke run away. The two have been chased by campus police at a nearby university, and by city police for stealing cars. One of their favorite pastimes is "clipping" things in downtown stores, and going through glove compartments of parked cars for items of value. The risk and excitement of these forays are reflected in Leroy's tone of voice in telling the interviewer about them, as well as in his choice of words.

Trouble follows Leroy to school, where he and Duke "fool around" to the point of being suspended, over and over again. Leroy claims that he liked school in the beginning. In the first grade, however, he "started fooling around" with another student. The principal gave him the stick, which angered Leroy:

I picked up a eraser, and threw it at him. He grabbed me, he started twistin' my arm . . . I started struggling to get it loose, and everything . . . so he just took me, you know, out of the school and just took me right home and told my mother and them about it. So he just told me to stay home and don't come to school . . . one day . . . so I went back, and I started more trouble, but he wasn't there. . . . then the other teacher started jumpin' on me. . . . that's when I started beginning to hate it, and . . . hate it more.

The principal's use of physical punishment and expulsion seems to have set the pattern for Leroy's subsequent career in school. He adds that the "reason why I hate school, really, is . . . they don't give you enough of sleep . . . when I get up in the morning, I feel dead and weak and everything . . . I be all tired." He and all his friends are chronically truant, and plan to drop out of school officially at age 16 so they can "sleep all day." As an afterthought Leroy adds, "when I go to school, I get all in trouble, the teachers get all on me the same way."

As with his trouble in the streets, Leroy feels that he has been labeled as a troublemaker in school, so that teachers often accuse him wrongly of misbehavior. Yet by his own admission, the label is deserved. He seems to get sucked into a whirlpool of his own making. He "fools around," a teacher yells at him, he yells back. A teacher grabs him, he hits back. Those in authority who think that getting tough with Leroy will reform him find, instead, that their toughness feeds his:

The math teacher . . . I get in a lot of trouble with him . . . I fool around the place, throw books at the other kids . . . I have a elastic on my hand, and pop the kids and, you know, look all innocent, like I didn't do it . . . I break out and start laughin', couldn't hold it, so he goes and tells the vice principal. So he comes . . . and starts grabbin' on me, and, you know, take the elastic off my wrist . . . starts shakin' me up and everything. Then I start, you know, pushin' on him . . . fighting back . . .

The degree to which Leroy is willing to go while fighting is exemplified by the following incident:

We gotta wear ties at the DuBois. One day I didn't have mine on; I had it hangin' out my back pocket. The vice principal came, yankin' on my shoulder . . . he said, put it on before I pick it out and hang it around your neck. So I told him to try it. He took the tie out, tried to get it around my neck, and I snatched it and pushed him; he leaned back on the table and flipped right over it [chuckle] . . .

The principal and the math teacher throw Leroy "right out the school." The interviewer asks Leroy what the math teacher thought of him: "I think he liked me, but . . . just when I do a little something wrong, you know, cough or something . . . he'd think I'd be doin' it for fun." As for the principal, the final authority to whom Leroy's teachers resort in exasperation, Leroy's toughness equals his: "He started . . . yellin' and talkin' his stuff, so we starts talkin' our stuff back to him."

The "we" refers to Leroy and Duke, who has been his classmate since the fourth grade. They are kicked out of the DuBois and sent back to the junior high school in their own district (the Carter), where they continue on their path of disrupting classes. Finally, they are expelled from all their classes. After a physical confrontation with one of the teachers, Leroy swears at him. The teacher responds with, "Don't you ever let me catch you in my room again, or I'll knock you dead in your jaw." In order to keep him in school but out of the classroom, Leroy is assigned the title of "monitor." Duke then gets himself into serious trouble as well, so that he can join Leroy. While other children are doing their lessons, Leroy and Duke help the janitors clean the corridors; after the others come inside from recess, Leroy and Duke clean up the yard. Leroy likes the job; when they finish their work, they are free to leave the school. More importantly, it allows Leroy to feel needed in an environment that is otherwise hostile and frustrating to him.

His favorite teachers all along have been those who allowed him to be milk monitor, or to clean the boards, and so forth. They have also been the ones who did not yell at Leroy, who helped him to get the right answers, and who gave him a second chance when he misbehaved. His behavior for this type of teacher has been quite different from that in other classrooms:

The English teacher—she helps you out . . . she made me monitor, she don't talk mean to no one; you know, when someone start talkin' bad to her, she just say, calm down . . . and she'd talk nice and everything to you. Everytime I do something wrong, I never let her see me. . . .

He does not start trouble in her class—she rewards him by "saying something proud about me to the other teachers." Leroy thinks she sees him as a "very nice boy when he wants to be," and as someone who can do the work when he wants to: "When she tells me to do something, I don't give her no back talk . . . I just do it right away." At home, too, Leroy finds peace in doing work for his mother. He cleans the kitchen—she says he does a better job than the other children do—and keeps his own room clean. He lists housework as something he does that makes his mother happy.

Leroy's preoccupation with aggression comes through in his preference for teachers. He would rather be taught by black teachers, because they "won't push on you like the white teachers do, help you with your work better." Female teachers are preferable because:

If . . . you get in a argument with a man teacher, he'll start pushing and beatin' on you . . . and give you the stick, and it hurt. But . . . a woman teacher, you get in a argument with her, she wouldn't wanna fight, 'cause she knows . . . that you'll whup her . . . or, if she give you the stick, it won't hurt that much. You know, you can take it.

Similarly, he prefers older teachers, because if they "mess with you, you can take care of 'em by yourself."

Leroy wants to leave school because "the teachers push around on you a lot . . . put you in court, get you sent up." That is his first response, however, to the question of how *he* would handle the worst troublemakers in the school: "Push 'em around a little bit, and just carry them to the office, get things settled there." The interviewer asks, "What if the trouble with the kid is that people have been getting tough with him all his life?" Leroy answers: "I don't know." Alternative orientations are foreign, but not totally so. He finally offers, when asked how he would get the student to respect him: "I'd start, you know, talkin' to him . . . kind and everything . . . try to make him understand you; he might start, you know, playing it cool and everything." It seems that this is precisely the kind of response from others that has been so tragically absent in Leroy's own life.

Although school has been his nemesis, Leroy is unwilling to let the "American dream" slip by him without at least a verbal fight. He says he might go to night school to complete his high school education so he can get a good job and lead the "good life." Night school would be ideal, he says, because he could sleep in late, watch his favorite daytime stories on television, and "clip" things from the stores while they are still open. Later in the interview, Leroy declares: "Sometime I wish that, if that man were still livin' who thought of school, I would kill him."

In describing his peers, as with his family, Leroy first and foremost relies on fighting ability and/or getting into trouble as defining characteristics. It is clear that he has selected a peer group that reflects and supports his troublemaker style. Duke, 15, is "all right once in a while, but . . . he gets me in some trouble . . . he made me get the stick twice, but I paid him back for that." He adds that Duke at 25 "might be a criminal or something, the way he is now." It is Duke whom he would trust the most, and whom he names as best friend. Jake, the group's leader, is a "very nice boy, but he gets on people's nerves." Leroy speaks of Jake's temper and his lack of playfulness. His orientation is suggested by Leroy's comment that Jake loathes school and teachers: "He just might end up killin' one of 'em." Arch is "all right, he never starts trouble, unless you start it with him . . . when you get in a fight, he help you try to whup the kids." Rip is the "meanest one in the bunch. He always starts trouble with you . . . he's gonna wanna fight you . . . even when you don't want to; he . . . punch you to try to make you." Clarence is "mean" also but cannot "whup" the others. Leroy especially likes those who share money with him and give him "things"

—generosity is a trait he himself is noted for among both family and peers.

The boys have constructed a shack near their homes, which serves as a secret hideout and base of operations both day and night. One of the rules of the group is not to tell anyone else about the location of the clubhouse (Leroy avoids telling the interviewer, even when pressed). The penalty for breaking that or any rule: 52 punches. In order to get into the group the boy must be a good fighter and loyal; arguments are resolved by fighting it out. Their activities include playing musical instruments (Leroy sings and plays the piano); several of the boys own matching shirts and slacks to identify themselves as members of the musical group. Leroy portrays their main activities succinctly when he says, "Sometimes we start trouble for nothin' . . . go to parties, get all boozed up, start some racket, start foolin' around the place . . . all that stuff." He says they go up to a group of boys and "start talkin' bad to 'em to make them fight"; if the boys say they do not want to fight, Leroy and his friends will "start pushin' 'em around, knock 'em down."

One incident, which Leroy remembers as the "most exciting" time he and his friends have had together, involves white boys from the projects nearby:

We saw some white kids on the railroad track. So they saw us, they started runnin' . . . so we started chasin' 'em. We caught up with 'em, we grabbed all of 'em, you know, threw 'em off the railroad track [chuckles] . . . and so we jumped down, and grabbed 'em again. And there were some empty trains over there . . . so we put 'em in the train, so we tell 'em to get on their knees and don't look . . . so we picked a big bag of newspaper [chuckle] and threw it dead on their heads.

The white boys begin yelling; Leroy's group begins laughing and hitting them on the jaw. "We threw 'em down, stomped 'em." The white boys are in tears, and the fight ends: "We always take our last hit off of 'em and then get out." This encounter apparently established the territory for Leroy and his friends, for they never fight again.

The singing group, which represents for Leroy a possible connection to the good life, also leads him into trouble. They have no support for their dream. The shack has no electricity for amplifiers, no piano. They go to the local YMCA (they are not members) and try to use the piano there. In the middle of a song, two janitors appear, asking if they have a pass to use the room. After a verbal confrontation in which the janitors accuse Duke of trying to "act big," they try to hold Duke while letting the others go. Leroy refuses to leave without Duke, the janitors threaten to call the police, and open fighting breaks out. Leroy and his friends throw bottles, chairs, ash trays at the two men as they run out of the room to the safety of their clubhouse. Later they dress up in their outfits and drop by another favorite hangout, the local pool-room. Leroy asks Duke for a dime to play a song on the juke box—"Stay by Me."

Leroy and his friends seem to constitute a conflict gang, as defined by Cloward and Ohlin, with most of their fighting occurring in the neighborhood (an unstable area) and with subgroup status as an immediate reward.[6] Leroy's story about avoiding apprehension brings to mind Short and Strodtbeck's conclusion that "the gang provides a strategic context for deviant behavior"—and affords a sense of belongingness and a "rep" of status—but becoming a "delinquent" is really the "result of having gambled with a risk and lost." Getting caught is a risk inherent in Leroy's forays; not getting caught is cause for celebration.

Leroy hints at a secondary strategic style, that of "withdrawn kid." Here and there throughout his interview are clues to the long hours spent alone in his room, reading comic books ("Hercules") and "army books," listening to records, or watching television. But it is only a hint, for Leroy seems to savor regaling the young, black, male interviewer with his action-packed Tough Guy stories. For example, he relates to the Roxbury riot of 1967 by recalling: "I would have thought it was fun to be in a riot, because I've been in one before in———. It's okay, you don't get hurt or nothing . . . you beat a few cops over the head." Yet parent and sibling interviews show us the other side of Leroy—the quiet, private, withdrawn boy whose fights with his brothers are stimulated by their invading his privacy as much as by anything else.

When other people are in the house, Leroy uses the television as a way to tune them out. He tells of a time at his uncle's house:

When you tell him you tryin' to look at television, he goes over to it and turn it off sometimes . . . I get mad and walk outa the house, and go home.

He resents Bart's bringing friends into the house ("most of the time I'm in the house alone"), and gets into a fight over it. His mother talks too much in trying to settle arguments:

So, I start gettin' all tired. . . . I tell her, oh, I forgot, I have to, uh, go and see about something. To get out the house so I won't have to hear what she have to say and things like that.

He shares a room with Bart. When he wants to be alone, "I just don't feel like talking to no one or doing anything, I just go into the room." Sometimes he goes to the upper floors of the project building and sits in the halls or on the steps. This is time for him to plan where he will go later, or simply to avoid talking with others.

Leroy sleeps twelve to fourteen hours a day—a withdrawal of major proportions which serves as a foil to his action-filled days, and provides relief from them as well.

Perhaps the most significant segment of Leroy's interview is that dealing with self-concept. The picture that emerges is a strange admixture of negative self-image and high sense of competence. The connection lies in the fact that Leroy *is* good at doing things, but, unfortunately for him, too many of them are defined by society and by him as wrong. He is ambivalent about the trouble he gets into: "Sometime—I like doin' it, doin' the bad things. You know, I think I'm not gonna get caught doin' them . . . but I do." In a response to a Peer section picture, he says a boy who appears to be caught by the police "feels all bad, or good, inside . . . thinkin' that he'll get off the hook." The "bad" is the fear, the "good" is the excitement of committing the act, and the optimistic hope that the consequences will not be waiting for him after all.

Leroy rates high on sense of competence. He says he is good in basketball, baseball, ping pong, pool, gym, wood work, English, history, geography, science, racing, wrestling, boxing, and stealing cars. He feels that he could become better at anything he does not do well, if he wished to do so. In some passages he appears to like himself. In response to the brainwash question, he immediately offers, "Oh, I'd fight hard, you know, to keep myself the same as I am now . . . I'd like to keep my life the way it is now." When pressed, he says he would fight hardest to keep his ability to "pop a car" (one might guess, his ability to get away, to be in control, to be free).

If the interview had ended at this point, one might get the impression that Leroy has a strong positive identity and high self-esteem. Yet later comments in which he discusses in negative terms the very qualities he uses to describe himself, reveal a strongly negative self-image slipping through his equally strong defensive stance regarding staying the way he is. This ambivalence is expressed well by Duke, who says that he would not want to change: "I mean, I really like the way I am . . . but, the point is, I don't like the way I'm gettin' into trouble. It ain't nobody's fault but my own fault." He goes on to say that he follows the crowd so they will not call him chicken, and that he goes with them while they "do the dirty work"; but they squeal on him when they get caught. Then, echoing Leroy's shift in self-presentation, he drops this line of reasoning and admits, "No, I'm doin' it on my own. Just only foolin' my own self." Similarly, Leroy says in one breath that he likes his life the way it is but in the next confesses that he wishes he could learn to stay out of trouble.

All this is reflected in some of Leroy's responses to projective-type questions. For instance, he would like to be the "boy who does well" in school rather than Johnny, the "boy in hot water": "If I was Johnny, I would've been put away three times [chuckle] . . . been all pushed around, you know . . . I would've got in fights with two kids and lost . . . but the other kid, he's okay." It is clear from his own account that his behavior and experience in school certainly have more in common with Johnny's than with that of the boy who is doing well. Similarly, when asked what he will want his son to be when he is Leroy's age, he replies: "I want him to get a job, go to school, you know, get a good education and [chuckle] stuff like that. And be good; don't—don't be like me, and that's all." He adds, "I hope he don't . . . steal, break in places, mug men, or snatch pocketbooks . . . curse at grownups, or get into fights."

In a passage strikingly reminiscent of this, Duke says he hopes *his* sons will not "pull jobs" (as he does)—"If they do, I'll get them out, get them a lawyer, and I'll break their necks." In comments such as these, Duke and Leroy reveal their ability to drop their fronts and be brutally honest about themselves, and also their deep dissatisfaction with who they are. Although their parents seem to blame "other kids" for their sons' deviance, the boys relinquish that rationalization rather quickly once the interviewer has gained their trust.

If Leroy could grow up to be like any person he knows, he would choose the father of a friend, Buddy: "He's a nice man; I never seen him, you know, come hittin' on us." In order to be like him, Leroy admits that he would have to "stop cursin', stop stealin' . . . stop hittin' on my brothers." In other words, stop being himself. If possible, he would like to switch places with Buddy: "He don't get in as much trouble as I do . . . his father and mother don't yell at him like . . . our mother do." Whom would he *hate* to be like?

Rip, because he's always mostly gettin' in fights with . . . kids . . . he wants to start some trouble with somebody so he can knock 'em down or something like that . . . so, uh, I don't really like to be him.

Responses to the "spy" question are one long and detailed testimony to Leroy's toughness. With family, friends, and teachers, the spy is to use force as the paramount orientation:

If they start gettin' on you, get mean, start talkin' back to 'em, and if they grab you or something . . . start swingin' . . . [toward his brother, Benny] start beatin' on him for nothin'. Benny'll think that's me [chuckle] 'cause I always do that stuff to him. Ain't gotta be kind to him or nothin', just beat on him.

Although Leroy's predominant style is tough, he is selective in choosing the objects of his aggressive behavior. He tells the "spy" not to start a fight with one particular teacher because he sends him to the principal "just like that"; he would not use force against the teacher who was nice to him, mentioned earlier; he instructs the spy to fight with his friends only if they start it first—but not with Duke, because Leroy can "whup" him. The distinctions are drawn, however, only in terms of when and how or with whom to use force.

About five months after Leroy's initial interview, he is contacted again as Duke's peer. In reference to a boy who lives in the housing projects with him, he says, "He's like me in a way . . . starting trouble." This states succinctly what appears to be the core of Leroy's identity. His "trouble" with the police has grown in severity, ranging from a stint in jail for car theft to getting into a fight with a policeman. The first three pages of the transcript consist of a nonstop recounting of his exploits (with Duke, Rip, and Bart) since the last interview.

Leroy speaks disdainfully of the police, charging that they hide behind their badges. One night he and Bart are sitting in the hallway of their building. A neighbor complains that they are making too much noise; the police arrive, and ask where they live. It becomes another example of the characteristic way in which Leroy creates a "spiral of violence" out of a fairly innocuous situation:

So my brother Bart, he started some stuff with them . . . so the cop grabbed my brother, so I stood up and told him to get his hands off of him. So the cop . . . told me to get the hell out of here or I'll bring you in. So I told him to step outside . . . I started, you know, boxing and everything. He kept reaching for his billy club.

Leroy then says to Bart, "See what I told you? The cops are nothing without their guns or their billy clubs." In a final provocation, Leroy slaps the policeman and challenges him with a rock: "Pull your club out now!" The policemen walk away, a reaction for which Leroy has no explanation.

The trouble does not always end so benignly. Leroy ends up in court on a car theft charge:

So the judge said, "nice seeing you again," and everything, talking to me. Said, "Here's my old friend Leroy again." So I started smiling, I couldn't help it. So he started yelling at me.

Leroy is sent to the youth detention center for two months (his second term), but his sentence seems mild compared to his friends'. Rip is jailed for five to seven years for purse-snatching and evading arrest. Duke is sent to a training school for nine months, but escapes after one week.

Leroy and his friends seem to be on a one-way street from boyhood troublemaking to adult criminality. To "clipping" things Leroy adds "hustling" (Duke says Leroy also runs numbers). A growing reliance on wine to numb the mind and relieve his pain replaces simple experimentation with it. With Duke on the lam, Leroy experiences some desire to work and stay out of trouble; he talks of going to night school or into the Job Corps, but nothing materializes out of these feeble attempts to break the pathway. Toward the end of Time I, Leroy's secondary style of retreatism becomes more pronounced as he spends countless hours watching television or holed up in his room reading and listening to records. The singing group is split up, with all its members incarcerated or on the run. Leroy is alone.

Characterizations by Others. "He gets a little mean."

During this moratorium on trouble, the other members of Leroy's cluster are interviewed. This timing, plus the fact that Leroy typically attempts to hide his troublemaking behavior— from his parents at least—results in more stress on his secondary style ("withdrawn kid") than we find in Leroy's own interviews. Both his family and his best friend perceive him as being quietly absent much of the time. There is a quality of hostility toward others suggested in their accounts of his quietness. All agree that when Leroy is angry, he is apt to withdraw into his room or wander out into the streets. Conversely, when they see that he is angry, they all concur that it is best to leave him alone. Says Mrs. Duncan:

Sometimes he stay in the house all day long, and say two or three words, all day. That's it. He'll just sit, look at TV, won't say nothing . . . to tell you the truth, I can hardly tell when Leroy is unhappy, 'cause he's quiet most of the time; and when he's mad, I know it . . . just let him alone.

Mrs. Duncan claims that she and Leroy are alike in their "quiet ways"—and that she can get along with him very well because of that (even though he "just gets on my nerves a lotta ways"). Bart says that his arguments with Leroy just as often end with silence and withdrawal as they do with a physical fight: "We just don't say nothin' to each other, and for a few days won't wear each other's clothes, so no one'll say anything." Similarly, Duke describes Leroy (his best and most trusted friend) as "comical, and he's a soft talker and quiet . . . stays in the house mostly." He adds that Leroy is more interested in working than "coming out"—a reflection of Duke's jeopardized position. Mr. Duncan says that Leroy is different in that "most boys of his age are always out, it seems to me—but he comes in the house and stays in." Compared to his three brothers, Mr. Duncan says Leroy is much quieter:

He's a lot quieter than the others, for one thing. And he'll get off to himself. You take, like the three of them will be in the front room watching

TV, Leroy will go in the bedroom with a book. And he'll stay back there till it's time to go to bed. If they leave then he'll come back out and sit in there by himself.

From Mr. Duncan's point of view, Leroy is jealous of his privacy. As an example he tells of an occasion when Leroy cut his leg and knuckles badly. His father asked him if he wanted to go to the hospital; Leroy declined; "but five minutes later, he was gone. He just went on his own." Mr. Duncan describes his son as an avid reader who does not appreciate being disturbed in his retreat:

I can go and open the door and look at him. He'll look right back at me. I don't say anything, I turn around and get out. One of the kids'll go in there and you'll hear him say, "get out of here." Because he's in there with that book, and he don't like nobody to bother him . . . he just loves his literature.

His favorite reading materials, according to Mr. Duncan, are *Life* magazine and *Reader's Digest*—a rather different picture than the one Leroy paints when the interviewer asks him what he reads. His father claims that he and Leroy do the "Word Power" section in one magazine together, looking up words and "always reading." Sometimes they play chess together. Often, it appears from the father's descriptions, these activities are designed to "stay clear" of Mrs. Duncan. This emphasis on Leroy's quietness is capped by Mr. Duncan's prediction that Leroy "should have a nice quiet life if he stays the way he is now."

Contradicting earlier statements, Mrs. Duncan claims that "most all the time, Leroy is very hard to get along with." Her attitude toward Leroy is suggested in her comment that she is "glad" that her brother no longer lives with them: "Leroy had too many ways like him. . . . and the ways that he had, I don't like, I didn't like."

Addressing Leroy's aggression, Bart says that he and his parents would all like to have Leroy cool his temper down. "He fights a lot. . . . he gets mad too easy." He describes one incident in which Leroy and his father were wrestling:

I was laying across the bed, reading. Leroy was high that night, and my father was too. They fell on me. So I say, "I wish I could stretch out." And Leroy jumped right up . . . he was really mad. And he started pushing me . . . and then he grabbed me. That's when I jumped up and threw him

down. . . . my father grabbed Leroy . . . he was breaking us up. Leroy
started crying, "Now you're teaming up on me," flew in the kitchen and
grabbed a knife.

Leroy does not use the knife; instead, he puts his hand through a
window. Bart says that Leroy goes downstairs to a neighbor's
apartment for the night. The neighbor calls the police, who take
him to the hospital for stitches. The next day, Bart goes down
there and asks Leroy if he is "trying to be Hercules and everything,
you know, doing all that. He just started laughing."

Bart says that Leroy will "fight anybody"—especially when he
has been drinking—but that he is "nice for a brother anyways."
He says Leroy's anger is just under the surface all the time, ready
to be expressed at the slightest provocation ("he don't have to be
in no certain mood"). He tried to knife Bart during the incident
described above, but Bart feels that beneath the anger is both a
semblance of self-control and affection for others:

I don't think he would kill nobody, anyway. There's times he could have
killed me; he tried . . . but by the way he looked, I know he didn't want
to . . . he would just cut at me, he wouldn't really even try to hit me with
the knife. Just scare me.

Mr. Duncan skirts the question of Leroy's angry outbursts. He
says that when his son is angry, he goes in his room and "pouts" or
"just runs the steam off":

He'll just take off. But he comes back to the house, and I don't see no
police car behind him, so I figure he's all right. Looks like he just goes out
and run it off or go play basketball.

These occasions may be Leroy's fighting and stealing forays.
What makes Leroy so angry? Mr. Duncan alludes to two sources
of intense irritation for Leroy. One, as suggested earlier, is when
someone breaks into the solitude he creates for himself when reading. The other is when someone (especially his mother) swears at
him. Mr. Duncan says he and his son are alike in their "temper"—
"one thing he hates is for a woman to swear at him, which I do
myself." Bart concurs, saying that Leroy "don't like you to call
him black." He admits to infuriating Leroy in this way frequently.
Being called "nigger" or even "black" is anathema for Leroy, who,
with his mother, is the darkest in the family. Leroy strikes back by

calling Bart "yellow." Or, in anger, "he'll grab something, throw it at you and try to hit you." Says Mr. Duncan of this situation, which obviously grieves him as well:

I get so sick and tired of her saying that word, "nigger." "Nigger," that's all I hear in the house, "nigger." It's got to be monotonous, you know? She'll turn around and ask them to do something, and they won't do it. Then she tells me, "Duncan, you better make that nigger do this!" I say "I'm not making him do nothing. You learn how to talk to them, they'll do what you want them to do."

He says Leroy's reaction to this kind of scene is to "get upset and walk out of the house." He refuses to speak to his mother. Sometimes, if Mrs. Duncan has been cursing her husband, Leroy will come into his father's room later and ask if he has any cigarettes; if the answer is no, he will go out and get a pack for his father in a simple gesture of solidarity, then retreat to his room again.

The demeaning tone of Mrs. Duncan's attacks has taken its toll on Leroy's racial identity and sense of pride in being black. Leroy earns a very low score in the Racial Awareness section; his lack of positive racial identification is expressed throughout the interview. Mr. Duncan tries to counteract this effect by telling Leroy that they are "Negro" not "niggers," that God wanted them that way, and that they must accept it with pride. When Mrs. Duncan is abusive, Mr. Duncan supports his son by telling him he does not have to leave: "She yells out, 'Get out of my house!' I say, 'You don't have to go anyplace. Just stay here.'" Unless his father encourages him to stay home, Leroy will leave and occasionally stay out all night.

The issue of swearing would seem commonplace were it not for two factors: one, the intricate linkage with racial and consequently general self-concept; two, the fact that Leroy is left with a cesspool of anger which is not entirely dissipated through running or retreating. Where does the anger go? His father eventually admits that Leroy "gets a little mean at times, but it's not his fault, really." Especially in response to the racial name-calling, he says Leroy gets "pretty evil" and swears himself: "It burns him up, makes him messed up . . . he'll go in the room, he's groaning to himself . . . I know myself that he don't like it."

This is a side of the family dynamics that Mrs. Duncan is either oblivious to or prefers to obscure from the interviewer. In response to a standard question—"Is the word nigger used often in your house?"—she replies, "Oh, yes [laughter] they don't know what the word Negro means . . . kids hardly say that." She is implying that her children are the ones who use "nigger." She notes that Leroy is darker than his brothers, but insists that it does not make any difference to him. When asked what she has told Leroy about being "Negro," she replies, "Well I haven't told him anything yet."

Later in the interview Mrs. Duncan reminisces about her pain in being called "nigger" in the South as a child. It might be hypothesized that her own racial identity is a negative one, stemming from the racist climate of the South she grew up in; that she lashes out at Leroy in particular because he, like herself, is so very dark; and that Leroy's negative identity stems from this shattered image *both* see reflected in each other's looking glass. It is difficult for Leroy to lash back to any great extent, for that would be to break the glass—she is, after all, his mother. Nor can he correct its image, since the only male to whom he can look for solace has, like himself, been defeated. In fury and frustration he leaves the house—the solution is clearly not there—and releases his feelings elsewhere.

Again contradicting Mr. Duncan's view, Mrs. Duncan contends that she has never heard her son swear: "I think I would knock the devil outa him." She also insists that he does not drink; Leroy, Bart, and Mr. Duncan all testify that he does, and, furthermore, attribute much of his fighting and hostile behavior (loss of control) to his drinking.

Best friend Duke emphasizes Leroy's fighting ability, his love of wine, and his bashfulness around girls. When asked if he knows anyone who makes a living from stealing, or anyone who runs numbers, Duke immediately replies, "Leroy." He claims that Leroy makes up to $200 per week: "Sometimes if he don't get that much he go back in, you know, keep lookin' for it till he gets it. Breaking into stores and snatching pocketbooks. As much as he wants . . . see he kinda greedy with the money. Money happy." Although Duke also says Leroy is generous, and points to helping each other out financially as a prime source of their friendship, he hints that Leroy is not always fair in splitting their "takes"—"that boy love his wine."

Bart says he would not hang out with Leroy and Duke—
"they're too crazy." He describes them as "messing around with
people," even "cripples," just for the fun of it. He thinks Duke and
Rip seem like "pros" and are better than Leroy at stealing, dancing, and driving. "Most of his good friends are in jail, 'cause they
were all thieves." It is clear that Bart, who is no stranger to trouble
himself, views Leroy and his friends as tough, troublemaking
youngsters who are dangerous to be around.

Duke concurs. He minimizes in his own interview as focal child
the trouble he has been in. But by the time of his interview as peer
for Leroy, Duke is frank about his own exploits:

It's been quite a while since you haven't seen me, 'cause most of the time I
been in trouble . . . I supposed to be calling myself "hustler" and making
money . . . it's no fun doing that. Go out, beating up guys, taking their
money . . . robbing stores.

He is on the lam from a boys' training school on a conviction for
armed robbery; he has decided at this point to give himself up
after Christmas, "if I ain't caught by then." He feels that "colored
persons" don't like to work, that whites can do things better than
they can, and so "colored persons probably get mad at them." He
speaks of stealing as "war" between him and the man who "wasted
his money buying a car":

Coloreds trying to be bad . . . white peoples trying to be bad . . . Have
their own ways, trying to make something out of themselves [What's
stopping them?] What's stopping them! Cops! The people trying to prove
how bad they can be. They walk around starting fights, breaking in
stores, get all kinds of clothes. . . . Sort of let everybody know he ain't
scared to do nothing.

As tribute to this view of life, Duke says he would fight hardest
to keep his "strength." And, like Leroy, he thinks his parents
would want him to change by "keepin' outa trouble and keepin'
outa cars . . . and stop hookin' school." He says he was one of the
"bad kids" at the DuBois. His way of treating a boy who is not
behaving in school, like Leroy's, is to use force: "Just . . . have a
nice long skinny stick, start hittin' him in the hand with it."

The others confirm that Leroy's primary way of handling disagreements is either to leave or to fight. Especially with Duke and
Bart, he resolves arguments with fisticuffs. Affection, too, is shown

through fighting or wrestling. Mr. Duncan says Leroy is closest to Bart and to himself. He and Leroy get along "just like two brothers, mostly." They wrestle, throw a few punches at each other: "sometimes he'll walk up and throw a punch at me, and he says, 'I got you didn't I'; I say, 'that's all right, I'll get even with you!'" He adds that they show affection toward each other by "hitting on" each other. Mrs. Duncan says she does not show affection toward her sons in a physical way—"Leroy, he don't let me get very close to him [laughter] he'll back away from me." She shows her caring by giving him things he wants or money to spend. Mrs. Duncan has difficulty answering a question about which adults seem important to Leroy. She concludes that "he just don't like too many people, period."

Analysis of the Tough Guy Style

In all focal clusters there is an obvious disparity between the points of view of cluster members—that is precisely what the focal-cluster method is designed to highlight. With the Duncan family, however, the disparities are deep chasms suggesting catastrophic distances between cluster members, both in perception and in emotional ties. Trying to make sense out of Leroy's cluster is like trying to solve a jigsaw puzzle whose parts don't fit. Bits and pieces of information, clues here and there, twist and push each other to create a picture of Leroy that is not available through reading only one transcript.[8]

Leroy is honest (for the most part) about his misbehavior—his parents minimize or deny it. Leroy says his parents like Duke and have no objection to their "hanging" together—both parents claim they have forbidden him to see Duke because he gets Leroy into trouble. Leroy acknowledges his father's drinking, but not his mother's—Duke says both "like drinking." Leroy never mentions his father's serious illness, chronic pancreatitis, which prevents him from working steadily.

While the others speak of fights and open conflict, Mrs. Duncan paints a rosy picture of a warm, happy family in which the children do not argue and their "trouble" is not serious or is someone else's fault anyway. Not only her interpretation, but the mere relating of facts is at variance with the other versions. She claims that she prepares her sons' lunches each morning and accompanies them to church on Sundays. Mr. Duncan describes how he gets up a five A.M. to iron, clean house, fix lunches, and get breakfast while she "just lays around." *He*, who has studied the Bible and sung in spiritual groups, is the one who takes Leroy to church.

Brother Bart is perhaps the most realistic and honest of all the members interviewed. For instance, Leroy seems more critical of his father than of his mother, whom he describes primarily as warm and kind. Mr. Duncan pictures his wife screaming obscenities at their children and wishing them out of existence. Bart says that when one of them is in trouble at school, his mother "would start off with hollerin' at us . . . and she wouldn't come up to the school neither . . . my father, now he'll ask what happened and everything." In first describing his mother, Bart says: "Now her, now . . . I think she's *sick*. She'll start drinking, she'll start hollerin', she'll call you all kinds of names . . . when she's *not* drinkin', she's kind of evil . . . you say something to her, she'll tell you to shut up."

These points may seem minor discrepancies, but I believe they form a pattern which reflects a deep and vicious hatred between Leroy's parents. This hatred permeates the fabric of the family constellation in a way that leaves an indelible mark on each member's personality, and forms a crucible in which Leroy's tough guy style was born.

The Family Matrix. In one way or another, all of Leroy's cluster members agree on his toughness and his tendency to withdraw. His primary strategic style does not escape his family or friends, although it is to some extent minimized by his parents. Mr. Duncan may see and emphasize the quiet, sensitive Leroy; over and over the others give witness to his anger, his temper, his toughness.

For Leroy, the central source of his style is the unresolved conflict which rages between his parents. To understand his anger, his own relentless sense of frustration and pain, we must understand the tension between his parents which spills over onto their children in countless ways, confounding everyone's search for peace of mind. We should explore this relationship in depth.

It has already been noted briefly that severe antiblack sentiments shaped Mrs. Duncan's life growing up in the South. Mr. Duncan ran away from his Southern home at age 15, riding the rails to the Midwest with a friend. For a misdemeanor the pair ended up working on a chain gang for a month. Later Mr. Duncan served in the Army and the Civilian Conservation Corps, worked in several menial jobs, and settled into a relatively stable work career as a meat cutter. He and Mrs. Duncan met and married.

Their trouble began early in the marriage when Mrs. Duncan took her husband to court for not giving her all of his earnings. She lost the case, and the event embittered both of them. After their four sons were born, Mr. Duncan was attacked in an alley in Boston. One of his attackers stabbed him; the other one Mr. Duncan knocked to the ground. The latter died of head injuries, and Mr. Duncan was convicted of manslaughter. He served five years of a four-to-seven year sentence. The injustice burned him; nonetheless in prison he studied stitching, automotive mechanics, barbering, and the Bible. He received diplomas for all of them. On another occasion he was sentenced to a year in jail for child molesting—he swears that a "friend" set him up with a minor-age girl whom he had just raped, leaving Mr. Duncan to take the rap. He served that term and another of several months for hitting a white man who called him "nigger."

The pain of being punished for self-defense against both verbal and physical attacks was magnified a thousand times by the fact that Mrs. Duncan never visited him in prison, nor would she bring his sons to see him. (They claimed they slipped in to see him anyway.) Instead of supporting him, Mrs. Duncan had an affair with his best friend and sent him the bills for several abortions. He says it was the worst thing that ever happened to him:

Them babies. I got a hospital bill . . . for the burial of Baby Duncan. What baby? I even got a bill for a white baby that she lost. When did I start putting out *white* babies! . . . a lot of time I just sit in the house and look at her, and think about that junk, and wish she was a man, sometimes, so I could get up and knock her down.

The agony of this period has had long-lasting effects on Mr. Duncan's life. Nor is it lost on Leroy, who, according to his father, will say in anger to his mother, "You didn't go see Daddy when he was in jail." Mr. Duncan graphically depicts Leroy's attitude toward women in this passage, which suggests a powerful source of conflict and anguish for his son: "Like if she'd be with somebody, and this guy would start a fight or something, he'd have to get Leroy just as quick as he would me . . . and he's pretty rough on girls now." Leroy confirms this, saying he will never marry: "I hate girls . . . they kill me."

This example related in one part of the interview comes to life in another. Mr. Duncan speaks of a time he and Leroy go downstairs in the housing project to visit a neighbor. They walk in the door, only to see Mrs. Duncan in a bedroom with another man:

They're in the bed, they're just kissing, man . . . so I made a statement. I says, "when you people get through, you come up there and get her clothes." She jumps up and *she's* gonna call the police on *me*. That burnt me. And I slapped her. This guy jumped up and Leroy grabbed him . . . I got busted that night.

The next day Mrs. Duncan drops the charges (on five other occasions she has followed through on assault and battery charges that held). Mr. Duncan leaves the house in disgust. It is Leroy who encourages him to return. He insists this is the last time he will submit to this humiliating process—"then I just gonna get me a place by myself . . . 'cause I think two times is enough . . . I'm not henpecked."

The pain in his life has left Mr. Duncan bitter and defeated, a model that Leroy can hardly overlook. He tells the interviewer, in summing up his life:

You ask yourself, well, why? Why did they do this? Well, why do you put up with it? Next thing, you're angry . . . in me, I am burning up. You can believe it. But I'm fighting against my own self. Then sooner or later I say to myself, what do I care?

His depression comes through in a comment about not feeling like washing or shaving in the morning: "It's not such a good feeling . . . who have I got to look good to? That's that old 'I don't care' feeling."

Although Mrs. Duncan attacks and degrades her husband in ways that sound straight out of a cheap novel, he stays with her in order to be close to his sons, whom he loves dearly and nurtures well. Yet he smolders with anger and humiliation, a broken man who was once competent and self-respecting. Leroy, not only witnessing this but experiencing it through the racial name-calling ("You ain't nothing but an old black nigger"), is usually reluctant to leave. He is held at home (during adolescence at least) because of the important emotional bonds between child and parent as well as financial dependency. But, like his father, inside Leroy is "burning up."

Critical Messages from Others. The family constellation serves as the primary source of Leroy's style in another sense as well. The messages and expectations directed toward Leroy tend to favor toughness and to retard the development of positive identifications or definitions of self.

When Leroy fails at something or disobeys his parents, he gets "yelled at and pushed around." Thus both verbal and physical violence are used to convey messages of disapproval. His parents, furthermore, confuse the issue of the consequences of getting into trouble. On one occasion they beat him for "yelling at grown-ups"—physical violence meets verbal violence—on another they protect him in his thievery. By doing so they add to the "excess of definitions favorable to violation of law over definitions unfavorable to violation of law"—a condition Sutherland points to as a cause of delinquency.[9] In both cases the use of force is supported as an acceptable way of handling interpersonal relationships.

Leroy's siblings share his combative approach to others, thus intensifying the atmosphere of hostility and violence. As we have seen, Leroy has in addition selected a peer group whose propensity for law-breaking and trouble-making matches and reinforces his own. With both siblings and peers, violence is used to express affection, anger, frustration, or the need for privacy.

Many of the expectations held of Leroy appear to be negative. Since Leroy tends to pay emotional heed to his mother, her expectations are particularly critical. For one thing she teaches him to steal and expects him to engage in dishonest behavior:

When the check comes, my father, he pays all the bills . . . he go get . . . some liquor, come back drunk . . . go in the room and fall asleep. So she go in there, you know, try to sneak some money out of his pocket. She can't do it, so she tells me to try and get about twenty dollars out of the wallet. So I go try it . . . while I was takin' twenty dollars out for my mother, I took five for me and stuck it in my pocket [chuckle].

She asks him how much he has taken for himself; Leroy says "nothing." She searches him (showing her lack of trust), he sticks the money up his sleeve, and Mrs. Duncan finally gives up with, "this is one time you didn't do it, huh."

In addition, Mrs. Duncan seems to squelch any positive expectations Leroy might hold for himself. He aspires to work in a department store, selling televisions and stereos. His mother wants him to be a doctor (Leroy laughs in relating this bit of information) and conveys this message in a way that tends to cancel out Leroy's own hopes: "She be saying, well, suppose I be in bed all sick and dying, and you don't know nothing about doctoring." She treats his second job choice, trolley car driver, with equal enthusiasm: "I told her I might work on one of those things, she said she better not catch me on one of those. So I said okay, okay."

Her reaction to his dreams is to warn him of what might happen to him if he does something wrong. For example, if he becomes a trolley or bus driver, he should not speed, for that will make the passengers nervous and he would be sent to court for it, or lose the job. As if this lack of support were not enough to frustrate Leroy in his quest for the "good life," later in the Work section Leroy lists trolley driver and salesman in a department store as jobs in which he does not see many blacks working.

His mother's pessimism pervades Leroy's responses to the Work Pictures, revealing an overriding expectation that violent things happen to one in the world of work. For example, he would not like to be a submarine captain, because he might "get a surprise attack in back of us . . . then it blows up, we be dead." Similarly, his response to a picture of a pilot describes in spectacular terms his otherwise unspoken attitude toward life in general:

I'd be all alone out in the sky, and everybody'd be busy fightin' the rest of 'em . . . two or three of 'em might see me, come at me, be three onto one, I wouldn't have a chance to turn around. Or, you know, while I be shootin' at one the other one come behind me, or above me, drop a bomb or something on me . . . and I just be blowed to bits.

This projective story is graphically reminiscent of Bart's description of Leroy flying into a rage when he thinks Bart and his father are "teaming up" on him. The story also gives us an insight into how Leroy sees the world around him: he feels alone, feels threatened, is convinced that he must attack before he himself is attacked.

Messages favoring Leroy's toughness are carried in the method of punishment and discipline utilized by his parents. Mr. Duncan says that he has no trouble with his boys at home; when he tells them to do something, they do it. (Mrs. Duncan apparently does not command the same respect.) When there is cause for discipline, Mr. Duncan says he prefers to handle it because "she just swears at them. That's not helping any, not to me, it's not." He takes the offender into the bedroom and tells him: "Whip me. If you can't do what I say, then you whip me, now." He claims that Leroy backs off and refuses to fight his father, and will obey the order, although he is angry.

Even though his way of dealing with his sons' disobedience is to take advantage of his superior physical strength, it seems that Mrs. Duncan's method would entail even more use of power. Says Mr. Duncan, "If I listen to her, it's always knock them down, kill them, or something like that. She don't care nothing about none of them no way, except that little one, Stevie." The suggestion that force (either father's or mother's threat of it) will solve problems and straighten out wayward children, is a clear message that Leroy hears. Mr. Duncan describes one incident with his oldest son:

Bart was down in Westland. So he came in late Saturday. So she said, "You going to kill him?" I said, "No. You want him dead, you kill him!" I say, "I'm not going to touch him. . . ." Now if she gets mad, that's the first thing she'll throw up in my face. "You won't even whip that boy."

Not only does Mrs. Duncan advocate the use of physical violence, using equally violent language, she also demeans her husband for failing to use her tactic. She complains that her husband will not punish Leroy because "that's his pet." She guesses that she could "beat him," but last time she tried it Leroy "almost wanna struck me back, and I stopped doing that now." She indicates some frustration when she relates that her husband can talk "so I can't even hear what he's saying," and Leroy will obey, whereas "the only way that Leroy knows that I really mean something, is by hollerin' at him."

While his parents yell at Leroy for his misbehavior, they also engage in some denial of their son's style. Whenever he gets into trouble, they blame it on Duke and tell Leroy not to hang with him. But, says Leroy, "I keep tellin' 'em Duke don't get me in trouble." He says he gets himself into it, or he happens to be around when others in his gang are caught. He says his mother is trying to make him into a "good person," but he does not listen to her most of the time. How does he make his decisions about whether to be "good" or "bad?" I just start thinkin' about it . . . and I come up with one of 'em . . . I do it, or my mind tells me not to do it, so I don't." It is significant that things which he thinks black children are better at than white children—fighting, running, stealing, and driving cars—are the very things he himself excels at, but in ways that may prevent him from reaching his goals.

The Impact of Role Models. The most salient role models for Leroy are problematic to say the least. He ignores his mother's swearing and yelling and chooses to identify with her as "kind, a soft talker, [a] sweet, and gentle" person—qualities he rarely shows to the interviewer, perhaps indicating that his "tough" style is somewhat exaggerated for the latter's benefit.

Leroy feels that he is not like his father at all (revealing an absence of positive identification with him), yet later in the interview speaks of his own drinking and fast temper. I surmise that to identify openly with his father is too threatening, for it would mean landing squarely on the side of trouble (convictions, drinking) and weakness. His identification with his mother is probably more "ideal self" imagery than true modeling. Another explanation of this perverse "blindness" to his overwhelming similarities with his father is that to admit his mother's rejection of him would be to admit that he, too, is being torn down and apart, being demeaned, being crushed, by the same woman who has all but destroyed his father.

Bart, another possible positive role model for Leroy, has followed a deviant and self-destructive route in and out of disciplinary school, detention centers, and prisons. He serves as a younger example of the pathway their father took throughout his life. As mentioned earlier, uncles and aunts for the most part are abusive and "rough" people.

Still, in a sense Leroy and his father share the same fate, as becomes clearer over the course of many interviews and years: both are tormented by Mrs. Duncan's destructive attacks; both use alcohol to escape that pain; both have severely bruised self-images;

both have wells of anger that are all too easily tapped; both spend impressive amounts of energy redirecting their anger away from wife and mother, since for different reasons they both still need her.

Mr. Duncan is a bitter and sad man, whose chances in life have soured, whose luck has all been bad. He offers Leroy the model of a forlorn and defeated man whose own violence (and weakness) have trapped him. Leroy is able to love his father but has little respect for him. Mingled with the love is perhaps some hate (probably more for his weakness than his violence). Mr. Duncan praises Leroy's helpfulness and caring, but adds that he also "picks on" him sometimes: "One time as a baby he almost swallowed a penny. I ran my finger down his throat. Maybe he's thinking about that, I don't know [laughter]." Furthermore, Leroy feels that his father does not pay enough attention to him, especially when his father drinks: "I wish he would stop gettin' mad fast and drinking so much . . . he don't listen and things like that."

The most salient role model for Leroy not only represents to him failure, violence, and trouble, but also uncertainty. We shall explore further this issue of Leroy's felt sense of rejection.

Other Issues.   Several other factors serve to reinforce Leroy's sense of isolation and his emerging "tough guy" strategic style. First is the subtle rejection, which works its way into the family dynamics. Leroy feels that his father favors Stevie, which suggests that, as the third of four sons, Leroy does not feel secure in being special and deserving equal attention. (Mr. Duncan claims, and Bart agrees, that *Mrs.* Duncan favors Stevie: "Well he's got a little curly hair and he's high yellow." At Christmas she is planning to buy him a bike, says Mr. Duncan: "She ain't buying the rest of them nothing . . . so I just take my time, and I'll get the other three something myself." He claims that he goes out of his way not to favor Stevie—"the boy is 11 years old, and to me he's not a baby. She didn't baby the rest of them like that.")

Although Mrs. Duncan does not comment on favoritism toward Stevie, she clearly expresses her feelings about her family throughout the interview. She blames Leroy's stubbornness on his being "just a teenager." She resents having to go to court over his fighting: "Sometime I get so mad I say, you know, Leroy you more trouble than you worth! . . . I just, you know, that just pops outa my mouth." Mrs. Duncan later claims that she does not really mean it, but then says that she feels the same way about her other sons and her husband as well. Mr. Duncan, in contrast, strongly denies feeling that his children are more trouble than they are worth:

Yeah, I've heard a lot of them curse their children out. I mean they act like it's the child's fault for being here . . . and actually it's not . . . I don't get tired of them. No. No. I do keep in mind someday that they're going to leave me.

He feels that his wife is more trouble than *she* is worth, however.

Added to this tension in the family, we find Leroy's discomfort in school. Much of his frustration in that setting, I suspect, comes from the fact that he finds it difficult to do the assignments and thus is doomed to failure in that sphere at least. He dreads the long tirades that greet his misbehavior there. One teacher yells at him for causing trouble—"I didn't under . . . really understand him, he was talking too fast for me." (At home, almost as painful as the beatings are the times when his parents "lecture" him. Speaking of his father, Leroy laments: "When he drinks, he . . . talk . . . me to death almost.") Because he finds the work difficult, he gets into trouble; because he gets into trouble, he is labeled "bad" and spends a lot of time out of the classroom, consequently making the work more difficult. This cycle is exacerbated, perhaps even caused, by Leroy's low mental capabilities.

Leroy's verbal IQ score of 80 at Time I was (with Duke's) the lowest in the Pathways sample. It is possible that Leroy received some brain damage when hit by a car at age 10. His mother says his head "was messed up," and he stayed in the hospital for three weeks. Yet his responses are full and detailed, among the most informative in the sample. This is especially true when he speaks of his adventures with his friends. His vocabulary, though limited, contains enough action words to hint at the quality of his everyday life. Perhaps most revealing of his intellectual capacity is the fact that Leroy frequently misunderstands questions asked him during the interview. For example, when asked who in his family he is most like, he answers in terms of whom in the family he likes the most. Undoubtedly the low IQ score reflects to some extent the amount of time he spends in school getting in trouble or being punished instead of learning. Being chosen to play "janitor" is hardly preparation for achievement. The complex interrelationship of trouble, intelligence, and school failure is obviously important in this case.

One final factor should be noted in trying to fathom the etiology of Leroy's "troublemaker" style. While it may be true that the family dynamics would have generated a tough style regardless of where the Duncans lived, undoubtedly living in the core of a high-crime neighborhood helped to provide opportunity, if not inspiration, for the particular form displayed by Leroy and his three brothers. Mr. Duncan refers to his neighborhood as a "whore's paradise," and confesses that he often lies about where he lives. Leroy says the police *expect* crime and vandalism to originate in his area, and patrol it regularly: "That's where most of the action is."

Leroy's Alternatives.   We examined a few of the situations at home and in school which throw Leroy's tough approach toward others into relief. It is difficult to do justice in a few pages to the richness and variety of his everyday experiences—almost without exception they testify to his toughness, and to his zest for trouble, risk, excitement.[10] Mixed as it is with feelings of guilt and anger, Leroy's orientation toward others is defined as combative. It is clear that his definition of self, and the perception of him by others, have crystallized into that of a trouble-making, violent youth.

Leroy's options for relating to others are severely limited by his background, by his significant others, and by himself. Being pushed around and pushing others around are familiar to him, and appear to serve the function of defense and of constructing a palpably strong self. There is little reward for his attempts to develop alternative styles, and much reinforcement of his toughness. His family, his friends, and his teachers, by and large, view Leroy as a fighter and a troublemaker—an image he accepts, even relishes.

His parents' alienation robs him of a clear example of intimacy, love, and respect. Lacking positive models, lacking reinforcement for constructive, autonomous behavior, and faced with "attacks" from parents and siblings alike, Leroy appears to have constructed a virtually impenetrable fortress, complete with cannon for fighting back and walls and moat for distancing himself from others. His parents, though protective of his deviant behavior, also expect it of him, thereby setting Leroy on a merry-go-round of trouble and fighting which does not seem to stop long enough for him to get off.

Leroy's evaluation of adult role models available to him is succinct: when asked which of the adults he knows he would like to resemble when he grows up, he replies: "I wouldn't know. All the grownups I know, they mostly do the same thing I do, go around cursing . . . and drinking." But the options are limited by himself as well as by the expectations others hold for him and the lack of positive role models. In two stories he tells about fighting, Leroy rejects open attempts by his brother to achieve a compromise: "I just wanna fight," he explains.

Analytical Dimensions. In terms of affiliation, Leroy's orientation toward others is essentially antipathetic. Yet his devotion to Duke is complete; and his affection for his parents, although tainted by disrespect and fear, is fairly strong. It is important to note that the two people with whom Leroy will not fight are Duke and his father, the two people with whom he feels most closely affiliated. He and Duke settled arguments physically until one day Leroy's hand slipped and he accidentally hit Duke hard enough to hurt him. Leroy was shaken and tells the interviewer, "I don't think we would fight anymore . . . we just argue with each other."

Whether Leroy will be able to build on his affiliations in later life is difficult to predict, since his style is grounded in the sense of rejection he has experienced from a woman who—if she could live her life over again—says she would not get married, and "I know I wouldn't have no kids."

In terms of the power dimension, it is clear that Leroy's tough style keeps him at the dominant end of the continuum in most situations. He sees force, or the threat of it, as a way of controlling others and gaining satisfaction or acceptance in interpersonal relationships. His environment tends to favor this style and to provide ample opportunity for its expression and its nurturance, and at the same time offers little to counter it.

Leroy's toughness seems relatively rigid, automatic, and spontaneous, the natural way for him to deal with others. His style seems relatively sincere as well. He believes in his toughness, prides himself on his strength, seeks out friends who share and understand his penchant for trouble. He tends to be open in regard to his misbehavior—he does not try to con the interviewer into thinking he is a "good kid"—yet I feel that much concealing takes place in Leroy's presentation of self. Underneath the rough texture of his everyday style, one senses hurt, pain, fear, which simmer until opportunity arises for an explosive confrontation with a sibling, a white gang, a policeman.

Leroy is not, I submit, operating from a secure, confident stance in which his toughness serves only to maintain integrity or to gain status in the eyes of his significant others. Rather, he operates from a basic insecurity created and perpetuated by a fundamentally hostile, threatening, and *attacking* environment. His toughness is a defense, a protective device—as is his secondary style of retreating. Both serve to make life tolerable.

Conclusion

A good deal of Leroy's energy is spent in being tough and causing trouble. Yet there is an underlying ambivalence and wish to be different which attest to the fact that for Leroy being a tough guy is a negative identity.

The significance of this ambivalence toward his use of force as a primary interpersonal tool should not be lost on educators, social workers, and corrections personnel when dealing with so-called tough guys or troublemakers. Especially in situations involving confrontation or sanction, the Tough Guy may be unable to reveal his ambivalence and is likely to present resolutely only his aggressive and trouble-oriented side. Because the style is defensive, the ambivalent feelings are unlikely to surface unless the person is approached in a nonthreatening, nonattacking manner. It appears that in attempts to counsel or rehabilitate tough guys, contrary to popular opinion, the last thing to do is use an equally tough approach.

This holds for educators as well. During the period of our interviews with Leroy, Jonathan Kozol had just published his muckraking *Death At An Early Age* (1967), which chronicled the continuing use of the rattan and other forms of physical punishment in the Boston schools. This method of discipline was often used on confused and troubled children who came from homes where beatings were the hallmark of interpersonal relations. Teachers, in their own frustration, are chagrined to find that hitting children is not particularly effective, especially with the most recalcitrant. I suspect that this is because hitting reinforces the Tough Guy style—the teacher is simply adding to a preponderance of violent messages in the child's life—and feeds into the child's negative self-image.

The teacher or parent who engages in physical expression of a violent nature—or perhaps even talks tough—may elicit momentary conformity. Ultimately, however, the risk is that violence begets violence, that the use of force fuels the "spiral of violence" that plays such a crucial role in the Tough Guy's strategic style. Earlier we saw how a policeman refused to participate in Leroy's attempt to establish a spiral—the situation was defused. Through another anecdote we witnessed a vice principal who, in trying to get Leroy to wear a tie, used force in a way that fed into the spiral.

My prediction regarding Leroy's future at this point, given the strength of Mr. Duncan's example, is that Leroy will maintain his "troublemaker" style throughout his early adulthood at least. It may eventually be supplanted by retreatism, probably in the form of heavy drinking or even alcoholism. As Mr. Duncan so wisely says, "Trouble—that's something that's easy to get into, but it's real tough getting out of it."

At the core of Leroy's style is the threatened or actual use of physical force. The Actor, on the other hand, relies on the force of words to provide a sense of control over others. In the case of Dave, we will see how powerful that strategic style can be.

What he wants you to know,
he'll let you know;
what he doesn't want to let you know,
you're not gonna know it.

— FATHER

5. The Actor *Dave Cooper*

Moving Over. The Put-On and the Con Artist

The Actor devotes much energy and attention to "staging" or "performing" in ways designed to make impressions on other people which are not always honest or true. His major motivational impetus is manipulation of others for the benefit of his own goals and gratification. This manipulation can take many forms: conning, gaming, hustling, lying, or trying to gain a primitive form of approval (attention) by being a clown or show-off.

This style falls into Rainwater's "expressive" category. It is "innovative" in Merton's sense—"rejecting of institutionalized norms at the same time that a high evaluation is placed upon the culturally prescribed goals." [1]

The two types of Actor to be discussed here are the "put-on" and the "con artist." The put-on typically treats people as though they were all the same; he does not control his expressiveness as well as the con artist—that is, he tends to act out his style for everyone, all the time. He is less slick than the con artist and possibly less convincing or effective in the impression he is trying to make.

At the same time, he probably reveals more of himself than does the "con artist," since his style is more spontaneous and less contrived than the latter's. He needs to "put people on" (get attention, sympathy, fear, respect, or whatever), and in doing so may push too hard and, so to speak, "lose his cool." He appears to be relatively immature and to have more self-doubts than many of the other styles.

The "con artist," on the other hand, is more controlled and clever in relation to others, skillfully molding his performance according to his needs and to the specific characteristics of various audiences. He is likely to be good at "rapping" with people, and exhibits excellent verbal facility (he may score very high on the verbal sections of IQ tests). He is described by people who know him as "slick," "smart," or even "sneaky." The con artist is confident that he can talk himself out of trouble if he is caught by his friends or family in a ruse (or later, if he becomes a criminal con man, by his victims or the police). He takes more risks than the put-on or the together guy, but assumes a front that is designed to indicate his coolness about doing so.

Typically, the Actor engages in a great deal of concealing behavior—far more than those who represent the other styles. He tries—through deceit, joking, lying, teasing, tricking, and other similar ploys—to control interpersonal situations. As with Dave Cooper, he may be perceived by others as "crazy" or a "clown." His predominant behavior involves masking of some sort. Other styles may involve occasional masking; for the Actor it is a central and key strategy which overshadows all others. Furthermore, especially for the boy who adopts the Actor style, it may be exceedingly difficult for him to *un*mask—a problem that may lead to his being perceived as "cold."

Weber says that action is social insofar as "the subjective meaning attached to it by the acting individual (or individuals) . . . takes account of the behavior of others and is thereby oriented in its course."[2] For the Actor this taking account is paramount, in terms of shaping his own behavior not only in response to that of others, but also in order to elicit a particular response *to* him *by* others. More than for other styles, the Actor's behavior seems specifically geared to this process. For example, he is likely to pout to gain sympathy, clown to evoke laughter, tease to elicit anger—in a self-conscious and purposeful fashion. The Actor is particularly adept at predicting the probable reaction of other people to his behavior, and this in turn shapes how he presents himself to them.[3]

The Actor's orientation places him toward the dominant end of the power dimension. He attempts to move over others, to manipulate, to control, to govern them and/or their perceptions of him and his behavior, often through subtle and typically through verbal means. Because others often see that he is trying to dominate them, their trust of him may drop to a low level. By the same token, I suspect that the boy whose dominant style is Actor is probably suffering from a loss of ability to trust or be open toward others.

In terms of affiliation the Actor seems to distance himself from others—both as a motivation for his style and as the consequence of it. He is not clearly affectionate or warm, nor does he *appear* to want their love and warmth. On the other hand, he is not clearly antipathetic toward others, nor overtly hostile. Rather, his affiliational needs appear to be expressed in terms of wanting attention (symbolic, to be sure, of love) and recognition. He relates to others primarily on the level of reciprocal favors, a device that tends to degenerate into using the other person. He is not viewed as someone to whom others would turn in an emotional crisis or on matters of intimacy—partly because he is too often the joker and cannot be trusted to take matters seriously, partly because of the emotional distance he maintains.

Occasionally the Actor will play the fool, as the epitome of expressing oneself as who one is *not*.[4] The thrust behind his orientation is to hide himself from the view of others and/or to manipulate them. For the put-on, the salient motivation is to manipulate impressions and to distance himself from others; he is basically self-conscious, self-centered, insecure, confused in who he is or would like to be. For the con artist the style has progressed to an extreme of manipulation of impressions and behaviors. Through his maneuvering and deceit, the con artist necessarily distances himself from others (although they may not realize it). He is self-centered and much more hip, confident, and secure in his style than is the put-on. In both styles, however, the person is "on"—in a false, concealing, contrived, and cynical sense—a good deal of the time. Says a friend, who spent ten years in New York City pimping and conning as a way of life—and who now has gone straight—"I just got tired of using people all the time, and never really being close to anyone, not even my girl." These are the salient issues for Dave Cooper.

Self-Characterization. "Just act like you didn't know what you did . . ."

Thirteen years old at Time I, Dave Cooper's primary strategic style of put-on is centered on teasing, fooling around, playing jokes on others, trying to get them to do what he wants them to do by persuasion and other verbal means. It might appear that Dave shifts to secondary styles of "withdrawn kid" with his family and "tough guy" with friends to help him maintain the distance he prefers between himself and others. In fact, I believe they are part and parcel of his put-on style—he is simply giving each audience what he thinks they want and what he believes will provide the most gains for him.

Dave thinks he is small for his age (others agree). He is the third of four children from his mother's first marriage to Cappy Cooper (siblings are Jim, 17, Sharon, 16, and Link, 11). He has two stepbrothers, Teddy, 5, and Sam, 2, from his mother's second marriage to Leo Gage. He speaks of his big brother, Jim, with disdain—"he thinks he's hip because he can fight"—yet looks up to him. Jim, he says, "hangs around with these bad boys like I do, but I don't go around stealing cars and breaking in houses like he do." Jim wants to be "a gangster," Dave declares—after he learns arithmetic in school.

Sharon is "okay." She and Dave do not spend much time together. It is Link to whom Dave is closest in his family. Link, he says, is "playful . . . and he gets mad." Teddy is "playful," Sam "acts stupid when he's mad." Dave mentions three cousins who live downstairs from him, whom he describes as thieves and tattletails. One in particular, Lois, 9, "likes to tell on people. Like if I go out and steal some ties, she'll tell on me, but she'll regret it afterwards."

Here we find the first hint of the enormous amount of concealing, physically and psychologically, that Dave engages in.

When his parents find out (perhaps through Lois) that Dave has stolen something, they tell him to return it. What does he do with it in fact?

Keep it. If it's something I can use, like a radio or something, keep it. [How do you get away with that?] Go and hide it in the cellar . . . I used to hide things outside, I had a big hole about that big, I used to put wood on top, and I'd hide my things in there.

(Yet, his mother, father, and stepfather all tell the interviewers that Dave, to their knowledge, does not steal.)

In another major area, we have evidence again of Dave's deceptive behavior. He visits his natural father (Mr. Cooper), but manages to keep that bit of information from his mother: "That's where I get all my money from. If she knew, she'd kill me." He claims his father takes him down to Cape Cod and back in one day: "Takes the shortcut down so we can get there, go swimming, and come back—and she won't know nothing."

When asked what happens when he gets into serious trouble, Dave replies: "You don't tell. You don't tell nobody. If they find out, act like you didn't know what you did . . . then they don't blame it on you because you don't know what you did." As an example, he tells of being accused of breaking a window at four o'clock: "I said, 'you lie . . . I wasn't around there at four o'clock'— and I wasn't, I was around there a little after four, that's when I broke the window." And when he is faced with parent-peer conflict, he does what he or his peers want him to, but not around his parents. After he does something he knows is wrong, such as stealing or fighting, he goes to confession.

Dave relies heavily on verbal skills to cope with interpersonal encounters. His style ranges from yelling to persuading, from teasing to verbal torment of others. One male teacher for whom Dave has little respect is unable to motivate Dave to work. The teacher's frustration elicits only a derisive reaction from Dave:

He got me mad, and I threw a pencil on the floor. He started yelling, and I yelled back; and I called his mother a ——— or something . . . then he came out there with a paddle, and I thought he was going to hit me, but he hit himself instead . . . I was laughing, I was having a fit, and ever since then, he never touched me.

In this case, as in so many, Dave's first reaction to threat is to yell or talk his way through it. Although he does fight, it is not his most immediate or comfortable way of dealing with others. He says his reaction to a teacher who "doesn't like colored kids" is to tease him: "We tell him he should comb his hair, like we go in his drawer and find all these mouthwashes, and we say, Mr. L., isn't it time you used your mouthwash, and all that . . . and he get mad."

The teasing stretches across audiences, from inept teachers to girls, from his closest brother to his favorite uncle. One uncle, whom Dave "liked the best," had a place on Cape Cod. Dave recalls this scene, which began in his kind of fun, but ended with Dave feeling rejected:

We used to kill his chickens and he'd run and chase us; and when he caught us, we paid for it! But we killed all his best chickens one day . . . one of the prize chickens, too. . . . we were playing with stones, just pebbles, so we hit it, Jim threw it hard . . . my uncle blamed it on me . . . I told him Jim did it, but he didn't believe me. He liked Jimmy best, that's all.

At another well-liked Uncle's house, Dave has fun by teasing the cats. He throws them down the hill and rides the cows. He enjoys it so much there that when his mother comes to take him back to Boston, he hides: "I'm just not home."

Dave teases his brother Link about "anything that gives an argument—school, girls, everything." The encounter ends with Link getting a knife and Dave running. Later he gets back at Link when the latter least suspects retaliation—he pushes him out of the top bunk: "It's a pretty long drop, too!" At his girl's house, Dave teases her and her mother, "fooling around," until a fight breaks out among her siblings: "That's when I leave. It gets too dangerous then."

Dave and his friends, Aggie, Wade, Mouse, and Butch, all 13 years old, go "any place, just to do something bad." Their trouble at Time I consists of minor theft, petty pranks, and mischievous "boys will be boys" behavior. Dave drifts away from another group of boys led by 14-year-old Bones, who steal cars, rob houses, and break into stores. Says Dave, "I got tired of that gang . . . it isn't worth it."

He and his current peer group go to the local park and steal bikes; they ride them, only to return them the next day at the same spot. At parties Dave smokes and drinks (his parents don't know, he says). The fooling around includes putting firecrackers in cigarettes and chairs. As a joke, he and Aggie give a girl some sleeping pills in her drink. After half an hour she does not wake up. The boys leave her in a ditch where they know police patrols will find her. On the way home he and his friends might ring a fire alarm and run, break a window, or ring strangers' doorbells and run. Dave's pranks often have a sense of the bizarre about them, as in this passage in which he describes his winter rounds:

Running around, ringing doorbells, throwing rocks at cars; but during the winters I throw snowballs, so it wouldn't break a window, then I throw rocks. Once I killed a couple of birds, and then brought them home and put them on the doorstep . . . my mother walks out in the morning and gets scared.

Dave claims that all his friends have passing grades in school, and at Time I they have no intention of dropping out. Dave predicts that Aggie will do "all right" as an adult, but the others will be thieves and bums. Bones, if he is not a gangster, will be a judge or a lawyer (Dave's own aspiration): "Because if he be a judge, he like sending people up; if he's a lawyer he'll lose every case he gets, just for fun; make the person go to the electric chair or something. . . . he likes beating up people . . . put them in bad condition."

From Dave's self-characterizations, a secondary strategic style of Tough Guy seems most apparent. His parents almost totally ignore this side of Dave and emphasize, rather, his quietness. In his own interview Dave scarcely gives a hint of the withdrawing style, which seems so obvious to others. This may simply be a reflection of the extraordinarily tight concealing system he has set up to shield his troublemaking behavior from his parents. It also is an indication of the care he takes in giving each audience what it wants to see and hear. In any case, on the street Dave dabbles in fighting and tough behavior, though cautiously. He says he and his friends have fights with "just any old boy . . . if he comes by and give you the eye, just hit him, just like in school." In particular, they fight with white boys across the railroad tracks:

White Boy Territory, that's what we call it. . . . sometimes we have gang fights to win the tracks . . . if we lose we can't go over there, and if we win, we *can* go over there, but they can't come over here unless they got our permission. And we always have some kids lined up because they try to sneak up . . . sometimes you might get hit with a B-B gun, or a rock they're throwing . . . sometimes you go all the way around and take the gun, come back and shoot at them. That's if you make it back.

The fights begin, he says, when someone calls one of his group a name, and they defend it. If the white boys are bigger (and they usually are) Dave will pick up a rock to fight with. He claims they fight every day. The fighting has a quality of gaming, however, more than serious fighting. They refuse to fight downtown (too many police, "you might get caught") or go to South Boston ("Too many kids got beat up"). Nor do they fight with "blades" since an acquaintance was stabbed to death in a fight.

When two boys in his group have a disagreement, they fight; the loser is hit with a stick—"you don't hit the kid too bad, though, just give him a knock on the head." When he expresses interest in having a girl, his friends tell him to "go find one . . . and don't come back without one, or else they'll give you a punch." By and large, the group seems more to be involved with fooling around and teasing than seeking out trouble. Two more replies point to toughness on Dave's part. When asked how he would handle the worst troublemakers in the school, he says he would take them out in the hall and "beat them up a little . . . make him fight back." In another passage, regarding race, he says that a little boy who is called "nigger" would probably say, "who are you talking to . . . he probably go try and kick him in the mouth or think he's getting funny." (Even here, a verbal response is first.) As if symbolically mixing the put-on and the Tough Guy styles, he lists as his favorite television shows and comic books "The Little Rascals," "The Flintstones," "Spiderman," and "Superheroes."

In his discussion of girls, Dave seems to prefer those with a slick, clever style rather than the overly direct or aggressive ones:

I quit one last night . . . she likes to fight too much . . . [His new one is "nice."] Some girls, they rush it to you, other girls they won't. Like some girls ask you, and some girls won't. [He prefers the latter.]

His verbal skills in defining a situation to his liking show in this exchange with the interviewer about getting a girl to go to bed with him:

I. Well, getting back to these girls now, you said that you had played; but make it plainer, say I'm a dummy.

D. Well, in that case it's kind of hard because you're a dummy . . . and you're clean, you don't know nothing, it's going to be kind of hard to put it to you.

I. Well, you just tell me, and I'll do the best I can.

D. You ever get close to a girl? Did you ever kiss them? Did you ever be over to her house for a while? Say till about one o'clock . . . and you're getting nervous?

I. Um hum.

D. Did you ever get sleepy, all of a sudden you find her in the bed with you, then you get nervous again. Oh, all of a sudden you want her to get out, and all of a sudden she don't want to, and all of a sudden you say it's all right to stay? And all of a sudden her mother walks in, you know, with ideas in her head because you been doing a little, you know. And all of a sudden she kicks you out and don't want to see you for a while, and then you come back in another day or so, and she's all sober again.

He adds that it may take a while longer for the father to come around.

If someone were trying to brainwash Dave, he would fight hardest to keep his personality. He has difficulty defining what he means by that, but his "spy" responses give some clues. For example, toward his sister, the spy would have to act "nice and mean." He should "yell at her and scream at her" if she tries to make him do something; otherwise he may act nice toward her. He should obey his mother, most of the time—but if she asks him to go to a store, go to a different one, or refuse to go. Toward Link he should act "nice, kind, most of the time." He should pretend to be tired when there is work to be done, so others will end up doing it. With his friends the spy should act nice most of the time but "act mean" when he is mad: "Like when I want something, and I can't have it." In school he should "fool around with all of them." And at parties the spy should "play with all the girls, any kind of girl, just flirt with her," and ignore the mother's request that they leave. And finally, toward his mother:

Have to come in a little late, when she tells you to come in about nine o'clock, come in about 9:30; when she tell you to come in at 9:30, come in at 11 o'clock. That's how it goes. [What's that for?] Just to get her mad.

Dave feels he is best at fixing things and horseback riding, but would like to be stronger and better able to swim. He thinks his parents would want him to be smarter (he would like to change in that way). His brother and sister would want him to be "taller, be stronger, smarter, that's all." Bones would want Dave "to be like him"—"stealing, murder"—but Dave makes it clear that he would not like to be like Bones or others in that crowd: "He's bad, he's too bad." He says he would like to be "a good guy, go straight," like his stepfather. His first occupational choice is judge (a "straight" job), so that he could "give people fines, they can't give me one."

Dave is generally vague in this area, however, claiming that he does not know what his parents would like him to be, other than "good." His second job choice is engineer, like his stepfather, but his real wish is to be—like so many other Pathways focal boys—a millionaire. In a simplified version of the Protestant Ethic, he claims that to be rich he would have to be "working, saving, go to church." He adds that his mother teaches him this.

It is symbolic of Dave's strategic style that he holds a very negative attitude toward sharing money with friends or family. If he were to become a millionaire, the money would all be for himself. He refuses to snatch pocketbooks with his friends: "I always do that by myself, because they split, fifty-fifty." He insists that he does not plan to get married—"I don't want no kids come nag me for money"—and if he were to marry, it would be to a "working girl, she has to work for *me*, be a lawyer or judge or something." This response is also indicative of his propensity for using people—getting them, by hook or by crook, to do his work for him. As we shall see in characterizations of him by others, his relationship with friend Aggie includes this factor.

Just as Dave predicts that if Bones were to become a judge, he would put people in the electric chair or lose cases "just for fun," it appears that Dave revels in manipulating other people, sometimes causing them discomfort, "just for fun." This is at the heart of his put-on strategic style at Time I. While he may not see himself as taking his adolescent forms of sadism as far as he predicts Bones will in the future, the element of using others for his own gain or amusement is clear, as is his tendency to contrive, conceal, and misrepresent his true feelings or intentions toward others. How do others in his cluster perceive Dave?

Characterizations by Others. "You can tell when he lies."

The adult members of Dave's focal cluster do not see, or do not publicly acknowledge, his troublemaking style, but all of them recognize in one way or another his dominant strategic style of put-on. From their point of view, Dave's secondary style is that of "withdrawn kid." They see Dave variously as sensitive, moody, teasing, cold, hard to know, fresh, and not altogether honest.

Because he hides from his parents his pranks, vandalism, fighting, and so on, they see him as a "good" child who is "no trouble." He hides his emotions from them, or tries to, causing them to feel shut out and cut off from him to some extent. His attempt to conceal his feelings from them is not totally successful, but serves nonetheless to construct a wall between them. Mr. Cooper expresses this most articulately and consistently:

I really don't get next to him like I'd like to . . . he's quieter and he keeps a lot of things to himself; he won't even open up to me. I could never get next to him, even as a kid. I could never pinpoint why, but I treated them all the same, there was no favorites . . . I mean, he's friendly and everything, but you always feel a little shyness and a little pulling away . . . he's reserved, really reserved. When he seems unhappy I'll try to set him down and try to find out what's wrong with him, and this is when he goes into his little shell.

Although he feels Dave is "gentle" and "honest"—qualities which he hopes Dave will not lose—he also is pained by this distance which he does not feel with his other children.

He testifies also to Dave's lack of directness. The other children will ask him "right out" for money or a favor. Dave will engage in "small talk . . . he's just leading around to small talk until he finally gets enough courage to ask me whatever it is he wants to ask me . . . he's leery about asking." Mr. Cooper later admits that Dave often goes to his mother for money—"he'd get it from her a lot quicker than he'd get it from me, 'cause I might ask him what he needs it for." Perhaps this reaction on his father's part encourages Dave to work up to the request slowly; or perhaps his mother is more susceptible to Dave's conning than Mr. Cooper is.

Mr. Gage, Dave's stepfather, comments that Dave is a "moody little kid," very sensitive, and relatively quiet. Small things upset him. Often Mr. Gage feels that Dave is keeping something from him . . . "I never know what he's thinking." He mentions that Dave argues quite a bit, but stresses his touchiness. He recalls one incident in which Dave's father asks him why he was visiting him (no indication here of motivation), and Dave responds by being very hurt:

> Even with the reaction that I was told concerning his father . . . his real father . . . this had its effect on him. He didn't believe it for quite a while. He didn't feel free to talk to me about it (he doesn't have enough confidence in me yet) so I let it slide . . . his father said something about, "why are you coming over here?" and this really shook him up.

This passage raises serious questions about Dave's insistence that he has positive and frequent visits with his father. Since no one else mentions the incident described by Mr. Gage, it is impossible to discern whether he misunderstood a situation, or Dave is conning the interviewer about his relationship with his father—or conning himself. This will be discussed below, page 143.

Mr. Gage offers another example of Dave's sensitivity. One day Mr. Gage makes a general invitation to the children to take them to a ball game. Dave wonders if he is included. Mr. Gage admits that he did not specifically invite Dave, but Dave was the only child who questioned being included. He says that Dave "was a little bit moody, and he didn't say anything, but I noticed it." Later, at the game, Dave wanders off for such an extended period that Mr. Gage has to send Link to find him. Apparently Dave wanted this kind of attention, for he accused his stepfather of only being interested in the game.

Further evidence of this sensitivity is Dave's reaction when he is sick. His mother describes looking in on him: "He says, 'you haven't been over here to see how I'm doing' . . . you can see the tears in his eyes." When he is angry with his mother, she says, he tries to ignore and avoid her; when he is punished, he becomes quiet and withdrawn, as if in defeat.

Mrs. Gage also points to Dave's craving for attention, "from just anybody." He likes to be praised "a lot." Sometimes this irritates her: "I don't know whether I praise him enough or not . . . he'll have his room cleaned when I come home from work . . . and if I don't notice it, he sorta gets all pouty." She adds that Dave complains that when he leaves his room a mess, she bawls him out for it, but when he straightens it, she does not notice. She asserts that most of the time Dave will not tell her that he is unhappy about something. He walks around with a "very unpleasant look on his face" until someone asks him what is wrong: "He wants you to ask, you know; he doesn't want to come and tell you. You don't have to coax him very much to find out what it is [laughs]."

The teasing and "fooling around" Dave relishes in the streets takes a different form with his family. The sensitivity, the "fishing," the subtle cues he gives others to engage their attention—all are signs of a mild form of gaming. This is coupled with his competitiveness, mentioned by most cluster members. He likes to do well at school and sports in order to "show" the others that he is as good as they are. He does not like to be criticized or restricted, as Mrs. Gage relates: "I don't usually say very much to let Dave know that I don't like for him to do things; he would become very hurt and . . . you can see he's fighting his tears back . . . he won't let you see him cry, but you know he's crying in his room."

Dave's siblings view him very differently, accentuating the careful audience segregation he practices. Sharon contends, in the first words she utters about Dave in her interview, that "he's a pain, he thinks he's grown." She associates more with Jim, who is closer in age, likes baby Sam the best, and argues most with Dave: "He's 13 years old and he thinks he can boss me around now." When he disobeys or talks back, she "hits him over the head or something," and he goes to his room to cry. Sharon's description is the first inkling we have of Dave's propensity for dominating and using others. She claims that they get along all right as long as she is "buddy-buddy" with him—if he cannot be boss, neither may she, despite her advantage in years. She says his temper is quick, but he gets over it quickly (Mr. Gage also mentions that Dave can go "from happy to unhappy" and back in a few minutes), he is small for his age, and he does not get "into too much trouble."

Sharon describes Dave as helpful and responsible when he wants to be. "When he wants to act right he helps out. . . . he really does a good job." When she is home, however, he does nothing. He tries to worm out of regularly assigned tasks, such as dishwashing, by insisting it is not his night. During the course of the interview, Sharon's attitude mellows somewhat, and she speaks of helping Dave with a party and buying him a telescope that he sorely wants: "I told him I'd get him one, you know, by June."

Jim's feelings toward Dave are not similarly tempered. His tone is harsh and critical, disdainful . . . unforgiving, cold. He says Dave is a "little fresh," and has "a big mouth." He argues most with Dave: "I tell him to do something, and he'll say do it yourself, after I told him to do it. He'll get a little smart about it." He says that Dave "lies his head off" in order to get others on his side during an argument with Jim. More importantly, he will argue interminably with Jim, but never with his parents:

He makes me nervous . . . too much talk, you know, he starts talking, you know, saying things that get you mad; and then you tell him to cut it out, and you know, he keeps it up. You have to go bat his head most of the time.

Dave, then, fails to respond to the cues others send him, ignoring the integrity of their boundaries. Jim alludes to Dave's attempts to dominate others in describing how he reacts when Jim watches him:

Oh, he's a little nasty about it. You know, he thinks he's a little older than me, a little bigger than me, and *I'm* supposed to do what *he* says. I have to straighten him out but quick.

That the dominating is an attempt to gain status as well as power is suggested in this account:

His girlfriend was at the house, you know, he started bossing me around in front of her . . . I told him to take it easy because he started to get on my nerves. I grabbed him, I felt like punching him in the face a few times, then we started arguing, and I told him to go to bed [counter-humiliation] and that's what really got him upset. His girl was there.

In a complete disavowal of Dave's claims to expertise with girls, Jim talks of his younger brother as a "faggot" and "stupid"—"he had so many hundred and lost them all, just because he wouldn't kiss them or else do something else with them." Jim thinks Dave is "afraid." If he criticizes him about his approach to girls, Dave becomes angry: "He tell me he did this, and he did that; and yet I know as well as he do that he didn't do nothing." Jim feels that Dave is "scared" to fight, that he "opens his mouth too much," that he tries to be someone he is not. He was doing well in school, for example, until he started trying to "act like big brother."

What can he be depended on to do at home? "Nothing." What things can Jim count on Dave for? "Never have any. I think we can skip that one." What things does he like best about his brother? "Not too many, really, not too many except when he's away . . . that's the main thing." In general, he and Dave "just leave each other alone."

Setting aside for the moment the intense hostility Jim seems to feel toward Dave, we are faced again with the credibility issue. Is Dave conning the interviewer in recounting his "exploits," or is Jim distorting Dave's behavior? The former is possible. The interviewer feels that Dave was exaggerating his prowess with girls, for example—but no more so than most boys did. The latter is possible also. After all, it is Jim whom Dave idolizes and desires to emulate; perhaps Jim, at 17, is not ready to relinquish his position as roué; perhaps he gains status (in his own eyes at least) by tearing Dave's down.

This would be compatible with Jim's view of Dave's peer group. It is interesting to note that he thinks they, too, are trying to act big by smoking, drinking, and fooling around: "A lot of them try to get up there with the big kids, but they don't make it." Of Bones and his gang, he says they are "off-beat kids, as bad as everything, the devil himself." (Dave concurs.) He does not confide in any of them, including Dave, for want of trust.

Aggie, Dave's best friend "for now," loves fishing. He and Dave go to the city piers, all year round. Aggie relates with excitement their experience of fishing in the dead of winter, freezing, catching nothing, trying to warm their hands over a fire that keeps going out, and having "fun." His affection for Dave is clear, although necessarily truncated by his lack of certainty about Dave's loyalty. He senses that although he is the best friend today, tomorrow he may be excluded. Worse, he may be used:

Dave, he don't call for me that much. I'll have to call him. He'll say, do this favor for me, that's the only time he come. Do me a favor, go to the store. I don't want to go to no store . . . I ain't going to no store for him.

You know, he's getting like his brother Jim. . . . he's kind of crazy too; Jimmy orders everybody. You know he's getting like that, ordering people, so I don't go for that. Use me for a slave—using me!

Still, the basis for their relationship is mutual aid and cooperation. They help each other with chores before and after school. Aggie is at Dave's house by six o'clock in the morning to help him take out the garbage, do the dishes. He says he helps Dave more often than vice versa, but the distinction seems acceptable to him: "he'll help me with everything." They play ball, swim, fish, steal, fight, and crash parties together. Of all his friends, he trusts Dave the most.

At parties, Aggie reports, they "dance a lot, show everybody off," rap to the girls, go with them. When asked if they have sex with them, Aggie says yes and asks for a cigarette. They call girls on the telephone, anonymously, "just for fun." They get into movies by lying about their ages. They change bad report cards and sign their parents' names. "Dave, I help him all the time, and he helps me, we're just good friends . . . stay together, go everywhere together, just good buddies."

Aggie confirms Dave's rapid mood swings: "He'll turn from mad to happy." He says that Dave is quick to anger, especially when Aggie teases him: "He gets mad and turns red like a piece of orange . . . redder than that or an apple." And he is absent-minded; he will misplace something and become angry that he cannot find it. When they are downtown and run out of money, they snatch a purse or shoplift. Aggie makes it appear that Dave is the instigator on these occasions. He says Dave comments, when they run out of money, "let's make the best of it." Aggie claims that Dave has stolen money from his mother. He was caught once:

His mother asked him how much money did she give him to go to the show, and I said $3. But I didn't know he stole it. I wouldn't have told if I had known. They said, well where did you get the other dollar, and he said I got it out of my bank. She didn't believe him. So somebody knew that he stole it, cousin named Ricky saw him.

Mrs. Gage makes Dave do the dishes and yells at him for stealing from her. As Aggie says, "you can tell when he lies, the way he turns red or something . . . I can tell when he lies."

Testifying to his own similar put-on style, Aggie admits that he follows Dave around when he has a girl, teasing and joking, talking too much. Aggie adds, "You know, I always drop into other people's conversations, and he don't like that and his mother don't either." If Dave becomes angry enough about it, he "start tearing up people." He cannot harm Aggie, however, who claims Dave is "too small for his age." He says Dave's sisters call him "punk" and "midget," and try to make Dave angry. They succeed.

In addition to helping each other out, Dave and Aggie apparently thrive on teasing, cajoling, joking. If Aggie drops some money, Dave will "make believe he's going to keep it." When they go places together, they call each other names "for the fun of it." At school they walk down the corridors, fooling around until apprehended by a teacher. They like to watch teachers get "beat up" by the students, says Aggie. "We don't do it, we just like to watch." The only thing that could break up their friendship is if Dave goes too far in trying to push Aggie around, "like he think he's the boss or something." Apparently sensitive and competitive like Dave, he does not like Dave to "brag" about working at the local gas station: "I got mad about that and said after I get my job I'll prove that I'm the man." He wishes Dave would not get mad "so easy." What would Aggie's "perfect friend" be like? "Do everything I tell him to do, and I'll do everything he tells me to do." Aggie concludes that Dave, in spite of his faults, will be successful in life because "he has an easy job, he'll probably make out better in life, but he have to have a small wife."

Although Dave has not, at age 13, developed into a full-blown "con artist," the elements of deceit and manipulativeness are present in sufficient quantity to warrant our overlooking his apparent lack of skill in pulling the style off, and focusing instead on his motivation for wanting to do so. The models and supports that propel him toward the Actor style, in one form or another, are as strong as his inclination toward it, as we shall see in the next section.

Analysis of the Actor Style

In Dave Cooper we find a young boy whose intimate relationships with others seem to be distorted by his need to dominate them. As we have seen, Dave's way of coping with others is often tinged with sadism, a quality discovered also in his brother Jim. If we define Dave's gaming, teasing, joking, lying as expressions of his need to dominate and control others—to have power over them—we see only half of the picture. The other half is drawn in the delicate lines of sensitivity, vulnerability, hurt. There is some evidence, especially in the family, of an insufficiency of freely given love and affection. Combined with parental deceptions, as we shall see in the next section, this creates Dave's pattern of "fencing" for affirmation of his existence and his worth. It is a sport not without its dangers. As he cuts, so too others cut him in return. Dave's defenses against rejection seem weak; his ability to reach out in spontaneous, sincere gestures of affection seems crippled.

The crucial discrepancies among cluster member interviews center on Dave's relationship with his natural father. As mentioned earlier, Dave claims to have a good relationship with him and to see him monthly. Mrs. Gage says Dave does *not* go to see his father—he always comes up with some reason not to go. Mr. Gage speaks of Dave's father rejecting him. As we examine the family matrix, we find reasons why Mrs. Gage might deceive the interviewer about this relationship. The question remains open, then, as to who is distorting the truth. The pattern of deceit and concealment is clear in the entire family. That factor emerges as the most critical one in the generation of Dave's Actor style.

The Family Matrix. Other than comments about Dave, perhaps the most enlightening material to emerge from his Time I focal cluster interviews is that dealing with parental relationships.

Mrs. Gage describes her first marriage in terms of "constant bickering, and never knowing when Daddy's coming home, what the next meal is gonna be like." Apparently it was a crushingly negative experience for parents and children alike. Mrs. Gage says the children "love family outings" in her second marriage, and feels that this kind of unity was missing during the first marriage. Even after the divorce (when Dave was five), the tension between Dave's parents does not recede. They do not speak to each other, except in dire emergencies involving the children, and even then they are "at each other's throats," to use Mr. Cooper's words.

The Coopers were married at an early age; Mr. Cooper says his wife "wanted too much too fast—I couldn't keep up." He says she was constantly pressuring him to "keep up with the Joneses"—his salary as a blue collar worker could not meet her expectations. He accepts most of the blame for their failure, although his bitterness is transparent: "things that you get hurt by you remember, things that you don't get hurt by you forget." He buckled under the pressure, stopped paying heat and rent bills, and eventually left:

Well, the reaction on the children's part, I thought they would resent me for leaving, but it didn't work out that way 'cause I used to come by and take them out and I used to take them anyplace I went . . . and then it got to the point we used to argue for a while, because I got up tight there for a while and I couldn't find a job, so I couldn't keep up the payment, so there were controversies and heartaches, and so it was affecting the children so I stopped coming by for a while.

The heartaches are spelled out in this story told by Mr. Cooper to explain how he came to be prosecuted for nonsupport and assault:

I had a truck, and I had to pay her $40 a week, which wasn't bad. My truck broke down and I had no job, and I tried to explain this to the court, but they didn't want to hear it, so they gave me ten days to get it up.

He borrows the money to pay most of it; then Link, who is staying with his father for the weekend, becomes ill with bronchitis. Mr. Cooper takes him to his mother to ask her to accompany them to the hospital. "She was having a party so she couldn't be bothered, so I was peeved . . . her party was more important." In anger, he strikes her, and receives nine months in prison. He says he "hated her for years" after this incident, but time has taken the edge off his feelings. Still, he crosses the street in order to avoid speaking to her.

Mr. Cooper feels that his wife's second husband is a "good fellow—him and I get along fine." He remarks that Mr. Gage "thinks the world of the kids and the kids think the world of him." His own second marriage has fared less well: He divorced his second wife the day after she failed to welcome his children into their home. He has married a third time and claims that "everybody gets along—she likes the kids, the kids like her." As the best event in his life, he lists the days his children were born. His dedication to his children appears to be strong.

Critical Messages from Others. This scenario of marriage, divorce, remarriage, divorce (by Time II Dave's mother has divorced Mr. Gage as well), provides the backdrop for a power struggle between Mr. Cooper and his wife—over their children. Mr. Cooper's strategy has been to engage in end runs around his wife's insistence that he not see their children. Although done out of love for his children, it has also served as an indelibly written message to Dave: if you want something others would deny you, trick them, fool them, lie to them.

After the time in prison, Mr. Cooper sought peace and work in Ohio and California. When he returned, his wife forbade him to see the children. His solution was to see them on the sly at their schools. She told the children she did not want them to see their father, so the deception of their visits was clear to Dave. Says Mr. Cooper, "many times they would want to come with me, she would perform all day and tell them that they can't; so when you deprive somebody of something that they want, it's gonna stick in the brain." He has been seeing his children since.

Mr. Cooper feels that he is vindicated through this battle because his children *want* to see him: "I got Jim and Sharon, and I'm pretty sure I'll get Dave and I'll get Link." He says he treats the children with respect and dignity, whereas his wife still tries to boss them around. The primary example of this is Sharon's preferring to live with her father when she becomes pregnant (age 16); her mother wants her to give the baby up and refuses to help her—her father counsels her to examine her feelings and to come to her own decision (she keeps it), and he will support her to the best of his ability. When asked what his attitude is now toward his first wife, Mr. Cooper replies: "I don't have any attitude towards her, I mean . . . now, it's the children that have the attitude towards her." By this he is implying that the children share some of the negative feelings he has harbored over the years.

Beyond the question of who has the most legitimate position in this tug-of-war is the more serious message that relationships consist of power struggles in which one either wins or loses. The children are the spoils which one parent or the other strives to win. The contrast between this pattern and the more positive and cooperative pattern established by Hank's mother, father, and stepfather is striking (see Chapter 6).

The divorce has also complicated messages to Dave about discipline. Mr. Cooper and Mr. Gage both leave punishment up to Dave's mother. She wavers and is easily conned, often in an effort to be fair. If the men punish Dave, it is considered tantamount to interference by his mother, thus diminishing its effect. The controls and limits on his behavior which Dave seems to need are absent or only inconsistently applied. Dave says that if his mother finds stolen goods in his pockets, he claims someone else must have put them there. She half believes the story but tells him he is to stay in the house after school for the next two weeks. But "the next day I'm outside playing." The message here is twofold: stealing is permissible, and mother's word is unreliable. Dave is also rewarded for telling a passable "story."

That Dave *needs* more limits is reflected by the fact that he often goes to confession after a misdeed. He respects the vice-principal at the DuBois because if he does something wrong, it is clearly unacceptable: "If he hits you, the swing is hard" and sure. As though he would like some assistance in controlling himself, he says his best teacher is good because "she make me sit down and do my work; all the other teachers, they let me fool around." At Time I Dave says his mother is the person he loves most. One way she shows her love is by protecting him from himself: "When I get hurt or something, she'll make me stay in the house; or if you come in the house to get a knife or something to go out and fight, she makes you stay in the house."

Because Dave is untrustworthy often enough, he finds that people don't always trust him. The message that he is not to be trusted feeds into his style, of course, and his own tendency not to trust others. He speaks of a school administrator who lurks outside Dave's classroom—"he don't trust us . . . we got a bad reputation"—because he and his classmates are always "clowning around" and giving the teacher "a lot of lip."

These are the critical messages in the formation of Dave's Actor style. He is growing up in a climate where emotional distance, people using other people for their own ends, and mutual lack of trust and respect are at the core of interpersonal relationships. He has several examples to follow.

The Impact of Role Models.   Dave's cluster is full of people who are struggling, as he is, with issues of affiliation and overdominance. Lying and distorting are familiar ploys for all cluster members. Dave describes himself as being like his mother and his natural father:

I like to bake and cook like she does, and I'm thin like my father used to be . . . I like to fight like my father . . . I like to drive, but not stolen cars. I like to watch TV, I like to play cards. I like fixing things like my second father, and I like to swim, and they don't.

Yet it is his older brother, Jim, whom he suspects he is most like. They share a love of partying and fooling with the girls. And he would most want to be like Jim, taking him as his most ideal male model (although he says he feels closest to his Uncle on the Cape). He feels his mother loved him most when he was younger, and loves him most now. Let us take a closer look at each of these people with whom Dave shares such a significant part of his life.

Dave's natural father, Mr. Cooper, seems to have well-developed affectional bonds with others; yet he has had to fight his own tendency to be a dominating person. Much of his interview is spent telling about his excruciating efforts to learn not to *tell* his children what to do, but to discuss things with them. Showing developing empathy, he says he was in trouble as a young man, a circumstance which now in midlife helps him to understand the difficulties his children get into: "I try to put myself in their position when I was their age, and what did I do—and I didn't think different; I stayed in trouble myself." Hinting at his wife's dominating tendencies, he says the one thing that will make Dave leave home is his "mother dominating, trying to tell him what isn't, instead of telling the truth." (It is fascinating that domination and lying are associated clearly in this statement.)

Mr. Cooper's example, although perhaps improving with the years, was not always admirable. As he admits, "Jim was starting to take after me until finally he's setting his own pattern—I'm glad 'cause I was no angel, and I was no pattern to follow." (He tells his children to be their own models.) His dream was to be a merchant marine, but he could not take the risk of being away from his family so often. As second choice, he tried to get into factory work by lying that he had experience—"I'd lie like hell to get in there, but I'm gonna get in." In this way, he learned a dozen trades from making foundations to roofing, and now works as a union carpenter. His skill in conning his way into jobs and acting competent until he actually was provides an intriguing model for Dave. He is secure now, financially and occupationally, owns his own home, and seems to have changed a great deal.

Mr. Cooper's years were marked by anger and aggressive acting out. (He almost stabbed a man to death at age 10; he says that when his wife locked him up for nonsupport, he wanted "to get inside her head and kill her.") Even at Time I, Mr. Cooper has difficulty controlling his temper. He slaps Jim's girl friend—"she was telling *me* what to do"—and is taken to court by the girl's mother. He says his relationship with Sharon is excellent, but Jim states that his father in fact has disowned her for supporting his girl friend in the conflict.

Although Mr. Cooper mentions being in prison for what he views as a "trumped-up" charge of nonsupport and assault against his wife, he never refers to other sentences. Dave claims he served time for breaking and entering and speaks of his "boys" at the city jail who served with him. Again, it is difficult to know which one is telling the truth, but it is possible that Mr. Cooper serves as a role model for Dave in stealing as well as lying.

Mrs. Gage speaks of herself as her children's "worst enemy." When it comes to helping them learn to read, for example, she admits that she "made a nervous wreck" of Dave and seemed not to be able to give him the "self-assurance" that he and her other children need in order to do well. She feels there is nothing that she can do better than the average person her age. Yet her transcript is full of colorful imagery and folk lore, as well as insight into herself and her children. She apparently is well read—and like so many of the Pathways parents is frustrated that she was not able to pursue her education and a career. Although others refer to her dominating tendencies, she presents herself as an even-tempered, calm egalitarian. Her real self and ideal self seem miles apart, a problem for her and her family. Her overdominance seems to stand in the way of forming close and stable bonds with anyone.

Mr. Gage is positive in his attitude toward the children. He says he plays with the children in the neighborhood, and is slow to react in terms of temper. His transcript is full of refusals to make judgments about other people or situations. He tries to weigh each issue carefully—so much so, one feels, that he avoids them altogether. As a young boy, he says he "was the biggest devil in the family, and everybody was happy when I was around because I amused them all." He grew up in the South, went to two years of college, and migrated North to find work. His occupational situation is stable and secure. He describes himself as "a practical joker . . . a lot of times something was sad, I'd try to find the bright side of it, and bring this out, and have people smiling." He appears to accept his wife's domination with a sense of humor: "Well, I'm married. And she's trying to change me, as she says . . . and, you know, it's the battle of the sexes that goes on, it keeps your life interesting . . . you have to expect it, you see." (They are divorced by Time III.) He adds that his wife tries to make him think he is making all the decisions: "She's already made this decision for you, but she's got to make you *think* that you made it, you know."

As a model of behavior and companion in the streets, Aggie is as complex as any of Dave's parents. He would not like to be Bones ("he is *very* bad"), nor would he use marijuana ("I don't want to get messed up"). Showing the same caution about getting into serious trouble like his friend Dave, Aggie says: "I gotta good record. I didn't never do nothing bad that the police ever found out." He also angers quickly, wants an easy millionaire's existence (something for nothing), and cons and teases his family. If his "spy" is caught in a misdeed, Aggie says he should "just look innocent, that's what I do." In general, he should "be respectful, have respect for others . . . don't go around acting like a punk. Be nice." This is, of course, in glaring contrast to the bulk of his actual activities with Dave.

Jim, whom Dave takes as his primary model, is described by everyone as "crazy," hard to get along with, "a big show-off," and "afraid of nobody." He wants to be a carpenter . . . like his father, and gets a job at 16 by lying about his age . . . like his father. He says he and his mother are "always arguing." She is afraid his behavior will land him in jail, and it does. His convictions include time for assault and battery and stealing cars. His school years are liberally sprinkled with assaults on teachers and principals alike. His toughness is accompanied by verbal lashings to "set things straight":

This teacher, he called me "yellow boy," and that's when I came back . . . and I laid him out right there on the floor . . . and later he came to, I said, you know my name, don't you, and he said no. I said you don't call me hey boy or hey you; everybody in the school knows me. If you want me, just ask somebody my name. And if you don't know, just shut up. . . . the principal said to my mother that I was a juvenile delinquent and this and that . . . I don't have no kind of control of myself.

As for affiliation, Jim is close to his father, but despises the rest of his family. He does not wish to see them when he is older: "I was thinking of leaving them all; that's the main idea, to get away."

Significantly, Jim is the one with whom Dave identifies most heavily. Jim's cold, hard, verbal exterior is expressed in brutal action as well. Within months of the first round of interviews, he is sent to prison for a murder which appears to have been committed in cold blood. Cluster members worry at Time I that Dave appears to be heading in Jim's direction. They are pleased that he seems to have changed course slightly, especially in terms of wanting to finish high school. At the same time, they admit their displeasure with Jim's behavior. Aggie describes Jim as "crazy—he'd do anything." It is likely that some of the sadistic edge to Dave's "fun" stems from Jim's example.

Two issues arise from this examination of Dave's available role models. First, it appears that the overwhelming thrust of their interpersonal relationships leans toward controlling, dominating, using, lying, teasing, joking, conning—the very scaffolding from which Dave has built his put-on style.

The second issue, equally important, is that of Dave's clear-cut identification with Jim. What twisted and perverse effect does it have on a young boy to wish to be like someone who despises him so? Dave adores Jim. Jim has no use for Dave and can hardly wait for the moment when he can escape the family—including Dave. One consequence of Jim's brutal coldness may be Dave's persistence in trying to "act big," something which many cluster members dislike in Dave. From Dave's point of view, however, acting big and engaging in cruel, manipulative behavior may seem like the surest way to worm his way into his big brother's heart—to be loved. Unfortunately for Dave, Jim seems more repelled and irritated by this behavior than impressed. Ironically, the fact that others worry over Dave following in Jim's footsteps may be rewarding to Dave, since that is exactly what he says he would like to do. And although at Time I Dave has not emulated Jim's fighting, the coldness is already his.

Other Issues.   The question of Dave's small stature must be considered. His father is short also, and refers to his size in negative terms. Dynamically speaking, it is possible that Dave's attempts to control and dominate others are a desperate attempt to guarantee that they do not do the same to him (cf. Jung's "inferiority complex"). He invests a great deal of emotional energy into proving himself, showing others that he is strong, competent, and "big." He appears to take the name-calling by his siblings ("punk," etc.) seriously enough to wish to prove them wrong. In addition, his size may be another impelling reason for his choosing verbal rather than physical means to dominate others.

Another issue is Dave's racial identity and pride. Aside from his prowess with girls, this seems to be the most salient area for him at Time I. His natural father's mother was Portuguese (white, rather than Cape Verdean). Dave is very light in color and calls himself a "mongrel." He recalls that when his mother and brother first called him this, he looked it up in a book and found that it means "a mixture of Negro and white." He also refers to himself as colored, and argues with Aggie (who refers to himself as black) that the latter is not black at all no matter how dark he is.

Dave's grandmother told him at age three he was "colored": "I walked out and I said I was colored, and a white boy came, and he beat me up, and ever since then I didn't tell it, that's all." While he may not announce it gratuitously, he apparently has been willing to fight verbally and physically to defend his being "colored": "We had three white kids in our class, and they said there were four. They said I was white, and I said if I beat you, I'm not white, and if you beat me, I'm white. They said okay, but they didn't win." Another time a substitute teacher asked how many white children were in the class; someone said none. One boy called out, "No sir, Dave . . . and I got up and threw a book at him." He says that when some white boys called him "nigger," he defended himself: "All of a sudden I turned around and said if you don't know our name, don't call us; and all of a sudden they started chasing us, so we ran . . . you can't beat 'em all the time." His parents have told him of incidents of racial discrimination in the South; he realizes that this might make black children wonder if they are as good as whites. On occasion, he has wondered.

Being neither black nor white is not simple for Dave. As with any marginal person, he has developed both anxieties and defenses to deal with his position. As if reflecting his own dilemma, he does not approve of interracial dating: "If they have a kid, what color is it going to be?" He says he is the same color as the other members of his family and is not treated differently from the others. In fact he is lighter.

How does Dave handle his marginal position? First of all, in response to several questions, he comes down squarely on the side of being black. He would not take a pill to make him white. He would throw it away: "What would you want to be white for; I want to be colored." Conversely, he would turn everyone in America black, "so then they couldn't be fighting each other." As if mapping out his own racial identity, he says he would live in an all-white neighborhood only if an all-black neighborhood were adjacent: "I'd live on the end of the street, near the end of the colored." Because he identifies himself as "colored" in so many ways, he was included as a Pathways subject despite his actual skin color and the attempts by certain others to define him as white.

Dave mentions twice that his parents and uncles yell at him in Portuguese when he does something wrong. Yet another verbal weapon is devised for wielding power over Dave. True to form, he responds by developing a little fluency in Portuguese by taking lessons from a boy in school, so that at least he might understand what they are yelling at him.

Stonequist's classic definition of marginality is instructive in Dave's case. He speaks of the "marginal man" as a person who is

poised in psychological uncertainty between two (or more) social worlds; reflecting in his soul the discords and harmonies, repulsions and attractions of these worlds, one of which is often "dominant" over the other; within which membership is implicitly if not explicitly based upon birth or ancestry (race or nationality); and where exclusion removes the individual from a system of group relations.[5]

Later work expanded the concept to include any situation in which a person identifies at least partially with two status or reference groups (such as child, adult), but is not accepted by either. The uncertainty of social belonging that ensues is linked with identity confusion, insecurity, anxiety, lack of inner harmony, even self-hatred or severe mental disorder.

In analyzing the genesis of Dave's strategic style, then, it is essential that we specify the ways in which he is a marginal person. By Stonequist's definition, he is clearly marginal by virtue of his racial background. In a school where only a handful out of almost 700 of his classmates are officially designated as "white," it is painful for Dave to be defined as "white," even in jest. Yet it is just as enigmatic for Dave to identify fully as a black person. He lacks clear-cut black role models in his family, and his skin color betrays him. His racial awareness is low, as he painfully tries to dredge names of black figures out of his memory. He comes up with a handful but begs off the questions with "that's all before I think my brains to death." He is, then, "colored." His favorite actor is Sidney Poitier.

The second level of marginality comes in Dave's tenuous connection with being Portuguese. Because of the language barrier, and because to identify with this part of his heritage is also to identify with being white, Dave finds himself on the fringes again. And finally, as with all the Pathways focal children, Dave experiences the classical marginality associated with being an adolescent, caught between two identity-providing groups—children and adults—and not feeling totally accepted by or comfortable with either. Perhaps this is reflected in Dave's attempts to act big and to prove to others that he is a young man rather than an old child.

One other factor must be included. When Dave was around ten years old, he contracted tuberculosis. The illness left him weak and sickly for a time, and accustomed him to sympathy and extra attention. As Bowlby notes:

persistent and apparently stable patterns of interaction between mother and child can be materially changed by events occurring in subsequent years. An accident or a chronic illness may make a child more demanding and/or his mother more protective.[7]

Unfortunately, not much was mentioned in any of the interviews about this incident. Since Dave mentions his mother's protectiveness as one of the things he likes about her, and since he spends so much time trying to command everyone's attention, we might surmise that the tuberculosis has been a contributing factor. As he enters adolescence, the put-on style may earn the attention for him that being sick did earlier on.

Dave's Alternatives.   The best clue we have to the likelihood of Dave's shifting away from his style is the pattern exhibited by his father. As Mr. Cooper passes into his forties, he seems to have settled into a stable work and family life. More importantly, he has worked steadily against his need to dominate others, which in turn has allowed him to get closer to his children and to a new wife. Compared to the manipulativeness and coldness enveloping Dave's everyday existence, however, Mr. Cooper's example seems puny. Although his father and stepfather provide some impetus toward autonomy, cooperativeness, and being a good person, Dave seems much too insecure to be able to risk charting a course that does not involve manipulation as its beacon. As with Ernie and Leroy, the paucity of significant others who provide modeling for alternative strategic styles is crucial to the early crystallization of a given style.

Analytical Dimensions.   At the heart of the put-on style is masking behavior that serves both to control and to distance others in Dave's life. He ranks high on the power dimension, seeking dominance in most of his relationships. His basic orientation toward others is to control them and/or to use them. He wants them to do his work for him; if he does theirs, it is only as a reciprocal event, not as a gift. When he cannot wield power over others, especially siblings and friends, he is upset and angry, frustrated, defeated. He uses his emotions to control others—the tears, the pouting, the sulking—and accepts equality only as a poor second to his dominating the other.

Yet, if we analyze his style in terms of the affiliation dimension, we find that he wishes to place himself not only over people but away from them as well. The obvious question, then, becomes whether his dominance and manipulativeness are more methods of distancing himself emotionally from others than pure power plays. He is neutral, cold, remote in his relationships with others, even his family. They sense this and are distressed by it; he seems to accept it as natural. He finds it difficult to commit himself to one person in an affectionate way. He leads Aggie to feel that he is Dave's friend only "for now." He goes with one girl and drops her because she teases him too much (competes with him in the power dimension) or, as Sharon relates, because she calls on him too much (presses him in the affiliation dimension). He is not particularly close to his father or his stepfather. They "get along." It is his mother and uncle to whom he is most closely attached, but even with them, teasing and stealing seem to violate the norms of love and trust.

One is forced to wonder if this pattern stems from his never feeling loved enough in the early years of his young life, or even during early adolescence. His mother offers her own explanation to the interviewer, hypothesizing that the children from her first marriage (Jim, Sharon, Dave, and Link) are less secure and even less intelligent because of the intensity of conflict between her first husband and herself. She feels she has had more time to give love and attention to her two boys by Mr. Gage, and describes in detail the differences between the two sets of children, all positively weighted toward the younger ones. Whatever the reason, Dave seems impoverished in the affiliation dimension at age 13; his prospects for growth in this area will be hampered to the extent that he remains high in manipulativeness—using others.

Dave is also high in concealing behavior—that he is often unsuccessful is immaterial. His intention is to outwit, trick, fool, hide, distort, cover. When Dave reveals his true feelings, it is usually in a way that is designed to extort a particular response from others. He lies when it is to his advantage, and seems to feel little guilt about doing so. On the other hand, Dave cannot keep a secret; in his hands someone else's concealment becomes a weapon of revelation to be aimed and fired.

Simmel says that human relationships are distinguished by the degree of mutual knowledge: "what is not concealed may be known"—"what is not revealed must not be known."[8] It is as though Dave were living his life according to these two principles. He allows others to know only what he wishes them to know, and much of that is false; he is angered and embarrassed when something he has tried not to reveal slips into others' awareness (as when he blushes upon lying). His self-protective lying and emotional coldness create barriers to others knowing him intimately.

Simmel theorizes also that confidence in another person comes somewhere between total knowledge of him and total ignorance.[9] In the first case, one does not need to speak of trust; in the second, one would be a fool to. In Dave's case, it appears that he tries to keep people closer toward total ignorance of him than total knowledge. Consequently, it is difficult for them to trust him—how little they know him!—just as it is difficult for him to trust them: he presumes they have the same motivational orientation in social relationships as he does.[10]

When it comes to the questions of sincere vs. cynical and contrived vs. spontaneous, it is clear that Dave's style is more cynical than not, and more contrived. He is relatively contrived in the area of clowning and joking. He anticipates the reactions he elicits in others; he appears purposely to set out to tease, annoy, pester them. Yet his need for attention, and the gaming he uses to get it, seem not entirely contrived; they are perhaps spontaneous in the sense that they are beyond his ability to control. His manipulativeness, by and large, seems to lead to conflicts with others in a battle of wills he is loath to lose. He refuses to be used, but consciously and knowingly sets out to get away with what he can interpersonally. In the sense that he believes that he is good at rapping, is slick and tough, and so forth, we could say his presentation of self is a sincere one. From Dave's words it is hard to know whether he is sincere or not. His distancing makes it impossible to see underneath his slippery exterior. My suspicion is that at age 13 he is at least in part sincere; as he grows older, he will probably become more cynical.

In discussing the "clown role," Pearson remarks that it allows a person to create an equilibrium between a negative self-image (size, parental rejection) and expected reactions from others: "He may attempt to make the best of a bad job by accepting the fact that he is clumsy and awkward and parading it in accentuating fashion before others in order to obtain the pleasure of their laughter." When laughter is not forthcoming, at least the satisfaction of their irritation is. Bales has carefully documented the tension-reducing and morale-lifting function of the clown or joker role in small groups.[12] There is some reward in any small group, of which the family is certainly an example, for this type of behavior—even if the reward is angry attention rather than approval.

Dave's style is comparatively rigid. When he is caught in a lie or reprimanded for teasing, his alternative response is to retreat into a sullen mood. He leaves the game, so to speak, at best attempting to continue to influence the situation through his antics, or, at worst, withdrawing from the scene altogether.

His style is defensive/protective, stemming from a basically insecure position spawned, I suspect, by a combination of anxiety-provoking early years, sickness, and unusually short stature during adolescence.

Conclusion

In discussing manipulativeness, Bursten says that "certain people use this exploitative relationship as a characteristic way of dealing with others."[13] Even at age 13, this seems to apply to Dave Cooper. In contrast to classical thinking about manipulativeness, Bursten feels it is not always pathological: "It is not a diagnostic syndrome; it is a way of thinking and acting which, like dramatization, may contribute to a variety of clinical pictures."[14] Dave seems high on both dramatization *and* manipulativeness, but not to the extent that this view of manipulators might suggest:

It has often been said that this group makes others suffer while they themselves, in contrast to neurotics, do not suffer. The confidence man, and indeed many charming scoundrels with an ability to overlook inhibitions and normal reticences, and an inability to feel real bonds, irresponsibly stirring the passions and bypassing the inhibitions of others, *leave havoc in their wake.*[15]

The con artist par excellence might fill this very demanding bill. But Dave is an amateur as yet, skillful in the management of others, often for the purpose of elevating himself and, as Webster's defines it, "able to control or play upon by artful, unfair, or insidious means, especially to one's advantage." The charm and ease are not yet his; the coldness is.

Bursten's definition is more stringent. In order to manipulate, four conditions must be present:

   a. initial conflict of goals;
   b. intention to influence the other . . . consciously;
   c. deception and insincerity (the element of fraud);
   d. feeling of "having put something over on the other."[16]

Several situations described by Dave and his significant others fit this definition. For example, in lying that he has washed the dishes the night before, Dave is consciously intending to influence his mother through deception; the conflict of goals is her demand that he wash dishes and his desire not to; the pleasure he takes in getting away with things (he brags about not getting caught) fulfills the last condition.

It is enormously difficult to make practical suggestions to parents and professionals regarding the Actor style, simply because so often one is not aware of being deceived. For a young adolescent with Dave's bent, it is essential that adults adhere scrupulously to standards of honesty and respect for others. If a child witnesses parents lying behind each other's backs, or a teacher using a child to meet his or her needs, the stage is set for emulation, internalization of dishonesty, and a utilitarian approach to social interaction. Dave respects the administrator who is brutally honest with him. He wants his parents to help him set limits; he feels unloved, rejected, hurt when they allow him to wheedle his way around them.

The Actor also needs very clear messages from others regarding their dismay when he teases, plays practical jokes on them, and so forth. Since he does these things for fun, those who laugh merely reward his behavior. Because the Actor is low on trusting others (and vice versa), it is important for adults to give him opportunities in which he can take responsibility or leadership. By showing trust in him, the adult has a chance to alter the negative, insecure sense of self that feeds the Actor's style.

People have been known to simulate quite successfully a variety of roles, even to the point of having others believe they are terminally ill or millionaires. The standard procedure in the event that a social worker or teacher suspects that he or she is being misled is to check out the facts. If the client/student is reluctant to reveal information that could be verified, this might suggest the presence of deception or conning. Perhaps the strongest medicine for the Actor is to be confronted with reality by those who are able to see through his gaming. Those who go along with it merely provide the applause the Actor is seeking.

Finally, since the Actor is usually as low in affiliation and intimacy as he is high in the tendency to dominate or control, it is incumbent upon adults to express affection openly—if genuinely felt—in as many situations as possible. In the classroom a teacher who notices a child's tendency to push others around and to dominate them might suspect that the child is being bossed around at home. Consequently, it would provide a constructive alternative for the child's repertoire if the teacher were to refrain from wielding his or her authority with a heavy hand. Requests instead of than "do it because I say to" are preferable ways of interacting with any child, but especially the Actor.[17] Otherwise, the teacher (or other adult in a position of power and authority) simply feeds into the Actor's need to engage others in a struggle over power, attention, and control.

Dave is starting out with a father who "lies like hell" to get what he wants, and a mother who admits she is his "worst enemy." At 13 the world for Dave is truly a stage—an arena in which the put-on style allows him to manipulate others to gain what he wants from them. He is the leading actor, of course, but it is significant that he relies on others to relate to him with their "fronts" as well.

With the addition of experience and finesse, Dave may move out of the put-on into the con artist style as he approaches manhood. I suspect the stakes will be higher but the pattern will be the same.

Because the Actor manipulates the environment from a defensive stance, his style is vulnerable. The Cool Guy, on the other hand, is theoretically the most solid strategic style. While the Actor creates a world with lies, deception, distortion, and applied fantasy, the Cool Guy shapes his life with action, sensitivity, directness, and a commitment to assertive openness. He is much more in touch with reality and with himself than is the Actor. Hank Nelson's life is not without its problems, but as we shall see in his portrait, his approach to coping with interpersonal relationships is unique in its delicate balancing between internal and external pressures.

Well, there's nobody I'd like to be
but myself, I guess.

—HANK

6. The Cool Guy *Hank Nelson*

Moving Toward. The Together Guy and the Super-Cool Cat

It seems crucial to include a portrait of a "together guy" in this book. Too many works on inner-city youth, especially black and poor youth, have emphasized the deviant, the defeated, the perverse, and the alienated. The case of Hank does more than remind us that black youth share at least the same range of styles as white youth (although perhaps not distributed in the same proportions); it also points up the incredible strength of the "together" style, arising in the present case out of unlikely origins: a family atmosphere permeated by apathy, punctuated by violence, and torn by an unrelenting rivalry and favoritism which renders Hank's position in the family tenuous and insecure. Yet the Cool Guy can be described primarily in terms of positive relations and attitudes toward others on the affiliation dimension, and autonomy on the power dimension.

The Cool Guy typically projects his personality into the definition of social situations. His motivational impetus in interpersonal relationships is the preservation of autonomy and the need for self-expression, which generally take precedence over needs for acceptance or status. "Cool" is used here to mean something beyond mere keeping one's "cool" in a "tight" situation. It indicates knowing what is happening, and knowing what one wants out of life and out of everyday social interactions. It implies self-respect, self-knowledge, and self-determination.

Within this style are two types, the "together guy" and the "super-cool" cat. Both partake of the expressive style which Rainwater defines as "an effort to make yourself interesting and attractive to others so that you are better able to manipulate their behavior along lines that will provide some immediate gratification."[1] There is no obvious place for the Cool Guy in Merton's terminology (it would fall somewhere between conformity and innovation). Rainwater's expressive style seems to compensate for this gap, however, in that it is a step beyond passive conformity but still focuses on legitimate means—and therefore is not innovation.

For participants in the Pathways study, "together" is perhaps the most positive and complimentary term they could use to describe another person. Although its exact meaning is best left to street definitions or intuitive grasp of qualities viewed positively and having to do with earned respect, I will attempt to connect the term broadly with standard definitions of mental health and well-being. (This raises another problem, since the question of *who* is mentally healthy and interpersonally adjusted is also difficult and even more so in an era when previously deviant behaviors—homosexuality and marijuana use, to cite only two—are being redefined by social movements and professionals as "variations.")

In terms of defining mental health, it seems inappropriate to apply Freud's conditions of being able to love and to work well to a youth in his early teens. Fromm's view of mental health as characterized by "the ability to love and to create" and by the "emergence from the incestuous ties to family and nature"[2] also seems stringent for a youth in the early stages of adolescence. Fromm's definition includes, however, "a sense of identity based on one's experience of self as the subject of one's powers, by the grasp of reality inside and outside of ourselves, that is, by the development of objectivity and reason."[3] These qualities seem more appropriate; yet they do not imply, as Fromm so wisely points out, *freedom* from insecurity or uncertainty—only the capacity to approach others from an initial position of insight, integrity, and self-determination.

Erikson's stages of the life cycle afford another way to view mental health. We could say that the "together guy" represents a psychologically and interpersonally healthy style because each crisis prior to adolescence (trust vs. mistrust, autonomy vs. shame/doubt, initiative vs. guilt, and industry vs. inferiority) has been met and resolved in a positive way—thus enabling the child to meet similarly the adolescent crisis of identity vs. identity confusion.[4]

Thus being "together" at age 13 is not quite the same as being together at age 23 or 53. Simmel's opinion that "one becomes an individual when one functions as an autonomous and integrated whole, which can if necessary become subordinate to a segment of itself,"[5] seems adequate, if interpreted to mean "integrated" considering the age and life-cycle stage of the person involved. Under the same qualification Jahoda's definition seems equally enlightening: a healthy person shows *active mastery* of his environment, *unity* of personality, and *accurate perception* of himself and others.[6] With these definitions in mind, let us turn to a more concrete examination of the qualities of the "together guy" as found in the Pathways study.

Although there was not at Time I a boy who could be described as wholly "together," several boys approached such a designation even though they were in the midst of the stresses and changes associated with adolescence and were living in a relatively hostile environment.

From many interviews a picture of the together guy emerges. He exhibits a balance in interpersonal relationships between conformity and individuality, between manipulating others and submitting to their whims, between violent aggression and passive victimization. The together guy will fight if his honor is called seriously into question, or to establish territorial or leadership rights, but resists fighting for the sake of fighting unless he is fairly certain that he will not be hurt or apprehended by the police. He approaches others with the expectation of a positive relationship, and has means other than force or conning to get what he wants from them. He is expressive, but can control his expressiveness; he does not panic or take unnecessarily high risks to achieve his goals. This indicates a sense of self-worth which mandates that he is not to be toyed with by himself or by others, nor to be thrown away recklessly in the name of excitement or fun.

The together guy is comfortable with himself and with others, and has a strong ego coupled with sureness and self-confidence. He seems mature for his age, and although he may at times be a loner or keep his own counsel (an expression of his need and capacity for autonomy), he is likely to have good relations in a flexible but close peer group. He can dress "sharp" but does not overdress or show off. As part of his strivings for self-expression, he can vary his behavior in different situations and seldom responds stereotypically to people or events. Yet underlying his behavior is a unity of style, intent, and sense of self. Although his behavior reflects his generally high level of self-esteem and caring for himself, he is not egocentric or narcissistic.

The together guy scores relatively high on the internal dimension of sense-of-control scales ("active mastery"). He views himself as being the primary guiding and acting force in his life, and is fairly optimistic about his chances of carrying out his hopes and plans. Yet if there is one significant characteristic about him that sets him off from the Conformist on the one hand and the Actor (who also has a very high sense of internal control) on the other, it is his sense of realism (Jahoda's "accurate perception of self") about his limitations and potentialities.[7] This is enhanced by a general feeling of trust and affection for others, and his capacity for being responsible. He can cope—and he is prepared to take the consequences of his own decisions.

The super-cool cat shares many of the same qualities as the together guy, especially the positive approach to others and his position toward the active rather than the passive end of the power dimension. He can be described further as a boy who utilizes the available cultural symbols and materials (cars, clothes, hairdos, music, etc.) to an extreme.[8] Although he may be admired by some (particularly younger boys, or his immediate peer group), he may be regarded by the together guy as flamboyant—and as having lost some of his autonomy in the pursuit of making an impression.

The dilemma of the super-cool cat who revels in expressiveness is matched by the together guy in his insistence on doing his own thing. Both run the risk of alienating those who would have them adhere closely to peer group norms, to follow the crowd, to engage in deviant behavior which the Cool Guy often finds perilously and senselessly ridiculous. As Riesman points out in *The Lonely Crowd*, although it is possible to achieve creativity and flexibility of behavior and values, there is also great pressure on the individual to adhere closely to peer group norms and expectations.[9] Not to conform—to be "your own man"—constitutes a deviation that is neither eccentric nor immoral but which bears its own penalty, as we shall see in the case of Hank.

Self-Characterization. "I got my own way in everything."

Hank's drive for independence and selfhood is apparent throughout his Time I interview. At age 14 he projects a sense of strength, of sureness, of uniqueness—qualities that are apparently salient for him. When asked whom he takes after, Hank responds: "I got my own way of talking, and everything. I got my own way in everything. I don't copy nothing from nobody."

Hank is a highly verbal respondent whose transcript from Time I is over 250 pages long. Much of the inner peace, self-confidence, and sense of internal control he presents in his interview is not confirmed by his mother, peer, or nephew—a problem dealt with below (page 172ff). It is by this very fact that Hank's "together" style is best demonstrated: he is his own man. Because he does not agonize over what others think of him, he often leaves the impression that he is "cold," as one friend puts it. Toward people he cares for deeply, however, Hank is warm, responsible, and giving. The capacity for affection and trusting others, and the realism about oneself and others which mark the Cool Guy, are well developed in him.

Hank's family is actually two intertwined. His mother was first married to a man named Roy, by whom she had two children, Pete, 25 at Time I, and Elsie, 38. After divorcing Roy, Hank's mother married Henry Nelson, Hank's natural father. At Time I they also have separated. Living in his house are Hank, his mother, and his 15-year-old nephew, Bert (Elsie's son), who has been raised as though he were Hank's brother. Elsie and her other six children live upstairs. Although Hank complains a great deal about his feeling that his mother favors Bert, and speaks of fighting between his mother and father when they drink too much, it appears that his view of his family life is very positive.

Hank defines the boundaries between himself and his significant others in perceptive terms. He distinguishes positive and negative qualities in others, is at once critical and appreciative of them; they are, like him, real and complex people whom he tries to fathom. For example, he likes it when his mother gets in a "lovey mood," but is quite honest in saying that he does not like everything about her. He does not want her to be different, however, in an unusual confirmation of another person's identity: "I don't think I could get used to any other ways. I'd think something was wrong if she were different." He likes his father, except for his drinking, which he could accept if it were "a little bit," but "it's going to his head . . . he's all messed up." He likes everything about Daddy Roy, except that he goes with teenage girls—"that don't make sense. Acts as if he's around 20 or so. That's what I like about him though. He understands me and I understand him."

Hank's sense of separateness from others is expressed by his enjoying quiet moments to himself occasionally. When he wants to be alone he sits in his room or on top of the fire escape at school: "I like to think about things, you know, the future and what I want to do and everything." This is more a time to recreate his sense of self than an escape from frightening or frustrating situations, as it was for Ernie.

Yet Hank is adept at establishing and maintaining intimacy with others. Along with his sense of separateness is an impressive capacity to share himself with others, and to love. One example is his story of a white boy named Danny. They met at a swimming pool, but did not become friends until they later fought at a party:

he was fooling around and bumped against me, and pushed me. I pushed him back and he went to hit me, and I said, are you playing for real? And he said, what do you think? And I said, if that's the way you feel . . . we fought until we got tangled up and couldn't hit each other. He couldn't loosen me and I couldn't loosen him. So we called it a tie and stood up, and then we became the best of friends . . . me and him.

Hank speaks of mutual loyalty and helping each other out; they were a team. "And then a couple of years ago he moved away. I never felt so sad in my life, man. That was someone I really looked toward. I never felt so sad in my life, though, when he left."

Another example is his relationship with his girl, Sally. He respects her, and says he does not like to play around:

She's good to me, and I'm good to her . . . I won't treat her wrong, she won't treat me wrong. I trust her if she trust me. If I see this girl, kiss her once or twice, I'll tell her about it. She just say, so what, and laugh it off. I don't mind her kissing other boys . . . just as long as it don't get too serious.

He treats Sally as an individual, and holds their relationship above arbitrary peer group pressures to follow the leader. When a member of his peer group has a falling out with his girl, another friend follows suit and tells his girl it is "quits"; Hank is astonished at their need to copy each other:

Man I told him you stupid ass. I'm sorry, but I just had to tell him that to his face. And then they come talk about, are you going to quit Sally? I told them, man, what would I look like quitting Sally just because you two fools going and quitting your good girls and everything. I'll look like a fool, quit her for no reason at all . . . I been going with Sally ever since.

A sense of competence permeates Hank's interview. He offers in passing that he loves to swim—"that's my game"—and to dive; he is called "sub-mariner" because he is the "best one in the crowd." He obviously feels comfortable rapping with girls, and feels that he belongs in the center of his peer group. The one thing he can do better than the average boy his age is talking—"come to talking to the girls I'm always ready."

His realism tones down other reported skills: "I'm not saying I'm better than kids my age, but I'm pretty good in swimming and playing basketball." Later in the interview he says he does not play on the school basketball team simply because he lacks the appropriate skill: "I'll tell you in a minute, that's something I don't have." On the street, he says he plays "regular," but is aware that team membership requires more than that. Hank is also "pretty good" at dancing, fighting, "carrying on." Many of Hank's skills are self-taught. He could improve by paying more attention (school work) or by practicing (baseball, running). His assessment of his abilities is based on a clear knowledge of his strengths and limitations, as well as a strong sense of internal control over his environment.

Coupled with his sense of competence is a high degree of self-esteem and respect for himself as he is. In response to the "brain-wash" question, Hank says he would not want to lose those skills that are so important to him—swimming abilities ("I like swimming better than anything else") and "the girls." When asked how his mother would change him, he replies: "For one thing she wouldn't, 'cause I wouldn't let her." His father wants him to be in the Coast Guard when he grows up: "But I tell him I don't want to be in the Coast Guard, I want to be in the Marines or the Air Force." And Daddy Roy would not want him to change even if he could—he simply wants Hank to be a "man." Hank interprets this to mean that he should treat others well and "do whatever you want to do and don't let anybody boss you around." His friend Rocky would not change Hank—"He wish he could be me." He adds that "they all like me the way I am now. I mean, it wouldn't be the same if I changed." Who would he like to grow up to be like? "Well, there's nobody I'd like to be but myself, I guess."

Hank's response to the "spy" question throws into relief his resistance to his parents and his proclivity for audience segregation:

I'd tell him, you know, every time my mother ask him to do something, to frown up and stuff like that. And when you're in a good mood, just act normal . . . if my father comes over when he starts to sit down beside you and starts talking and everything, frown, and say "quit it, dad." When I come in late my mother'll . . . holler at you. Just stand there and look simple . . . and when she get finished, do whatever I want. [With his girl] . . . play around regular . . . do good with 'em. [In school] Just act regular, fool around with the fellas and what not.

Hank is average in racial awareness at Time I, but his racial identity as yet is a strange admixture of pride and stereotypical thinking. He would not take the pill to make himself white—"I'd stay just the way I am now . . . I like it that way." Nor would he press a magic button to make everyone in America black: "You wouldn't have no house the next day, or anything else." He seems to view blacks as being irresponsible, an attitude that reflects his mother's feelings. (Statistics on crime support his perception that blacks tend to commit crimes against one another more than they do against whites.)

If blacks were rioting in their own section of the city, Hank would "think the Negroes were going mad . . . that's the way they blew it, going into a Negro section." Hank applies the same self-protective principles to his race as he does to himself. He calls himself "Negro," resents a white person calling him "nigger" (he speaks of not being able to control himself—"I end up beating the hell out of them"). Stereotypically, he thinks whites cannot dance or play sports as well as blacks, and, surprisingly, are "slow in learnings." Blacks "got a better style than they do." He feels that whites do not trust blacks generally and that the former end up being richer and having jobs in higher places than blacks do.

Yet Hank feels that blacks are "just as good as whites," and apparently perceives the "system" as being open to his strivings. Hank wants to be a businessman, an occupation that would afford him good pay and would allow him to have "a good family . . . to have a good name, and to be able to know something, to do something." His second choice is crane operator—Daddy Roy's occupation. He feels he is capable of graduating from high school plus two years of college: "I think I'm going all the way. Matter of fact I know I'm going all the way."

Unlike many of the Pathways focals, who often seem stymied in the face of adult authority and lack of responsiveness, Hank is willing to make a case, verbally and otherwise, for what he wants. For example, when a neighbor invites him to go horseback riding on a Sunday afternoon and Hank knows a good movie is playing at the local cinema that day, he asks her if they could go on a Saturday instead. He mentions debating with his mother about the merits of a particular pair of shoes and why he should be allowed to have them.

When his mother catches him disobeying her (e.g., smoking), Hank does not hesitate to leave if she scolds him unnecessarily: "She'll say, well, what did you do this for? Or, I told you about that. If she went a little too far, I just walk out." Or, when he brings home a poor report card: "She might slap me around a few times. When I get tired of the slapping, I just walk out and come back later." While he might appear from these examples to use withdrawal as a primary way of coping with unpleasant situations, I think it is rather an extension of his caring well for himself. Hank does not leave out of fear, or in order to avoid confrontation. He does not run away or hide, as in the case of Ernie. He terminates interaction that threatens to demean him or to violate the boundaries that protect his integrity and his dignity. He leaves in order to define and control the situation, not to run from it.

Just as he insists that others respect his integrity, he respects others for theirs. But when others play roles and act like someone they are not, he feels disdainful toward them, as in this account of his mother's behavior when she is called up to Hank's school:

> She'll start showing off in front of the teacher, yelling and hollering at me. I just don't listen to her, I just stand there and act simple. And she'll just be talking and the teachers will be gabbing. I just don't listen. She'll say, don't do it again, or sometime she'll put me on punishment. When I get tired of that, I just say, ma, I'm going to go out anyway.

He appreciates the authenticity projected by his shop teacher: "He don't try to be like no one but himself." Another teacher, who tries to act like a big shot and is nosey and unfair, falls short because he "makes a fool of himself." Similarly, the "boy who is doing well" is not a positive reference figure for Hank, in spite of his fine grades: "He tries to follow behind Rocky [a tough friend] too much . . . I told him, you know, he was going to get himself messed up . . . I don't see why he should try to be something he ain't."

Supporting Hank's primary "together guy" style is a secondary style of "real tough guy." Hank does not usually seek out trouble, but the use of force is well within his repertoire of ways of coping with others. When Bert bothers him and "acts all stupid," Hank says, "I just grab something and hit him, and he don't bother me no more."

The toughness is reflected in his peer group at Time I, whose members he describes in terms of being good athletes and good fighters, loyal to the group. The group consists of Mark, 15, Vince, 15 ("then comes me . . . I'm just regular"), Lucky, 15, Rocky, 14, and Lee, 13, as well as several peripheral figures. The boys refer to themselves as the "In-Crowd." The group is close-knit in terms of loyalty (especially when it comes to refraining from "squealing" on each other), but is rather fluid in a sociometric sense. (For Times I and II sociograms for Hank's peer group, see below, pages 175 and 176.)

Hank emphasizes that the group sticks together in case of trouble, and resolves conflicts through stating respective positions clearly. Fighting occurs if necessary to prove his point or to save face. For Hank, force is used to preserve identity, not to create it, as in Leroy's case. Hank's gang, though in many ways a "fighting" or "conflict" gang, shares his reluctance to start fights:

We don't go around starting nothing. But if someone come around and start something, we'll fight him up and up. They want to get some boys, all of us together, and if we lose, no hard feelings. You know, you see these cats, always jumping people and things. We don't do that.

Hank controls very carefully his participation in activities that could get him into trouble. He drinks, but his mother "never caught me drinking, never will." He will not steal, but rides occasionally in a stolen car with his friends—"I know they can get away." According to one peer, Hank has either slipped through police awareness when his peers were apprehended, or, if caught, was released because he had not participated in the misbehavior. At age 14, much of his relationship with his peer group is focused on keeping a certain distance between his identity and the group's. This results in his not being fully accepted or trusted by his friends, and vice versa. He speaks of this distance in slightly different terms as well:

Well sometimes I . . . like, see, I'm in a way strange from the rest of them because I do what I want, and I'm by myself most of the time. Like at night, me and my dog will go out for a walk . . . just keep going around, just walk and think, you know, plan about . . . you know, daydream about things.

Hank's toughness is evident from his early experiences in nursery school, when he and his cousin attended together:

One day, we got swinging on the swings . . . so Freddy, his big mouth, got me in a fight, fist fight; all of a sudden, I saw this kid draw back and hit Freddy in the jaw. I jumped off the swing, and I said, What did you hit him for? Cat said, well . . . 'cause I wanted to. Talking like that, you know. I was scared at first, and then I just hit him in the jaw. He went down and started crying and went and told the teacher . . . and the teacher asked me what I hit him for. And we got it all straightened out.

Since then, Hank has been willing to fight for what he feels are his rights, both in and out of school. When his report card shows a "D" in shop after his teacher had told him that he was doing well, Hank confronts the teacher, who admits he has made a mistake.

On another occasion, Hank and his friends play hookey on a Monday, but are not apprehended. The next morning, when Hank arrives late, Mr. Smith begins writing out a "truant card" for Tuesday:

I said, What's that for? He said, Well, you could've been. I could've been, but I wasn't, I said . . . there's no reason for that. And, I said, I'm going to tell you to your face what's going to happen if it comes in the mail— I'm going to take it and rip it up and if you come to my house, I'm going to slam the door in your face. Well, he . . . he just kept on writing, but the truant officer ain't came, and it ain't came in the mail either.

Others in his focal cluster refer to Hank's temper. Hank recognizes that he is quick to anger, but, as with other forms of getting into trouble, seems to have his temper under control. He relates one incident involving Rocky, who became so angry at a teacher that he was calling her a "white bitch":

I couldn'ta did that, no matter how mad I was. Getting ready to knock her out, man, and then he would have been in serious trouble, man, if he hit her. I just grabbed him, threw him in his room, and kept him there until he cooled off.

As he matures, Hank appears to be increasingly willing to shift from physical to verbal means of controlling others. Similarly, he notes that his father no longer beats him for hooking school but relies on words, telling him that he is old enough to learn and to know what he means. His scenario of how he would handle the "boy in hot water" in his school reflects this shift: "I'd treat him just as equal as I would, you know, the other cats." Hank would listen to him, try to be his friend:

I. How would you get him to respect you?
H. I'd respect him.

He adds that he believes in giving people a second chance—thus allowing others the same opportunity to get themselves "together" that he demands for himself. His favorite teachers, predictably, have been those who showed no favorites, but were flexible, fair, firm, and understanding. The shop teacher is at the top of his list: "If he tells the kids to stay away from something and he goes out of the room, everyone stays away from it. You know, just . . . he treat us well and we treat him well."

Finally, Hank's realism about his flaws as well as his strengths is indicative of his potential for full autonomy. He repeated the third grade: "Girls as usual. Try to show off and carry on . . . but I got hip to that and I haven't repeated since." His grades hover around average, yet he wants his teachers to tell him exactly how he is doing: "Straight to my face, you know, if I'm passing or not. No beating around the bush or nothing." He predicts his grade in music will not be high because "I blew it with my conduct." He would like to improve his grades; in order to do so he would have to stop "playing around so much . . . sometimes I can't even trust my own self . . . I get in school and all of a sudden, bam, there I am . . . you know, end up fooling around." Similarly, after agreeing with his "old lady" (Sally) not to get serious with anyone else, Hank allows himself to get involved with another girl. "I got this girl digging me and I don't know what to do, man, to tell the truth . . . 'cause they meet up and compare notes . . . I just blew my game."

At 14, then, we see a young man developing strength, self-assurance, independence, and a sense of uniqueness—and in the throes, as well, of learning to fight for those qualities and how to take the consequences they often bring.

Characterization by Others. "He's very determined."

Although Hank in his interview exhibits insight, a keen sense of fair play, realism, and a positive view of himself, the reference interviews show that his most autonomous and "together" qualities also serve to create a distance between Hank and others. For example, Mark, a key member of the "In-Crowd," expresses some of the disdain other group members feel toward Hank because he refuses to take high risks or to pursue trouble-making behavior openly. The strength Hank shows in making decisions that are right for him, regardless of peer pressures, Mark says, is interpreted by the others as hostile neutrality:

I. Does Hank ever let the guys down?
M. Yeah, he let us down one night, all of us . . . we was going to this party, he was in front of us, and we were walking behind so he crossed the street, so he turned up this street, and the next thing we know we didn't see him no more so we just didn't bother with him.

I. What did the guys say about that?

M. They all said he was cold . . . didn't want him hanging around us.

This coldness is referred to in another exchange:

I. Well, how do other guys in the group feel about Hank?

M. I don't think they like him.

I. What makes you feel this way?

M. He never hang around with us; the only time he hang around with us is on Friday nights.

I. Um hum.

M. That's when we can get something to drink, but he always puts in money.

I. What do you think he, you know, why do you think he just gets around on Friday night?

M. So he can get drunk.

These comments seem puzzling at first, since Hank in his interview gives no hint that he is actively seeking to *avoid* the In-Crowd—in fact he says at one point he is in the center of it. Yet his values and attitudes toward violence and stealing even then constrain him from full participation in some of the gang's activities.

Apparently, between his interview and Mark's a few months later, Hank has shifted away from the In-Crowd and his ties with Rocky, and toward a closer friendship with Vince, who shares Hank's disdain for open deviance, and his positive attitudes toward school, work, and being "cool." In his subsequent interviews, Hank (who six months earlier had called Rocky his best friend) tells Mark that Rocky makes him sick and that he likes Rocky least of all. His link with the In-Crowd has grown more tenuous and narrow, his affiliation with Vince more salient. Drinking remains an activity he can freely engage in with the In-Crowd— (at both Time I and Time II he feels he has it under control)—but this self-limited participation seems disloyal and threatens his position as a member of the group. This is confirmed by Mark's statement that Hank "don't hardly hang with us when we go downtown" to steal. Says Mark, "I never got in any trouble with Hank." Mark claims that Rocky is now leader of the In-Crowd. Mark quit because "I didn't want it, we were getting into too much trouble . . . stealing cars, stuff like that." (To support this explanation, see Figures 5 and 6, which show Hank's peer group memberships at Time I and Time II. Although I shall discuss Hank's strategic style at Time II more fully in Chapter 7, below, it is clear from these figures that when Mark is interviewed, Hank is in the process of shifting his allegiances from one peer orientation, which focuses on his secondary style, tough guy, to a new orientation, which allows fuller expression of his primary style, together guy.)[10]

During Time I, Mark, Rocky, Mrs. Nelson, and Bert, all of them significant others, were also interviewed. Though trouble may be a primary concern for the In-Crowd, being cool is a close second; that serves partially to explain Hank's attraction to, and position in, the group in the first place. For example, when he is asked if there is anyone in the group who is "not too together at all, not too clean," Mark replies flatly, "They don't hang around with us." Mark reports that Hank is respected for the way he dresses: "See, we're all supposed to be hip, you know, not being shy . . . start talking with a girl . . . we all have the latest stuff, you know, stuff that's in style." Bert thinks that Hank dresses better than the others: "He takes after his brother there. His brother dresses up real nice, models in clothes, you know." Mrs. Nelson, Bert, and Mark all acknowledge Hank's skill and ease with girls: "He's a good mixer with people, he's not bashful or shy or anything like that."

In his peer section Rocky speaks of Hank as a "nice" guy who is the most trustworthy and the "cleanest" of all his friends. When asked what Hank will be like when he grows up, Rocky says, "he'll be like a man." It is apparent that coolness as a value is coupled in the In-Crowd with quickness of temper, lack of tact, and stubbornness, which offer Hank a legitimate place to express those qualities as well. Mark says that Hank has "a bad temper, you know. When something happens, he gets mad and starts turning red, so I just don't bother him, just leave him alone." Rocky, too, has a quick temper, but, adds Mark, "mine I think is worser." He says his friends would have him change that, but "when I get mad, I'll fight anybody. Thàt's why they don't mess with me."

Temper and toughness are virtuous in the In-Crowd, and are symbolized by the central role of fighting. Membership in the gang is determined initially by the ability to fight. Loyalty is measured by willingness to help a buddy out of a tough spot by fighting with him. If there is a disagreement among members, it is settled by a fight. Mark is asked what could break his friendship with Hank, and he replies, "A fight, you know, if he's doing something that I don't like." (Obviously, he means only the most violent transgres-

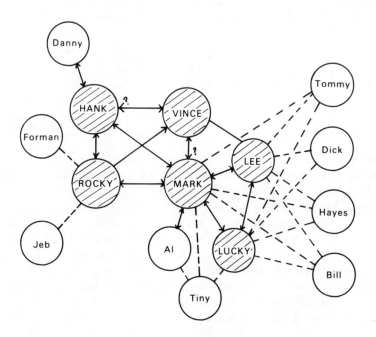

FIGURE 5. Hank's Peer Group Membership—Time I. The *solid lines* between boys indicate relatively high frequency of interaction: *broken lines* indicate regular but less frequent interaction. *Arrows* indicate designations of "best friend," "most trusted," "leader," or "boy who gets things started," as derived from interviews with those underlined as well as with Hank's mother and nephew. Hank and Rocky choose each other as best friend since Danny has moved away, but occasionally they hang with Forman; primary activities—biking, building models, listening to music. Shading shows boys who are considered to be members of the "In-Crowd;" primary activities—playing basketball, swimming, going to parties, and drinking on Friday nights. The "In-Crowd," minus Hank and Vince, also engages in car theft and purse-snatching. Mark is obviously the sociometric "star" who links the various cliques together. He also joins with Lucky, Al, and Tiny in a peripheral clique which engages heavily in serious illegal activities such as assault, breaking and entering, and dope traffic.

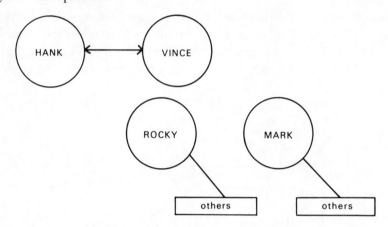

FIGURE 6: Hank's Peer Group Membership—Time II. Three years after the first interview, Hank has made his choice. When asked what Rocky is doing, he says he does not know or care. One thing he does know—Mark and Rocky are both "hoods," into dope, theft, assault, and so on. He and Vince are the closest of friends, understand each other. Both are still in school and are aiming toward some college and stable work futures. The others have dropped out, are in trouble with the police, have lost their dreams. Hank says he has not seen Mark and Rocky for about two and a half years, confirming my hypothesis that it was the process of shifting groups that created the sense of alienation felt by other members of the "In-Crowd" at Time I.

sion, for he lists as an example of what might cause them to fight the possibility of someone saying something about his eight-year-old sister, who is crippled and destined to spend the rest of her life in a hospital near Boston.) As stressed in Hank's and Mark's interviews, the group does not seek out fights with other gangs or individuals. Mark puts it aptly: "We just wait for somebody to mess with us."

The toughness carries over into school, which all of them hold at arm's length as a purely functional place where one must bide one's time in order to become employed later in life. Like Hank, Mark takes very little from teachers. On one occasion, when Mark tells a boy to "shut up" and the teacher thinks the comment is directed toward him, the teacher punches Mark in the arm: "I told him to keep his fucking hands off me or he'd get his ass kicked."

Mrs. Nelson acknowledges Hank's temper—he likes to argue

and is quick to express his anger—which she sees as a youthful version of her own:

Certain times I have a temper myself. They all have that. That's why sometimes I can understand it in them. I can control mine much better, because I'm older, and I can understand what a temper can get you into.

At best, Hank is determined. He will try to convince his mother of the reasonableness of his requests ("He's going to try to win over his side"). She will "come to an agreement" when she is able (thus rewarding Hank's efforts) and stands firm when she feels that would be best for him. Hank, she feels, is very outspoken with his family and friends: "If there is something he dislikes, he'll speak up in a minute." She does not see this causing a problem with Hank's friends, since "most of them are the same way . . . they agree and disagree, you know."

Nonetheless, Hank's mother and nephew would have him tone down. Says Bert of Mrs. Nelson: "She'll call him and he'll say 'what' real loud, you know . . . and when he walk out the door, he slam the door, he's mad or something." Bert feels that Hank should learn to control his temper, that it can get Hank into unnecessary trouble. He speaks of one incident in which someone falsely accused Hank of stealing a television set during the 1967 riots in Roxbury. Hank started yelling indignantly—it was Bert who stepped in and quietly persuaded the storekeeper that Hank did not take it: "He don't know how to talk to nobody quiet."

School is of concern to Mrs. Nelson. She would like to see Hank improve (as would he), but "he's a little girl-crazy now." She attributes Hank's neutral, often negative, attitude toward school to his determination and tendency to be outspoken. She feels Hank is afraid to speak his mind at school, at least not as often as he does with family or his friends, with whom he apparently feels "safer":

And instead of coming out with it, he'll take it out in stubbornness . . . if the teacher yells at him or something (that really gets next to him, more than anything), right away he's going to clam up . . . he'll refuse to talk, and then he gets a stubborn look on his face and he won't come out with anything.

In the face of what Hank perceives as a losing game, he "clams up" and refuses to play, all the while revealing his resentment. This infuriates principals and teachers alike, and Hank skirts the edges of being a "discipline problem." Yet Mrs. Nelson, like Mark and Rocky, has high expectations for Hank's school performance. They all believe that he will follow his brother Pete's footsteps through high school graduation and some college, then into a good job. His aspirations apparently are strong enough to enable him to curb his temper if he deems it necessary for school success. In fact, Mark's expectations for Hank are higher than for anyone in their group, because "he's determined." The others, he predicts, will be pushing dope and out of work within two years (a prediction that comes true for himself as well).

That Hank has control over his temper is further indicated by a comment his mother made: "When something is bothering him, it's very hard to really get it out of him. He stays with himself. He don't like to talk about it too much . . . he goes off by himself, doesn't have very much to say. Quiet." These may be the times when Hank says he needs and wants to be alone, private, to daydream and work things through for himself. To others this is a gate that has been shut, cutting them off from Hank; to him it is that all-important breathing space in which he explores his feelings and needs. This capacity to deal with feelings both internally and externally is one reason I have typed him as a "together guy," since it allows him to cope with himself and others in a reflective as well as spontaneous manner.

In terms of the community's definitions, a "together guy" must, as he grows into adulthood, "have his head together" about racial and social-system questions. At Time I, Hank is relatively naive and unaware of racial issues but, at least in his own interviews, exhibits a solid sense of pride in being "Negro" and views his color as a positive quality. By Time II (age 17), he has grown toward radicalism and is relatively high in racial awareness and sophistication. This is another area in which his efforts to preserve his integrity have caused him trouble. Mrs. Nelson recalls:

. . . one time in particular one of the little white girls in his school told Hank, "you look like a little black teddy bear." I said to Hank, "Well, what did you say?" He says, "I didn't say anything to her, but I looked at her, but what really made me angry is when Joey, this little white boy, took it up—little black teddy bear, little black teddy bear. I just knocked him down."

The teacher sent Mrs. Nelson a note stating that Hank was "disturbing the class," whereupon Mrs. Nelson visited the teacher to explain the situation. When the teacher said, "The kids read these things in the books and they really don't mean any harm," Mrs. Nelson tried unsuccessfully to convince her that in fact the potential for harm is there.

Mrs. Nelson adds that Hank gets "very disgusted" when his friends call one another "nigger," an appellation he abhors. Hank insists (as his mother says she has taught him) that blacks are as good as whites, and in some ways better.

Hank's positive attitude toward himself is mirrored by the positive self-concepts of Mark, Bert, and Rocky. When asked how he would like to change, Mark says that he prefers to "stay the way I am." He would not like to switch places with anyone—"I just want to be myself, I don't want to be like nobody else." Bert and Rocky express similar sentiments.

Analysis of the Together Style

In pleasing himself, Hank has not always pleased those others who weave the fabric of his daily life. Nevertheless, respect for his integrity is expressed fairly consistently by those who know him well. He has strength, sureness, insight, high self-esteem, and a certain expressiveness which render him "together."

Returning to the criteria of mental health, we see that Hank fulfills most of them remarkably well. Interviews with other focals suggest that "together" is equated with self-respect, self-knowledge, self-determination. Hank exhibits these qualities.

Following Erikson, we see that Hank has resolved the childhood crises in the direction of trust, autonomy, initiative, and industry—allowing him to continue positively through the adolescent crisis of identity vs. identity confusion (as exemplified by his leaving a basically incongruent peer group). Freud's criteria of loving and working well seem to be met by Hank's affectionate relationship with Danny and his girl friend, and by his determination to finish school (which he dislikes) and establish his own business. Finally, we see that Hank's style also meets Jahoda's criteria of active mastery, unity, and accurate perception of self and others. His self-esteem is protected by strong coping skills; his uniqueness is coupled with great concern for authenticity; his temper is balanced by realism and empathy toward others.

We look to the family to gain some insight into the genesis of these elements of the together style, and find a profusion of positive role models, love, good times, and companionship, intermingled with favoritism, nagging, instability, episodic violence, and alcohol-induced brawls.

The Family Matrix. There is a distinctly positive tone to Hank's projective picture stories after the Family Section of the interviews. In real life, the positive tone similarly prevails. When asked how he felt about his family on the most recent Christmas, Hank responds, "The same way I always do . . . just felt good." He mentions hours spent with his mother and Val (the woman next door), who "is just like a sister to us," playing cards, drinking coffee, "talking about what happened back in their days and all . . . having a good time." His dreams of his own future family center on a wife and children, dogs and horses, living in the country in a warm and loving environment.

Although he cares for all of his family members in some way, most of all Hank loves his paternal grandmother, who lives in New Hampshire: She is "like a regular grandmother, she gives you everything . . . you talk about it, and she tells you to get it." (This is in sharp contrast to his mother, who, in Hank's eyes, is somewhat withholding.) His parents have told him that when he was small, they would visit her and "she'd hold me in her arms and she wouldn't put me down for nothing, she wanted me to stay with her." This made a deep impression on Hank; when the going gets rough at home, particularly when he feels rejected by his mother, Hank talks of running away. Grandmother offers a haven of trust and reliability—"if I ask her not to tell my mother where I am, she won't tell her."

Haven from what? Mainly from the nagging and partiality which Hank perceives emanating from the triangle formed by him, Bert, and his mother.

The issue that pierces Hank's family from his point of view so painfully is the favoritism he feels his mother shows toward Bert. Mrs. Nelson does not confirm this, and seems to feel that any privilege Bert receives above Hank is merely due to their age difference. Bert, in turn, senses favoritism from Mrs. Nelson, but in the reverse. When asked if he and Hank are treated differently, he replies:

Not too much . . . just a little, that's all. She treats him like he's a baby, you know . . . when she tells us to clean up the house, he'll walk out . . . and she don't say nothing to him, and I have to clean it up you know . . . she say, don't argue, just do it.

Bert adds that Hank will not take orders from Bert when Mrs. Nelson leaves him in charge. It is clear from this and other passages that Hank resists helping out around the house, and especially resents Bert's being placed above him in any way.

Bert, then, is the thorn in Hank's side. They have lived together since they were both about seven years old. Bert was in so much trouble (beating people up, breaking windows, "hanging around with the wrong crowd") that Hank's mother decided to take her grandson in. "He'd go around and steal, and as he got older he got badder . . . go around breaking parking meters, snatching pocketbooks, stealing cars." He was sent to reform school for six months, and "when he came back, he'd surely growed, so he's been living with us ever since."

Hank claims that Bert continues to steal from whites and from Mrs. Nelson's purse, but when she asks Bert how he gets his money, he claims that he found it. "She believes him, too. But if it was me, she wouldn't believe me an inch." Hank feels that his mother favors Bert—"he gets away with anything":

If I do something, she starts screaming . . . but with Bert, she don't do nothing, she just asks him, why didn't you do this, why didn't you do that. But with me, she just gets all over me. I don't like that. Quite a few times, I was going to run away, and I thought, no, you'd better wait until summer.

He complains that his mother allows Bert to buy more expensive suits and shoes than Hank receives. "I don't like that either. A lot of the time I feel like getting out of there. Like to do what I want."

To this perception of injustice, add violence. Hank says his father is "normal, but he drinks a lot." Hank has learned how to drink from both his parents; he also has gained insight into the problems and confusion drinking can precipitate. One night his father came home "messed up" from drinking. He teased his wife, who "didn't want to be bothered,"

so he started hitting her and she grabbed a can opener and hit him across the face. She chased him out of the house, pushing him down the stairs. He returned a few minutes later. She threw a fist at him, knocked him completely out the door . . . and threw him down the stairs again.

Another incident, which Hank describes as one of the worst times he ever spent with his family, reveals both Mrs. Nelson's temper and Hank's love for his father—to say nothing of his being caught between the two of them:

One night—it was a grown-up party—all of a sudden, I heard a lot of screaming. I ran downstairs. My father and my mother got into it. She just got mad and jumped on my father. My mother took a glass of whiskey and threw it in his eyes. And I didn't know what to do because I felt bad for my father, then, you see, so I just—you know, my father's falling down and blinded—and I just picked him up and threw him in my uncle's car . . . and me and my uncle drove him to the hospital.

These nightmarish scenes are full of anguish for Hank. The favoritism toward Bert, whether perceived by others or not, is painfully real to Hank. Yet, there appears to be such a substantial base of loving, caring, listening, and supporting in the family that these situations do not destroy Hank. In fact, there is some suggestion that the fierce fighting between his parents has contributed to his strength and his empathic nature.

Critical Messages from Others. Counterpointing the tough friends, rivalry with Bert, and fragmented parental relationships is the relatively positive and accepting home atmosphere in which Mrs. Nelson treats Hank as an individual. Mrs. Nelson's comments about her family suggest a distinct warmth and closeness underlying the family interaction. Positive regard for Hank is prominent in Mrs. Nelson's thinking. When asked to describe the best or happiest day with him, she replies: "They're all that way I guess." To the question of whether she has ever felt Hank was more trouble than he was worth, her answer is unequivocal: "I think I never felt that way about any of mine."

Mrs. Nelson claims that she openly expresses affection toward

Hank (he says he likes it when his mother is "lovey"); a broken home has not meant loss of love or positive feedback. In addition, three major factors serve to counteract the negative forces in Hank's life: being the "baby," clear authority of the mother, and a push toward responsibility. We will examine each.

Mrs. Nelson claims that her family is small—just herself, her three children, grandson Bert, and upstairs the younger grandchildren. Not until the interviewer probes does she include the two husbands in her life. More important, she says that because of the age difference between her three children (38, 24, and 14 at Time I), each one has been the baby of the family; each one has been raised separately; each one has had a long period of being shown singular attention, and in her word being "spoiled." Though all of them got "all of the attention" as a baby, Hank received even more, since he had two older siblings to contribute to that attention. That Hank is an individual, respected as a person in his own right, is reflected in this dialogue:

> *I.* Who does Hank try to take after?
> *M.* He just has his own ways.
>
> *I.* What kind of work do you think he wants to do?
> *M.* I've asked him several times, and he'll say, "I don't know, I'm not far enough in school yet to decide what I want."
>
> *I.* What would you like him to be?
> *M.* It's his future, and so I would like what he wants. . . . I couldn't see myself working at a job I disliked.

The second factor, clear authority of the mother, is important for Hank's development of his own capacities for setting standards and limits on his behavior. Mrs. Nelson's expectations of him are clear and, for the most part, reasonable. The interviewer asks if her daughter or friends ever disagree on how Hank should be raised. She replies:

No, that's one thing I've never had any interference with; I mean, my children will have one boss over them, and that's myself. I don't believe in two or three people trying to tell children what to do.

That Mrs. Nelson handles discipline in the family without relying on either of her husbands for intermittent authority or punishment may make it easier for Hank to derive support from the affectionate and uncomplicated companionship of Daddy Roy and his father. Also, her method of discipline allows room for Hank to develop a sense of effectiveness or control in his environment. When he transgresses, she removes privileges and gives him a "talking to," so that he will "think twice the next time."[11] Hank, she says, will try to talk his way in and out of privileges, but in the end he will obey her: "If I tell him not to do a thing, he won't." The limits, initially negotiable, are not infinitely so, allowing Hank room to define the situation, and providing him with ultimately clear-cut restrictions.

Responsibility is impressed on Hank through his mother's example and through her expectation that all her children will contribute to the family when they begin to work. When asked if she thinks Hank will mind, she says, "no, I'm quite sure he won't." She feels a job after school helps the children "later on" by teaching them responsibility. Her hopes for his future life and work reflect this faith that he will be responsible and do well, without imposing specific work categories on him: "I hope it will be something good, honest, and worthwhile—that's good enough for me." She feels that Hank has taken her values as his own: "He will consider a family and a home first." When they talk about boys who get into trouble with the law or have no hopes of their own, she adds that he says he has never been in trouble; he sees what happens to the rest of them and does not want that.

Closely related to the push toward responsibility is a concomitant expectation of competence. Mrs. Nelson encourages Hank to do better even as she praises his improvements. She helps with his homework when she understands it, and suggests that he tell his teachers he needs help, communicating to him the message that the world will respond to him. Her own sense of competence is reflected in her repeated attempts to get Hank out of the DuBois (a "terrible" school). Although unsuccessful, Mrs. Nelson has not given up trying. She encourages Hank not to give up on school even though he finds it boring.

Her realism, like Hank's, is balanced with optimism and an expectation that things can be changed: "I've always been able to adjust myself most anywhere. If I'm there, all right; if I want to up and leave, just up and leave." Regarding her neighborhood, for example, she feels it has become dangerous and rundown. She feels "suffocated" in their apartment and is trying to get out: "Here's hoping that I can find something else and I think I will."

Mrs. Nelson looks to "the children, both black and white," to affect changes in American life. She feels black children will feel secure vis-à-vis whites if their home life has been secure, regardless of poverty. It seems that her beliefs have been transmitted successfully to Hank, who even at 14, shares her optimism, determination, tolerance for others, and positive self-regard.

The Impact of Role Models.   Census workers would count Hank's family as a father-absent family. It is quite the contrary. Not only does he have two fathers, whom he sees regularly, but his older brother, Pete, offers a model of success and accomplishment in the outside world. Hank looks up to Pete, who served in the armed forces and lives on his own.

Hank's natural father, Mr. Nelson, usually stays at the mother's apartment from Friday night through Sunday; he and Hank go out for a beer and sandwich on Friday nights. Similarly, his mother is still friendly toward Roy—"he comes over whenever he wants to . . . he wants anything, she gives it to him." Hank likes Daddy Roy "a lot." They ride around in his fancy car and "just talk." "Whatever I need, he's glad to give it to me. If anything happens, he's always there." Hank looks to both men: he wants to be like his father, and feels closest to Daddy Roy, who he thinks loves him most.

When asked directly if there is an adult male Hank admires, Mrs. Nelson flatly replies, "no." She claims he does not talk much about such matters—and perhaps he does not to her. It appears that Hank's feelings for his father and Daddy Roy are private and have nothing to do with his mother. His interview testifies to secure, loving relationships with both men. His outings with them may be islands of masculine activity and banter which Hank, in his strivings for independence and autonomy, does not choose to share with his mother.

Gary T. Marx has found that morale, sophistication, and pride in oneself (all of which are developing well in Hank) are correlated positively with militancy among black males. He also found that these qualities are associated with "the most privileged and least socially isolated" blacks. While little argument could be made for Hank's family being numbered among the "most privileged," perhaps his lines into the world through father, Daddy Roy, and Pete help to reduce social isolation and to account for the relatively strong militancy which has evolved by Time II.[12]

Hank identifies with his mother because of her temper and because "she's not scared of anything . . . she knows what she wants and . . . things like that." The modeling goes further: Hank begins to say that he is different from his mother because she drinks a lot, "but I forgot, I drink too. We do mostly the same thing—but I can't do it in front of her face."

He goes on to note that he and his mother and father "are pretty much the same" especially when it comes to a fast temper and drinking. This may partially explain Hank's empathetic attitude toward his father: when his father starts yelling at him for something, Hank says, "I don't pay no attention to him, because he's messed up from the drink." Living through this experience has made Hank vulnerable to liquor, but also extremely cautious in preventing it from overwhelming his own life.

There is one way Hank takes his father as a negative role model. He feels that Mr. Nelson made a mistake by dropping out of school before graduation. When asked how he would feel if he were his father's age and had not become what he had wanted to be, Hank replies in one word which hints at the depth of his insight into his father's state of mind: "Disappointed."

Despite the favoritism problem, Bert serves as another influential model for Hank. He is tough, bitter, cold, resolute, good with the girls, and, like Hank, determined to get out of the house and on his own. Although they do not share many activities, they talk every night; more important, Bert had schooled Hank by age nine in the art of getting a girl to go to bed with him. Whenever Hank complains that he is discouraged by a girl's protestations, Bert tells him, "Don't do that, try and get what *you* want. Don't be a square."

Bert's attitude toward school also serves as a model for Hank. Bert has little use for school. He claims that (at age 16) he reads at the second grade level, because teachers have not helped him to learn. He never had a teacher he liked. He prides himself on never saying yes sir or no sir. Bert left the "special sixth" grade at the Boston disciplinary school at age 16, and refuses to engage in the job training programs offered him unless they include at least 50 percent reading—"I can't do it by myself." In spite of a physical disability (arthritis in his legs), Bert's toughness and determination are clear examples for Hank to follow. When asked if Hank helps him when he gets into a fight, Bert replies, "No. I don't need no help when I get in a fight."

Bert describes Hank's friends at Time I as "bad," especially Rocky—"he's the worsest one of them." He admires Hank's refusal to engage in the stealing: "When he's with his friends, you know, they get ready to do something, you know . . . I see him, and he don't do nothing with them." He feels that Hank is like his grandmother in being very generous, and predicts that Hank will not stay with the same peers for very long. "He want to be like the rest of them, you know, but he just ain't got it in him. . . . he ain't slick enough"—that is, Hank wants to be a part of the group but is not enough of a troublemaker to feel comfortable with it. As we have seen, Hank does find a more congruent peer group.

The decisive factor in the genesis of Hank's "together guy" style, I believe, is the presence of so many auxiliary role models in his set of significant others. When he is irritated with his mother, when he feels she is pressing him too hard, he can turn to Val or to his grandmother. They offer unconditional love and total acceptance of him as a person. This enables him to accept the qualities he loves in his mother—her stubbornness and determination, for example—without having to buy into her negative qualities. When he and his father cannot be together, Daddy Roy, who loves him "the most," takes him for a ride in his car. If his older brother Pete is away from the house, Hank still has Bert to teach him how to be a man in ways he can relate to. Even in his peer group, Hank has a set of friends he can shift toward when he finds the In-Crowd too deviant for him. Essentially, then, Hank is in the enviable position of being able to choose from among many loved and respected persons—who care deeply about him in return—for guidance and blueprints for growing up as a together guy.

Other Issues.   Control is a central issue for Hank. Being a together person implies being aware of one's ego boundaries, and being able to establish and preserve them even in the most intimate situations.

Hank controls his behavior and his temper in order to create an image of himself which he can live with and which will help him achieve his long-term goals. He limits his mother's ability to define him, by walking away from abusive encounters. Less than we could expect of a 14-year-old, he does not permit others to intrude into the space he carves for himself. He is adept at assessing social situations and thus paves the way for the most appropriate and effective responses to them. As Sites points out:

The well person, from both a social and a psychological point of view, is in control of himself in relation to a situation. He can judge social situations for what they are in terms of his relationship to them and use the necessary control devices to realistically optimize his position both socially and psychologically. These, of necessity, always operate together, in terms of perception and of action; a feedback loop is always present between the social and the psychological.[13]

Although Hank is not enamored of school, he plods on, realizing that he must finish his diploma in order to attain his goals. He has learned how to work and discipline himself without becoming compulsive; his determination is a quality which, everyone agrees, will pave his way to a fulfilling future. Keith Sutton, our Conformist, works hard to finish high school as well. The difference is that Keith is working for others as much as for himself (if not more so); there is no evidence in Hank's transcript that he pursues his goals, controls his less constructive impulses, in order to please anyone but himself.

Hank's Alternatives. The major alternative to Hank's dominant "together" style is the tough style of many people around him. If it had not been for his auxiliary models and the expressions of love from his family, he would have walked a pathway much closer to Leroy's.

Aside from the violence in his family, Hank is enmeshed in what Cloward and Ohlin refer to as a conflict gang; the use of fighting to gain or retain status is common. It is also to some extent a retreatist gang because of the extensive use of alcohol by most of the members, including Hank. Both types Cloward and Ohlin see originating in communities in which social disorganization is high and social control is low or weak. Out of frustration at not being able to "make it" in terms of conventional norms and means, boys in such areas are drawn into neighborhood gangs through a need for achievement.[14] This seems to be true of Leroy Duncan and his friend Duke.

Though Hank's status in the gang was enhanced by his sexual exploits, his ability to fight, his participation in sports, and his loyalty, that he pulled away can be explained by his increasing perception of himself as *able* to work within more conventional means and norms and therefore, with increasing age, his decreasing need of the gang for status and a sense of achievement. Walter B. Miller's view is similar. He describes tough behavior, with its focal concerns of trouble, smartness, excitement, fate, luck, and autonomy, as a product of socialization into the American "slum subculture." He claims that boys in a setting like Hank's in Roxbury are so isolated from middle-class culture that they ignore conventional norms and values, substituting their own aggressive masculine toughness.[15]

Yet, as Short and Strodtbeck point out, it is not so much that these youths are isolated from mainstream values. The mass media infiltrate every corner of American life, and the schools proclaim them even in so-called ghetto areas. Nor is it that they do not in fact share them—the boys in Short and Strodtbeck's study in Chicago held stable jobs and family life high in their aspirations, just as almost every Pathways youth holds the good life of suburban marital and job success as primary values. Having these values is not attaining them, however, and the gang provides a "strategic context in which deviant behavior, with its attendant risks, serves as a means of status-management and success."[16]

For Hank the concerns of trouble and excitement are slowly annulled by his personal growth in the direction of autonomy. Eventually, risk-taking—which confers status in the gang—becomes too costly and incongruous. He opts for success through school and work, which he knows can be threatened by his remaining in "conflict" gang activities. Thus his most viable alternative to being together loses out; he shifts away from the In-Crowd and throws his time and loyalty toward the less deviant Vince.

Analytical Dimensions. Hank's interpersonal orientation lies toward the positive end of the affiliation dimension. In moving toward others, he shows respect for himself and for them. With room to grow in, Hank will love and work well. Evidence for this can be found in his mother's description of him as caring, playful, attentive, "soft" toward her younger grandchildren; at the time of her last interview, she reported that Hank was trying to get a job at the YMCA for the summer, "watching over young children." Hank feels good about himself; positive social interaction is familiar to him. He shows the capacity for empathic and sensitive understanding of himself and others which should enable him to form meaningful bonds in the future without violating his ego boundaries.

In terms of power, Hank is neither dominant nor submissive. He copes with everyday situations well, showing a strong sense of agency and effectiveness. His orientation is motivated by a wish to express himself, not to dominate others or to be dominated by them. He is high on initiative, independence, and willingness to take the consequences of his choices. Conversely, he is low on guilt feelings and is able to tolerate the anxiety that stems from failing consistently to meet the expectations of significant others.

Hank is also low on maneuvering, manipulation, posturing, and deception. His concern for personal integrity and authenticity indicates a sincere and spontaneous orientation. He places an extremely high value on honesty, and appears to believe in who he is. His style is less rigid than others. He is able to fight, withdraw, conform, and so forth as he sees fit—always in the service of preserving his integrity. He is not trapped in a fixed way of interacting with others. The range of alternatives available to him is limited only by his realism and sense of autonomy.

On the secure/defensive dimension, it is obvious that Hank is secure, competent, self-respecting, and equipped with enough internal strength and insight to avoid the need for defensive behavior. His self-image is positive and graced with a clarity that belies his years. He knows who he is and who he wants to be, and is not afraid to try hard to achieve his goals. One feels after reading his transcript that Hank will remain together, and will indeed "be a man."

Conclusion

We see the "together guy" style emerging from a family situation that, while problematic in some ways, also provides positive modeling from both male and female adults, and support for the development of autonomy, self-esteem, and authenticity.

The broken relationships among the adults in his family and the open rivalry between Hank and his nephew appear to be counterbalanced by the positive elements in his family life. Hank has derived a fundamentally positive orientation toward others—mainly, I believe, through his fathers and brother; this orientation appears to serve him well in his relationships with others outside his family.

The greatest lesson in Hank's case is that the people around him—by and large—have accepted him on his own terms. Glaringly absent are messages from others denying his personhood, his uniqueness, his ability to do well. In addition, no one has tried to program Hank to be a doctor or lawyer or mechanic or anything but a good person who is responsible for himself and respectful of others. He, among all our cases, has been given freedom. Even though it has been offered within certain clear-cut limitations, because the limitations lack rigidity and derive from genuine concern about Hank, his freedom has been emotionally significant.

Toward Times II and III

We have seen how each of five boys has dealt with the internal and external pressures we spoke of in the first chapter in defining strategic style.

Each of them has had to cope with unique and sometimes excruciatingly complex family constellations. For each one the critical issue in generating his strategic style has been different: guilt for Keith, rejection for Ernie, violence for Leroy, normative lying for Dave, favoritism for Hank. As we visit the boys later in their adolescence, we have the opportunity to discern the legacy these issues have carried with them.

I just got older, that's all.

—KEITH

My own mind changed me.

—DAVE

7. Toward Manhood *Growth and Change in Styles over Time*

Strategic Styles Revisited

Three to five years after Time I, we take another look at the lives of the five boys.[1] Although life circumstances and maturity have altered the picture somewhat, portraits drawn in their late teens bear a striking resemblance to the earlier ones.

Keith is still the Conformist, Leroy is still the Tough Guy, and so on for all five boys. The strategic styles evident in early adolescence were not spurious by-products of a particular stage in the process of identity formation. The same styles are still very much operative in late adolescence—indelibly drawn, it seems, from the original portraits.

Keith. "I have a nice personality."

Keith Sutton, "all right guy" (Conformist) at Time I, is an "all right guy" at Time II, age 17. He has become more militant racially, more aware of black issues and figures, and seems much surer of himself than at Time I. As predicted, he appears to be moving slowly toward the "together guy," but is still very much bound up in following parental prescriptions and proscriptions.

As at Time I, Keith appreciates "nice" people (his parents and friends) and a "nice" neighborhood. He wants to live in the suburbs, where it is quiet and clean. When asked if any major incidents have occurred in his life since Time I, he replies: "I just got older, that's all." This statement seems innocently and incredibly accurate; it is as though Keith had been set on a one-directional track at age 12 (or earlier), which he continues to follow unwaveringly. The only obvious thing that has changed significantly about Keith is his age. He is cooperative, "nice," kind, responsible—a striving, achievement-oriented youth whose focal concerns are, without question, school, work, and sports. The "whininess" and "sneakiness" significant others mentioned at Time I seem to have given over to a forthright self-assurance.

Keith's relationship with his parents and grandfather remain positive. He feels equally loved by both parents, although he is a little closer to his father ("he's not too hard on me"), whom he confides in and wants to be like. He argues a little with his grandfather over which television program will be watched; his mother "fusses" at him about going to church on Sundays (he complies). Other than this mild tension, Keith describes his parents' marriage and general family atmosphere as "pretty happy." His girl friend has a "good personality," and they get along well. He predicts that he will get married someday to someone who will "agree with me," reflecting the high value he places on harmony and getting along with others. He sees himself in terms very similar to Time I: "I have a nice personality; I don't argue much; I'm usually nice to everyone." He is hard pressed to say how others would describe him, but settles for "I'm a nice guy . . . I do a lot of work." Symbolically, he would tell the spy at Time II to "act, you know, natural . . . like quiet and everything . . . real good." He does not drink or smoke, fight, steal, or violate the law in any way. In response to questions dealing with infractions of the law or trouble of any sort, he responds, consistently and emphatically, "Never."

Keith's self-concept remains high: "Anything I like I can do." He scores 37 high answers out of 50 on a self-esteem scale given at Time II. His perseverance and motivation seem to have strengthened since we first talked with him, when others wished he had a little more ambition. Now Keith seems ready to make his school and occupational choices on the basis of *his* likes and dislikes rather than predominantly on the basis of parental pressures. He also seems able to work toward achieving his goals with determination and creativity.

Keith and his parents seldom disagree violently. If they do, Keith says, "I always go by what they say." This is as much out of love and respect at Time II as it was out of duty and lack of strength at Time I. If his peers want him to do something his parents would disapprove of, he "wouldn't do it . . . I usually think about it myself, I just make my own decision, that's all." His development appears to be in the direction of increased autonomy and strong affiliation with others.

Perhaps the most significant factor in his life—complementing his affectionate and supportive family—is the friendship of Mr. Shore, a black store owner for whom Keith has worked since age 12. Mr. Shore, who attended two years of college and intends to complete his own education in the near future, encourages Keith to earn a college degree. This serendipitous relationship is paving the way to Keith's dreams of the "good life." Mr. Shore is instrumental in getting Keith into an Upward Bound program at a local college, and promises to pay half of Keith's tuition if he decides to go to the city university after high school. Although Keith tests out at Time I at a relatively low IQ of 88—96 on the Verbal Section and 82 on the Performance—support from others and his conformist style enable him to work toward fulfilling his aspirations and his potential (which, of course, may be much higher than the IQ tests indicated).

Mr. Shore adds to Keith's already very positive set of male role models. He takes Keith everywhere he goes, even to pick up fresh vegetables at 5 A.M. three days a week. He trusts Keith, allowing him to run the store for days at a time when he takes a vacation. This enables Keith to develop a greater sense of competence and responsibility, and provides an important message toward his growing autonomy.

It is not surprising that Keith wants to own and manage his own store after college or business school. He says he knows what it is like, feels competent in dealing with people and figures, and enjoys the work. He claims Mr. Shore will help him set up his own store when the time comes, another gesture of support which rewards Keith for his increasing maturity. It is significant, and certainly in keeping with Keith's strategic style, that he has found a man to work for who has land, money, connections, and the interest in Keith to help propel him toward his goals.

The messages from others reinforce his conformist style. Mr. Sutton tells his son that he is different from other boys his age because he is responsible and "straight." Keith shares this view of himself and shows a great deal of pride in his accomplishments. He has worked extremely hard to keep up with the students in his suburban high school (to which he has been bused since the eighth grade). As predicted, his tendency toward "moving with" others has facilitated success for him there. Despite the blindness of his left eye, he is first-string quarterback for the high school football team.

There is a shift toward more autonomy. Keith associates with white people, mostly from his school, but his friends are all black. He says he would have a white friend if he wanted to, even if others criticized him for it: "I figure it's my business what I do anyway." He wears an Afro, calls himself "black," shows higher than average racial awareness, and seems to have a high degree of racial pride: "I'm happy the color I am." As his brother Frank predicted at Time I, Keith has been able to get along with "whitey" in a way that Frank thought he would not be able to do himself. Yet Keith has not "moved with" the whites, regardless of their behavior. He has participated in two separate (nonviolent) protests at his school against a white teacher and a white janitor who allegedly made disparaging remarks about blacks. When asked how a teacher earns his respect, he replies: "Well, if she respects me, I'll respect her . . . if she treats me right."

As at Time I, Keith's friends at Time II support and reinforce his "all right guy" style. They all have good personalities, work, play sports, and attend school regularly. (Keith claims that he does not hook school—when he does not feel like going, he simply tells his parents and does not go. They respect his judgment and trust him not to miss more school than he should—and he does not.) He still hangs out with Alfie, though only on weekends. He is friendly with three black boys from his school and another boy who works at the variety store with him. None is involved in theft, drug use, playing hookey, or any other sort of trouble, in or out of school.

Echoing his sentiments at Time I, Keith at 17 tells the interviewer that if a "spy" were to take his place for a week, he would have to act "natural . . . like quiet and everything, you know. Real good." At school the spy would have "to keep pace with them kids, and don't be arguin' with them and everything." It is clear that he sees his own conformist style as an asset and a strategy.

With his clarity of aspirations, the support of family and of Mr. Shore, his personal stamina, and his determination, I expect that Keith will eventually become a "together guy." He is resolving his adolescent identity crisis in the direction of initiative, industry, and positive self-concept. He is increasingly able to express himself as an individual separate from the adult forces and models who propel him toward the good life of stable family and career. Yet he remains openly affectionate with those he loves—his moving away from submissiveness is not paralleled by diminished affiliation.

The picture at Time II is quite the opposite for Ernie Hayes, also 17.

Ernie. "I don't go out too often."

Ernie is still the "withdrawn kid" whose quiet, shy ways remain pivotal in his orientation toward others. At the heart of his strategic style are fear, insecurity, guilt, inferiority, and confusion about who he is. Ernie continues to distance himself from most others, ensconced in a cocoon from which contacts with people seem more like unwelcome skirmishes than customary sociability. In fear and mistrust he has restricted his aspirations and his efforts in the realms of school, work, and interpersonal relationships.

Mr. Hayes has turned the third-floor attic of their home into an apartment for Ernie and brother Teddy, thereby legitimizing their escape to this isolated and safe refuge from family quarrels and inner strife. By Time II, Teddy has moved out; he has fathered a child and is on the run from police for truancy charges. Ernie shifts his alliance from Teddy to young Pam next door, who has had a child by someone else.

Ernie and Pam spend hours in their third-floor hideaway. Ac-

cording to the interviewer, he treats Pam and her baby with love
and care. It is almost as if he keeps them as compatible pets, who
help to ward off the loneliness that inevitably stems from Ernie's
self-imposed exile. With Teddy gone, Ernie names Pam as his best
friend: "She's not too noisy." (He still sees Paul, his "best friend"
from Time I; Paul visits him and falls asleep on the couch while
Ernie writes a letter or builds a model.) Later in the interview he
says he really does not have any friends (echoing his father)—he
just sees people on occasion.

His father further legitimizes Ernie's inclination to retreat by allowing him to drink when they go out together. Ernie drinks a
great deal at home also, having switched from glue-sniffing. Other
than visits to bars with his father, Ernie restricts his social activities carefully: "I don't go out too often." He says his mother
would describe him as "a little bashful . . . a little shy . . . that I try
to dress nice . . . and she might say it's hard for me to say something." (She would be correct on all counts.) His father would say
he is "shy"—and "He might say I'm bright, but I don't think that's
right." His best friend would say, "I'm quiet and probably say I
don't like a lot of noise and I don't like to play a lot." His worst
enemy, if he had one, might say, "I don't jive around or say, like,
that I only like one girl friend and if I have a girl friend I don't play
around with no other girls."

As at Time I, Ernie sketches his family in broad strokes of hostility, passiveness, lack of trust, and a paucity of affection. He says
he is like his father in that they both collect old junk, hoarding it
in their rooms until Mrs. Hayes asks them to throw it out. If they
refuse, she will throw it out right in front of their eyes. When
asked how often he and his family do things together, he says,
"never," then amends that to "very seldom," adding that they play
badminton in the yard in warm weather. He says that a social
worker comes to their house once a week "to talk about costs and
tries to find out why we don't like living together or what, or why
we do, and all that junk."

That his mother throws his "junk" out is matched in kind by his
father's lack of responsiveness. Ernie mentions that his father "just
lays resting on the table" when his little sister misbehaves. This is
reminiscent of Mishler's finding that families of schizophrenic
sons showed lower responsiveness or "acknowledgment" toward

their children than did control families.[2] He also found "an absence of genuine warmth and expressiveness," a kind of "pseudo-mutuality" and coldness among family members.[3] Ernie claims that when his parents do notice misbehavior, it is, as before, greeted with beatings or being banished to one's room. He is hard pressed to choose which parent loves him the most.

Except for the hoarding, Ernie denies taking after either parent. He feels closest to older brother Abby and feels there are few others to whom he could turn if he were in trouble: "There would only be a few people that I would turn to, and then I got reasons why I wouldn't turn to them—so that leaves only Abby." Ernie does not mention Pam in this regard. He says that if the police were chasing him, Teddy would tell him to turn himself in—rather than protect him—and his parents would tell them, "He's upstairs sleeping or something."

Thus Ernie lives in a hostile environment, which he reduces to manageable size by restricting the number of people he must deal with. He drops out of school in the ninth grade. He works "a little" for his uncle, painting and plastering. After work he comes home and sleeps. If it is warm, he sits out in the yard with books and puzzles . . . he has no street life to speak of.

In stark contrast to the life he leads at Time I and II, with its shrunken boundaries and troubled apathy, is the life Ernie says he would like to lead in the future: "*Active* . . . working a lot and moving around a lot . . . work, and when you get out from work, take a quick ride someplace and on the weekend go to Canada, the Cape . . . do a lot of sports." He attempts to put this image into reality. Ironically, though, as if nailing the last peg into his battened-down existence, he pulls a ligament in his knee when he tries to play a game of ball. He is hospitalized for a week—a "terrible experience"—"I just wanted to be at home." He has been told that his other knee may develop the same problem. The injury makes it difficult to play or to help his uncle. This physical lameness, added to the interpersonal element, threatens to prevent him from leading the active life he dreams of.

Ernie laments quitting school, realizing that being a drop-out will further hamper his chances of success in life. That he dropped out is no surprise, however. He responded to the anxieties in school the same way he responds to them in other arenas—he "moves away." It is school that has been his nemesis all along, in spite of his IQ score of 128 at Time I. He can barely remember the sequence of schools he has attended since Time I. When he left the DuBois, he tried to go to Boston Trade, but the step was enormous for him: "I'd walk right up to the school and turn around and go up someplace else." Someplace else was usually the attic.

He was sent to a disciplinary school for chronic truancy; when he later tried to reenter Trade, they refused to admit him. He ploughed through red tape, fulfilling requests that one school normally makes of another (transcripts, records, etc.), in an unusual demonstration of determination. Every move was an obstacle of major proportions. The school wins: when they ask him to bring a teacher down to Trade to *prove* he has taken a certain course, Ernie folds under the pressure and gives up—"I just said, forget it." As with his family, trust and concern about him as a person are woefully absent.

His fear of failure indicates his lack of security. He tries to make sense of this harrowing experience by making the best of it. He adds that he really did not want to go to school anyway, because he had to get up so early and because he thought he would fail English ("I didn't even understand their way"). But he admits that he should have persisted since he knows that to be a carpenter (his first job choice), he must finish high school. Now he is two years behind and is toying with the notion of returning, even though school is painful for him. His parents called him "idiot, idiot" when he dropped out. Some of his teachers said it was a shame, since he did well in school despite his poor attendance. He claims that in art and printing he attended only about a quarter of the time, but could make the work up so well and so quickly that the teachers passed him.

Ernie has little insight into why he has hooked school during his teen years. He says school is not particularly boring; sometimes it was more fun outside, sometimes more fun inside. Occasionally he could make a little money working on his afternoons away from school, but he does not list that as a prime reason for hooking. Occasionally he would ride in a friend's car, but that, too, seems like a peripheral activity. More important is that he did not like to get up early, did not like to be called on (dreaded it, in fact), could not pay attention (the glue?), would arrive late and not know what the assignments were, hence failed or became confused, was un-prepared because he would not take down homework assignments . . . or forgot to do them. Lack of effort, motivation, and involve-ment (fear of failure?) seem to have combined to create feelings of apathy and anxiety in their own right, making school an over-whelmingly threatening place for Ernie. As though symbolic of his whole school experience, he states emphatically that he "hated music—they made me sing in front of the class."

Reflective of his own retreatist style is that all his friends from Time I have left school, as has sister Donna. All have drifted from one menial job to another. When asked how he feels about this, Ernie replies: "I don't have that many friends anyway, 'cause I don't go around that much you know. But I think they should go back if they're not going to get a job."

Ernie's self-esteem is only slightly lower than Keith's at Time II—34 high answers out of 50 questions. He feels he is good in art and building models. He says he is "serious" when he does his art—other boys are too busy rapping with the girls—and when he works on his models, he is patient and careful, waiting for the glue to dry on one section before proceeding to the next. Other boys try to rush it. He feels inept at sports, rapping with girls, or getting along with others. He feels proud, though, that at least he can be "polite," something that other boys are short on: "I can't stand it, not to be polite." This is his only interpersonal skill. I surmise that his proficiency in physical/mechanical skills (which produces the high self-esteem score) is far outweighed in everyday living by his paralysis when it comes to dealing with people.

Ernie's racial awareness is still relatively low, although he feels "black power" is important and wants blacks to be equal to whites. As in other areas of the interview, his answers are often confused and contradictory. He changes them often and fre-quently relies on "I don't know." He feels blacks are more likely to attack whites than vice versa, because he hears boys on his street saying "let's get him" when a white man walks by. He says he does not hate whites, yet admits that he and Teddy took pleasure in throwing rocks at whites during the 1967 Roxbury riot. He would not go to a white person's house, as at Time I, more because it implies a social situation than a racial one. Typically, Ernie says that the rioting makes him want to leave the country altogether. He would not take the pill to make him white:

I might hide it in a real safe place because if I took it I might be sorry . . . but there might be a real emergency, like say they were going to kill all the niggers; I wouldn't take it then 'cause I'd die with my people. I'd probably just hide it just to keep it there, but don't think I'd take it.

He says his neighborhood has deteriorated drastically since Time I—he seems to connect this in his own mind with the fact that the area has gone from almost all-white to almost all-black.

Ernie feels things are opening up occupationally for blacks, but his own rejection of school as a means of upward mobility has left him empty-handed. He has made some attempts to get work through job training programs, but is easily discouraged and frightened away by having to make connections. One job as a rough carpenter on a high-rise building downtown paid well and pleased Ernie. It was cold and windy, but he appreciated the good pay. (As one of the jobs he does not see many blacks working in, Ernie lists carpentry first.) If he does not return to school, he thinks he may get a job working with his father in electronics. Conspicuously absent is his dream of becoming a chemist.

Ernie, then, has not changed much since Time I. He is perhaps a little more articulate about himself, perhaps somewhat more willing to make at least a tentative, initial effort to carve his place in the world. But he lacks the determination, the self-confidence, the internal security, and the support from others which he needs to break out of his family's ghetto cage and the cocoon he has woven to protect himself from the elements of his everyday life. Unless some dramatic event occurs in his life to help him gain the assurance and trust he so sorely lacks, I expect he will continue to be the "withdrawn kid" into his adult years—following, as it were, the restricted path his father has taken before him.

Leroy, too, has not changed his strategic style.

Leroy. "I just bust out."

At 17 Leroy Duncan is a carbon copy of himself at age 13. At 20 the copy is the same, except that the impression is drawn with sharper and bolder lines. He is still fighting, making trouble, battling himself and others, hurtling headlong toward jail, death, self-destruction.

The words in these later interviews seem all too familiar, spoken in tone and intention as they were at Time I. The trouble is more serious, the fighting leads to a more violent climax than before. Leroy seems to have lost some of the self-control he had at Time I—he laments that he is getting "too fresh," talking back even to relatives—"I never used to do that. [I'd] like to be like I used to be, in a way. Go to work every day, be more frank with people. Now I am not."

Leroy still relishes telling the interviewer about his trouble-making exploits. The risk, the excitement, the challenge are still there. But a coldness runs through the stories that was only suggested at Time I. Leroy seems no longer to have any guilt, any fear. The fighting is automatic, emotionless—he is seemingly impervious to the grotesque realities of the risks and possible consequences to which his behavior lead. He relates one incident:

Happened about four weeks ago. There was this white dude at Washington Street. This was around three A.M. in the morning; I was coming from the Hill. No one was out there. I bumped into him because I didn't see him—it was too dark. So he said, "Aren't you going to say anything?" You know, he started it. I said, "You better get the hell away from me." I didn't feel like being bothered with anyone. So he came up to me and grabbed me and started punching me. So I said, "Wow!" I grabbed him and threw him down, stomped on him. Just left him there. I didn't even know if he was dead or alive. I know his last name 'cause I knew him from someplace. Next thing I heard was . . . I saw on the police blotter he had a broken neck.

This experience bears a striking resemblance to his father's so many years ago on those same Roxbury streets, when white men attacked him and in self-defense he accidentally killed one of them, and was sent up for manslaughter. Yet Leroy does not seem to feel the agony that his father did, or the screaming sense of injustice. Leroy, of course, is lucky—he is not apprehended. It is just another fight that he walks away from unscathed.

Fights with Bart, at Time I his closest sibling, have taken on a similarly cold and compelling tone. Now they fight until someone breaks them up or until they are too tired to fight any longer. He and Bart both drink heavily. They live in their own apartments away from their parents. When Bart is drunk, he thinks he "can whip the world," says Leroy. Stevie remains at home, where Mr. Duncan routinely beats him. Leroy feels protective toward Stevie and tells of pulling his father off the young boy. His father has returned to drinking, in spite of his stomach ailments, bent apparently on self-destruction and oblivion. Says Leroy: "Can't understand him the way he is now. The liquor is messin' up his mind . . . forgets quickly. Before, you could, you used to be able to talk with him, ask his advice. But now all he wants to do is hang on street corners and drink; he don't want to be bothered with anyone." He tells Leroy he is old enough to solve his own problems. Apparently Mr. Duncan, who fought to keep himself sober and sane enough to care for and protect his children through their early years, has given up, put his children in the hands of fate. His failure rate is high and must in itself be devastating: Bart is in jail by Time III for armed robbery; Benny is married, runs around with other men's wives, drinks, and fights; Leroy brushes imprisonment and death at every turn; Stevie is a thief but is slick enough not to get caught. In many ways the story of Leroy is the story of his father, relived and retold a generation later.

At age 17 Leroy feels that he has changed for the worse. He is more short-tempered than ever. He is deeply embroiled in trouble: "a lot of things—fights, jail, arguments—more than I ever had." He is supersensitive, tough, touchy, a walking stick of dynamite that can be ignited at any moment by the smallest thing: "I just bust out." He says his mother might describe him as "O.K., but don't get me rowdy sometimes 'cause then I might cut your throat." His father would say that he was "evil." "I don't like people to put their hands on me and what not. Oh yeah, he would talk nasty, just nasty about me. Oh, he'll say I'm a thief." He says he has heard both his parents say these things about him—the questions and answers are not hypothetical.

He sees Duke occasionally, most often to pull a job; but his best friend now is Buddy, 18, who, Leroy claims, would describe him in this way: "O.K. You can get along with me—get in trouble, I'll help you out. I think he'd tell a person maybe 'keep on guard,' that I'm short-tempered or something." He concurs with this characterization of him. Others must be on guard around him, as he himself is always on guard in a hostile and injurious environment. He says he is good at running, wrestling, playing basketball, joking around with his friends, making them laugh. As at Time I, he feels relatively competent in dealing with the physical world; but his score on the Coopersmith is low (27 high answers out of 50), pointing to his generally negative self-image.

His secondary style of retreatism is exemplified at Time II by his reluctance to socialize with his three roommates. He is close to Buddy, but prefers watching television or sleeping to going out with the roommates: "I don't want to go . . . you know, and I don't know why . . . I don't have anything to do." He and Buddy spend their time drinking and fighting—each other and anyone who gets in their way. He has found a man in his twenties, Roger, who in some ways replaces the father he has "lost." Roger takes him riding in his car; they "talk to women, have a ball." It is Roger to whom Leroy feels closest:

Roger helps me out more than anyone else does when I get into trouble; he always asks me if I want to borrow his rifle . . . blow a person away. Offers to help me in fights—twice when I was going to have a fight with someone else, he ask me if I wanted him to take my place.

Both his friends share his troublemaker style and his preoccupation with violence, at once rewarding and reinforcing it.

At Time I, Leroy said he would rather work than steal. He has long been out of school, but tries through Manpower to work at odd jobs in the Boston area. He says he likes being a stock boy, and indeed works at that for stretches of a month at a time. He wants to be a plasterer but says he is "nervous" and lacks the "spirit" needed to learn it. His hold on work seems tenuous at best, relying on others for rides and landing in jail too often to stay at one place very long. (He spent two months in city jail for breaking and entering; other skirmishes with the law take him out of circulation for a day or two.)

Leroy looks forward to the good life, "living good—clean house, good job, good pay, do what I want to do. Have a nice house, car, maybe a wife." But he also says he would "shack up" with a girl but not marry; if he were to marry, it would be to a woman who is unlike "most of the women I know who go into barrooms every night, mess with different boys." (His father met his mother in a bar.) He wants a "nice, easygoing girl, not too rowdy, clean," but he still is afraid of women, and is painfully shy when sober:

I see girls occasionally, only when I'm high. That's the only time I can face them. I don't have to worry about what to say to them, about having a relationship with them. When I'm high I just come out with it.

He does not want children: "The way kids are today, I just don't want any, period. I don't think I am a father image, that's all." In the distant future, he might like a daughter . . . "be less trouble than a boy." He says later that he knows a woman with boys and they are "wild—sometimes I just feel like pressin' their brains out, you know."

He regrets not having a high school diploma. That is the second strike against him, he knows, in addition to his color. Some of Stevie's female friends were admiring Stevie's diploma—"they went crazy over it. They asked me where mine was and I told 'em I lost it. I wish I woulda had one then . . . all I had to show was a happy and sad face." He is referring to the mask he made in woodworking shop back in the seventh grade. (The symbolism of the mask is powerful, paralleling his own words at Time I regarding feeling happy and sad about being in trouble.) He thinks white people are smarter—"they seem like they have learned more than us, 'cause they've been taught better . . . they pay more attention than us blacks do in their work." (At Time I he spoke of his inability to pay attention in school.) The good life seems unattainable in the face of all these societal and personal obstacles. One feels that he knows this but simply cannot utter the words, lest he verbally seal his fate.

We are fortunate that Leroy is one of the boys interviewed at Time III. At the age of 20 he is on general relief, working on and off, living alone, with others, or with his parents, a few days or weeks at a time, never settling down to one place and one routine. Only the fighting and trouble persist, forming a thread he can hold on to, the warp through which all other events and activities are woven. When asked what has been going on in his life since Time II, he replies:

Me and these other fellows would gather around with Joe, get drunk, go out, start some shit, you know [laughs]. Have a little party. Fight a while. Me and him have a little beef some time ago, got busted up and what not, went to jail . . . from then on I kept on gettin' in trouble, drinkin' practically every day, um hum.

He is on a four-year suspended sentence for his implication in the stabbing of a young woman. He has put his hand through another window, this time receiving 30 stitches and permanently damaging some tendons. He robs with Duke, the victims always white. The coldness remains. He tells of robbing a man in the subway station:

When he turned his back, Duke grabbed him, and I went into his pocket and got his loose change and a white envelope that contained $600. He yelled out: "This is my vacation money!" We said, "We don't give a damn," and stomped him in his mouth and kept him crying 'til we got away [laughs].

Having had contact with Leroy over a six-year period, the interviewer tries to fathom Leroy's motivation for trouble-making. He claims that the cause is "the booze"—yet at Time I, long before he drank regularly, he was a tough and trouble-oriented person. The drinking seems to legitimize his behavior in Leroy's eyes: it isn't really me, it's the rosé or the vodka. But he knows he is only fooling himself. Why does he steal? "I guess I kept doin' it 'cause they was there. And afterwards I wish I had never did it. Um hum" (laughs). Why does he put his hand through a window? "You don't think about it, you know, you so mad that it's right there and you just knock it out [laughs] and that's it. After you're cut you think about what you did, you look at the window. Then you're bleeding so bad you go to the hospital." What makes him get into trouble?

Well, I don't know, it just happens. We go outside, you know, when I have a fight, go places. . . . we go to a party or whatever, or a lounge . . . and a fight starts, and we all grab bottles, you know, and get ready to beef and beat each other's brains out right there . . . or we just go out looking for trouble [laughs]. That's with the whities . . . bump into persons and knock them down for fun, try and upset cars, tear off car antennas [laughs] for no reason at all. That's trouble right there.

How does he feel about it? "I don't feel any guilt" (laughs). He claims that the trouble is fun, exciting. He adds that he does not like whites. "They're just there, so we mess with them . . . I'm not getting even, I'm just bothering them." The cost is hangovers, beatings by the police, upset stomach in the morning. He can lay off the liquor for a couple of days if he needs to (the interviewer probes enough to determine that Leroy is not actually an alcoholic in the physiological sense)—but "when I don't drink, I don't have any fun." When he is sober, he is "shy"—"when I'm high, I would tire you" (much laughter). Drinking gives him "more courage, don't give a damn then."

In the midst of this introspectiveness, and at the very end of the Time III interview, Leroy finally admits that he fights with his mother. When they argue, he gets "nervous"—"sometimes I feel like I want to hit her, I walk away; sometimes I lose my temper. That's it." This is a vital revelation (for himself as much as for the research); at this point the interviewer very cautiously (and wisely) asks him about his mother calling him names:

I used to really lose my temper; I call her bitch, get the hell out of my sight or I'll kill ya. Yeah. She called me son of a bitches, white mother-fuckers, she used to call me every name in the book, some names I never even heard of sometimes comin' out of her mouth! [Why?] Only 'cause we can't get along sometimes, you know, we look alike, and we both be black, you know.

The prediction that Leroy will continue "moving against" others seems gratuitous and pointlessly technical. The wounds he has suffered are abysmally deep and monumentally crushing. The real question is what alternative does he have but to continue fighting and cutting and stealing, letting the anger out, purging himself of the urge to kill? Guilt, inferiority, and identity confusion are wrapped up for him in the clenched fist and the slow burn that pull him along a path of self-destruction and ultimate defeat.

Gelles concludes from his research into the nature of family violence that the family provides "basic training for violence":

The empirical data . . . on homicide, assault, child abuse, violent crimes, and violence between family members definitely tend to indicate that violent individuals grew up in violent families and were frequent victims of family violence as children.[4]

Leroy has received excellent training.

Dave. "I just can't hook up and stay hooked up."

At 13, Dave Cooper was sneaky, devious, manipulative, high in dominance, and relatively low in affiliation. These characteristics, which mark his "put-on" style at Time I, have remained salient and bring him closer to "con artist" as he approaches later adolescence.

Dave says he has changed a lot since he was 13. Sixteen at Time II, he likes to be by himself quite a bit: "I got a lot to think about." Early in the interview he reveals the source of this dramatic statement: "I'm a junkie, for about a year now . . . I'm always that way." As at Time I, Dave does what he pleases, and hides his behavior from those who would not approve:

I woulda been like that today, but my girl friend was coming over and she don't like to see me that way. She gets mad. Folks don't know, but my brother knows. First I used to snort it, but now it's shooting it. Most of my friends are doing it, too, except for one friend. So if I do it, I don't tell him.

He claims that his real father (who once was a "junkie," he now reveals) knows about his drug use, and threatens to "beat his ass." Nothing comes of that threat, however, and Dave later says discipline in his family is almost never followed through. In fact, he says he gets along with mother, father, and stepfather because they all try to "give me what I want."

His attitude has changed over the years, Dave says. Now he gets high and does not want to be "bothered." Little things annoy him. He hits his girl friend in the face for "talking a little" to another boy. What bothers Dave the most, however, is a nagging sensation that he will not live long. His tuberculosis has flared up again; the doctors tell him not to smoke or use drugs because of a "bad lung." He persists. "Even before I started shooting up, I knew I wasn't going to live. They said I wasn't going to live too long. That's how come my mother don't yell at me like she used to." He says that sometimes when he goes to sleep he is afraid he will not awaken: "That's why I stay high." His prediction comes true. One day he overdoses: "I was sleeping and wouldn't wake up, and I had a fever." He spent a week in the hospital, barely squeaking through. This frightened him even more, but he tries to be philosophical about it: "What's the use? Just die a little younger. There ain't nobody that can help me about taking drugs, really, but myself."

His habit is costly in more ways than one, for it must be supported. "I'm a thief. I used to work, but one day I got high and just didn't go back." He claims to make from $65 to $300 per week, "stealing, robbing houses, people." Most of the money goes for drugs, the rest is spent on other people. He says his money "goes quick." He cannot seem to get ahead of himself. Dave's confusion and depression at this point in his life seem almost overwhelming. The sense of impending doom, the cycle of oblivion and theft which the drugs entail, seem to have blocked out the less self-destructive activities he used to engage in. He can no longer enjoy playing basketball, for example, because he is "too nervous" and "shaky." Stealing eats up his time as well. He is "in and out of the clink" for breaking and entering, disorderly conduct, and so forth. The stays are short (most cases against him are dismissed or yield only probation), but they interfere with his ability to go to school or work steadily.

Dave says he wants the "good life—if I live that long." He insists that he does not want to change his life or the way he is. His protestations notwithstanding, he seems at Time II to have a clearly negative self-image. He says he would advise sons (if he ever had any) to "watch out—and I wouldn't want them shooting up or nothing; become a junkie. Don't steal." As if to explain why he has not followed his own advice, he adds that he will give his children the money they need: "Money ain't nothing. That's what my mother says, too. But I need a *lot* of money, I'm greedy." Later, in response to a question about changes he would make if he could live his life over again, he immediately replies, "I wouldn't be a junkie." If he had his way, he would be "a child again," without the worries and responsibilities he has now.

Miraculously, in light of his drug use, Dave is officially still in high school. He has become very close to Mr. Capri, whom he knew at the DuBois also. Mr. Capri encourages Dave to stay in school, telling him that he knows he can do the work and understands that he is bored and tired. Dave visits him through the summer, talking to Mr. Capri and his wife ("she says she finds me interesting"). Mr. Capri is "different." Dave says, "He's got his own thing, he's straightforward, and he'll explain it to you if you got a problem." (This teacher happens to be very expressive and "cool," often a joker—a teacher many Pathways focal subjects choose as their favorite.)

Dave knows he "needs his education," and says his parents want him to graduate from high school "so they can brag." He likes school, in a way, for he can see "the girls." He feels he would have to get up just as early to go to work—and staying home is not a viable alternative—"My mother's home, and she'd be gabbing all the time, after me to do something, get out of the house. She hate me to be in the house." His temper keeps him on the brink of suspension, however; he strikes out at teachers who try to wake him up at his desk. At one high school he attended briefly, he started a riot when he punched a teacher.

Dave's old friend Aggie is still in school also. He "smokes grass, snorts heroin." Mouse, Butch, and Bones he no longer sees. They are in jail, he thinks. Another unnamed friend is a pool hustler. His closest friend, Carter, he describes as "cold." ("We grew up together and we do everything just alike.") The relationship is as close as any Dave forms (at one point he says he really has no *friends*, just acquaintances). The lack of trust and trustworthiness on Dave's part is evident. For example, Dave and Carter steal from some coats, one of which contains $2000. Dave tells Carter he finds only $50—"He would have wanted half, so I didn't tell him."

In any case, most of his time is spent with girls. He feels he is most loved by Terri and Louise, the two girls he is simultaneously dating. He is "in love" with Terri and wants to marry her, but Louise is pregnant, he says by him. (He and two friends were all having relations with her during the same period.) Dave rejects the child and cons a friend into thinking it is *his* child. The friend believes it and marries Louise, who goes along with the "deal." (She later dies of an overdose.) Her parents also support the deception: "They say let him think the baby is his."

His "spy" responses reveal the same acting and manipulativeness evident at Time I, as well as his high capacity for audience segregation:

[Around the house] act quiet, do what you're told, don't do it right away—give her a little lip. . . . get a girl up the house and say, "Don't bother me," things like that. [With friends] when they want money, beat around the bush—"I don't got any money." Later on . . . you give it to them . . . fool around first. [With girls] act hard and smooth at the same time. Can't let her boss you around. You do what she tells you once in a while, but when somebody's looking, you do it, do it smooth, so everybody won't say, "Oh, she's ordering you." You have to treat her nice, too. [At school] certain people you say "hi" to. When you get to class late, throw a smooth answer to the teacher, say "I'm sorry," like that.

The spy, at work, should do as he is told for the first few weeks, then if he is told what to do by the boss, should say, "Don't be on my back all the time."

He says he has thought about himself a great deal. He shows increasing insight into himself:

I got a different attitude; personality. Sometimes I'm quiet, sometimes I'm noisy . . . depends on my mood. I'm crazy, that's what they say. Always doing something funny . . . some people say I'm *too* crazy. I play around too much. I don't beat around the bush. I tell what I want . . . when I want something I just take it.

Dave says he is good at "rapping" with girls. He reads the newspapers avidly and feels that helps him: "It's being able to make conversation—I was always like that." He is a good thief, he says, because he is small and has a "rubber body." Yet despite his general expressiveness, his self-esteem may be low, judging by only 24 high answers out of 48 on that scale. He thinks he takes after his father—"I like to be free"—and describes him as "crazy," among other things: "He's always chasing somebody, mostly girls. He likes to drink. Likes to fool around too much. Gets too high. He's mean. I'd make him a little bit nicer." Initially he says he wants most to be like himself. After describing his parents (his mother is "weird"—likes to party and move around), he says he wants to be just like his mother: "Everybody likes her." His parents would agree that he has a "quick attitude" and "jokes around"—but it is his friend, Carter, who would give the most accurate description of him: "Dave, he's a smooth nigger. He's bad as . . . he's light-skinned. Got a big pretty Afro. Always making somebody laugh; he's nice to be with . . . a nice dude." His worst enemy would say, "he's bad . . . he's a homely little . . . he's smooth, but he's too smooth for his own good. He's gonna get cut some day." It is this last comment that is pivotal in Dave's life between Time II and III.

At Time II he reports that he has worked through Manpower, on and off, but has run into friction because he could not stand to be bossed around. His ideal job was still to be a judge, where his power over others is unchallenged—"I tell somebody they got to go away, and they can't say nothing." He was toying with the idea of pimping—it would make him the kind of money he needs— "but I don't want to . . . like Terri, she'd do it, but I like her too much." Yet by Time III (age 19) he admits that he has been pushing drugs and pimping for "four or five years," having only recently extricated himself from this highly dangerous and exploitative life.

This indicates that Dave was not being entirely frank at Time II (any more than he was at Time I). He was open about his drug use, but glossed over the fact that he was deep into pushing. He skirted the issue of pimping, claiming affection; but by his own admission three years later he has been at it for quite some time, *including* Time II: "Takin' money from women . . . that was the easiest thing to do, though, was take a broad's money, 'cause they so willing, you know, they gullible. All women is gullible."

At Time III Dave's strategic style remains that of "con artist"— yet he has managed to get himself off drugs and is bent on making it through high school and into a "good job." When the interviewer asks what has happened since he was 16, Dave replies "Wow! That's a long time, long time." He says at 16 he "just didn't have any sense." He was a "hell raiser," in a stage where he wanted others to pay attention to him:

You know, when you just hit that age and think you're cool. You go out in the streets and you be bip-bopping here and there. I was a "Watch me, I'm cool" person. I was takin' drugs, messin' around heavy, stealin' heavy, wasn't goin' to school . . . a lot went down. . . . I was one of them, you know, finga-poppin' niggers, walking around, doing what I wanna do, catch what I wanna catch, say what I wanna say . . . now it's a little different. I still do what I wanna do though, but I'm a little quieter.

He says he was "all the way into drugs." "I got in places that I had no business stickin' my dirty little nose into." The danger started getting to him. He was involved with too many people, he says, referring to other pushers he associated with:

I'd be a lieutenant. I had so many niggers under me. I was just rackin' up the money. I got away like a bandit all my life . . . I was hangin' out with niggers, you know, pimps, and prostitutes . . . I was out with the fast life.

Many of the people he was terrified of: Dave is "slick," not violent. One man pushed a gun into his stomach in the dead of night, demanding drugs. Dave insisted he was clean, but the man, desperate as he was, started leading him into the bushes. A friend intervened in a true cinematic *deus ex machina*. This incident and the drug overdose served to wake Dave up: "It really shook me up, and I really got over. And the year before that I got busted three times in one month, so I really straightened the nigger out [meaning himself]."

Getting older helps straighten Dave out, too. Alluding to stiffer sentencing for adults, Dave says "when you're young, you can hustle for a while and get over, but once you hit that 18 mark, it's over with . . . and I got away until I was 18 years old, then I took that fall [16 months probation for grand larceny] you ain't no kid no more, and you don't get treated like no kid." He feels he grew up too fast, knew too much too soon. Now he is legally an adult, out on his own, and he feels he must take care of himself. No one else will.

Part of the caring is laying off drugs; he relies on marijuana to relieve his anxieties. It is a "sedative." When asked how he got off hard drugs, he replies, "My own mind developed me." He says, in addition, people "taught me a lot." He mentions Mr. Capri and an older woman who is very straightforward and blunt, not a "phony." She befriended him, helped him, cared for him (he attributes his addiction in the first place to the fact that he "didn't dig" his home life).

He is facing the fact now that he has difficulty being close and loyal to anyone. He has no male friends to speak of; women are more useful to him, he says. He speaks of being tired of "drifting." He cannot maintain a relationship with a woman for more than six months; he leaves abruptly, "it's over." He sees the woman on the streets a few weeks later, and she asks him what went wrong: "I just got tired." This disturbs him. Later in the interview he says he has figured out what is missing in his relationship with his present girl, Amy:

Like I tried to hook up with this girl, right. Everything was cool, but one thing was missing was we really trust each other—but I really don't trust her . . . I just can't hook up and stay hooked up, you know, something's missing. I don't know what it is half the time.

This problem in affiliational poverty extends into other areas of his life as well. Dave shuts out the memory of the baby he had by Louise at age 17. It died of pneumonia, he thinks; he never speaks of Louise or the baby. He feels close to his younger brother ("that nigger's my heart") but he does not trust him. ("He's like a tape recorder, he runs off at the mouth too much.") He goes to the Cape to be with his father, caring for him before and after an operation, but admits to being annoyed with his father's ways. His oldest brother is in jail for murder—"He blew some nigger's head off"—and Dave has not been to visit him, although the prison is nearby. He rarely sees his sister (who now has seven children) and does not recognize his nephews and nieces when they approach him at his mother's house. He rarely visits his mother and refuses to give her his apartment telephone number.

Apart from trust and affiliation, the issue of domination persists for Dave. He complains of his mother's dominating ways:

It would be cool if she'd just lay low, stop trying to run somebody's life all the time . . . she's got my younger brother wrapped up doing what she wants, but I just can't do it. I'm not used to takin' orders.

This interferes with his relationships with women in general. To be close means to be dominated. He prefers to give orders or have no relationship at all, which he is quick to point out to anyone he dates.

As Dave enters early adulthood, he is still battling the legacy of insufficient affection and trust that has plagued him since early childhood. Until he can find ways of establishing these bonds, he will continue to approach others according to their usefulness to him. His manipulative tendencies will persist, and block, in their own right, his chances for establishing permanent and meaningful affectional bonds. The style is unchanged; only the means have shifted. After drugs and pimping he looks to opening a child care center to make his money. He speaks of twisting things financially to fill his pockets (primarily manipulating government funds). He says he would not neglect the children, as some centers do (although he "hates kids"); but he would work the system to his advantage. After pimping and pushing, he lists "government and politics" as ways to make big money. Interpersonally, the shift is similar. He does not "go through that violence trip" anymore: "I'd rather just work it out. You know, I felt like if you get back at somebody through their brain, that hurts more. You know, that's just what I been doin', play with somebody's mind, let it kill them." This manipulativeness, using such verbal means as questioning and challenging the other's motivation and state of mind, takes on a psychological bent which, he admits, "backfires" on occasion. He thinks this is what happened to Amy, who had a nervous breakdown in front of him one night. "I'm up there, blam! You know, throwing things at her she never heard before." He says he tries to "look into people," see what makes them tick. He has learned how "people react, see when somebody's lyin' . . . I learned to see right through that, see when somebody's schemin' on me." Perhaps if Dave can see through his own "scheming," he will be able eventually to relinquish his "con artist" strategic style.

Hank. "I know how to act . . . know how to talk."

Hank Nelson is 17 at Time II, a "together guy" who has continued to show strong coping skills and a capacity for close emotional ties. He is married, having fathered a child out of wedlock. He and his wife, Norma, decided to wait until after the baby was born to take their vows, in order to allow Hank to work full time for the summer months.

Hank is still in school, although he dislikes it and has never done particularly well. He has landed a job as assistant to a veterinarian and attends school at night to finish his diploma. Like Dave, he has grown up "too fast." Giving his baby daughter a name is a duty he would not shirk (he always spoke of his willingness to take the consequences of his choices), but when asked what he would change if he could live his life over, he says he would not choose this route again: "I wouldn't get married."

His choices are his, though, and apparently well thought out. He received advice from his brother and his mother—"they're tellin' me 'no school, no job' and stuff like that. And I think about it and everything and figure, well I might as well go ahead." He says he felt like dropping out in the tenth grade; he looked around and saw what was happening to his friends who had left school, and said to himself, "No, I'd better keep going." His dislike of school, plus feeling tired in the morning, tempt him to play hookey. When he feels he is getting too far behind, however, he attends consistently enough to catch up. Hank says he gets along with the teachers, but apparently is willing to stand up to them if necessary:

The vice principal at the DuBois, he was famous for that—kicking kids—every time you turn around you hear of him sticking his foot up somebody's behind . . . I was waitin' for him to try it, you know, 'cause I'd break his leg, or try—honest to God!

He will respect a teacher if the teacher respects him: "It's as simple as that." (Hank had participated in a protest march in the sixth grade when the school system fired Jonathan Kozol for reading poetry by Langston Hughes: "I felt, they teach white poetry, so why not black poetry.") At his high school he is involved in establishing a Black Student Union. He protested the fact that they had to agree to allow white students in: "Now, what kind of shit is that . . . that's what we was arguing about!" He would protest (nonviolently) again for a "cause worthwhile."

In spite of his mediocre academic performance, Hank has been willing to fight for a reasonable learning situation based on his needs and pace. In the tenth grade he runs into difficulty with the geometry class he is assigned to; he analyzes the situation and comes to the conclusion that he lacks the necessary algebra to do the geometry. He approaches the teacher: "Listen, I mean I never even had algebra, so how am I supposed to do this here?" He is transferred into a special algebra class, but "you couldn't learn nothing in there." The teacher is afraid of the students and evidently has little or no control over them. This angers Hank, but instead of giving up, he follows through, getting himself into a tutoring program until he catches up to the geometry class. "I got the hang of it."

As before, Hank is realistic about his limitations. He has given up the idea of college, replacing it by business school or computer training. His brother-in-law is manager of a computer operation and promises that he will arrange things for Hank. The only thing standing in the way of success in school and work is himself, says Hank, indicating that he feels he, rather than outside forces, is in control of his fate. He knows his school performance and his attitude have not prepared him for serious academic study. He feels he *could* do it if he tried, "but then again I might just get frustrated . . . I couldn't see me studying no four or five hours a day after school and stuff like that." He says he reads very little and loses interest in a book quickly. (His verbal IQ at Time I was 90, Performance 93, for an overall score of 91, so perhaps reading is arduous.) If something interests him, however, he will wade through it to the end. Presumably his interest in computers will enable him to concentrate enough to learn that field well.

As suggested by his comments above, Hank is relatively high on racial identity (although only average in racial awareness). He feels that courses like Black History should be taught by blacks, because they have more insight into the subject matter:

All I can say is this is a white man's world and that's what they teachin' in school—what the white man wants . . . that's why blacks are finally waking up and gettin' themselves together and trying.

Hank calls himself "black" and wears an Afro. He has had white friends, but feels strongly that no matter how close a white friend is, "as the time lingers on he'll always seem to, like, end up wantin' to be the boss . . . it never fails . . . he'll always be, like, tryin' to embarrass you unconsciously."

Hank would not take the magic pill to make him white: "I'd leave it alone—what do I want to be somebody else for?" Upon reflection he says he would try it if he could turn right back, just to get himself "some of them white broads—'cause, like, the majority of white boys is lame to the bone anyway [laughter] and I could just move on in—wow!" Neither would he turn the world all black, because he feels "it takes all kind of people to make a world." He feels that whites have more advantages than blacks, can go wherever they want, get jobs more easily. He says he does not see blacks in politics and high-paying or high-skill jobs—although "most blacks have the skill for it." This he lays to discrimination. "That's just the way white people take blacks—they still think they're under their feet."

He feels blacks are different from whites in that the former have their "own style, have their own ways, even have their own way of talkin' . . . and really, I think being black you have more fun." He says that whites are "steady up in this 'high society' and they still think they're king of all blacks—they're living in a dream world. They can't do what we can do—that's all."

Hank says he has changed since Time I. He has "grown up":

Back then . . . I had a pretty good thing with the ladies . . . I mean, I didn't have no static or nothing. I got what I wanted . . . and as far as street life is concerned, the way I feel about it is, I know as much about that as, like, in other words, I know more than I'm supposed to know. Let's put it that way, because the way I was raised and stuff like that, was right in the heart of the action.

Since he has married, his life style has changed radically. He and wife Norma go to quieter parties, take in the Boston Pops from time to time. He does not own a car, which limits his mobility.

The most important thing that has happened to Hank since Time I is his daughter. He helps feed and change her, likes to play with her. He and his wife get along well: "If I didn't care for her or the baby, I mean I wouldn't have gave her a second thought." They live with his mother; Hank wants very much to save enough money to move his new family into a place of their own.

Looking back on his family of orientation, Hank says his mother and father have "done all they can" to help him over the years. Although he says sometimes he feels like cussing his mother out, he likes her, and says that when he needs her, "she's always there." His father is a heavy drinker but is trying to stop: "I feel good when I see him sober." He says he used to be hurt that his father was a little nasty toward him. "I used to always say, well, hell with him, you know." One day he and Hank fought over giving Hank some money. His mother sat him down and told him about his father's life:

I really felt bad, 'cause, like, my old man been through a hell of a lot of jams . . . he started supporting his mother and the rest of his family when he was 13 . . . during the depression . . . the old man died . . . after that I could understand it, because he really wouldn't have that much money . . . and he's never hardly had nothing for himself.

This compassion and capacity for understanding extend to his mother as well. Hank says she "don't like nobody to know too much about her . . . she's had it kind of hard, too." He says he can get along with her, she has a nice personality, and "she ain't going to take nothing; once you get out of hand she gonna let you know."

Hank feels he is more like his mother than his father: "She don't bother nobody unless nobody bothers her . . . she can get along with anyone, and that's just about the same way I am . . . she don't like nobody railroading her . . . and that's the same way I am." He still feels very close to Daddy Roy (mother's first husband). They talk, and Hank feels they understand each other.

At the core of Hank's "together guy" style are his capacity for affection, his sense of autonomy, and his worldliness. He says his mother would describe him as "no angel, she knows me right well. And she could see something that was done and I say that *I* didn't do it, and like, she know that, and that's why she wouldn't have nothing bad to say about me, 'cause since I was real small, that's all I can remember—whatever I did, I always told her the truth."

Hank's closest friend is Vince, toward whom he was leaning at Time I. Vince is planning to graduate from high school and is oriented toward a stable work career. Hank says Vince would describe him as "trustworthy": "He would say that I know what to do when I'm out, when I'm with people, I know how to act . . . know how to talk. He could get along with me." Hank is selective in whom he befriends. He no longer hangs out with Rocky and Mark—they are all "hoods" who had "big ideas about being gangsters . . . so I said no, that ain't for me." As though describing himself, he says Vince is "smooth—that's why I like him, 'cause he knows what he's doing . . . he's the only one that I thought was smart . . . he knew when to move when it was time to, and he knew what was happening, and knows how to cope with everything."

Getting jobs, working, playing basketball, swimming, diving, and hustling (he did some light stealing when younger, never was caught), rapping with girls, and dancing—all are Hank's fortes. He has taught himself to do all these things, and feels he is willing to "try anything once . . . I can handle myself." (His self-esteem scores confirm his verbal description of himself: 35 high answers out of 46, a very high score compared to the other boys.)

Hank believes a person can be what he wants to if he tries hard enough. He feels he will "make it" occupationally and otherwise. "I try to be very successful, I'll do just fine." His success rests partly on the fact that he "thinks ahead." He chooses to go into computer work, for example, because "it's going to be machines and they'll need someone to take care of the stuff." The only reason he might not get the job he wants is his color—and he would fight that.

Hank's advice to his children is to "have fun . . . go places." He has been given emotional support and freedom to develop competence and expressiveness, and the trust that has allowed him to grow. He would tell his children to "keep the pants up and her dress down," reflecting his realization that he has been edged into marriage too soon. But in spite of his own mistakes, he is (at age 17 at least) willing to allow his offspring the same room to grow that he has been fortunate enough to have: "I don't think I'd stand in the way, you know, stop them, not unless I see somethin' wrong and I'd *strongly* object." (Setting limits, as his mother has.)

Hank's sense of self is strong and positive; his need for independence and autonomy equally so. If his parents do not agree with him, "he finds out for himself." When the baby came up, he stood his ground, letting them know what he and Norma wanted. "What was done was done, so they couldn't say nothing . . . the best thing to do was to work together. To my surprise, everything worked out all right . . . now everybody's happy and they can't put the baby down." Similarly, he would not want his daughter to do things differently from the way he has: "Just be cool until she gets on her own, and then I wouldn't be able to tell her nothing."

Interaction, Meaning, and Strategic Styles

Through these portraits we have seen emerging identity as a product of the interaction between self and other definitions. The development of a person's strategic style is a product of his (or her) attempt to handle conflict between internal and external pressures, and between affiliation and power needs.

The strategic style is vested with meaning in terms of emotional impact and interpersonal orientation as the person copes with everyday social situations. Moving away from, against, with, over, or toward others can be seen as ways of dealing with competing pressures and the instability of adolescence.

In all five cases, messages from significant others serve to help create identities and, further, to label and help perpetuate them. For Keith, we have seen how persistent messages to be good, nice, and kind have built up in him both the need and the capacity to be just that. The messages—which alone might not be sufficient to define Keith's style—are buttressed by a system of interpersonal rewards for achieving and conforming to parental values and expectations. For Ernie, descriptions of him by others that focus on his shy, quiet ways serve to nurture that view of himself. The investment of meaning in social interaction is translated into both expectation and behavior, thus creating the strategic style. For the Tough Guy and the Retreater, social interaction means threat, harm, fear, antipathy. For the Cool Guy and the Conformist, social interaction is interpreted as potentially gratifying and self-confirming. For the Actor, social interaction is defined as an occasion to use or to be used.

The portraits show these meanings to be generated in the immediate family first, through messages, modeling, and direct or indirect treatment of the child which tends to elicit complementary behavior (for example, ignoring the child, which encourages him to invent attention-getting mechanisms).[5] Later the messages are reinforced by the selection of a peer group that is consonant with the child's values, self-image, expectations, and interpersonal orientation. School, the other major source of meaning, is more apt (at least in the inner city) to reinforce retreatism, rebellion, manipulation, and conformity than autonomy, tending to feed into initial orientations brought to school by the child in his early years. If peer and parent messages conflict, the child may become frustrated and confused until he allows one set to be more meaningful for him than the other. This phenomenon is a critical part of identity formation during early adolescence in particular, when the peer group becomes more significant as a reference for both behavior and self-identification.

To summarize, the particular strategic style exhibited by each youth is a product of: (a) messages from others; (b) rewards for fitting the messages; (c) models among significant others; (d) interaction patterns which tend to elicit complementary or reactive behavior; and (e) the relative absence or low valence of alternative styles in the child's immediate environment.

An assumption implicit in this book is that differences in *strate-*

gic styles will be as predictive as the *situation* in determining the individual's action. Have the cases supported this notion? Several examples come to mind. The third-floor attic apartment becomes a hideaway and retreat for Ernie, the perfect opportunity for him to deal with his feelings and a hostile environment. Would it have been used in the same manner and with the same meaning and frequency by Keith or Hank? For Leroy, bumping into a half-stranger on a dark street in the middle of the night becomes a mandate for struggle and unthinking violence. Would Dave or Keith, Ernie or Hank have propelled the encounter to the same murderous crime? The occasion of fathering a child becomes a classic opportunity for Dave to manipulate and use others in his own definition of responsibility. Would the other boys have so slickly and coldly slipped out of the predicament? Would Dave, Leroy, or Ernie have been able to make what Keith made out of an ordinary job at the corner store?

Just as important as the situation, then, is the boy's predisposition toward others (and self). For Ernie, to retreat is to retreat from parents, from a kindergarten playground, or a new high school. For Leroy, the battles are fought on every front, some created by his own aggressiveness. For Dave, every social encounter is a potential opportunity for exploitation, regardless of how close he is to his victims. For Keith, every challenge deserves the same effort and cooperativeness. And for Hank, self-respect, autonomy, and coolness are an integral part of every encounter.

Although the boys exhibit varying degrees of flexibility of style, I suggest that the clearer the messages and models, and the more stressful or rigid the interaction patterns with significant others, the more fixed the strategic style will become. We need to learn more about how to supply a child with alternative and varied meanings and interpersonal experiences to enable him to create an identity characterized by insight, autonomy, and a balance between affiliation and power needs. This is the role of a body of literature supportive of clinical sociology.

Further research and analysis are called for in order to test the relationship of strategic styles to other variables—family size, birth order, school achievement, IQ, and so forth. (See Appendix C for some initial efforts in that direction.) For example, the Pathways study suggests that intellectual potential may be greatly affected by a person's strategic style: in describing Ernie (whose IQ score of 125 at Time I was the highest in the study), his mother used the term "shy" again and again. His twin sister she portrays as "smart." Clearly, to those around him Ernie's withdrawn style becomes more significant than his brightness; conversely, the perception of him as shy and withdrawn is fed back to him in messages from others which reinforce his self-image and retreatist behavior. Ernie's withdrawn style has extended to school, where his fear of interpersonal interaction and his chronic truancy have rendered his intellectual potential inoperative in that setting. He is the underachiever *par excellence.* Had his style been conformist or together, he undoubtedly would have excelled in school and perhaps would have become a chemist—his childhood dream—rather than a dropout.

For Leroy, we've seen how a low IQ (tested at 80) may be part of the frustration that, in tandem with the pressures from home, creates a tough and violent style. Keith, whose IQ tests out in the low 90's, has tended toward overachievement. That is, his willingness to conform to teacher and parent expectations, and his self-discipline, enable him to achieve in school at a level he might never have reached with a tough or withdrawn style. The relationship between IQ and strategic style is one that bears further and meticulous research.

Suffice it to say that strategic styles are self-reinforcing. The consequences that follow upon a person's way of coping with the facts and circumstances of his life in time themselves become antecedents. The process of reformulation and redefinition of self is ongoing. For example, stealing, drug use, and dropping out of school undoubtedly feed a sense of failure and defeat into a boy's identity; this becomes a circumstance in its own right, which then must be managed. Strategic styles, it follows, may shift over time: The "con artist" goes straight; the "withdrawn kid" comes out of his shell; the "too-good guy" loosens up; the "troublemaker" turns over a new leaf; the "together guy" slips into the wrong crowd.

In the five cases reported here, with the possible exception of Keith, the styles appear to have crystallized, rather than shifted, but their permanence is open to further research. This and many other questions generated by the present study might be pursued further, using larger and different groups. Other questions include:

(a) Do styles which emerge during adolescence generally remain stable into adulthood, or are they normally a temporary adaptation to adolescence itself? Are there distinctions among styles according to their longevity?

(b) Do adolescents tend to seek out peer groups which tolerate, reinforce, complement, or conflict with their styles?

(c) Do certain dominant and secondary strategic styles tend to be associated with one another (i.e., do they tend to appear in sets)?

(d) Do groups or patterns of antecedent variables cluster to predict certain styles? If so, how early can we predict the development of a particular style, based on analysis of antecedent factors?

(e) What styles show the greatest sense of internal control? What other psychological traits or qualities are associated with each style?

(f) How strong is the correlation between the strategic styles of parents and children (both same-sex and opposite sex)? How strong is the correlation between strategic styles of siblings?

(g) For black youth, which styles are predominant and which are associated with a high sense of racial awareness and pride?

(h) Can teachers, parents, social workers, etc. be taught to recognize styles and their probable antecedents and consequences, so that they can respond in ways that do not reinforce styles destructive to self and others?

Finally, strategic styles should be seen as ways people use to define situations for themselves. The behaviors associated with those definitions might best be recognized as *symptomatic* of a strategic style rather than isolated phenomenon.

Clinical Sociology Revisited

It seems clear from the five case studies examined in this book that strategic styles are passed down from generation to generation. As the child is raised, so will he raise his own, unless he gains insight into the patterns of family interaction which created his own style. Thus intervention should take into account not only the child who presents disturbing symptoms, but the entire family.

The need for research into the contexts in which people live out the daily struggles of their lives is a crucial one. We must focus not only on description, but on analysis of patterns which emerge in various family constellations. I hope this work will not be taken as a mere accounting of the lives of five young boys, but will spur the reader to make comparisons with others—both male and fe-male—to uncover the regularized ways of interrelating which we evolve in our intimate contacts.

Harry Stack Sullivan believed that people make people sick— and people could make them well again. He saw the formation of emotional health and disorder as the product of interaction with others. Mental illness he defined as a "miscarriage of human rela-tions," the product of anxiety-ridden experiences with significant others who participate in the child's socialization process. Pro-longed exposure to "warped relational experiences" can cause mental illness or at least great personal unhappiness. Particularly significant, he felt, was lack of tenderness, loss of security, and re-sponses from others which cause a person's "self-system" to work overtime in a defensive mode.

We have seen in the cases of Ernie, Leroy, and Dave that each of them has felt a lack of tenderness and genuine affection from their families; each has felt terribly insecure; and each has developed a strong self-system to defend himself from the emotional and some-times physical attacks from others in their worlds.

Studies have found that schismatic marital relationships, in which parents are chronically engaged in open conflict and hostile attacks against each other, tend to produce emotionally disturbed children.[6] We have seen the devastating effects on Dave, Ernie, and Leroy of such parental conflict.

Others have found that the absence of genuine warmth and ex-pressiveness contribute to interpersonal distortions.[7] Again, Dave, Ernie, and Leroy, who suffer most from an inability to love others, come to mind. Along these same lines, Truax and Carkhuff found that several qualities *enhance* a therapist's effectiveness:

Being . . . high in empathy, warmth, and genuineness are more effective in psychotherapy because they themselves are more potent positive rein-forcers; *and* also because they elicit through reciprocal effect a high de-gree of positive affect in the patient, which increases the level of the pa-tient's positive self-reinforcement, decreases anxiety, and increases the level of positive affect and positive reinforcement from others.[8]

This is an excellent conceptualization of a positive feedback loop. We can see immediately that it is the opposite of the process that occurs in Leroy's family—or Dave's or Ernie's. In their cases the interaction follows a negative feedback loop—similar in its consequences to one described by the authors in relation to *ineffective* therapists:

By contrast, counselors or therapists who are low in communicated accurate empathy, nonpossessive warmth and genuineness are ineffective, and produce negative or deteriorative change in the patient because they are noxious stimuli who serve primarily as aversive reinforcers *and* also because they elicit negative affect in the patient . . .[9]

If these processes can be documented in therapy settings, it is likely they can be documented in families, schoolrooms, peer groups, work settings, and so on. For example, it is interesting that the very qualities that make Hank a "together guy" are "communicated accurate empathy, nonpossessive warmth, and genuiness"—qualities he is developing himself, and whose absence in others he detests. The negative vs. positive feedback loop plays a central role in the genesis of strategic styles, a person's sense of identity, self-concept, and sense of mastery in his psychosocial matrix.

The kind of holistic approach to family interaction we have used here could also be used in other settings. For example, a boss who operates in the primary style of "tough guy" may help create a gulf between workers and the boss, who exacerbates the retreatism of the more withdrawn employees, stimulates the toughness in the more aggressive and belligerent ones, and demoralizes the conformist and together guy, who feel a lack of reward for their competencies because of the tough-guy boss's insensitivity in interpersonal matters.

A clinical sociologist could soften the lines of the situation by encouraging the withdrawn workers to practice higher participation in non-threatening areas; to make the other "tough" employees (and the boss) aware of the ways in which their reciprocal aggression reinforces itself; and so forth.

As sociologists and social psychologists, we see the origins of personal and group difficulties in *social* rather than *individual* pathology. By better understanding the etiology of that pathology, we can intervene in meaningful ways.

As Glassner and Freedman say, "It is usually possible for persons and groups to change their social conditions and, at times, clinicians who are sensitive to sociology can be instrumental in analyzing this change."[10] We must not wallow in pessimism because so many problems have seemed resistant to change in response to other kinds of intervention strategies. Sociology is not the last word either; sociological clinicians must not forget what they choose to ignore. They must work hand in hand with those who emphasize different perspectives in shaping and implementing a more comprehensive, integrative model of human interaction and growth.

The Family Blueprint

Although, as mentioned earlier, I did not begin this study with the intention of focusing specifically on the family, the extent to which the family appears to be instrumental in generating and perpetuating strategic styles is too striking to ignore. Indeed, it is the "crucible of identity." Other forces and influences certainly play their part in shaping the style of young boys as they discover who they are—especially peers and adults outside the family. But the blueprint appears to be firmly lodged in the interaction matrix of the family—not simply its demography.

Its lines are clear and compelling forces in the creation of the young person's strategic style. As Dave Cooper's father commented, in a reflective mood,

That's why I say it goes back to the home in the beginning, because this is the first society . . . the family group . . . *there's* a society!

Appendixes

Appendix A
Focal Child Interview Schedule (Time I) *

I. GENERAL INFORMATION

1. What is your full name?
   Do you have any nicknames?
2. When were you born?
   How old are you?
   Where were you born?
3. Where do you live? (Street Address)
4. Do you have a phone? (*If yes, ask for number. If no, is there a phone number at which your family can be reached?*)
5. How long have you lived at (address given)?
6. Where did you live before that?
   Why did you move? (*Explore what happened.*)
   Where did you live before that?

---

* Time II and Time III Interview Schedules are parallel, with appropriate update questions. They are available on request. The term "Negro" was used in the interviews, reflecting common usage in the community during Time I. If the subject indicated that he or she used another term for his or her racial identification (usually "colored"), the interviewers were instructed to shift to that term.

(*Continue to inquire until S seems to have recalled all the places he has lived.*)

7. Have you ever lived away from your family?
   (*If yes*) When was that?

8. Have you ever spent any time in a hospital?
   (*If yes*) How long?
   How old were you then?
   What were you in the hospital for?

9. Have you had any serious diseases or illnesses?

10. Have you ever had an operation?
    (*If yes*) Will you tell me about it?

11. Have you ever been hurt in an accident? If so, what happened?

12. Do you think you are small or large for your age or just about average?

II. PRESENT FAMILY

1. Can you tell me something about *each* person who lives in your house, starting with the oldest person?
   Give me their names, ages, and tell me something about them.
   Does anybody else live there—anybody who is not related to you?

2. Do you have any brothers or sisters who don't live at your house?
   If yes: What are their names and ages and tell me something about them.
   How often do you see them, and where do you usually see them?
   Do you have any brothers or sisters who are dead? *Ask for names.*
   How old was your brother (sister) when he (she) died?
   How old were you then?

3. (a) *If father or mother is not mentioned in response to 1. ask this question*:
   What is your father's (mother's) name?
   Is he (she) living?
   If parent is dead, continue with 3(b).
   Where does he (she) live?
   How old is he (she)?
   Tell me something about him (her).
   How often do you see him (her) and where do you usually see him (her)?
   What do you do when you and he (she) get together?

   (b) When did he (she) die?
   What did he (she) die of?
   What do you remember about him (her)?
   When people in your family talk about him (her) now, what kinds of things do they recall?
   Where was he (she) living before his (her) death?

4. (a) Are your grandparents living? *Ask about the living:*
Tell me their names, about how old they are, and something about them.
Where do they live?
How often do you see them?

   (b) *If any grandparents have died, ask:*
What do you know about or remember about your grandparents who died?

5. (a) Do you have a favorite uncle or aunt or other relative?
If yes: Tell me something about him (her).
What do you like about him (her)?
How often do you see him (her)?
What do you do when you are with him (her)?
Have you ever lived in the same house?
Has he (she) ever helped in raising you or taking care of you?
If yes: In what way?

   (b) Have you an uncle or aunt or other relative that you don't like very much or don't like to be around?
If yes: Tell me something about him (her).
What is it you don't like about him (her)?
How often do you see him (her)?
What do you do when you are with him (her)?
Have you ever lived in the same house?
Has he (she) ever helped in raising you or taking care of you?
If yes: In what way?

   (c) Do you know any of your other relatives very well?
If yes: Who are they and how are they related to you?
How often do you see them?
What do you do when you are together?

6. Who in your family are you most like?

7. (a) In what ways are you like your mother?
   (b) In what ways are you different from your mother?

8. *If a child has or remembers his father:*
   (a) In what ways are you like your father?
   (b) In what ways are you different from your father?

9. *If child says he is most like someone other than his mother or father, ask:*
Who are you most like—your mother or father?
If he mentions physical resemblance only, ask:
What about in personality—who are you most like?

10. Who in your family would you most want to be like?

11. Of all the men you know, who do you feel the closest to now?
(*Probe:* How often do you see him? What do you do together? Why do you feel close to him?)

12. When you were younger, who took care of you most of the time?
How old were you then?
What are some of the things he (she) did for you?
Was there anyone that took care of you after that?
When did ———— start taking care of you?

13. (a) When you were younger, who was most likely to get after you or
punish you?
What kinds of things do you remember being punished or scold-
ed for?
How were you punished?
What did he (she) say when you were being scolded?

    (b) Who is it who gets after you or punishes you now?
What kinds of things does he (she) get after you about?
What does he (she) say?
How are you punished now?
What happens after that?

14. What things do you do that your mother likes most?
Is there something else you do that she likes a lot?
How does she show that she likes it (those things)?
Repeat question for father and/or mother or father surrogate.

15. When you were younger who seemed to love or care about you
most?
How did he (she) show it?
When was this?
Who would you say likes or loves you most now?
How does he (she) show it?
Who is it you like or care about the most? Why?

16. *Ask for each important adult the following questions:*
How do you get along with (person discussed above) in general?
What kinds of things do you and she agree about?
What kinds of things do you and she disagree about?
What do you like most about her?
Is there any way that you wish she would be different?
Would you say you get along with her better than or worse than your
brothers and sisters? Can you explain this?
Is there a particular child she seems to favor?
If yes: Which one and what makes you think so?
Do your other brothers and sisters know that he (or she; i.e., the sib-
ling mentioned) is favored?
What do they think about it? (*Repeat for male adults.*)

17. *If child has siblings of both sexes, then ask:*
Are boys and girls treated differently in your family?
If yes: In what ways? By whom?
Ask if child has brothers only or brothers and sisters.

Are you treated differently from your brothers sometimes?
If yes: In what ways? By whom?

18. *Ask if child remembers a time when his parents lived together. Rephrase to ask about mother's relationship with stepfather or regular boyfriend.*
    How do (did) your parents get along with each other generally?
    All parents disagree sometimes. What kinds of things do (did) your parents disagree about most often?
    Give an example of one disagreement and what happened?
    What kinds of things make your mother upset or angry?
    What kinds of things make your father (or appropriate male) upset or angry?

19. How do you get along with your brothers and sisters?
    Ask specifically about each one.
    Which one of them do you talk with or do things with most?
    How come?
    Which one do you talk with least and don't do many things with?
    How come?
    Which one do you like best? Why?
    Which one do you like least? Why?
    Which of your brothers and sisters get along best with each other?
    How come?
    Which ones have the most arguments or fights?
    What causes it?
    What usually happens after they argue or fight?
    Is there any way you think *each one* would like you to be different?

20. *Ask with regard to each family member.*
    When you get into an argument or fight with ———, what is it usually about?
    How does it start?
    Who is on your side and who is on his (her) side?
    How does it usually end?

21. Who makes most of the decisions in your family?
    What kinds of things does she (he) have to make decisions about?
    Does he (she) talk about it with other people in the family?
    If yes: With whom?
    Give an example of something he (she, they) had to make a decision about.

22. Who handles the money in your family? What things does ———
    have to spend money for?
    Where does the money come from?
    Tell me about a time when there wasn't enough money for something.
    Who argues about money in your family?
    Who says what in those arguments?

23. Now I would like to get an idea of what life is generally like in your family.

    Tell me everything that you can remember about what you and everybody else did yesterday (or most recent weekday).

    Try to account for the activities of everybody. If others (i.e., non-family) are mentioned, inquire about their activities. Try to find out about the nature of conversations as well as what each person did.

    (a) What was the best time you ever had with your family? The worst?

    (b) What was the best time you ever had with your father? The worst?

        Ask the same questions about other important male.

    (c) What did you and everybody else do last Christmas Eve and Christmas Day? Who was there? How did you feel about your family?

    (d) What was the best Christmas you ever had?

    (e) What did you and everybody else do last Sunday (or "yesterday," if interview is on Monday)? *Probe as suggested above.*

24. I am going to ask you about some events or incidents. Tell me what happens in your family when such things occur.

    If it is something that hasn't actually happened in your family, tell me what your family would probably do if it should happen.

    What happens . . .

    (a) When somebody has to go to school to see a teacher or the principal about you?

    (b) When you ask for money?

    (c) When you get sick or just aren't feeling good?

    (d) When your mother is sick?

    (e) When somebody else in the family is sick?

    (f) When you bring home a good report card? *Probe for reactions of important grown-ups.*

    (g) When you bring home a poor report card?

    (h) When you stay out too late in the evening?

    (i) When you get real angry with your mother?

    (j) With father (stepfather or mother's friend)?

    (k) When you get into serious trouble?

25. Who do you go to when you need help with your homework?

26. Is there someone who you can talk to who really understands you?

27. What does your mother want you to be when you grow up?

    What kind of a person does she want you to be?

    Is there someone she would like you to be like?

    Ask same questions about father or any other important adults.

28. Do you ever go to church?
    (How often?)
    Where?
    What kind of church is that?
    Do both whites and Negroes go there? *Probe for proportion.*
    Who do you go with?
29. What do you think about church?
    Probe for why child does or doesn't go to or like church.
30. *If child goes to church:*
    Do you know the minister?
    What's he like?
31. Do you belong to any church groups?
    If yes: What does the group do?
32. If you have children would you want them to go to church?
    What church?
    Why?

III. FUTURE FAMILY

1. When you have grown up and are on your own, what kind of life do
   you want to have?
   *Probe for details and for his plans for arranging for the kind of life
   he hopes to have.*
2. *Ask if marriage is not mentioned in response to 1:*
   (a) Do you plan to get married when you grow up?
       Why or why not? *Ask about conditions and qualifications if any
       and about preparation or readiness for marriage if his response
       suggests it.*
   (b) What kind of girl would make a good wife for you?
       What kinds of things would you like her to do or expect her to
       do?
       Do you know anybody whom you would like her to be like?
3. How many children do you want to have when you grow up?
   How many boys?
   How many girls?
   Why?
4. What kinds of things will you want your sons to do when they are
   your age?
   What kinds of things do you hope they will not do?
   What advice will you give them when they are your age?

IV. PEER GROUP

(NOTE: *Ask for specific examples, anecdotes, whenever appropriate.*)
  1. Who do you hang with?
     Ask respondent to name each member of his usual group and to describe each one. Probe for whether group is school or neighborhood based.
     (a) Do you think of yourselves as a gang or club or just a bunch of guys?
     (b) How did you join this group?
     (c) What do you usually do together?
         Probe: Are there two or more groups? Which is most important to focal child? If more than one group, ask question 2, below, for each.
  2. *Try to find out what different roles exist in the group and who fills these roles; for example:*
     (a) Is there anybody who usually is the one who decides what to do? Would you say he's the leader? *Probe for respondent's distinctions.*
     (b) Is there anyone besides ——— who usually plans the action—whatever you're going to do?
     (c) Who's your best friend of these you've mentioned? What's he like?
     (d) Which (boy, kid, guy, cat, stud, dude) do you like the least and why?
     (e) Who would you trust most if you were in trouble?
     (f) Who's the cleanest, most together guy in the bunch?
  3. What sort of things do you do together?
     (a) Do you get together for parties?
         i. Who comes? Can kids outside the group come? Who?
         ii. What are your parties like? *Probe for drinking, smoking, sex, fighting.*
         iii. Do you and your friends ever fool around with girls?
              If he says he doesn't but some friends do, ask: What do they do with the girls? Do they make out? Elaborate on question if necessary.
              If he says he does, ask him some of the things he's done, and probe to better understand his present sexual activities. If he has a girl friend, we will be interested if he still does things with other girls and if he treats them differently than he does his girl friend.
         iv. *If not previously answered:* Are there any girls who hang with you sometimes?

(b) What about sports? (teams, casual games, chance playing; give specific examples)

(c) *Ask about things they do together in general for each relevant area, for example; hanging out, going down-town. Get specific examples.*

4. (a) What happens when two guys disagree or get mad at each other? *Probe for specific example.*

(b) Are there any kids in the (gang, group) who seem to be constantly bugging each other?

5. Every group has some kind of rules.

(a) What sort of rules does your group have?

(b) What happens if you don't live up to them or like them? Has this ever happened to you?

6. Is there anything that your friends would like you to do differently from the way that you do it? *Probe.*

7. Which ones in your group does your mother know? How often does she see (each of them)? What does she think of (each of them)?

8. Which ones does your (father or other close relative or surrogate) know? How often does he see (each of them)? What does he think of them?

9. What about your brothers and sisters? Do they know your friends?

10. Are there any other kids that you see a lot of but aren't in the group? When do you see them? What do you do together? If they know boys in your group, how do they get along with the other boys in your group?

11. Are there any kids your (group, gang) fights with? Who are they? How does it start? How often?

12. How does your group get money? *Probe for breaking and entering, etc.*

13. (a) Have you ever been in trouble together (in or out of school)?

(b) Have you (or any others in the group) been in trouble with the cops?

(c) What happened?

(d) Did your folks find out? What did (whoever it was) do?

14. How are your friends doing in school? *Probe for each cited friend:*

(a) How are his grades?

(b) Does he like school?

(c) How does he feel about going to the DuBois?

(d) How far do you think he'll go in school?
Has he talked about dropping out? *Explore fully reasons why or why not.*

(e) *If appropriate*: Where does he want to go to high school?
Do you think he'll go there?

(f) What kind of work do you think he'll do after he's out of school?
How'll he'll make out in his work?

(g) What do you think he'll be like when he's twenty-five?
Thirty-five?
Probe for work, family, place of residence, etc.

V. SCHOOL

A. *School History*:

For each school ask where it is if you don't know and how long he went there.

1. Where you have gone to school?

   (a) Pre-school: Nursery schools, day care centers, church schools?

   (b) Elementary schools: How long for each school?

   (c) Junior high: Could you have gone to any other junior high?

   (d) Do you wish you had gone to some other school this year?
   If yes: Why?

   (e) High school:
   If they haven't gotten this far, find out where they expect to go and why.

   (f) What tracks? Type of course?

   (g) Have you ever been skipped a grade or made to repeat?

2. What's the first thing you remember about school?
   Probe for details of experience and feelings, quality of the teachers, and the kid's expectations.

3. Who was the best teacher you ever had?
   When did you have her or him?

   (a) Why was s(he) good?

   (b) What grade and subject did s(he) teach?

   (c) What did s(he) think of you?
   Did s(he) see you as you are?

   (d) Was s(he) fair with the kids? *Examples.*

   (e) Did s(he) expect a lot of work from the kids?
   Was s(he) strict?

(f) Did s(he) call on you often? *Probe the circumstances.*

(g) Did s(he) help you to get the answer right?
Did s(he) give you enough time to answer?
What did s(he) do if you said you didn't know the answer or if you got it wrong?

(h) How was your work in that subject?

4. Who is the best teacher you have had this year? *If not covered above.*

   (a) Why is s(he) good?

   (b) What subject does s(he) teach?

   (c) What does s(he) think of you?
   Does s(he) see you as you are?

   (d) Is s(he) fair with the kids? *Examples.*

   (e) Does s(he) expect a lot of work from the kids?
   Is s(he) strict?

   (f) Does s(he) call on you often? *Probe for circumstances.*

   (g) Does s(he) help you get the answers right?
   Does she give you enough time to answer?
   What does she do if you say you don't know the answer or if you get it wrong?

   (h) How is your work in that subject?

5. Is there any teacher this year that you're having trouble with? *If not, ask*: Well, think about the teacher you had the most trouble with before.

   (a) What grade and subject did s(he) teach?

   (b) What was the trouble? What happened? *Give an example.*
   How did you feel about it?
   If appropriate: What did the other kids say?
   Did your parents find out?

   (c) Did any of the other students have trouble with her (him)?
   What sort?
   Do you think most kids thought s(he) was bad?
   Optional probe: Was there anyone who stuck up for the teacher?

   (d) What did s(he) think of you?
   Did s(he) see you as you are?

   (e) Who got most of the attention in that class?
   Why?

   (f) How was your work in that subject?

   (g) What teacher do you dislike the most this year?
   Explore unless it's the same as above.
   If none given, ask for the teacher he'd most like to have a substitute for.

6. Have there been many times when your teacher left your school during the term?
Do you have substitute teachers very often?
In what class and why?

7. Would you like any of your teachers to give you more attention or help? *Ask for specific examples.*

   (a) Is ——— (the teacher mentioned) interested in helping you when the work is difficult?

   (b) Think of an instance. What did s(he) do?
   What was the effect of this?

   (c) What happens when you need help and s(he) doesn't come through?
   Why do you think s(he) doesn't help?
   How does s(he) let you know—what does s(he) say to you?

   (d) If you needed extra help in a subject, who could you go to?
   Have you done this? *Example.*
   Do you have a tutor? *If yes:* How did you get the tutor?
   If no: How would you go about getting one?
   Do any of your friends have tutors?

B. *Discipline*:

8. Tell me about a boy who is always in hot water in school.
Have subject really describe such a boy.

   (a) How does he get along with the teachers?
   Is there any teacher he gets along with well?
   Why do you think that is?

   (b) What do the other students think about him?
   Do some admire him because of what he does?

   (c) How is he treated?

   (d) Is he getting anything out of school? *Probe.*
   Will he stay in school?

   (e) Why do you think things go badly for him at school?
   (Is it him or the school system?)

   (f) What could happen that would make it better?
   How could the teachers and the kids treat him and teach him that would get him going, make him happier, and help him learn better?

   (g) If you were his teacher and wanted him to do better and to like school more, what would you do?
   Probe for any relevance of this for subject.

9. What sorts of things seem to bother teachers most at your school?
Give me an example.
How do they handle that?

What is discipline like at your school?
Do they use the rattan much? *Probe.*

10. If you were a teacher, how would you handle the worst troublemakers?
Probe: If subject gives mainly "Get tough" answers, try
What if the kid's trouble is that people have been tough with him all his life?
Another important probe is, How would you get him to respect you?
We have to be able to differentiate between the teacher who gets tough and is then beaten up and the teacher whose toughness pays off ultimately in rapport.

11. What kinds of trouble have you had in school?
Probe for consequences.

12. Has there been any racial trouble in your school?
(a) What happened?
(b) Have you had any trouble because you're a Negro?
(Have you ever been called out of your name at school?)

13. Now think about a boy who does very well in school.
(a) What is he like?
(b) Why does he do so well?
(c) How does he get along with teachers?
Other kids?
Which is more important to subject?
Probe for how the subject feels about such a kid. Is the good guy a fairy and a sell out? Does the subject feel more like this kid or the kid who's in trouble?

C. *Interest and Performances:*

14. What have you liked most in school?
Why?
Were you especially good at that?
Possible probes: If he answers with an academic subject, ask him what the teacher was like. If he answers with an activity or sport, ask who supervised or coached it and what other friends were in it. Then ask, after (b), about favorite subject.
(a) Does the interest continue?
(b) Do you get recognition from it?
How?
(c) What do you like to study the most, if not the above?
(d) What do your teachers think you're best at?
(e) What do you think you're best at?

15. What have you hated (or disliked) most in school?
    (a) Why?
        Was there anything you could do about it?
        Areas of probing: If a subject is not mentioned initially, ask about the subject he hated most, what the teacher was like. Was his dislike linked to a feeling of frustration or failure?
        (b) What do your teachers think you're worst at?
    (c) Do they know what you're really best at?
16. How are you doing in your courses this year?
    (a) *Probe: Get course comments. For each course ask if he expected to do differently or wants to improve his grades in the course now.*
    (b) *Probe: If he says he wants to do better, try to determine whether he cares about getting a better grade, as opposed to thinking he ought to because of external pressures.*
        What would he need to do to do better in the course?
    (c) Do you think your marks on tests and school grades really show how well you know the stuff you're supposed to be learning?
    (d) Are there any courses you wish you had taken?
        Any you wish you hadn't taken?
    (e) Have you had any special classes?
        What were they like?
        Probe for remedial or enrichment classes and programs.
    (f) Would you say it's easier for you to learn school subjects than others in your class, or harder for you to learn than for other kids, or just about the same?
17. Is your school different in any way from other schools you know about?
    If he can't think of other schools, suggest others.
    (a) *If he doesn't mention the present difficulties at the DuBois, ask specifically:*
        What do you think is going on with the DuBois?
    (b) *Probe to find out his perception of what's happening in the Du-Bois, especially in regard to discipline. Get specific examples:*
        i. *Is he involved?*
        ii. *What students do what?*
        iii. *How do individual teachers act and react?*
        iv. *Which teachers does he respect and which is he down on?*
        v. *What does he think of the administration?*
    (c) *It will be very important to get at his reasons for why such problems arise and his perception of the points of view of teachers and students.*
    (d) *Probe to find out what he thinks of the publicity.*

(e) *Do his friends and family talk about it?*

(f) *How would he go about fixing things up?*

18. Has your mother ever gone to school to talk to a teacher or the principal about you and/or your brothers and sisters?
If father is present, repeat the question, asking if father has gone to the school, etc.
Ask for description of instances.

19. Have you talked with any teacher about:
(*For each section, ask with whom, what teacher said, and how it came up.*)
(a) What high school you would go to?
(b) What you should do when you grow up?
(c) What courses you should take in junior high school and high school?
Ask about guidance teacher if he doesn't mention him (her).

20. (a) How far do your teachers think you should or could go in school?
(b) How far do they think you will actually go?

21. (a) How far does your mother (and father, if present) think you should or could go in school?
(b) How far does she (and he) want you to go in school?
(c) How far does she (and he) think you will actually go in school?
(d) How important is it to your mother (and father) that you get good grades?
(e) What does she (and he) say about how you're doing in school?
(f) Does she (or he) ever say that she (he) wishes you would do as well as some other kid?

22. (a) How far do most of your friends want to go in school?
(b) How far do you think most of them will actually go?

23. Is there any one person in particular who you think has a special interest in how well you do in school?
What do they say about your schoolwork?

24. (a) If you were able to go as far in school as you wanted to, how far would you go? Why?
(b) How far do you think you will actually go in school? Why?
(c) *If the subject does not expect to finish high school, ask him why.*
(d) What would have to happen in order for you to graduate from high school?
If the subject expects to go to high school, be sure that we know what high school he expects and wants to go to and why.
If the subject plans to graduate from high school but does not plan to go to college, ask:

(e) Have you ever thought of going to college?

(f) Do you think you have or could have the ability to go through college?

If he would like to go to college, ask:

(g) What kind of college do you imagine going to?

If the subject expects to go to college, ask:

(h) What kind of college do you expect to go to?

(i) What do you have to do to get in?
What courses do you have to have in high school?
What kind of marks do you have to get?

(j) Would anything prevent you from going to college?

25. Do you ever think of dropping out of school?
If yes: When did you first think of dropping out?

(a) What might make you decide to drop out?
What keeps you from dropping out?

(b) What do your friends think about dropping out for you or for themselves?

(c) Do you think getting through high school will make any real difference in your life?

(d) What about the school—do you think that the teachers and staff would mind if you quit?

(e) Would your folks mind?

(f) If you quit, what would you do (after you were 16)?
If no: Why not?

D. *Teachers, race, etc.:*

26. Do the teachers here ever treat Negro kids differently from white kids?

27. Is there any difference between Negro teachers here and white teachers in how they treat kids?

28. If you could be taught by mainly Negro teachers or mainly white teachers, which would you pick?
Why?
If there's no preference, ask:

(a) What would be the best ratio of Negro to white teachers?

(b) Can you think of any courses that might be taught better by a Negro than a white teacher or better by a white teacher than a Negro teacher?
Why?

29. Would you rather be in an integrated school, one that had mostly Negro students, or one that had mainly white students in it?

30. Would you rather be in a school run by a Negro teacher or a white teacher?

31. If you had a choice, would you rather be taught by:
    (a) Men teachers or women teachers? Why?
    (b) Teachers in their 20's and 30's or teachers 40 years or older? Why?
    (c) Married teachers or single teachers? Why?

32. In your courses have you had anything about Negro History or civil rights?
    Probe for detail and subject's reaction.

33. Do you learn anything about Africa as it is now? What?
    Probe for image of Africa, African Negroes.

E. Extra Curricular Activities:

34. Have you ever gotten involved in any clubs, committees, teams, special responsibilities?
    What?
    When?
    How did you get involved in that?
    Probe carefully and for details regarding athletics.

35. Have there been things that you would have liked to do but didn't?

36. What does it take to be a part of these things?
    (a) In many schools there is one group that seems to have in it most of the leaders, the most popular kids, or smartest, or best athletes.
    (b) Is there a group like this in your school?
        What is it like?
    (c) Are you in that group?
        Would you like to be?
        What would it take to be part of that group?

37. Are there any other activities you would enjoy in school but which are not available in your school?

38. (a) Is there anything connected with school that you can't do as well as you'd like because you don't have the money to keep up?
    (b) Are there other kids who have a hard time in school because their families just don't have enough money?
        What happens?
        What do they do when they don't have the money they need?

F. Reading:

39. Did anyone read to you when you were younger?
    Explore memories of who read, what sort of things were read, child's interest.
    Do you read much now?
    If yes:
    (a) What kinds of books, newspapers, magazines, comics?

How frequently?

How do you find out what's happening in the news?

(b) Who do you like to talk with about the things you read?

(c) Does anyone suggest interesting books for you to read?
Do you enjoy the things they give you?
Do you hash these books out with them?
If no:

(d) Do you find it hard to read stuff?
Why? Because you're not a good reader, or is it that books have never seemed interesting?

(e) Do you read the sports page? Comics? Mysteries? Etc.

40. What about hookey?
Do you stay out much?
How did you get started?
Who do you play hookey with?
What did you do when you skipped school?
Probe for what kid got out of skipping school—independence?
Gang solidarity? Money? Etc.

41. *Optional introduction*: We've talked to lots of high school and junior high boys now. Some say they think school is OK; others think it's a drag and the whole system is for the birds.
How do you feel about school (and the school system?)

42. (a) If you could build a school to be any way you wanted, what would it be like?

(b) Do you know of any schools in or around Boston that are like that?

43. (a) If you were running this research program (and wanted to find out how school is for kids your age), is there anything you'd ask them that we haven't?

(b) Is there anything you think we asked the wrong way or we should have left out?

VI. WORK

1. What do you want to do for a living when you grow up?

2. What exactly does a ——— do? *Ask about job mentioned.*

3. What is it you'd like about being a ———?
What is there about being a ——— that you think you might not like?

4. Let's say you're grown up and you're a ———.
What do you think an average work day might be like for you?

5. What do you have to do to become a ———?
What kind of training do you need?
Where would you go to school for this?
Are you thinking of the service as a possibility for training?

6. What made you first think of becoming a ————?
   If subject gives an answer that is not a person, then ask:
   What was it about ————'s that you liked?
   If a person is given, then ask: Did you talk with him about being a
   ————?
   What did you ask?
   If not a person, then ask: Did you know anyone who is a ————?
   If yes: Have you talked to him about his work?
   What did you ask him?
   If not: If you had a chance to meet a ————, what kinds of questions
   would you ask him?
   If a person, ask: Do you know of any ————'s from TV or movies,
   books or comic books?
   If yes: What was it about them that you liked?
7. What does your mother want you to be?
   What does she like about that job?
   What job would she not like for you?
   What does your father want you to be?
   What does he like about that job?
   What job would he not like for you?
   Would your mother like you to do what your father does?
   Why?
   *If there is another important person in the household besides the fa-
   ther, ask about him:*
   What do they think about your being a ————?
   Do they ever disagree about the kind of job that they want you to
   have?
   Is there any other grownup you've talked to about jobs? *Probe in
   similar manner.*
8. Have you received any advice or counselling in school about this?
   From whom?
   What did he say?
   If not a guidance counselor: Have you ever talked with a guidance
   counselor?
   What did he say?
9. You've said you'd like to be a ————? Let's say that for some reason
   you couldn't be a ————, what would be your second choice?
   Repeat questions 2–6 for second choice.
10. How long have you wanted to be a ————? (First choice)
    Before that, what did you want to be?
    What made you change your mind?
    Before that what was the first thing you remember wanting to be?
11. Do you think that there are jobs that you might want that you might
    not be able to get because you are a Negro?
    If yes: Probe for specific jobs and ask why.
    If no: Are there any jobs that you don't see many Negroes in?

12. Are there any exciting or unusual jobs that you might like but you don't see many Negroes in?

13. Can you think of some types of work you would *not* like to do? Why not?
    For each job mentioned, probe for both social status reasons and reasons of personal capability. Do not settle for financial reasons only.

14. Are you working now?
    If no, go on to question 15.
    If yes, continue with:
    (a) What do you do? *Probe for specific activities and job description.*
    (b) How many hours per week do you work on this job? What are your hours each day?
    (c) What is the pay . . . (per hour?)
                                    (per week?)
                                    (per month?)
                                    (per year?)
    (d) How long have you had this job? How did you find out about this job?
    (e) Do you expect your present job to end in the near future?
    If yes: Why? *Probe for specifics.*
    What will you do when this job ends?
    If no: Why not?

15. *If no to question 14 ask:*
    (a) Have you ever tried to get a job?
    If yes: Please give an example—*Probe for type of job, method of trying to obtain it, what happened as a result of his efforts.*
    If no: How do you think you might go about getting a job if you wanted one?
    (b) Have you had any other jobs in the past?
    If yes: Probe for job description.
                hours
                pay
                length of time held and reason for leaving
                how the job was discovered and obtained
    NOTE: *If the child had not had any previous work experience and is not working presently, continue with the regular Work Schedule. The following questions are only for students who have been or are now employed:*

16. Now I'd like you to think about all the jobs you have held in the past and the job you hold now. Tell me:
    (a) What you liked and disliked about each.

For instance: What did you think about the pay, the type of work, the hours, the people you worked with, the physical setting.

(b) How would you describe your boss (es)?
Did/do you have to see him often during the day? *Probe for the specific nature of his contact with the boss and his feelings about this contact.*
What does your boss normally do?

(c) What was most important to you when you were deciding whether or not to take the job(s)?

(d) Did you know much about the job(s) before you took it (them)? *Probe for what he knows and how he knew it.*

(e) Why do you think you were hired?
Do you think there was something "special" about you that helped you get this job(s)?
What do you think your boss took into consideration when he hired you?

(f) How did you do on the job?

(g) If your boss didn't treat you fairly, what could you do about it?

17. Is your employer white or Negro?

(a) Have you ever had a Negro boss? If so, was he different in any way from the white bosses you have had?

(b) How many people work on your job?

(c) How many of these are white? Negro?

(d) Are there differences between white jobs and Negro jobs?
What's the difference?
What jobs are for whites?
What jobs are for Negroes?

(e) Are whites treated differently from Negroes?
If so, in what way and why do you think this is so?

18. If you were thinking about taking a job, what are some of the things you'd try to find out about the job?

19. When someone is thinking about hiring you, what things about you do you think he should take into consideration?

20. If you could have a wish to become anything you wanted, what would it be?
Why?
Could you ever become that?

ADDENDUM TO VI. Family Work

N O T E: *If father is absent, but you think subject may know something about his father's work, ask these questions:*

1. Do you think your father has abilities he never got to use in work?
   Is your father working now?
   If yes:
   What kind of work does he do?
   Where?
   How long has he been working there?
   What does he have to do when he is at work?
   What does he say about his work?
   How much does his job pay?
   Have you ever gone to work with him?
   Do you have any idea how he learned to do this particular type of work?
   If special training was required, ask where he got his training, inquire about the nature of the training. Probe to find out if parent is trained to do something else. If so, ask why he is not working at the kind of job for which he was trained.
   (a) Does he likes his job?
       What does he like/dislike about it?
       Would you like to do this type of work?
       Why/why not?
   (b) Does he have a second job or extra job?
       If yes: Use the questions above as a guide.
   (c) Before working at this job (these jobs) where did your father work?
       Ask the questions above about previous jobs.
       If no: Has he ever worked?
       If he has, ask questions above about previous jobs.
       When did he stop working?
       Why?
       Has there been a (another) period when your father was unemployed?
       If yes: When was that?
       How long was he unemployed?
       How did he spend his time when he wasn't working?
       What does (did) he have to do in order to find another job?
       How do you think he feels when he is not working?

2. When your father was growing up, what did he want to be?
   Probe: Try to cover the following three items:
   (a) Was it something he once did, but then gave it up?
   (b) Was it something he never did, but always wanted to do?

(c) What were his explanations as to why he never did it, or why he left it?

3. *Where there is an easily accessible history of something the father wanted to be, ask the following questions:*
   (a) How do you think your father feels about the way things turned out, about not being a ————?
   (b) What do you think he should have done with himself, in terms of work?
   (c) How would you feel if, when you're his age, you haven't become what you wanted to be?

4. *Where the subject cannot report some specific job aspiration of father's, probe for idealistic jobs the father might have liked.*
   If your father could have been anything he wanted to be, what do you think he would have been?
   What stopped him from doing that?
   Would he have been good at being a ————?
   Why?
   Probe here for either a YES or NO answer, for the personal qualities the boy feels his father had or lacked, qualities that would in the boy's mind have been important to being a ————.

   N O T E : *If there is no father present or working, but if the mother is working, ask these questions about the mother.*

VII. SELF-CONCEPT

1. Everybody has some things that he's especially good at and other things he's pretty bad at.
   (a) What things would you say you can do much better than the average boy your age?
       First get spontaneous list; then, if necessary, probe for different areas: School, sports, street life, work, hobbies, social skills.
   (b) *For each such activity probe for:*
       What makes you better at that?
       We want to know if he thinks his competence is just natural, learned, imitative, etc.
   (c) What sorts of things are you not so good at, compared with the average boy your age?
   (d) *For each activity mentioned:*
       What would it take for you to become better at that?

2. Now, there are probably some things that you're lousy at but you don't really care about because other things are more important.
   But of those things you said you weren't very good at, which ones would you want to change if you could?

Why?

Do you think you can?

3. If you could be different in any *other* ways, how would you like to be different?

   Why?

4. If somebody was trying to brainwash you in order to change you as much as possible from what you are now, what about your self would you fight hardest to keep the same?

5. If your mother could have you change in any ways she wanted, how do you think she'd have you be different?

   Would you want to change to be that way?

   If he sounds as if he's giving a pat answer, try something like, Come on now, do you really mean that?

6. If your father (father-surrogate, or any other important person charged with raising the boy) could change you, how would he want you to be different?

   Would you want to be like that?

7. What about your (sister or brother)?

   Here ask about brother(s) and sister(s) who seem most important.

8. If your best friend could have you be different in any ways, how do you think he'd want you to change?

9. Are there any things your folks want you to do that your friends don't want or don't like you to do?

   (What do you do about that?

   How do you decide?

   How do you feel about it?)

10. Are there any things your friends want or like you to do that your folks don't like?

    (What do you do in that case?

    How do you decide?

    How do you feel about it?)

11. Are there any things that other adults want or expect from you that your folks are against or don't care about?

    Utilize similar probes; if no response, ask what about teachers, employers.

12. *If answer is "No" to above questions, one last valiant effort:*

    Do you ever find yourself in situations where two people disagree about how you should be or what you should do?

13. If you could grow up to be like any person you *know*, who would you pick?

    Why?

    What would you have to do to become more like him?

    Make sure he is telling you about someone he knows as opposed to a celebrity or someone he "knows of."

14. (a) If you had a chance to change places with any boy your age that you know—be like him and live his life—who would you switch with?
Why?

(b) Do you know of families that you like so much sometimes that you think it would be nice to be a member of that family?
Explore.

15. Who of the boys your age that you know, would you most hate to be like?
Why?

16. Let's pretend you wanted to disappear from the scene for a while, but you had to get someone to take your place so that no one would know you were gone. You have to teach him, like with a spy, how to act like you so that no one would know the difference.
How would you tell him to act around home? With your friends? At school? (etc.)

17. If you could be changed into any famous person who ever lived, who would you pick?
Why?

VIII. RACE

1. We are interested in finding out how teen-agers think of themselves racially. First of all, what do you call yourself in terms of race?
Remember the term used by S and use it subsequently in the interview. If the question is not clear even after re-wordings, ask: "Do you think of yourself as being colored, Negro, black, Afro-American, West Indian, or what?"

2. Some of the boys we've interviewed have referred to themselves as Negro and some kids said that they were black. Other kids called themselves colored and some have called themselves "Afro."

(a) Do you think that a person who calls himself black or Afro-American thinks about his race differently than one who calls himself colored or Negro?

(b) Do you think there's any difference between a person who calls himself colored and one who calls himself Negro?

(c) What about your family, your friends . . .
How do they refer to themselves racially?

3. When did you first realize that you were ———?
What happened?
How did you feel about it?
How old were you then?
Did you tell any of your family about it? (or anyone else?)
What did they say?

If the subject relates a very early incident without much detail, and it looks as though probing won't elicit more, then ask for later incidents:

When was the next time that made you aware that you were a ———?
When was the last time you thought about being a ———?
What made you think about it?

4. Have you ever been called *nigger* or any names like that?

   Explore specific circumstances. If subject only mentions being called nigger by other Negroes, still explore it but ask him if he's ever been called that by whites.

5. Have there been any times when something bad or unpleasant happened to you just because you are ———?

   Suggested probes: What happened then? (How old were you?)
   How did you feel?
   Why did it happen?
   Did you tell anybody about it?
   What did that make you think?

6. *If subject mentions an incident*:
   Did this sort of thing ever make you wonder if Negroes were maybe not as good as whites?

   If subject does not mention an incident:
   Do you think that some Negro children sometimes wonder if they are as good as white children? *Explore.*
   Have you ever wondered that about yourself?

7. Do you ever discuss the racial situation or racial problems at home? Give me some examples.
   When was the last family discussion about ———s and things that happen with them?
   What was it all about? *Find out who participated, who said what, what started it.*
   If father is in household: Do your mother and father ever disagree about the racial situation or civil rights?
   Do you ever disagree with your mother (or, if present, your father) about these things?

8. Imagine that you and your family were watching the news on T.V. and there was a report that a Negro civil rights leader had been shot and killed by a white man.
   What would you think and feel?
   What would (each family member) say?
   (*Probes*: How would you feel about whites?
   How would you feel about America?)

9. Imagine that you were watching T.V. and there was a news flash that there was rioting in the Negro section of a large city.
   Repeat above probes.

10. Let's pretend that a little boy is playing on the sidewalk and some white boys push past him. One of the white boys says "Hey, nigger, get out of the way." Now, the little boy had never heard that before. He never even knew he was Negro.
How does he react to this? What does he think, do, feel?

11. Now let's imagine that you go downtown with some friends and you go into a store to look at the merchandise. Then you notice the store manager looking at you.
What's happening? (What is the manager thinking? What are you thinking? Your friends? What happens?)

12. When you see a Negro guy dating a white girl, what do you think about it?

13. When you see a Negro girl dating a white boy what do you think about it?

14. If there was an injection or a pill you could take that would make you white, what would you do? Why? *Explore.*

15. If you could press a button and by magic it would turn everyone in America into Negroes, would you do it? Why?
Explore.

16. What is the difference between white kids you know and Negro kids you know?

17. What are the differences between Negro people and white people in general?

18. What are some advantages of being ———?
Why are they advantages? *Ask about each.*

19. What are some disadvantages of being ———?
Why are they disadvantages? *Ask about each.*

20. Are there some things that you know of that Negroes can't do or that they are not allowed or encouraged to do?

21. Is life for Negroes different from life for whites?

22. Do you have any close friends who are white?
If not: Why not?
Have you ever had any white friends?
If yes: How do you (did you) get along with them?

23. How would you feel if you were invited to a party and you were pretty sure you'd be the only ——— there?
Would you invite a white boy or girl to a party if you knew everyone else there would be ———?
Why or why not?

24. Would you:
    (a) live in an all-white neighborhood? In an integrated neighborhood?
    (b) go to an all-white school?

(c) belong to the same social club with some white boys your age?
(d) belong to the same gang with some white boys your age?
(e) invite a white boy to watch TV at your house?
(f) go to his house to watch TV?
(g) go to a party with some white boys your age?

25. Do you know what a *do* is?
If he doesn't know what a do is, suggest "hair process."
What kind of dos have you seen?
Would you like to have a *do* yourself?
Explore to find out what kind of do he would like, and when, and why he'd like to get his hair done.
Have you ever had a do?
Is there any difference between kids who wear *dos* and those who don't?

26. (a) Are you lighter or darker or about the same color as other members of your family?
If lighter or darker: Do they treat you differently because of it?
If yes: How?
(b) What about your friends—are you lighter or darker or about the same color as your friends?
If lighter or darker: Are you treated differently because of it?

27. Were any members of your family white people or Indians or Africans?
If yes: Do you feel you are part (white, Indian, or African, depending on what *S* mentioned)?

28. Have you heard of Negro History Week?
Where did you hear about it?
What do people do during that week?
Have you ever heard the Negro National Athem?

29. Tell me about some famous Negroes from history.
Ask what they are famous for.

30. Name some well-known or famous Negroes who are living today.
Ask what they are famous for.
Have you ever read any books about Negroes or books written by Negroes?
If yes: Which ones?

31. *After subject has named and described some contemporary Negroes, ask him to name and describe some Negroes in the following areas:*
(a) Sports
(b) Entertainment (music, movies, TV, etc.)
(c) Civil rights
(d) Writing, painting, arts
(e) Science

(f) Famous Africans

(g) *Any other area you think of*

(h) *Ask him if there is anyone or any category that was left out.*

32. Are there some well-known Negroes that you know about who live in Boston? *If he doesn't name one ask him if he has heard of Mel King, Noel Day, Royal Bolling, Rev. Virgil Wood and any other specific persons you feel may give us an idea of what he knows about the community.*

33. Do you know of any guys who are into Numbers (or policy) or who are making it as pimps (alternate wordings: "who have a string of hustlers") or who are making some money through stealing?
Assure him that names are not necessary.
For each: How do you know about him?
Some of the kids we interviewed last year said that they had thought about being pimps or getting into Numbers.
Did you ever think of doing that?

34. Do you know about any civil rights groups or organizations?
If the question is not clear, give the NAACP as an example and ask if he knows what it does.
Inquire specifically as to what he knows about the following groups and what they do:

(a) CORE

(b) SNCC

(c) The Urban League

(d) The Black Muslims

(e) Operation Exodus

(f) METCO

35. Do you know about the following people? (*if he has not already talked about them*)
What do you think about them?
How did you find out about them?

(a) Martin Luther King

(b) Malcolm X

(c) Stokely Carmichael

(d) Louis X (or Louis Farrakahn)

(e) Rap Brown

(f) *anyone else you'd like to ask about*

Do your family, friends think the same as you do about these groups and people?

36. There's a lot of talk nowadays about Black Power.
What do you think people mean by it?
What do you think about it?

37. Do you think things are changing for ——— in America?
    If yes: In what ways?
    What changes do you hope for by the time you grow up?
38. Do you think that your being in America will make it harder for you to get what you want out of life?
39. Do you think there is ever any conflict between being ——— and being an American?
40. If you weren't ———, what race or group would you like to be a member of?
    What race or group would you hate to be a member of?
41. Is there any other country you'd rather live in than the U.S.A.?
42. Are there any questions we should have asked about race but didn't?

IX. NEIGHBORHOOD, HOUSE, AND TRAVEL

1. When you think about your neighborhood, what first comes to your mind?
   What else stands out in your neighborhood?
2. How would you describe your neighborhood? *If child has not answered the questions below in his response, then ask*:
   (a) What does your neighborhood look like?
   (b) What kinds of buildings are there?
   (c) What kinds of people live in your neighborhood?
   (d) What goes on in your neighborhood?
   (e) What is your neighborhood called?
   (f) In what section of town is it?
3. (a) Draw a map of your neighborhood. *Use black felt tipped pen for this drawing.*
   (b) *When the subject has completed his drawing give him the base map.*
       There are a number of places I am going to ask you to find on this map. First, find the street where you live on the map and mark it with an "X" (*Color: black pencil*)
       Draw a circle around the area you call your neighborhood. (*Color: black*)
4. Where do you usually hang out in your neighborhood?
   (a) Do you have any favorite places for hanging out?
   (b) *If yes*: Where are they?
       Draw a circle around those areas on the (base) map. (*Color: green*)
   (c) Why do you like to hang out there?
   (d) What do you do there?

Where are special places you go to have a good time?
Draw circles around them. (*Color: orange*)

5. Are there some places in your neighborhood where you are not allowed to go?
   (a) *If yes:* Where are they?
   (b) Who told you not to go there?
   (c) Why are you not supposed to go there?
   (d) Do you go anyway?
   (e) Draw a circle around those places on the (base) map.
       (*Color: blue*)

6. Are there some places in your neighborhood where some people feel are not safe places to go at night?
   Where? Draw a circle around them. (*Color: red*)
   Why do they think they are not safe?
   Are there some places where people do not feel safe during the day?
   Where? Draw a circle around them. (*Color: red*)
   Why do they think they are not safe?

   N O T E: *The Interviewer is to indicate with brackets the areas unsafe at night and unsafe during the day. Pencil in "N" in the area unsafe at night, "D" the area unsafe during the day.*

7. Is your school in your neighborhood? Show me where your school is on the (base) map. Draw a circle around it (*Color: black*)
   (a) Do you walk or ride from where you live to your school?
       If he rides ascertain mode of transportation.
   (b) Show me the streets you take when you go to school with a heavy dotted line on the map. (*Color: black*)
   (c) Do you usually go this way?
       Why?
   (d) Are there any short-cuts you sometimes take to school?
   (e) What kinds of things do you do on the way to and from school?
   (f) What are some of the places where you stop in between school and home?
   (g) Where do you hang out around the school?

8. When you go outside of your neighborhood, what are some of the places you go? *If necessary clarify by saying "in the Boston area."* Draw circles around them on the (base) map. (*Color: purple*)
   (a) How often do you go to ———? *Ask about each place.*
   (b) How do you get there?
   (c) What do you go there for?
   (d) What streets are included in the downtown area?
       Ask subject to write the word "downtown" across the area he has indicated. (Color: purple)

(e) Why do you go downtown?

(f) What do you do when you are there?

(g) How often would you say you go downtown?

(h) Have you ever had any unusual experiences downtown?

(i) Has anything that has happened to you downtown ever bothered you?

(j) Have you ever felt you were lost when you were downtown?
     If yes: Will you explain what happened?

9. Where is the center of Boston? (*Purple "X" on map*)
   If not "downtown" ask: How often do you go there?

10. Do you like the neighborhood where you live now?
    Will you explain that somewhat?

11. What kind of reputation does your neighborhood have?
    How do you know this?
    What do people who live outside of your neighborhood think of it?
    How do you know this?

12. Tell me about your house (or apartment) where you live.
    What does it look like on the outside?
    What is it like on the inside?
    How many rooms for sleeping?
    Where do you sleep?
    Where does everyone else sleep?
    What are some things you like about your house (apartment) and what are some things you don't like about it?

13. Where do you go when you want to be alone?
    Where do you like to sit in your house when you want to be by yourself or just don't feel like being bothered with other people?

14. What is the busiest room in your house?
    What goes on there?

15. When you're older and on your own, what kind of house would you like to live in?
    What would you want it to look like on the outside?
    What do you want it to be like inside?
    Where do you want it to be?
    Why do you want to live in a place like that?
    Do you know anybody who lives in a house like that?
    Who?
    Have you ever visited them?
    Where is their house?
    Who do you want to live with you?
    Why?
    Who do you want to live nearby?
    Why?
    Who do you not want to live nearby?
    Why not?

16. Have you ever been to any cities or towns near Boston?
    If yes: Which ones?
    How did you happen to go? (*Or*: Why did you go?)
    How did you get there—bus, subway, car?
    Have you been to some places outside of Massachusetts?
    If yes: Where?
    How did you happen to go?
    How did you get there (car, bus, plane, train)?
    Which ones did you visit and which ones did you just travel
    through?
    What did you do there?
    How long did you stay?
    How old were you then?
    When was this?

17. If you won a free trip to any place in the world, where would you
    like to go?
    Why?
    How did you know about ———?
    Anyplace else?
    Why?
    How do you know about it?
    If you could *live* anywhere in the world you would like, what place
    would you choose?
    Why?
    Any place else?
    Why?
    Can you think of some places where you never want to live or even
    visit?
    Why?
    Anyplace else?
    Why?

Appendix B
Reference Group Interview Schedules (Time I) *

PART I. Parent Interview

I. PRESENT FAMILY—description of children and their interaction
  1. *If child is an only child, modify questions appropriately.*
     (a) Starting with the oldest, will you tell me something about them:
        i. their names, ages
        ii. where they were born
        iii. what each child is like
     (b) *Ask about each*:
        Does (name of child) go to school?
        If yes: What school, grade, course?
        If no: What grade was he (she) in when he (she) stopped going?
        What has he (she) been doing since then?
     (c) *About children above 18 years attending school, ask*:
        Does (name of child) work?

---

* Sibling and Teacher Interview Schedules from Time I are similar; Time II and Time III Interviews are parallel to Time I, with appropriate update questions. All are available on request.

      If no: Has he (she) ever tried to get a job or to make some money?

    If yes: Where does he (she) work?

           What are his (her) hours?

           How did he (she) happen to get this job?

2. Do any of the children seem to take after or act like somebody in the family?

   If yes: Which ones, and in what respect?

3. What are some ways in which the children seem to be alike and in what ways are they different?

4. How do your children get along together?

   (a) Which ones seem to work well together or to help each other?

   (b) Can you give some examples of this?

   (c) Who does (focal child) get along with best?

   (d) Who is (focal child) closest to in the family?

       Why do you think that is?

5. How do arguments between the children start in your house? Is (focal child) often involved in arguments?

   If yes: With whom?

          What are the arguments about?

6. How is (focal child) different from your other children? *Omit if he has no siblings.*

   Probe in some specific areas.

   (a) health, size, athletic abilities

   (b) school performance, intellectual abilities

   (c) temperament and general decorum

   (d) motivation, energy out-put and determination

7. Has (focal child) lived with you all of his life?

   If no: Probe for details.

8. What was he like as a baby and a young child?

9. As a baby and a young child, did he have any serious accidents or illnesses?

   If yes: Probe for nature of accident or illness.

10. How has he changed?

   Probe if necessary: In terms of personality?

11. Has there ever been a period when he was hard to get along with?

   If yes: Tell me what was going on and how you handled it.

12. (a) In what ways is (focal child) like you?

       Different from you?

   (b) In what ways is he like his father?

       Different from his father?

13. Have his grandparents helped out with rearing him in some way? Has anyone else?

14. Could you tell me how you and (focal child) get along together now?
15. Are there any ways you get on each other's nerves?
16. How is affection generally shown in your family?
    (*Optional probe*: Do you show affection quite a bit or would you say you are fairly reserved people?)
17. Do you ever have time to do things together?
    If yes: What do you do together?
              When can you usually spend time together? (How much time?)
18. Who does (focal child) seem to imitate or try to be like?
19. Who does he really take after?
20. In what ways would you like him to change?
21. What are some traits or habits he has that you hope will *not* change?
22. *Ask the parent to describe the most recent happy or good day and the most recent bad day that they've had.*
23. What adults seem to be most important to him?
    When they are together, what do they do?
    Who are the men (focal child) has contact with?

Ask Only of Mothers

24. What man seems to influence your son most?
25. *If not subject's father*: How and when did he and your son become acquainted?
26. Do you encourage their relationship? Why or why not?
27. Give me an example of an activity that he and your son have shared in.

II. SITUATIONS

Now we want to learn something about typical reactions of (focal child) in certain kinds of situations.
   1. What happens when . . .
      (a) he does something that you don't want him to do?
      (b) he wants to go some place or do something and you want him to do something else?
      (c) you are ill or are not feeling well?
      (d) he is ill?
      (e) he gets angry with you?
      (f) he seems unhappy about something?
   2. Do you and (other parent) ever disagree on how to raise him or disagree on how to handle him?

3. When he has done something wrong or hasn't done something that he ought to have done, who usually punishes him?

4. How is he punished?
   How does (focal child) react to this kind of punishment?

5. What sort of things might he get punished for?
   Get examples.

6. (a) What things does he do that really make you happy?
   (b) How do you show your reaction to him?

7. I'd like to get some idea of the sort of general rules you have for (focal child). What sort of things is he allowed to do and what sort of things isn't he allowed to do?
   Suggested probe: How about going to certain places?

8. How late may he stay out at night?

9. How about the amount of time he watches TV?
   How many hours and days is the TV set on and someone is watching?

10. How about cursing and swearing?

11. What are your feelings about his smoking?
    What about drinking?

12. Some families have difficulty dealing with questions about sex with their children. How has this been handled with (focal child)? *Probe.*

13. Sometimes even the most loving and patient parent feels her (his) children are more trouble than they are worth. When do you feel that way about (focal child)?
    Do you ever feel like that towards your other child (or children)?
    Ask about other parent or someone else who shares responsibility for rearing the child.

III. SCHOOL—*The Parent's Perception of the Focal Child's School Life*

1. Does (focal child) talk about school much?

2. What does he say about it?

3. What is your opinion of the DuBois School?
   (a) What has been happening there?
   (b) Why has there been so much trouble?
   (c) Who do you think is involved in the trouble?
   (d) Who's responsible for it?

4. Has your child said much about the current trouble at the DuBois?
   Inquire in detail about what child has reported.

5. Have you or any of your family ever gone to the school to talk to a teacher or the principal about (focal child)?

Ask for description of instances.
Have you ever been called by the school about your child?

6. Have you met any of his teachers (past or present)?
   What are they like? *Ask for descriptions of individual teachers.*

7. Which one of your son's teachers at the DuBois School did he like the most or dislike the most?
   Why?
   How did you find out about this?
   How did you react to it?

8. Who at the DuBois School do you think understands your son best?

9. Who is the principal of the school and what's he like?

10. Does your son have any Negro teachers?

11. Do you think there is any difference between Negro teachers at the DuBois and white teachers in how they treat kids or how they teach?

12. Have you seen anything about the DuBois in the papers or on TV?
    (a) Have you talked about the news with (focal child)?
        Ask about specifics.
    (b) Have you talked about the DuBois with any neighbors, friends, or other parents?

13. What do you think is the effect that this trouble has on the children?
    . . . on (focal child)?

14. Have you been approached by any parents' group or community group like Exodus to do anything or go to meetings about the DuBois?
    If so: What have they said? *Get specifics.*

15. What about this issue of combat pay for teachers at the DuBois—do you think a teacher should get more pay to teach there?

16. What do you think about the teachers at the DuBois—are they better, worse, or the same as other Boston school teachers?

17. What do you think ought to be done to solve the problems at the DuBois?
    If Negro staff is not mentioned:
    Do you think that more Negro teachers would help?
    Do you think a Negro principal would help?

18. (a) Have any nice things happened at school for your son?
    (b) Any problems?
        Ask for examples of each.

19. How is your son different from your other children who have been in your son's grade?

20. Does your son ever ask for help with his school work?
    If necessary, then ask: Who helps the child and how does it turn out?

21. If your son has a problem with this school work or otherwise, what does he generally do?

22. What do you do?
    (*This can also include questions about future.*)
23. Has he ever been held back a grade?
    If yes: What grade was it? Why?
24. What happens when he brings home a poor report card?
25. What happens when he brings home a good report card?
26. What were his grades like on his last report?
27. Does he seem to find school interesting, or is he bored with it?
    Why do you think he finds it interesting? (or, why is he bored with it?)
28. Does (focal child) stay out of school much?
    Why does he stay out?
    Is he sick often?
    Does he play hookey?
    What happens when you find out he's been playing hookey?
    (*Or*: What would you do if he played hookey and you found out about it?)
29. Do you think he has ever considered dropping out of school?
    If so, explore for reasons and parents' or others' responses to this.
30. How does the child find out what is possible for him, regarding the choice of courses, choice of other schools, job, or other academic possibilities?
    Probe to find out what the child or parent may have been told by teachers or guidance counselor.
31. How did he get into the school he is in now?
32. Did you think of his going to a different school?
33. Did he have a chance to go to a different school?
    If yes: How is it he is attending ——— school?
34. Has (focal child) said anything about what high school he might like to go to?
    If yes: Which one?
        Why does he seem interested in ——— school?
35. What high school do you think he should attend?
    Why?
36. Do you think (focal child) has the ability to graduate from high school?
37. How do you think his school work compares to the work of the other students in his class?
    Probes: Is it as good, not as good, or about the same?
        Are you satisfied with it?
38. Do you think he works as hard as the average student in his class?
    (a) Does he work as hard as he ought to?
        If not: What do you say or do about it?

(b) Is he doing as well as he could?

39. Do you think his marks really show how much he knows or understands?
(*Optional probe*: Do you think his teachers mark him fairly?)
If not: What would give a better idea of how he's doing or what he knows?

40. How does he feel he's doing in school?

41. Do you think that has any effect on how he views his future?

42. How far do you hope he will go in school?
If appropriate:
(a) Do you want him to go to college?
(b) What kind of college and what course?
(c) Do you think he has the ability to graduate from college?
If not: What would need to happen for him to be able to make it through college?

43. How far do you think he will actually go in school?

44. Compare your schooling to your child's schooling today.

45. If you were a teacher, how would you handle discipline problems? How would you deal with the worst trouble-makers?
If firmness or punishment is suggested: How would you get it across without stirring up more anger?

46. (a) If you were planning a school for your child, to be any way you wanted, what would it be like?
(b) Do you know of any schools in or around Boston that are like that?

IV. PEERS AND THEIR ACTIVITIES

1. What does your son usually do after school?
Probe for difference in playing and hanging out.

2. Who are his best friends? *Get their full names.*
Who does he spent most time with?

3. What are they like?
Are any of them boys you would prefer he did not spend time with? Why?
Are there any kids you wish he would spend more time with? Why?
Which of his friends do you like most?

4. Where do they usually play or hang out?

5. How often do you see his friends?

6. What kind of trouble does he seem to get into?
Who does he get in trouble with?

7. Do any girls hang around with (focal child) and the other boys?

8. Are there things that you want your son to do that his friends don't want or like him to do?

9. Are there things that his friends want or like him to do that you don't want him to do?

10. What are his favorite activities?

11. Does he belong to any clubs or groups?
    If yes: What does he do there?

12. How is (focal child) different from most boys his age?
    Comparisons with specific peers may sharpen the contrasts.

13. What advantages does (focal child) have over most boys his age?

14. What kinds of things does he do especially well?

15. What are some of his handicaps or disadvantages in comparison to other boys his age?

16. What are some things he doesn't seem to do well at all?

V. WORK—*The Focal Child's Work and Expenses*

1. Does (focal child) work?
   If no: Has he ever worked?
   If no: Has he ever tried to find a job?
   Probe for information about his looking for jobs.

2. *If the focal child is working, or if he has worked in the past, ask:*
   What kind of work does/did he do?
   What does/did he like about his job, and what is/was it that he does/did not like about it?
   What else has he told you about it?
   What does/did he say about his boss?

3. How did he find this job?

4. Is his employer white or Negro?
   (a) Are there differences between jobs for Negroes and jobs for whites where he works?
   (b) What are the differences?
       What jobs are for Negroes? What jobs are for whites?
   (c) Are whites treated differently from Negroes on the job?

5. How much does/did he earn?

6. What does/did he do with this money?

7. *If child doesn't work*: How does he get extra spending money?
   If child does work, ask: Is there any other way he gets spending money?
   If appropriate, ask: Whom does he ask for money and what happens when he asks?

8. (a) Can you give me an estimate of the amount of money (focal child) spends every week for lunch?

(b) How much does he spend for carfare or busfare?

(c) What does he spend on recreation—movies, and so forth?

(d) Does he save any money?
Is he encouraged to save money?

9. (a) Who selects and pays for his clothes?

(b) Does he ask for things to wear that you think are unnecessary?
If yes: Can you give an example?
Did he get them?
What is the added expense of something like that?

NOTE: *If focal child worked previously, ask questions 1 through 5 about previous jobs.*

10. How do you feel about his working?

11. Do you think that this will help him later on?
If not: Why not?

12. (a) What kind of work do you hope he will get when he grows up?

(b) What kind of life do you want (focal child) to lead when he grows up?

(c) What do you hope he will be doing when he is 21 years old? When he is 40 years old?

13. (a) What kind of work will he probably have when he grows up?

(b) What kind of life is he likely to have?

(c) What do you expect him to be doing when he is 21 years old? 40 years old?

(d) What are some of the things that you hope he will not be involved in when he grows up?

VI. RELIGION

1. Do you or your children have any contact with religion?

2. What is your religious affiliation?

3. (a) What church do you attend? What is that church like?

(b) How often do you attend?

(c) Do you go to church together?
If not, find out which family members attend.

4. Is (focal child) encouraged to participate in any religious activities?

5. What type of relationship does your family have with your minister or priest?

6. What do you think religion means in the life of (focal child)?

VII. NEIGHBORHOOD

1. How would you describe your neighborhood?

2. Do you like the neighborhood where you are living?
   Will you explain this somewhat?
   Find out what aspects are desirable and which ones are undesirable.
3. (a) What kind of reputation does your neighborhood have?
      How do you know this?
   (b) What do people who live outside of your neighborhood think of it?
      How do you know this?
4. Are there some places in your neighborhood where (focal child) is not allowed to go?
   Why?
5. Are there some places in your neighborhood where you don't feel safe?
   Why?
6. (a) What are some things you like about your house?
   (b) What are some things you don't like about it?
   (c) How long have you lived at (address given)?
   (d) Where did you live before that?
      Why did you move? *Explore what happened.*
      Where did you live before that?
      Continue to inquire until parent seems to have recalled all the places she (he) has lived.
   (e) How long do you expect to live here (at your present address)?
   (f) Ideally, what kind of housing would you like?
      Where would you like it to be?
      Why?
7. *Ask only if parent migrated from South:*
   (a) What made you decide to come North?
   (b) Why did you pick Boston instead of a place like New York, Philadelphia, Chicago . . . ?
   (c) What are the main differences between living in the North and in the South?
   (d) Do you ever miss the South or wish you were back there?

VIII. RACIAL AWARENESS

1. Can you recall the first time (focal child) became aware of being Negro (colored)?
   (a) What happened at the time?
   (b) How old was he then?
2. Has he had any experiences since then that have made an impression on him?

3. Is the word *nigger* used often in your home?
   How is it used?
   When did the child become aware of its meaning?
   Will you tell me about it?

4. Has (focal child) ever been treated differently in school because of his race?
   If yes: What happened?
             How did you find out about it?
             What was the outcome?

5. Is (focal child) lighter or darker than his brothers and sisters (or others in the family)?
   Does it seem to make a difference?

6. What do you tell your son about being Negro?

7. What advice do you give him?

8. Is he treated differently by anyone because of it?

9. Do you think that some Negro children sometimes wonder if they are as good as white children?
   Explore, especially in relation to self and own children.

10. Do you think life for Negroes is going to be different when your son grows up?
    If yes: In what ways?
    If no: Why not?

11. Do you ever discuss the racial situation or racial problems at home?
    Give me some examples.

12. When was the last family discussion about Negroes and things that happen with them?

13. (a) Are there any famous Negroes in the news who (focal child) seems to admire?
    (b) Regardless of race, what person (not necessarily famous) does he seem to admire the most, want to take after?

14. What do you think of the following:
    (a) Operation Exodus
    (b) METCO
    (c) CORE and SNCC
    (d) NAACP and the Urban League
    (e) The Black Muslims
    (f) Martin Luther King
    (g) Malcolm X
    (h) Mel King
    (i) Adam Clayton Powell
    (j) Stokely Carmichael

(k) Edward Brooke

(l) Royal Bolling

(m) Black Power

15. Do any of the members of your family have any white friends?
    Do you encourage it?

16. What are your feelings on your son dating a white girl?

17. Would you ever live in an all-white neighborhood?
    In an integrated neighborhood?
    Where?

18. (a) How has being Negro affected your life?

    (b) Can you recall the first time you became aware that you were Negro?
        Same probe as for #1

    (c) How did your parents react?

19. Have you noticed changes in your life?
    In your neighborhood?
    Among your friends?
    Will you give me some examples?

20. Do you think there's any conflict between being an American and being a Negro?

IX. PARENT'S SELF-CONCEPT

1. We've been talking a lot about (focal child). It would be nice to talk some more about your own life.

   (a) Where were you born?

   (b) What is your date of birth?

   (c) Where have you spent most of your life?

   (d) Could you tell me a little about your family?

   (i) Are your parents still living?

   (ii) What is (was) your father like?
        What was his work?
        How far did he go in school?
        What did he want for you to do and be?

   (iii) What is (was) your mother like?
        Did she work?
        How far did she go in school?
        What did she want for you to do and be?

   (iv) Do you have any brothers or sisters?
        What are their names and how old are they?
        Where do they live?
        How far did they go in school?
        What are they doing now?

      (v) What do you remember most about your grandparents?

      (vi) Were any members of your family white people or Indians or Africans?

         If yes: Do you feel you are part (white—Indian—African, depending on what Subject mentioned)?

   (e) Do you ever tell your children about things that happened to you before they were born?

     What sorts of things have you told them?

   (f) How long have you lived in Boston?

     If Boston-born, ask: Have you always lived in Boston?

   (g) How far did you go in school?

     Did you consider going further in school?

     How far did you want to go in school?

   (h) Do you think about going back to school?

     If yes: What would you study? Why?

     When you were in school, what were your future plans?

2. What did you want to do for a living when you were growing up?
   What were some other occupations you were interested in?

3. How old were you when you first went to work?
   What kind of job was it?

4. What have you done since then?

5. Are you working now?
   What does the job involve?

6. *If working, ask*: How did you get your present job?
                     Are you satisfied with it?

7. What was the best job you ever had (it doesn't make any difference how long you had it)?

8. *If unemployed*: When did you last work?
                What type of job was it?

9. Do you expect to go back to work?

10. What kind of work would you most like to do?

11. When would you be going back to work?

12. When you are not working (outside or around the house), how do you spend your time?
    Probe: Watch TV, movies, read, visit with neighbors, friends, going to nightclubs.

13. Do you belong to any clubs or organizations? Which?

14. Have you ever worked with a civil rights group?
    Which one?
    What did you do?

15. What things do you think you're better at than the average person your age?

16. What things do you do less well than the average person your age?

17. In what ways are you most different from other people—most unique compared to the average person?

18. If you could be different in any way you wanted, how would you like to be different?

19. If your children could have you be different in any ways they wanted, how do you think they'd want you to be different?
Would you want to change that way?

20. *If husband or wife is present, ask*:
How would your husband (wife) want you to be different?
Would you want to change that way?

21. If your friends could have you be different in any ways, how might they want you to change?
Would you want to change that way?

22. If you could be like anyone you know personally, who would you want to be like? Why? What are they like?

X. PARENTS' MARITAL STATUS (Modify for Father)

1. How did you and (spouse or child's father) meet each other, and what happened?
If father of focal child is not available for interviewing, inquire about his birthplace, birthdate, education, occupation. Try to elicit personality description: What do you remember best about him? What were some of his strong points and some of his weak points?

2. How old were you then?

3. How did things go after that?
Probe history of relationship and reactions of offspring to critical events.

4. *If parents are separated or divorced*:
   (a) When did the relationship break up? Why?
   (b) What was the age of (focal child) at that time?
   (c) What has happened since with regard to visiting?
   (d) What support does your ex-spouse give?
       Is it on a voluntary basis?
   (e) What are your attitudes towards your ex-spouse?
   (f) What is your present relationship with him, especially in regard to (focal child)?
   (g) What does (focal child) think of his (real) father?
   (h) What are your prospects and plans or hopes concerning marriage?

5. *If there is another man in the picture*:
   (a) How did you and Mr. ——— become acquainted?
   (b) How long have you known him?

(c) What are some of the things you like about him?
Probe for his strengths and weaknesses.

(d) Would you consider him as a prospective husband?

(e) What effect do you think this will have on your son?

(f) How much time does Mr. ——— spend with your son?

(g) Do you encourage this relationship?
If yes: Why?
If no: Why not?

(h) What are some of the things that Mr. ——— and your son do together?

(i) Do you approve or disapprove?

(j) Are there any other males that your son is influenced by?

(k) How do the other males compare to the one that has the most influence on your son?

(l) Of all the men you have come in contact with, which one would you like your son to be like? Explain in detail.

6. What is it like bringing up a child without his father being there?
What effect do you think it has on (focal child): How does he feel?

7. What is your attitude towards welfare (ADC)?

8. *If mother wants to get off welfare*:
What is your reason for trying to get off welfare?

9. When you are not at home, who manages your household?
Which of your children seems more responsible for that kind of task?

10. Who makes most of the decisions in your family?
What kinds of things does she (he) have to make decisions about?
Does she (he) talk about it with other people in the family?
If yes: With whom?
Give an example of something she (he, they) had to make a decision about.

PART II. Peer Interview *

I. PRIMARY GROUP

1. Who do you hang with? (*Get names and description of each member of respondent's primary group.*)
2. Do you think of yourselves as a gang or a club, or just a bunch of guys?
3. How did you first get into this group? When was that? How is it decided who will be allowed to join the group?
   (*Probe for history and structure of the group before FC joined.*)
4. What kinds of things do you usually do together? (*Get nature and location of activities.*)
5. Where do you hang with them? (School, home, etc.)
   N O T E: *If FC is not listed as a member of this group, ask if respondent (P) belongs to any other groups. Is FC a member of that group too? If not, then ask if P ever hangs with FC at all. If he does, then continue interview concentrating on FC-P relationship; if he doesn't, then ask what he does know about FC and what kind of contact has he had with him.*
6. In this group (or groups) is there anybody who usually is the one who decides what to do? Would you say he is the leader? (*Probe for hierarchy within the group. Get a recent example of a decision made, who made it, whether it was followed through, etc.*)
7. Is there anyone else who makes plans or decisions? Is there anyone who usually gets things going?
8. Does your group have any rules about how you should act around each other? (*Probe for different levels, e.g., smoking, drinking, girls, swearing, etc. and symbolic requirements, e.g., insignia, dress, do's, etc.*)
9. Who is your best friend of all the guys you mentioned? What's he like?
10. Who would you trust the most if you were in trouble? Why is that? Who would you trust the least? Why?
11. Which of these guys would you say you like the least? What's he like?
12. Who's the cleanest, most "together" guy in your group? Is there anyone who is really not "together" at all?
    (*Description.*)
13. Who do you think likes you most? Why? Who likes you the least? Why?

---

* "FC" refers to "Focal Child." Interviewers substituted the boy's first name.

II. FOCAL CHILD—*General*

1. How did you happen to get to know FC? (*If FC is not in any of P's groups, does P know who FC hangs with?*)
2. How long have you known him?
3. What kind of guy is he? (*Encourage a free description of FC here.*)
4. How often do you get together with FC? What kinds of things do you do? Where do you go? (*Probe for parties, sports, general things such as going downtown. Also probe for cooperative ventures—and for things FC and P have done together which no one else knows about.*)
5. What kinds of things would you rather do with FC than with anyone else? Why is that?
6. Are there any things you'd rather not do with him? Why?
7. What kinds of things do you and FC talk about? Does he come to you when he has something on his mind? Do you ever talk to him when something's bugging you?
8. Who do you think is FC's best friend? Why is that?
9. Who would you say he trusts the most?
10. Do you know who he likes the least? Why is that?
11. Are there any girls who hang with you and FC? Who are they? What kinds of things do you do together?
12. Have you ever been in trouble with FC? (What happened and where: How did it turn out? Were the police involved?)
13. Does FC get into trouble very much? What kind?
14. What happens if you and FC disagree about something? (*Examples: Probe for contests, competition, rivalry, etc.*)
15. Have you and FC ever had a real fight? (Fist-fight) What started it, and how did it turn out?
16. Are there any groups or kids you and FC fight with? (*Get example of an incident and how it turned out.*)
17. How long have you and FC been friends? What do you think is the basis of your relationship? Are there some things you guys just wouldn't do to each other? What? How come? (*Probe for rules and agreements with each other, how they come about, and whether there have been disagreements about these rules.*)
18. What could (or did) happen to make you split?

III. SELF-CONCEPT/COMPARISON

1. If you could be different in any way, how would you like to be different?
2. If you could grow up to be like any person *you know*, who would you pick? Why? What is it that you like about that person?

3. If you had a chance to change places with any boy your age that you *know*—be like him and live his life—who would you switch with? Why?

4. Who, of the boys your age you *know*, would you most hate to be like? Why?

5. If you could be changed into any famous person who ever lived, who would you pick? Why is that?

6. In what ways do you think you and FC are the same?

7. How do you think you and FC are different?

8. Are there things FC does better than you do?

9. What are some things you can do better than FC?

10. Are there any things you wish FC would change about himself?

11. Are there things he'd like you to change about yourself? (*Probe for why and whether FC and P would agree on these changes.*)

12. How do the other guys in your group feel about FC?

13. What are some things that FC does well or that the group counts on him to do?

14. Are there things he just doesn't do well enough?

15. Does FC ever let the guys down?

16. If you could have an ideal friend, what would he be like?

IV. RACIAL AWARENESS

1. What do you call yourself in terms of race?

2. How does FC refer to himself?

3. Have you ever been called "nigger," or any names like that? (*Probe for circumstances and reactions.*)

4. Has that ever happened when you and FC were someplace together? What happened? (*How did P respond, and how did FC respond?*)

5. Has there been a time when something bad happened to you and FC just because you were Negro?

6. What do you think are the differences between Negro and white people in general?

7. What are some of the advantages of being Negro? Why?

8. What are some of the disadvantages of being Negro? How come?

9. What does FC think about the advantages and disadvantages of being Negro? Do you agree on these things?

10. Do you think life is different for Negroes than for whites? How?

11. Do you think you are lighter or darker than most of your friends? What about FC? Does this make any difference?

V. SCHOOL, OCCUPATION

1. Some kids we've talked to think school is a drag. Others think it's okay, and some really dig it. How do you feel? What about FC?

2. Have you been in any classes with FC? Which?

3. Is there any teacher you and FC especially like, or have gotten into trouble with? Over what? How did it turn out?

4. Did any of the other guys in your group have trouble with that teacher?

5. How does FC get along with his teachers in general?

6. How is he doing in school? (Grades) How about you? (*Probe for last report card.*)

7. How far do you think FC will go in school? What about you and the rest of the guys?

8. Has FC ever talked about dropping out? (*Probe for when, why.*)

9. How does he feel about going to the DuBois? (If now in high school, how did he feel.)

10. Where does he want to go to high school? (If in a high school now, what does he think of it?)

11. If you could build a school any way you wanted, what would it be like?

12. If FC would build a dream school, how do you think it might differ from yours?

13. Do you play hookey much? Ever with FC? How often, and where do you go?

14. Of the guys in your group, who do you think will be the most successful? Why?

15. Which one will be "happiest"? Why?

16. Who will earn the most money? How come?

17. Will any of them be pretty much unemployed? (Sent up, into drugs, anything like that?)

18. What do you think FC will be doing when he's 25 or 30? Will he be married, have a job, etc.?

VI. FAMILY

1. Do you know FC's family? What are they like? (*Include FC's brothers and sisters here.*)

2. Does he know your family?

3. Whose house do you hang around more often?

4. How do FC and his parents get along?

5. Do they ever disapprove of some of the things you and FC do? What happens then?
6. Do your mother and father know FC? What do they think of him?
7. How do your parents feel about your hanging with FC?
8. How do FC's parents feel about his hanging with you?
9. Do your brothers and sisters know FC? What do they think of him?
10. When you have grown up and are on your own, what kind of a life do you want to have?
    Probe for details and for his plans for arranging for the kind of life he hopes to have.
11. What kinds of things will you want your sons to do when they are your age?
    What kinds of things do you hope they will not do?
    What advice will you give them when they are your age?

Appendix C *Strategic Styles versus Selected Variables*

1. ANTECEDENTS AND CONSEQUENCES OF STRATEGIC STYLES

I have been treating "strategic style" as an organizing variable, in the sense that a style represents an attempt by the individual to take into account, adapt to, and deal with, in a way that is most satisfactory to him, the messages he receives from significant others, as well as with his (a) life chances (determined by birth, residence, color, etc.); (b) personal abilities and potentials (IQ, health, talents, etc.); (c) personal, emotional sets (attitudes, values, etc.); (d) needs, goals, wishes, and dreams; (e) beliefs about the system (whether he views it as open or closed, subject to his control and access, etc.).

It is of interest to determine which antecedent variables, such as environmental factors, family size, birth order, IQ, critical experiences, are associated with specific styles. Furthermore, it should be determined which styles are most often associated with specific consequences—that is, behavioral consequences like school performance, involvement with girls, peer-group activities, drug use, working. For the Pathways Final Report (1970), project staff tested the association of several variables with strategic styles of all seventh- and ninth-grade focal subjects. Computer runs are available for several of these; I shall discuss them briefly here for their heuristic value. (The relevant tables are reproduced below.) Suggestive findings include the following:

a. As might be expected, Conformists and Retreaters tend not to be associated with participation in *nonschool trouble*. Cool Guys and Actors are as likely as not to be involved in this type of trouble, reflecting both reluctance to engage in self-destructive activities or activities that might damage their reputation, and their capacity for controlling their behavior to fit the demands of the situation. The Tough Guy, on the other hand, is almost invariably associated with trouble. In a sense this category begs the question, since in the first place it measures a behavior that heavily influences determination of the style (especially conformist and tough). Although computer data are not available for *school trouble vs. strategic styles*, a general reading of seventh and ninth grade transcripts suggests a similar trend. (Table C: 1.)

b. Conformists and Retreaters are highly unlikely to be associated with the commission of *specified illegal acts* (breaking and entering, car theft, disorderly conduct, etc.); the Tough Guy's involvement is high; the Cool Guy and Actor tend to keep their illegal acts to a minimum (and/or are more careful not to be caught). (Table C: 2.)

c. Contrary to extensive popular and social-science literature on the plight of the middle child, the Cool Guys overwhelmingly hold *middle positions in the family*—as do Conformists. The Actors hold predominantly middle and oldest positions, while Tough Guys tend to be middle or youngest children. Only Retreaters are overrepresented in the only-child category. These findings are complicated by the fact that a high proportion of boys with older brothers tend to follow the same strategic styles exhibited by them (as we saw with Hank, Ernie, Keith, and Leroy). (Table C: 3.)

d. Conformists tend overwhelmingly to come from *father-present homes*; Actors and Tough Guys are primarily from father-absent homes. The Cool Guy and Retreater are about as likely to come from one as the other (as we saw in the case of Hank). (Table C: 4.)

e. *Quality of family life*, as estimated by interviewers and staff, is an interesting category. Excessively stressful family situations are able to produce all styles, although more frequently the Tough Guy (four out of six) and the Conformist (seven out of fourteen). No Actor comes from an above average family situation—but a surprising two out of five Retreaters do. (Table C: 5.)

f. *Racial identity* appears to be highest for the Cool Guy and Tough Guy (probably for "real tough guys" or rebels rather than for "troublemakers"), and lowest for the Retreater, Actor, and Conformist. This trend was evident in the five portraits, and indicates that positive racial identity (including sense of pride) is an integral part of total positive self-esteem and sense of identity. (Table C: 6.)

g. The Retreater, Conformist, and Cool Guy are far more likely to *stay in school* than are the Tough Guy or the Actor. (Further data indicate that the latter two are also more likely to drop out earlier than the first three—i.e., before the tenth grade.) (Table C: 7.)

h. The Conformist, reflecting his conventional values, is more positively-oriented toward *college* than any other style; the Tough Guy is the least inclined to want to pursue higher education. (Table C: 8.)

i. The Tough Guy and the Actor have lower *grades* than the other three styles, reflecting their difficulty in adjusting to traditional school situations. (Table C: 9.)

j. Of those for whom *grades* were available in June 1968, the Cool Guys and the Retreaters tend to have slightly better grades. (Table C: 10.)

Naturally, these associations do not indicate the direction of causality. Furthermore, I was not involved in helping to designate styles for all subjects; hence, my use of the concept and the staff's may not be entirely the same, although they followed guidelines I had written for an earlier progress report. Data analysis is available for the five basic styles, not for sub-styles, making it somewhat less accurate. An even greater stumbling block is that several runs were made using collapsed categories of "expressive and rebellious" (Cool Guy, Actor, and Tough Guy) and "conformist and withdrawn." For my purposes, treating expressive and rebellious styles as comparable is misleading. Therefore, findings from tables arranged in that manner have been omitted from the discussion here.

TABLE C:1 *Strategic Styles and Non-School Trouble**

	Cool Guy	Actor	Tough Guy	Conformist	Retreater	Total
Low	8	10	1	14	5	38
High	11	6	5	-	-	22
Total	19	16	6	14	5	60

p level = .001

TABLE C:2 *Strategic Styles and Specified Illegal Acts*

	Cool Guy	Actor	Tough Guy	Conformist	Retreater	Total
Low	7	9	1	12	5	34
Medium	8	4	1	2	-	15
High	4	3	4	-	-	11
Total	19	16	6	14	5	60

p level = .005

TABLE C:3 *Strategic Styles and Family Position*

	Cool Guy	Actor	Tough Guy	Conformist	Retreater	Total
Only	1	-	-	-	2	3
Youngest	3	2	2	1	-	8
Middle	13	7	4	11	2	37
Oldest	2	7	-	2	1	12
Total	19	16	6	14	5	60

p level = .012

* The total number (N) varies because information was not available or was unclear for some subjects. Significance levels are indicated below each table ("p level"); a level of .05 or less in contingency tables such as these is generally considered to be a strong indication of association of variables.

TABLE C:4 *Strategic Styles and Father-Presence*

	Cool Guy	Actor	Tough Guy	Conformist	Retreater	Total
Father Absent	10	12	4	1	3	30
Father Present	9	4	2	13	2	30
Total	19	16	6	14	5	60

p level = .004

TABLE C:5 *Strategic Styles and Family Situation*

	Cool Guy	Actor	Tough Guy	Conformist	Retreater	Total
Excessively Stressful	4	5	4	7	2	22
Average	11	11	1	5	1	29
Above Average	3	-	1	2	2	8
Total	18	16	6	14	5	59

p level = .126

TABLE C:6 *Strategic Styles and Racial Identity*

	Cool Guy	Actor	Tough Guy	Conformist	Retreater	Total
Low	7	10	2	10	4	33
High	12	5	4	4	1	26
Total	19	15	6	14	5	59

p level = .122

TABLE C:7 *Strategic Styles and Dropping Out of School*

	Cool Guy	Actor	Tough Guy	Conformist	Retreater	Total
Drop-outs	5	10	6	4	-	25
Stay-ins	14	6	-	10	5	35
Total	19	16	6	14	5	60

p level = .009

TABLE C:8 *Strategic Styles and College Orientation*

	Cool Guy	Actor	Tough Guy	Conformist	Retreater	Total
Negative	2	1	2	-	-	5
Mixed	8	9	2	4	2	25
Positive	5	4	-	8	2	19
Total	15	14	4	12	4	49

p level not significant

TABLE C:9 *Strategic Styles and Academic Performance (1967)*

	Cool Guy	Actor	Tough Guy	Conformist	Retreater	Total
Fail	-	-	-	-	-	-
					(no drop-outs)	
D	-	2	4	-	-	6
C	13	7	1	11	1	33
B$^-$/B	5	3	-	3	3	14
B$^+$/A	1	-	-	-	1	2
Total	19	12	5	14	5	55

p level = .008

TABLE C:10 *Strategic Styles and Academic Performance (1968)*

	Cool Guy	Actor	Tough Guy	Conformist	Retreater	Total
Drop-outs	1	4	4	1	2	10
Fail	1	1	-	-	-	2
D	1	-	1	4	-	6
C	7	7	1	8	1	24
B$^-$/B	4	1	-	-	2	7
B$^+$/A	-	-	-	-	-	-
Total	14	13	6	13	5	49

p level = .067

Notes

1. Strategic Styles: Individual Responses to Social Reality

1. I make a distinction between "processual" marginality (as in the case of the adolescent who at some time "arrives" at adulthood) and "essential" marginality (as in the case of a youth who belongs through birth to a racial minority). Logically, the white American youth participates in the former only; the black American youth shares in both types of marginality. This distinction is elaborated in my paper "No Owner of Soil: A Discussion of Marginality," presented at the Eastern Sociological Association Annual Meeting, March 1980, Boston.

2. This term, coined by Harry Stack Sullivan to stress *selectivity* in identifying with "others," was discussed originally by C. H. Cooley and G. H. Mead. See Sullivan's *Conceptions of Modern Psychiatry* (Washington, D.C., William Alanson White Psychiatric Foundation, 1940), pp. 18–22. For an example of its systematic application in research, see Norman K. Denzin, "The Significant Others of a College Population," *Sociological Quarterly*, 7 (1966), 298–310.

3. Pathways to Identity, Harvard Graduate School of Education; Robert A. Rosenthal, Bernard E. Bruce, and Florence S. Ladd, codirectors. Time I interviews were conducted between 1967 and 1968; Time II, between 1970 and 1971; Time III, in 1973. "Final Report, Pathways to Identity: Aspects of the Experience of Black Youth (unpublished, 1971). See also the same authors' *Different Strokes: Pathways to Maturity in the Boston Ghetto: A Report to the Ford Foundation* (Boulder, Colorado, Westview Press, 1976). Alfred Adler used the term "portraits" to mean "composite pictures of individuals," which he wrote to illustrate their "style of life." See Donald H. Ford and Hugh B. Urban, *Systems of Psychotherapy* (New York, Wiley, 1965), pp. 311–312.

4. Tamotsu Shibutani, *Society and Personality: An Interactionist Approach to Social Psychology* (Englewood Cliffs, N.J., Prentice-Hall, 1961), pp. 20–23. The symbolic interactionist line of thought moves through the works of William James, C. H. Cooley, G. H. Mead, John Dewey, Robert Park, Ellsworth Faris, Erving Goffman, Anselm Strauss, and Arnold M. Rose. A concise history of the perspective is presented by Manford Kuhn in "Major Trends in Symbolic Interaction in the Past Twenty-Five Years," *Sociological Quarterly*, 5 (1964), 61–84; it has been systematized to some extent by Shibutani (above); George McCall and J. L. Simmons in *Identities and Interactions* (New York, Free Press, 1966); by Herbert Blumer in *Symbolic Interactionism: Perspective and Method* (Englewood Cliffs, N.J., Prentice-Hall, 1969); by Norman K. Denzin in "Symbolic Interactionism and Ethnomethodology," *American Sociological Review*, 34 (1969), 922–934; and by Peter Hall in "A Symbolic Interactionist Analysis of Politics," in Andrew Effrat, ed., *Perspectives in Political Sociology* (Indianapolis, Bobbs-Merrill, 1973), pp. 35–75. See also Jerome Manis and Bernard Meltzer, eds., *Symbolic Interaction: A Reader in Social Psychology* (Boston, Allyn and Bacon, 1967), Michael Argyle, ed., *Social Encounters: Readings in Social Interaction* (Chicago, Aldine, 1973), and Earl Rubington and Martin S. Weinberg, *Deviance: The Interactionist Perspective* (New York, Macmillan, 1973).

5. Shibutani, p. 2. Symbolic interactionist theory rests on three central premises: emergence, voluntarism, and process. *Emergence* refers to the primary distinction between humans and all other animals—the capacity for language, speech, thought, and communication which allow for expression of expectations and, consequently, the molding of behavior to meet those expectations; *voluntarism* assumes that people are actors rather than reactors, capable of creation and invention as well as responding to stimuli; *process* centers on activity and change as the normal course of events for humans, rather than equilibrium, stasis, or structure. See Hall, "A Symbolic Interactionist Analysis of Politics," in Effrat, p. 36.

6. From the interactionist perspective, meaning is extrinsic to any given act (that is, must be arrived at by definition) and arises out of communication and interaction. It determines how we continue to act toward certain objects; it can be redefined. The self is viewed as an object as well, which takes on meaning in interaction with other selves and with which we interact (self-concept).

7. Hall, "A Symbolic Interactionist Analysis of Politics," in Effrat, p. 39.

8. Gerth and Mills note that "according to the principle of the confirming other, persons will present themselves in one way to one set of persons and in another way to another set. The ways in which the person presents himself will vary according to what he believes these various others think of him. In general, his style of self-presentation will be a bridge from the image of self which he believes these various others hold of him and the self-image he would like to have them confirm." Hans Gerth and C. Wright Mills, *Character and Social Structure* (New York, Harcourt, Brace and World, 1953), pp. 94–95.

9. George Herbert Mead, *Mind Self and Society* (Chicago, University of Chicago Press, 1934).

10. Erving Goffman, *The Presentation of Self in Everyday Life* (New York, Doubleday, 1959), p. 49.

11. R. D. Laing and A. Esterson, *Sanity, Madness, and the Family*, 2nd ed. (New York, Basic Books, 1971), p. 6.

12. Blumer, *Symbolic Interactionism*, p. 20.

13. Erik Erikson, *Identity: Youth and Crisis* (New York, W. W. Norton, 1968), p. 50.

14. Blumer, *Symbolic Interactionism*, p. 15.

15. Ibid., p. 74.

16. Some notable exceptions in recent years include Ronald Akers, *Deviant Behavior: A Social Learning Approach* (Belmont, Calif., Wadsworth, 1973); Robert C. Carson, *Interaction Concepts of Personality* (Chicago, Aldine, 1969); Chad Gordon and Kenneth L. Gergen, eds., *The Self in Social Interaction* (New York, Wiley, 1968); George Kaluger and Charles M. Unkovic, *Psychology and Sociology: An Integrated Approach to Understanding Human Behavior* (St. Louis, Mosby, 1969); and McCall and Simmons, *Identities and Interactions*, 1966.

17. Lee Rainwater, "The Crucible of Identity: The Negro Lower-Class Family," in Talcott Parsons and Kenneth B. Clark, eds. *The Negro-American* (Boston, Beacon Press, 1965), pp. 194–195.

18. See Don D. Jackson, "The Study of the Family," in Paul Watzlawick and John H. Weakland, eds., *The Interactional View* (New York, W. W. Norton, 1977), pp. 2–21. He comments (p. 5) that, "The family is the most influential learning context."

19. Ibid., p. 11.

20. Elliot G. Mishler and Nancy E. Waxler, *Interaction in Families: An Experimental Study of Family Processes and Schizophrenia* (New York, Wiley, 1968), p. 96.

21. Ibid.; also Laing and Esterson, *Sanity, Madness, and the Family,* and Watzlawick and Weakland, *The Interactional View.*

22. An excellent example is Stuart T. Hauser's *Black and White Identity Formation: Studies in the Psychosocial Development of Lower Socioeconomic Class Adolescent Boys* (New York, Wiley, 1971).

23. Jackson, "The Study of the Family," p. 5.

24. Jay Haley, "Toward a Theory of Pathological Systems," in Watzlawick and Weakland, p. 33.

25. Sullivan was one of the first psychiatrists to insist that the *mode* of transmitting information between people is as important as intrapsychic conflicts or "internal" problems. He saw the self as an "experiential matrix"—to be understood in terms of interaction with others—rather than as a "core insular personality." He disparaged the "illusion of individual personality" and emphasized an "ecological point of view" in understanding the individual. What is "intrapsychic or extrapsychic" is a "phantom problem" which cannot be answered on an either/or basis—the line between our "inner world" and "outer world" is not clearly demarcated. For an excellent discussion of this seminal thinker, see Gerard Chrzanowski, "Implications of Interpersonal Theory," in Earl G. Witenberg, ed., *Interpersonal Explorations in Psychoanalysis* (New York, Basic Books, 1973), pp. 133 ff.

26. Mishler and Waxler, *Interaction in Families*, p. 7.

27. Louis Wirth, "Clinical Sociology," *American Journal of Sociology*, 371 (1931), 49–66.

28. This trend is reflected in the work of Henry L. Lennard and Arnold Bernstein, *Patterns in Human Interaction: An Introduction to Clinical Sociology* (San Francisco: Jossey-Bass, 1969); Hugh Gardner, "Some 'Real' Doctoring for Sick Societies," *Human Behavior*, (September 1978), 68–69; Alfred McClung Lee,

"On Context and Relevance," in John Glass and John Staude, eds., *Humanistic Society* (Pacific Palisades, Calif., Goodyear, 1972), pp. 247–257; Alvin W. Gouldner and S. M. Miller, eds., *Applied Sociology: Opportunities and Problems* (New York, Free Press, 1965); and most recently, Charlotte Green Schwartz, "Clinical Sociology as Practice in Everyday Life," *New England Sociologist*, (Fall, 1978), 4ff.

29. Barry Glassner and Jonathan A. Freedman, *Clinical Sociology* (New York, Longmans, 1979), p. 5.

30. Ibid., p. 27.

31. Robert F. Bales, *Interaction Process Analysis* (Cambridge, Addison-Wesley, 1970). The model for observation developed by Bales in his work with "laboratory" groups was utilized by Mishler and Waxler in their study of family interaction patterns, and can be used to observe any small group systematically.

32. Glassner and Freedman, *Clinical Sociology*, p. 46, emphasize the interplay of "linkages" between groups and their members: "When the head of a family has a nervous breakdown, the entire family suffers and needs help."

33. Cf. Sullivan's Principle of Redundancy, in Chrzanowski, "Implications of Interpersonal Theory," in Witenberg.

34. John Bowlby, *Attachment* (New York, Basic Books, 1969), pp. 348–349.

35. Glassner and Freedman, *Clinical Sociology*, p. 135.

36. After interviewing began, a few members of various focal clusters, especially fathers and older brothers, left the Boston area. Many interviews later in the study were conducted in prisons, at army bases, or work places out of the state and/or region.

37. For examples, see Thomas Pettigrew's summary of such studies made prior to 1964 in *A Profile of the Negro American* (New York, Von Nostrand Reinhold, 1964); also R. M. Dreger and K. S. Miller, "Comparative Psychological Studies of Negroes and Whites in the United States," *Psychological Bulletin*, 57 (1960), 361–402; Parsons and Clark, *The Negro-American*; and Elizabeth W. Miller, *The Negro in America: A Bibliography* (Cambridge, Mass., Harvard University Press, 1966). In addition, massive government studies such as the so-called "Coleman," "Moynihan," and "Kerner" reports have compared black and white experiences in major areas of life such as family, school opportunity, and the system of criminal justice. See James S. Coleman, et al., *Equality of Educational Opportunity* (Washington, D.C., Government Printing Office, 1966); Otto Kerner, *Report of the National Advisory Commission on Civil Disorders* (New York, Bantam Books, 1968); and Daniel P. Moynihan, *The Negro Family: The Case for National Action* (Washington, D.C., Government Printing Office, 1967).

38. These are reviewed succinctly by Rosenthal, et al., in their "Final Report."

39. Representative of these are Allison Davis and John Dollard, *Children of Bondage* (Washington, D.C., American Council on Education, 1940); E. Franklin Frazier, *Negro Youth at the Crossways* (Washington, D.C., American Council on Education, 1940); Charles S. Johnson, *Growing Up in the Black Belt* (Washington, D.C., American Council on Education, 1941); St. Clair Drake and Horace Cayton, *Black Metropolis* (New York, Harcourt Brace, 1945); Kenneth Clark, *Dark Ghetto* (New York, Harper and Row, 1965); Elliot Liebow, *Tally's Corner* (Boston, Little, Brown, 1967); William McCord, et al., *Life Styles in the Black Ghetto* (New York, W. W. Norton, 1969). Autobiographical/novelistic works include Richard Wright, *Black Boy* (New York, Harper, 1965) and "The Psychological Reactions of Oppressed Peoples," in his *White Man, Listen!* (Gar-

den City, N.Y., Doubleday, Anchor, 1957); Ralph Ellison, *Invisible Man* (New York, Random House, 1952) and *Shadow and Act* (New York, Signet, 1964), particularly the section, "Harlem is Nowhere"; James Baldwin, *Go Tell It on the Mountain* (New York, Knopf, 1953), *Nobody Knows My Name* (New York, Dial Press, 1961), *Another Country* (New York, Dial Press, 1962), and *The Fire Next Time* (New York, Dial Press, 1963); Malcolm X, *The Autobiography of Malcolm X* (New York, Grove Press, 1964); Claude Brown, *Manchild in the Promised Land* (New York, Macmillan, 1965); Eldridge Cleaver, *Soul on Ice* (New York, Delta, 1968); and George Jackson, *Soledad Brother* (New York, Bantam, 1970). Other important anecdotal material can be found in Robert Coles, *Children of Crisis* (Boston, Little, Brown, 1967), and Thomas B. Cottle, *Black Children, White Dreams* (Boston, Houghton Mifflin, 1974).

40. Developed by Robert L. Kahn, et al., *Organizational Stress: Studies in Role Conflict and Ambiguity* (New York: Wiley, 1964), pp. 44–49.

41. Studs Terkel, author of *Hard Times* (New York, Pantheon, 1970) and *Working* (New York, Avon, 1975), pays his man-in-the-street interviewees: "You see, I'm taking their lives . . . even when they're happy with how the interview comes out, I still know I've stolen from them." *Providence Sunday Journal* (June 30, 1974), p. 23. Pathways viewed the respondents as "co-collaborators" and accordingly "paid them for their time." As co-director Bruce recalls, the general reaction was one of surprise: "You mean you're going to pay me just for rapping?" For many, being paid was an inconsequential reward for participating in the study; most felt pleased with being able to discuss their family and work situations with a neutral person.

42. Effrat, *Perspectives in Political Sociology*, p. 42.

43. Julian B. Rotter, "Generalized Expectancies for Internal versus External Control of Reinforcement," *Psychological Monographs*, 80 (1966), 1–28.

44. "Power is control over environment—both the physical and the social environment. In a real sense, power represents survival. Unless the individual can exercise a certain minimal level of control, he is at the mercy of other people and of external forces." Howard M. Bahr, *Skid Row: An Introduction to Disaffiliation* (New York, Oxford University Press, 1973), p. 31. Bowlby (*Attachment*, p. 229), says that "affiliation," as introduced by Henry A. Murray in 1938, includes all manifestations of "friendliness and goodwill, and the desire to do things in company with others," and must be distinguished from "attachment" and "dependency." These two dimensions—power and affiliation—have been singled out by many theorists (including Freud) as being central to interpersonal relationships. David Bakan, in *The Duality of Human Existence* (Boston, Beacon Press, 1966), uses the terms "agency" and "communion" to "characterize two fundamental modalities in the existence of living forms: agency for the existence of an organism as an individual, and communion for the participation of the individual in some larger organism of which the individual is a part" (p. 15, emphasis added). See also Dorothy Lee, on autonomy and community, in *Freedom and Culture: Essays* (Englewood Cliffs, N.J., Prentice-Hall, 1968).

45. Timothy Leary, *Interpersonal Diagnosis of Personality* (New York, Ronald Press, 1957); see especially his discussion of "interpersonal themes," p. 71.

46. The cell produced by Insulation/Activity includes both competitive behavior (in which the other is neither liked nor disliked, but merely coped with), and masking behavior (in which the individual typically "puts on" a front of tough, clowning behavior in order to conceal his "real" self). Some boys in the study

appeared to use the "tough put-on" or the "clown" as a smokescreen to protect their predominant style. The notion of "impersonal competition" is delineated by Robert E. Park and Ernest W. Burgess in *Introduction to the Science of Sociology* (Chicago, University of Chicago Press, 1937), p. 574. Such behavior remains in the Insulation/Activity cell until the individual personalizes the competition (begins to dislike, even hate the other), in which case it moves into "conflict" and properly belongs in the Antipathy/Overactivity or the Antipathy/Activity cell. For a discussion of "action modes," see R. G. Barker and H. F. Wright, *Midwest and Its Children: The Psychological Factors of an American Town* (Evanston, Ill., Row, Peterson, 1954).

47. Robert K. Merton, *Social Theory and Social Structure* (New York, Free Press, 1957), chapter 4.

48. Rainwater, "The Crucible of Identity," in Parsons and Clark, pp. 194–195.

49. Erving Goffman, *The Presentation of Self in Everyday Life* (New York, Doubleday, 1959), and *Strategic Interaction* (Philadelphia, University of Pennsylvania Press, 1969).

50. I focused especially on the following questions from the focal boys' transcripts: the entire Self-Concept section; questions 7, 8, 16, 17, 19, 20, 24, and 27 (Family); 1, 2, 3, 4, 5, 6, 11, and 13 (Peer); 4, 5, 10, 11, and 13 (School); 1, 3, 4, 8, 10, 14, and 15 (Race); and 1, 2, 3, 7, 19, and 20 (Work).

51. Laing and Esterson, *Sanity, Madness, and the Family,* p. 11.

52. Cf. ibid., p. 56, and Beulah Parker, *A Mingled Yarn: Chronicle of A Troubled Family* (New Haven, Yale University Press, 1972), p. 14, for further discussion of discrepancies in family reports and "the official version" of family history offered by many people, at least until trust has been established with the professional worker. In describing her own family's distortions of reality, Parker says, "eventually the discrepancies wove such a confused pattern in our minds that we all approached the brink of disaster."

53. Goffman notes: "When an individual appears before others, he knowingly and unwittingly projects a definition of the situation of which a conception of himself is an important part." *The Presentation of Self in Everyday Life*, p. 242.

2. The Conformist: Keith Sutton

1. The "too-good guy" is an example of overconformity or, in Merton's terminology, "ritualism"—"A private escape from the dangers and frustrations which seem to be inherent in the competition for major cultural goals by abandoning these goals and clinging all the more closely to the safe routines and the institutionalized norms . . . conformity, for the sake of conformity, becomes a central value." In Charles P. and Zona K. Loomis, *Modern Social Theories* (Princeton, Van Nostrand, 1961), p. 275.

2. See Lillian Kovar's description of the "adult-oriented girl," in *Faces of the Adolescent Girl* (Englewood Cliffs, N.J., Prentice-Hall, 1968), p. 53.

3. Loomis, *Modern Social Theories,* p. 273.

4. A recurrent theme in interviews of Keith, Mr. Sutton, and Grandfather is an emphasis on provident planning coupled with an ever-present feeling that things might change so that those plans might not be carried out after all. This is the only evidence of pessimism in otherwise optimistic interviews.

5. In her study of adolescent girls, Kovar draws a distinction between two types of relations: "reciprocal," in which the person is tied to another "through

mutual giving or sharing . . . this for that"; and "personal," in which intimacy and caring or love are present regardless of reciprocity (*Faces of the Adolescent Girl*, p. 3). Compare Abraham Maslow's "dependency-love" versus "being-love" in *Toward a Psychology of Being* (Princeton, Van Nostrand, 1968). Keith's relations with his family involve both, but at Time I appear to be weighted in the "reciprocal" direction. See also Alvin W. Gouldner, "Reciprocity and Autonomy in Functional Theory," in Llewellyn Gross, ed., *Symposium on Sociological Theory* (Evanston, Harper and Row, 1958), pp. 241–270.

6. Richard Dewey and W. J. Humber, in reviewing material from Drake and Cayton's *Black Metropolis*, identify a personality type among blacks which they call the "striving, conforming personality," characterized by strong need for achievement and high aspirations. *An Introduction to Social Psychology* (New York, Macmillan, 1966), p. 387. One might expect, of course, to find the same type among whites; the important point is that when blacks fall into this category, they may experience some distancing from their racial as well as their social-class background.

7. See Coleman, et al., *Equality of Educational Opportunity*.

8. Several researchers have found that middle-class teachers tend to reward students who are most passive, docile, and obedient with higher grades and more attention. These traits are easier for the middle-class child to exhibit; thus a pattern emerges in which lower-class children are less likely to "please" the teacher (that is, fit mainstream expectations) and are therefore less likely to achieve well academically.

9. Cf. Robert Rosenthal and Lenore Jacobsen, *Pygmalion in the Classroom: Teacher Expectation and Pupil's Intellectual Development* (New York, Holt, Rinehart, and Winston, 1968). They offer evidence that teachers evaluate students' performance at least in part on the basis of how they expect them to perform. That is, if their expectations of a student are low (because of reputation, race, or other prior information), they are likely to treat the student in a way that in fact elicits a lowered performance level—the "self-fulfilling prophecy." The consequences of this are devastating for children being educated in a racist or sexist atmosphere.

10. Mrs. Sutton claims that students who do well in inner-city schools such as the DuBois do poorly on city-wide tests. (The evidence supports her.) Although Keith was on the honor roll at the DuBois, she questions what that really means: "I wonder actually if he's really that good." This disparity between inner-city and other educational systems was apparently rendered true for Keith. Later interviews with the family indicate that he had a great deal of difficulty in keeping up with the academic work in the suburbs.

11. *Racial awareness* as utilized by Pathways was determined by a set of questions designed to elicit knowledge of national, state, and local black figures and organizations. *Racial identity* is another category based on responses to questions focusing on the importance of being black.

12. Rainwater, "The Crucible of Identity," p. 195.

13. Hyman Rodman, "The Lower-Class Value Stretch," *Social Forces*, 42 (1963), 405–415.

14. Rainwater, p. 194.

15. One study shows that nondelinquents in high-delinquency neighborhoods usually come from exceptionally stable and intact families. See F. R. Scarpitti, Ellen Murray, S. Dinitz, and Walter C. Reckless, "The 'Good' Boy in a High Delinquency Area: Four Years Later," *American Sociological Review*, 25 (1960)

555–558. An earlier study by Reckless, Dinitz, and Murray indicated that a strong positive self-concept served to help boys resist deviant behavior in high-delinquency neighborhoods: "Self-Concept as an Insulator against Delinquency," *American Sociological Review,* 21 (1956), 744–746.

16. Harry Stack Sullivan, *The Interpersonal Theory of Psychiatry* (New York, W. W. Norton, 1953), pp. 213–216.

17. An early analytical tool used by Pathways was to divide the subjects into two groups, "reactors" and "initiators." This was developed by Charlotte Weissberg in her unpublished doctoral dissertation, "Self-Evaluations and School Withdrawal: The Subjective Views of Lower-Income Black Adolescents" (University of Chicago, 1973). Keith was classified as a "reactor."

18. Kovar, *Faces of the Adolescent Girl,* p. 3.

19. Ruth Shonle Cavan, "The Concepts of Tolerance and Contraculture as Applied to Delinquency," *Sociological Quarterly,* 2 (1961), 243–258.

3. The Retreater: Ernie Hayes

1. Rainwater, "The Crucible of Identity," in Parsons and Clark, p. 195.

2. Loomis, *Modern Social Theories,* p. 276.

3. Archie Towle is perhaps the most clear-cut example of the "loner." He was not chosen for the portrait because of his age at Time I (16), his ninth grade status, and because his strategic style in combination with his life circumstances (deceased father, no siblings) produced a focal cluster of two—Archie and his mother. I will describe Archie briefly to provide a comparison with Ernie's "withdrawn kid" style. Archie's social contacts are restricted at every level. He has no friends; his activities consist of solitary pastimes, like reading, building models, and watching television alone in his room. Archie describes himself as a "loner" (his term), and in fact is probably as close to that as any person could be without becoming a hermit. When asked how his mother would have him change, he recalls that when he was younger, she wanted him to go outside and play with other children: "I didn't want to. She lost that. That's one battle she lost." In response to the "spy" question, first he insists that he could go away without even being missed, except by his mother. Then he says that no one could stand replacing him, even for one day: "It wouldn't work, it would drive him mad if he know how to be like me . . . after being normal . . . I mean after doing what other kids do, he couldn't take it." He would risk being driven crazy: "first of all most people are used to having contact with others. Me, I stay in the house all the time except for when I go out and get my books . . . no contact with anybody except my mother . . . he'd go nuts." At school, Archie's "spy" would "have to contend with one person, my chess partner." The spy would have to be "a fairly lousy chess player, but would have to beat my partner a couple of times. As far as all the rest, all he'd have to do is keep his mouth shut, and don't talk to anybody; and especially don't talk to girls . . . and don't talk to the boys either. If he started a conversation, he'd give himself away." For a discussion of the psychological dynamics of the withdrawn style, see Helen Pallister, *The Negative or Withdrawal Attitude: A Study in Personality Organization* (New York, Archives of Psychology, 1933).

4. Talcott Parsons, *The Social System* (New York, Free Press, 1951), pp. 390ff.

5. Lee Doerries conducted a study to examine levels of social interaction. His hypothesis—that people suffering from "existential frustration" and/or "pur-

poselessness" would tend to withdraw from interaction with others—was con-firmed. "Purpose in Life and Social Participation," *Journal of Individual Psychology*, 26 (1970), 50–53. On the other hand, if frustration exceeds a person's "tolerance" level, aggression may result. See John Dollard, et al., *Frustration and Aggression* (New Haven, Yale University Press, 1939). It appears that Ernie's strategic styles reflect both of these reactions to pervasive frustration.

6. A methodological hitch emerges in Ernie's cluster interviews. He was first interviewed in February 1967, at which time his closest "friends," Will and Paul, were engaging with him in glue-sniffing. His parents were interviewed later that same year, and told of putting pressure on Ernie to stop hanging with these boys. Apparently by April 1968 he had done so, having found a new friend, Peter, who is interviewed in August 1968. By then the glue-sniffing is a thing of the past. Ernie has switched to drinking wine—not with Peter, but with his brother Teddy and sister Donna. Furthermore, Will and Paul were never interviewed; nor was Teddy, with whom Ernie shared a room and retreatist activities. Donna was interviewed in 1969. The unfortunate spread of the interviews over time, as well as the absence of interviews with Will, Paul, and Teddy, are balanced, I think, by the opportunity to see how some issues, such as hooking school, sniffing glue, and Ernie's interest in chemistry, have persisted over a two-year period.

7. "The junkies *have* to use drugs, man, to stand this life. I couldn't do it myself, man, without using drugs . . . everybody with a little bit of sensitivity would have to use something or else kill himself." Brown, *Manchild in the Promised Land*, p. 334, quoting an ex-addict who joined the Black Muslims.

8. Erik Erikson, "Growth and Crises of 'Healthy' Personality," *Psychological Issues*, 1 (1959), 87–88.

9. Hauser, *Black and White Identity Formation*, p. 121.

10. Ibid.

11. Erikson, *Identity: Youth and Crisis*, p. 120.

12. Ibid., p. 122.

13. Hauser, *Black and White Identity Formation*, p. 122.

14. Erikson, *Identity: Youth and Crisis*, p. 184.

15. McCord, et al., *Life Styles in the Black Ghetto*, p. 157. They describe black psychotics (and others who are "defeated") as people who share the American middle-class dream but are "frustrated" in their "search for fulfillment."

16. Ibid., See also H. Edward Ransford, "Isolation, Powerlessness, and Violence," *American Journal of Sociology*, 73 (1968), 581–591.

17. Lennard and Bernstein, *Patterns in Human Interaction: An Introduction to Clinical Sociology.*

18. Bowlby, *Attachment*, p. 334.

19. Ibid., p. 335.

4. The Tough Guy: Leroy Duncan

1. Rainwater, "The Crucible of Identity," in Parsons and Clark, p. 195.

2. Loomis, *Modern Social Theories*, p. 275. Merton distinguishes between "aberrant" behavior, in which norms are violated ("troublemaker" style), and "nonconformity," in which a person tries to change norms ("tough guy"). William McCord, et al. distinguish between the "activist" who is a rebel, who has "chosen the reformer's path rather than the way of individual or mass violence," and the "revolutionaries," who, whether open or hidden, are likely to en-

gage in the activities of such organizations as the Black Panthers or the Black Muslims, which are rigid and even paramilitary in structure, providing a sense of manliness and identity—tough and unconventional. *Life Styles in the Black Ghetto*, chapters 11 and 12.

3. They characterize the rebels without a cause as people who "aggressively lash out at their world in an apparently senseless way, who express their rage through overt violence." They seldom know *why* they behave as they do, nor do they "rebel under the flag of some movement or cause." Ibid., pp. 195–96. See also Albert Camus, *The Rebel* (New York, Random House, 1956), for distinctions between rebellion and revolution. Regarding the "troublemaker" style, compare Herbert Gans in *The Urban Villagers* (New York, Free Press, 1962), p. 29, where he makes a distinction between "action-seekers" and "routine-seekers" among the young men he studied in the West End of Boston. For the "action-seekers," he says, "life is episodic. The rhythm of life is dominated by the adventurous episode, in which heights of activity and feeling are reached through exciting and sometimes riotous behavior. The goal is action, an opportunity for thrills, and for the chance to face and overcome a challenge . . . Whatever the episode, the action-seeker pursues it with a vengeance, and lives the rest of his life in quiet—and often sullen—preparation for this climax, in which he is usually said to be 'killing time.'"

4. Brewton Berry, *Race and Ethnic Relations* (Boston, Houghton Mifflin, 1958), p. 494.

5. Duke was interviewed both as Leroy's best friend and in his own right as one of the Pathways focal subjects. He consistently denies any involvement in stealing pocketbooks, cars, or merchandise from downtown stores—all of which Leroy talks about freely, naming Duke as his companion. Duke finally admits to truancy and car theft when his mother tells the interviewer about it in front of Duke.

6. Richard W. Cloward and Lloyd E. Ohlin, *Delinquency and Opportunity: A Theory of Delinquent Gangs* (New York, Free Press, 1960).

7. James K. Short and Fred L. Strodtbeck, *Group Process and Gang Delinquency* (Chicago, University of Chicago Press, 1965).

8. Credit must be given to the male interviewer who probed and rephrased questions diligently to get at information he was aware of from talking to others in the cluster, without letting the interviewee know he was aware of it. The male interviewer who spoke to the father, Leroy, Bart, and Duke, probably would have done a better job interviewing the mother as well. As it was, the female interviewer, who was not as aware of the intricacies of the male responses, was unable to elicit much information from Mrs. Duncan, who resisted the interviewer by almost falling asleep shortly after the beginning of one session, and by denying trouble in the family which other family members freely report. Mr. Duncan comments to the interviewer: "I don't know how she [his wife] was, but whatever it was, she [the interviewer] didn't get nothing out of it." During the first interview, which was conducted at the Duncan apartment, several interruptions took place. Mrs. Duncan's reactions to them were consistently hostile and abrupt, revealing a lack of control over her children, who persisted in interrupting. Later interviews were conducted in the project's Roxbury office.

9. See his theory of "differential association" in E. H. Sutherland, *Principles of Criminology*, 5th ed., revised by Donald R. Cressey (New York, Lippincott, 1959), pp. 74–81.

10. Cf., Walter B. Miller, "Lower Class Culture As A Generating Milieu of Gang Delinquency," *Journal of Social Issues*, 14 (1958), 5–19.

5. *The Actor: Dave Cooper*

1. Loomis and Loomis, *Modern Social Theories*, p. 274.
2. Max Weber, "Subjective Meaning in the Social Situation," in Lewis A. Coser and Bernard Rosenberg, eds., *Sociological Theory: A Book of Readings* (New York, Macmillan, 1964).
3. Cf. Parsons: "Part of ego's expectation, in many cases the most crucial part, consists in the probable reaction of alter to ego's possible action, a reaction which comes to be anticipated in advance and thus to affect ego's own choices." *The Social System*, p. 5.
4. Orrin E. Klapp, in *Heroes, Fools, and Villains* (Englewood Cliffs, N.J., Spectrum, 1962).
5. Everett V. Stonequist, *The Marginal Man* (New York, Scribner's, 1937), p. 8.
6. See for example the work of Merton in *Social Theory and Social Structure*.
7. Bowlby, *Attachment*, p. 348.
8. Georg Simmel, "Types of Social Relationships by Degrees of Reciprocal Knowledge of Their Participants," in Kurt H. Wolff, ed., *The Sociology of Georg Simmel* (New York, Free Press, 1950), p. 32.
9. Ibid., p. 318.
10. See John P. Spiegel's article on "masking" and "unmasking" in relation to disorganization and re-equilibration in families. "The Resolution of Role Conflict within the Family," in Norman W. Bell and Ezra Vogel, eds., *A Modern Introduction to the Family* (Glencoe, Free Press, 1960), pp. 375–377.
11. Gerald R. Pearson, *Adolescence and the Conflict of Generations* (New York, W. W. Norton, 1958).
12. Bales, *Interaction Process Analysis*, especially the chapter on the group style, "Toward Material Success and Power."
13. Ben Bursten, *The Manipulator* (New Haven, Yale University Press, 1973), p. 6.
14. Ibid., p. 2.
15. Ibid.
16. Ibid., p. 8.
17. Basil Bernstein, *Class, Codes, and Control* (London, Routledge and Kegan Paul, 1971).

6. *The Cool Guy: Hank Nelson*

1. Rainwater, "The Crucible of Identity," in Parsons and Clark, p. 194.
2. Erich Fromm, *The Sane Society* (New York, Holt, Rinehart, and Winston, 1955), p. 203.
3. Ibid., p. 196. For a broad discussion of the concept of mental health, see Marie Jahoda, *Current Concepts of Positive Mental Health* (New York, Basic Books, 1958), and John A. Clausen, *Sociology and the Field of Mental Health* (New York, Russell Sage Foundation, 1956). See also Edwin D. Driver's *The Sociology and Anthropology of Mental Illness: A Reference Guide* (Amherst, University of Massachusetts Press, 1965).

4. Erikson, *Identity: Youth and Crisis*, p. 94. As Erikson warns, we must not consider positive resolution a final and static achievement: these crises are in fact renegotiated through life, albeit in lesser proportions. "What the child acquires at a given stage is a certain *ratio* between the positive and the negative which, if the balance is toward the positive, will help him to meet later crises with a predisposition toward the sources of vitality" (p. 324n.).

5. From Mathew Lipman, "Some Aspects of Simmel's Conception of the Individual," in Kurt H. Wolff, ed., *Essays on Sociology, Philosophy, and Aesthetics* (New York, Harper Torchbooks, 1965), p. 125.

6. Marie Jahoda, "Toward a Social Psychology of Mental Health," in M. J. E. Benn, ed., Symposium on the Healthy Personality, Supplement II: Problems of Infancy and Childhood. Transactions of Fourth Conference, Josiah Macy, Jr. Foundation (New York, Josiah Macy, Jr. Foundation, March 1950).

7. "The key to autonomy is heightened self-awareness or self-consciousness. A person must respect his own feelings, potentialities, and limitations." John and Mavis Biesanz, *Modern Society* (Englewood Cliffs, N.J., Prentice-Hall, 1968), p. 207. Hank appears to meet these criteria.

8. For elaboration on "super-cool cat" characteristics, see Bernard Wolfe, *The Late Risers* (New York, Random House, 1954) on "hip" New York City males; he says blacks (regardless of style) are seldom out of sight of a white audience and therefore "spend most of their lives *on* . . . every Negro is to some extent a performer" (p. 202). See also Walter B. Miller, *The Cool World* (Boston, Little, Brown, 1959); Le Roi Jones, *Blues People* (New York, William Morrow, 1963); Charles Keil, *Urban Blues* (Chicago, University of Chicago Press, 1966); and John Horton, "Time and Cool People," in Saul Feldman and Gerald W. Thielbar, eds., *Life Styles: Diversity in American Society* (Boston, Little, Brown, 1972), pp. 317–326, on expressive black male roles; and several pieces on "playing the dozens," a ritualistic exchange of name-calling and insults which demands a "coolness" and expressiveness of highest caliber: R. F. B. Berdie, "Playing the Dozens," *Journal of Abnormal and Social Psychology*, 42 (1947), 120–121; Roger D. Abrahams, "Playing the Dozens," *Journal of American Folklore*, 75 (1962), 209–20; and Stanford M. Lyman and Marvin B. Scott, "Coolness in Everyday Life," in Marcello Truzzi, ed., *Sociology and Everyday Life* (Englewood Cliffs, N.J., Prentice-Hall, 1968), pp. 92–101.

9. David Riesman, Nathan Glazer, and Reuel Denney, *The Lonely Crowd* (New Haven, Yale University Press, 1961).

10. Further complicating the reference view is the fact that, through a series of misunderstandings and difficulties in locating certain others, in a sense the "wrong" people were interviewed for Hank's cluster. The most important people from his point of view—grandmother, father, Daddy Roy, Peter—were not interviewed. Rocky was not interviewed as best friend (although Hank so named him in July); rather, Mark, who for Hank is an influential but not particularly "close" friend, was interviewed on Bert's and Mrs. Nelson's suggestion. Fortunately, Rocky happens to be a focal child in his own right, so his Peer section reveals a very positive view of Hank's "together" qualities. The loss of the interviews with Mr. Nelson, Daddy Roy, and Pete, is an inestimable one, and is why I looked at the Time II interviews after writing the first version of Hank's portrait in order to untangle the peer group problem.

11. Kovar says the "autonomous" girls she studied came from homes where the parents provided a "nonthreatening, nonpressuring haven" and a sense of un-

conditional love and acceptance. They also encouraged independence and varied experiences. The autonomous girl can "think and feel for herself," as can Hank. *Faces of the Adolescent Girl*, pp. 107–109.

12. "The Psychological Context of Militancy," in Stanley S. Guterman, ed., *Black Psyche: Modal Personality Patterns of Black Americans* (Berkeley, Calif., Glendessary Press, 1974), p. 214.

13. Paul L. Sites, *Control: The Basis of Social Order* (Port Washington, N.Y., Dunellen Publishing, 1963), p. 49.

14. Cloward and Ohlin, *Delinquency and Opportunity*.

15. "Lower-Class Culture as a Generating Milieu of Gang Delinquency," *Journal of Social Issues*, 14 (1958), 5–19.

16. Short and Strodtbeck. *Group Process and Gang Delinquency*.

7. Toward Manhood: Growth and Change in Styles over Time

1. Time II transcripts are the source of data for Keith, Ernie, and Hank; Time II and Time III transcripts provide information for Leroy and Dave. Only focal subjects were interviewed at Times II and III.

2. Mishler and Waxler, *Interaction in Families*, p. 192.

3. Ibid., pp. 104, 81.

4. Richard Gelles, *The Violent Home* (Beverly Hills, Calif., Sage Publications, 1973), p. 169.

5. Mishler and Waxler, pp. 119–120.

6. Theodore Lidz, reported in Mishler, p. 162.

7. Ibid., p. 81.

8. Truax and Carkhuff, quoted in Glassner and Freedman, *Clinical Sociology*, p. 37.

9. Ibid.

10. Ibid., p. 4. The focal cluster method of open-ended interviewing may be a good vehicle for eliciting everyday interaction patterns before intervention is attempted. While there is much value to be gained from joint interviews, or direct observation of a family in interaction, it is also beneficial for the clinician to determine the conflicting "definitions of the situation" *independently* of the power plays that may occur in joint settings. As the research in family myths suggests, the family may present a collective front supporting a prevailing myth in front of the therapists—but when questioned separately, may hold quite disparate feelings. Questions may not need to be extensive, but merely designed so as to evoke interactional responses.

References

Abrahams, Roger D. *Deep Down in the Jungle . . . Negro Narrative Folklore from the Streets of Philadelphia.* Hawthorne, N.Y.: Aldine, 1964.

———. "Playing the Dozens," *Journal of American Folklore*, 75 (1962), 209–220.

Ackerman, N. W. "Social Role and Total Personality," *American Journal of Orthopsychiatry*, 21 (1951), 1–17.

Adler, Alfred. *What Life Should Mean to You.* Boston: Little, Brown, 1931.

Akers, Ronald L. *Deviant Behavior: A Social Learning Approach.* Belmont, Calif.: Wadsworth, 1973.

Ahlstrom, Winton M., and Robert J. Havighurst. *Four Hundred Losers: Delinquent Boys in High School.* San Francisco: Jossey-Bass, 1977.

Allport, Floyd H. "A Structuronomic Conception of Behavior: Individual and Collective: I. Structural Theory and the Master Problem of Social Psychology," *Journal of Abnormal and Social Psychology*, 64 (1962), 3–30.

Allport, Gordon W. *Pattern and Growth in Personality.* New York: Holt, Rinehart, and Winston, 1961.

———. *The Person in Psychology: Selected Essays.* Boston: Beacon Press, 1968.

———. *Studies in Expressive Movement.* New York: Macmillan, 1933.

Anderson, Ralph E., and Irl E. Carter. *Human Behavior in the Social Environment.* Chicago: Aldine, 1974.

Ansbacher, H., and Rowena Ansbacher. *The Individual Psychology of Alfred Adler.* New York: Basic Books, 1956.

Antonovsky, A., and M. Lerner, "Occupational Aspirations of Lower Class Negro and White Youth," *Social Problems,* 7 (1959), 132–138.

Argyle, Michael. *Social Encounters: Readings in Social Interaction.* Chicago: Aldine, 1973.

Arnspiger, Varney C. *Personality in Social Process: Values and Strategies of Individuals in a Free Society.* Dubuque, Iowa: W. C. Brown, 1969.

Aronfreed, Justin. *Conduct and Conscience: The Socialization of Internalized Control over Behavior.* New York: Academic Press, 1968.

Aronson, Elliot. *The Social Animal.* San Francisco: W. H. Freeman, 1972.

Atchley, Robert C., ed. *Understanding American Society.* Belmont, Calif.: Wadsworth, 1971.

Ausubel, D. P. *Theory and Problems of Adolescent Development.* New York: Grune and Stratton, 1954.

Bachman, Jerald G., Patrick M. O'Malley, and Jerome Johnston. *Adolescent to Adulthood: Stability and Change in the Lives of Young Men.* Ann Arbor, Mich.: Institute for Social Research, University of Michigan, 1978.

Backman, Carl W., Paul F. Secord, and Jerry R. Peirce. "Resistance to Change in the Self-Concept as a Function of Consensus among Significant Others," *Sociometry,* 26 (1963), 102–111.

Bahr, Howard M. *Skid Row: An Introduction to Disaffiliation.* New York: Oxford University Press, 1973.

Bakan, David. *The Duality of Human Existence.* Boston: Beacon Press, 1966.

Baldwin, Alfred L. "The Parsonian Theory of Personality," in Black, ed. (see below), *The Social Theories of Talcott Parsons,* pp. 153–190.

Baldwin, James. *Another Country.* New York: Dial Press, 1962.

———. *The Fire Next Time.* New York: Dial Press, 1963.

———. *Go Tell It on the Mountain.* New York: Knopf, 1953.

———. *Nobody Knows My Name.* New York: Dial Press, 1961.

Baldwin, James Mark. *Social and Ethical Interpretations in Mental Development.* New York: Macmillan, 1897.

Bales, Robert F. *Interaction Process Analysis.* Cambridge: Addison-Wesley, 1970.

———. "Roles in Problem-Solving Groups," in Maccoby, et al., eds. (see below), *Readings in Social Psychology,* pp. 437–446.

Ball, John C. *Social Deviancy and Adolescent Personality.* Lexington: University of Kentucky Press, 1962.

Bandura, Albert. "The Role of Modeling Processes in Personality Development," in Fowley, et al., eds. (see below), *Contemporary Readings in Psychology,* pp. 328–338.

————, and R. H. Walters. *Adolescent Aggression.* New York: Ronald Press, 1959.

————. *Social Learning and Personality Development.* New York: Holt, Rinehart, and Winston, 1963.

Barker, R. G., and H. F. Wright. *Midwest and Its Children: The Psychological Ecology of an American Town.* Evanston, Ill.: Row, Peterson, 1954.

Barron, Milton L., ed. *American Minorities.* New York: Knopf, 1958.

Baughman, E. Earl. *Black Americans: A Psychological Analysis.* New York: Academic Press, 1971.

————, and W. Grant Dahlstrom. *Negro and White Children: A Psychological Study in the Rural South.* New York: Academic Press, 1968.

Becker, Howard S. *Outsiders: Studies in the Sociology of Deviance.* New York: Free Press, 1963.

Bell, Norman W., and Ezra F. Vogel, eds. *A Modern Introduction to the Family.* Glencoe: Free Press, 1960.

Bennis, Warren G., et al., eds. *Interpersonal Dynamics: Essays and Readings on Human Interaction.* Homewood, Ill.: Dorsey Press, 1964.

Berdie, R. F. B. "Playing the Dozens," *Journal of Abnormal and Social Psychology,* 42 (1947), 120–121.

Berger, Bennett M. "Soul Searching: Review of Urban Blues (Keil, 1966)," *Transaction,* 4 (1967), 54–57.

Berger, Peter L. *Invitation to Sociology.* Garden City, N.Y.: Doubleday Anchor Books, 1963.

————, and Thomas Luckmann. *The Social Construction of Reality.* Garden City, N.Y.: Doubleday Anchor Books, 1966.

Berkowitz, Leonard. *Roots of Aggression: A Re-Examination of the Frustration-Aggression Hypothesis.* New York: Atherton Press, 1968.

————, and Richard M. Lundy. "Personality Characteristics Related to Susceptibility to Influence by Peers or Authority Figures," *Journal of Personality,* 25 (1956), 306–316.

Berlyne, D. "Uncertainty and Conflict: A Point of Contact between Information Theory and Behavior Theory Concepts," *Psychological Review,* 64 (1957), 329–339.

Bernfeld, S. "Types of Adolescence," *Psychoanalytic Quarterly,* 7 (1938), 243–253.

Bernstein, Basil. *Class, Codes, and Control.* London: Routledge and Kegan Paul, 1971.

Berry, Brewton. *Race and Ethnic Relations.* Boston: Houghton Mifflin, 1958.

Biddle, Bruce J., and Edwin J. Thomas, eds. *Role Theory: Concepts and Research.* New York: Wiley, 1966.

————. *Social Role: Readings in Theory and Application.* New York: Wiley, 1964.

Biesanz, John, and Mavis Biesanz. *Modern Society.* Englewood Cliffs, N.J.: Prentice-Hall, 1968.

Billingsley, Andrew. *Black Families in White America.* Englewood Cliffs, N.J.: Prentice-Hall, 1968.

Black, Max, ed. *The Social Theories of Talcott Parsons: A Critical Examination.* Englewood Cliffs, N.J.: Prentice-Hall, 1961.

Blake, R. R., and C. V. Ramsey, eds. *Perception: An Approach to Personality.* New York: Ronald Press, 1951.

Blitsten, Dorothy R. *The Social Theories of H. S. Sullivan.* New York: William-Frederick Press, 1953.

Blos, Peter. *The Adolescent Personality.* New York: Appleton-Century, 1941.

————. *On Adolescence: A Psychoanalytic Interpretation.* New York: Free Press, 1962.

Blumer, Herbert. "Sociological Implications of the Thought of George Herbert Mead," in Perry and Seidler, eds. (see below), *Contemporary Society,* pp. 134–144.

————. *Symbolic Interactionism: Perspective and Method.* Englewood Cliffs, N.J.: Prentice-Hall, 1969.

Bordua, D. J. "Delinquent Subcultures," *Annals of the American Academy of Political and Social Sciences,* 338 (1961), 119–136.

Borgatta, Edgar F. "Role and Reference Group Theory," in Borgatta, ed., *Social Psychology: Readings and Perspective* (Chicago: Rand McNally, 1969), pp. 286–296.

Bowerman, Charles E., and John W. Kinch. "Changes in Family and Peer Orientation of Children between Fourth and Tenth Grades," *Social Forces,* 37 (1959), 206–211.

Bowlby, John. *Attachment.* New York: Basic Books, 1969.

Brim, Orville G., Jr. "Personality Development as Role-Learning," in Iscoe and Stevenson, eds. (see below), *Personality Development in Children,* pp. 127–159.

Brittain, Clay V. "Adolescent Choices and Parent-Peer Cross Pressures," *American Sociological Review,* 28 (1963), 385–391.

Brittan, Arthur. *Meanings and Situations.* London: Routledge and Kegan Paul, 1973.

Brody, E. B. "Color and Identity Conflict in Young Boys," *Archives of General Psychiatry,* 10 (1963), 354–360.

————, ed., *Minority Group Adolescents in the United States.* Baltimore: Williams and Wilkins, 1968.

————. "Social Conflict and Schizophrenic Behavior in Young Adult Negro Males," *Psychiatry,* 24 (1961), 337–346.

Bronfenbrenner, Urie. "Freudian Theories of Identification and Their Derivatives," *Child Development,* 31 (1960), 15–40.

————. "Parsons' Theory of Identification," in Black, ed. (see above), *The Social Theories of Talcott Parsons,* pp. 191–213.

————. "Toward an Integrated Theory of Personality," in Blake and Ramsey, eds. (see above), *Perception,* pp. 206–257.

Brown, Claude. *Manchild in the Promised Land.* New York: Macmillan, 1965.

————. "Playing Hookey and Catting," in Atchley, ed. (see above), *Understanding American Society*, pp. 17–23.

Brown, J. A. C. *Freud and the Post-Freudians*. Baltimore: Penguin Books, 1961.

Brown, Judson S. "Principles of Interpersonal Conflict," *Journal of Conflict Resolution*, 1 (1957), 135–154.

Bullough, Bonnie. "Alienation in the Ghetto," *American Journal of Sociology*, 72 (1967), 469–478.

Burgess, Ernest W. *Personality and the Social Group*. Chicago: University of Chicago Press, 1929.

Burke, Kenneth. *A Grammar of Motives*. Berkeley: University of California Press, 1969.

Bursten, Ben. *The Manipulator*. New Haven: Yale University Press, 1973.

Buxton, Claude E. *Adolescents in School*. New Haven: Yale University Press, 1973.

Cain, Maureen E. "Some Suggested Developments for Role and Reference Group Analysis," *British Journal of Sociology*, 19 (1968), 191–205.

Campbell, Ernest Q. "The Internalization of Moral Norms," *Sociometry*, 27 (1964), 391–412.

Camus, Albert. *The Rebel: An Essay on Man in Revolt*. New York: Random House, 1956.

Carson, Robert C. *Interaction Concepts of Personality*. Chicago: Aldine, 1969.

Cavan, Ruth Shonle. "The Concepts of Tolerance and Contraculture as Applied to Delinquency," *Sociological Quarterly*, 2 (1961), 243–258.

Chinoy, Ely. *Sociological Perspective*. New York: Random House, 1968.

Chrzanowski, Gerard. "Implications of Interpersonal Theory," in Witenberg, ed. (see below), *Interpersonal Explorations*, pp. 132–146.

Clark, Kenneth. *Dark Ghetto: Dilemmas of Social Power*. New York: Harper and Row, 1965.

Clark, Robert E. *Reference Group Theory and Delinquency*. New York: Behavioral Publications, 1972.

Clausen, John A. *Sociology and the Field of Mental Health*. New York: Russell Sage Foundation, 1956.

Cleaver, Eldridge. *Soul on Ice*. New York: Delta, 1968.

Cloward, Richard. "Illegitimate Means, Anomie, and Deviant Behavior," in Coser and Rosenberg, eds. (see below), *Sociological Theory*, pp. 562–582.

————, and Lloyd E. Ohlin. *Delinquency and Opportunity: A Theory of Delinquent Gangs*. New York: Free Press, 1960.

————. "Norms of Delinquent Subcultures," in Coser and Rosenberg, eds. (see below), *Sociological Theory*, pp. 144–150.

Cohen, Albert K. *Delinquent Boys*. New York: Glencoe Press, 1955.

————. "The Sociology of the Deviant Act: Anomie Theory and Beyond," *American Sociological Review*, 30 (1965), 5–14.

————. "The Study of Social Disorganization and Deviant Behavior," in Coser and Rosenberg, eds. (see below), *Sociological Theory*, pp. 604–614.

————, and James F. Short, Jr. "Crime and Juvenile Delinquency," in Merton and Nisbet, eds. (see below), *Contemporary Social Problems*, pp. 89–146.

Cohen, Yehudi A. *Social Structure and Personality: A Casebook*. New York: Holt, Rinehart, and Winston, 1961.

Coleman, James C. "Types of Adjustive Reactions," in Dyal, ed. (see below), *Readings in Psychology*, pp. 368–370.

Coleman, James S. *The Adolescent Society*. New York: Macmillan, 1961.

————, et al. *Equality of Educational Opportunity*. Washington, D.C.: Government Printing Office, 1966.

Coles, Robert. *Children of Crisis*. Boston: Little, Brown, 1967.

Conger, John J., and Wilbur C. Miller et al. *Personality, Social Class, and Delinquency*. New York: Wiley, 1966.

————, and C. R. Walsmith. "Antecedents of Delinquency, Personality, Social Class, and Intelligence," in Mussen, et al. (see below), *Readings in Child Development and Personality*, pp. 442–467.

Cooley, Charles Horton. *Human Nature and the Social Order*, revised ed. New York: Scribner's, 1922.

————. *Social Organization*. New York: Scribner's, 1909.

Coser, Lewis A., and Bernard Rosenberg, eds. *Sociological Theory: A Book of Readings*. New York: Macmillan, 1964.

Coser, Rose Laub. "Insulation from Observability and Types of Social Conformity," *American Sociological Review*, 26 (1961), 28–39.

Cottle, Thomas J. *Black Children, White Dreams*. Boston: Houghton Mifflin, 1974.

Cressey, Donald R. "Delinquent and Criminal Structures," in Merton and Nisbet, eds. (see below), *Contemporary Social Problems*, pp. 147–183.

Crow, Lester D., and Alice Crow. "Some Explanations of Personality," in their *Readings in General Psychology*, (New York: Barnes and Noble, 1954), pp. 392–395.

Cumming, John, and Elaine Cumming. *Ego and Milieu*. New York: Atherton Press, 1966.

Dahrendorf, Ralph. "Out of Utopia; Toward a Reorientation of Sociological Analysis," in Coser and Rosenberg, eds. (see above), *Sociological Theory*, pp. 209–227.

Dai, Bingham. "A Socio-Psychiatric Approach to Personality Organization," *American Sociological Review*, 17 (1952), 44–49.

————. "Some Problems of Personality Development among Negro Children," in Kluckhohn et al. (see below), *Personality in Nature, Society, and Culture*, pp. 545–566.

David, Jay, ed. *Growing Up Black*. New York: William Morrow, 1968.

Davis, Allison, and John Dollard. *Children of Bondage*. Washington, D.C.: American Council on Education, 1940.

Dennis, N. *Cards of Identity*. New York: Meridian, 1960.

Denzin, Norman K. *Childhood Socialization: Studies in the Development of Language, Social Behavior, and Identity*. San Francisco: Jossey-Bass, 1978.

———. "The Methodologies of Symbolic Interaction: A Critical Review of Research Techniques," in Stone and Farberman, eds. (see below), *Social Psychology through Symbolic Interaction*, pp. 451–452.

———. "The Significant Others of a College Population," *Sociological Quarterly*, 7 (1966), 298–310.

———. "Symbolic Interactionism and Ethnomethodology," in Douglas, ed. (see below), *Understanding Everyday Life*, pp. 261–287.

Derbyshire, R. L., and E. Brody. "Marginality, Identity and Behavior in the American Negro: A Functional Analysis," *International Journal of Psychiatry*, 10 (1964), 7–13.

Deutsch, Helen. *Selected Problems of Adolescence*. New York: International Universities Press, 1967.

Deutsch, Martin, et al., eds. *Social Class, Race, and Psychological Development*. New York: Holt, Rinehart, and Winston, 1968.

Dewey, John. *Experience and Nature*. Chicago: Open Court, 1925.

Dewey, Richard, and W. J. Humber. *Introduction to Social Psychology*. New York: Macmillan, 1966.

Dixon, Vernon J., and Badi Foster. *Beyond Black or White: An Alternate America*. Boston: Little, Brown, 1971.

Doerries, Lee E. "Purpose in Life and Social Participation," *Journal of Individual Psychology*, 26 (1970), 50–53.

Dolci, Danilo. *Outlaws*. New York: Orion Press, 1961.

Dollard, John. *Criteria for the Life History*. New Haven: Yale University Press, 1935.

———, and Leonard Doob, N. E. Miller, O. H. Mowrer, and R. R. Sears. *Frustration and Aggression*. New Haven: Yale University Press, 1939.

Douglas, Jack D., ed. *Understanding Everyday Life*. Chicago: Aldine, 1970.

Douvan, E. A., and J. Adelson. *The Adolescent Experience*. New York: Wiley, 1966.

Drake, St. Clair, and Horace R. Cayton. *Black Metropolis: A Study of Negro Life in a Northern City*. New York: Harcourt Brace, 1945.

Dreger, R. M., and K. S. Miller. "Comparative Psychological Studies of Negroes and Whites in the United States," *Psychological Bulletin*, 57 (1960), 361–402.

Driver, Edwin D. *The Sociology and Anthropology of Mental Illness*. Amherst: University of Massachusetts Press, 1965.

Dubois, W. E. *The Souls of Black Folk: Essays and Sketches*. Chicago: McClurg, 1903.

Duncan, Hugh D. *Communication and Social Order.* New York: Bedminster Press, 1962.

Durkheim, Emile. *The Rules of Sociological Method,* 2nd ed. Chicago: University of Chicago Press, 1938.

Dyal, James A., ed. *Readings in Psychology: Understanding Human Behavior.* New York: McGraw-Hill, 1962.

Effrat, Andrew, ed. *Perspectives in Political Sociology.* Indianapolis: Bobbs-Merrill, 1973.

Eisenstadt, S. N. "Studies in Reference Group Behavior: I. Reference Norms and the Social Structure," *Human Relations,* 7 (1954), 191–216.

Elkin, F., and W. A. Westley. "The Myth of Adolescent Culture," *American Sociological Review,* 20 (1955), 680–684.

Ellison, Ralph. *Invisible Man.* New York: Random House, 1952.

———. *Shadow and Act.* New York: Signet, 1964.

Erikson, Erik H. *Childhood and Society.* New York: W. W. Norton, 1963.

———. "Growth and Crises of 'Healthy' Personality," *Psychological Issues,* 1 (1959) 87–88.

———. "Identity and the Life Cycle," *Psychological Issues,* 1 (1959), 1–171.

———. "Identity and Uprootedness in Our Time," in Ruitenbeek, ed. (see below), *Varieties of Modern Social Theory,* pp. 55–68.

———. *Identity: Youth and Crisis.* New York: W. W. Norton, 1968.

———. "Memorandum on Identity and Negro Youth," *Journal of Social Issues,* 20 (1964), 29–42.

———. *Young Man Luther.* New York: W. W. Norton, 1958.

———. and Kai T. Erikson. "The Confirmation of the Delinquent," *Chicago Review,* 10 (1957), 15–23.

Fanon, Franz. *Black Skin, White Masks.* New York: Grove Press, 1962.

Faris, Ellsworth. *The Nature of Human Nature.* New York: W. C. Brown, 1937.

Feldman, Fred A. "Some Problems Concerning Identity," dissertation, Brown University, Providence, R.I., 1969.

Feldman, Saul D., and Gerald W. Thielbar, eds. *Life Styles: Diversity in American Society.* Boston: Little, Brown, 1972.

Ferdinand, Theodore N. *Typologies of Delinquency: A Critical Analysis.* New York: Random House, 1966.

Ficker, Victor B., and H. S. Graves, eds. *Social Science and Urban Crisis.* New York: W. W. Norton, 1971.

Fiske, Donald W. *Strategies for Personality Research: The Observation Versus Interpretation of Behavior.* San Francisco: Jossey-Bass, 1978.

Fitts, William H. *The Self Concept and Behavior: Overview and Supplement,* Research Monograph 7. Nashville: Dede Wallace Center, 1972.

Flynn, John T. *Identification and Individuality (Instincts Fundamental to Human Behavior).* New York: Beekman Press, 1968.

Foley, John M., Russell A. Lockhart, and David M. Messick, eds., *Contemporary Readings in Psychology*. New York: Harper and Row, 1970.

Foote, Nelson. "Identification as the Basis for the Theory of Motivation," *American Sociological Review*, 16 (1951), 14–21.

————, and Leonard S. Cottrell, Jr. *Identity and Interpersonal Competence: A New Direction in Family Research*. Chicago: University of Chicago Press, 1955.

Ford, Donald H., and Hugh B. Urban. *Systems of Psychotherapy*. New York: Wiley, 1965.

Forman, Robert E. *Black Ghettos, White Ghettos, and Slums*. Englewood Cliffs, N.J.: Prentice-Hall, 1971.

Forward, John R., and Jay R. Williams. "Internal-External Control and Black Militancy," *Journal of Social Issues*, 26 (1970), 75–92.

Frazier, E. Franklin. *Negro Youth at the Crossways: Their Personality Development in the Middle States*. Washington, D.C.: American Council on Education, 1940.

————. "Problems and Needs of Negro Children and Youth Resulting from Family Disorganization," *Journal of Negro Education*, 19 (1950), 269–277.

Freed, Leonard. *Black in White America*. New York: Grossman, 1969.

Freeman, Howard E., and Norman R. Kurtz, eds. *America's Troubles: A Casebook on Social Conflict*. Englewood Cliffs, N.J.: Prentice-Hall, 1969.

French, J. "A Formal Theory of Social Power," *Psychological Review*, 63 (1956), 181–194.

Freud, Anna. "Adolescence," in *Psychoanalytic Study of the Child*, Vol. 13 (New York: International Universities Press, 1958), pp. 255–278.

Freud, Sigmund. *Civilization and Its Discontents*, trans. James Strachey. New York: W. W. Norton, 1962.

————. *Group Psychology and Analysis of the Ego*, trans. James Strachey. New York: W. W. Norton, 1975.

————. "Instincts and Their Vicissitudes," in Joan Rivière, ed., *Sigmund Freud: Collected Papers*, Vol. 4. New York: Basic Books, 1959.

————. "The Transformations of Puberty," in Joan Rivière, ed., *Three Contributions to the Theory of Sex*, Nervous and Mental Disease Monographs, 7. London: Hogarth Press, 1953.

Freund, Julien. *The Sociology of Max Weber*. New York: Random House, 1968.

Friedenberg, Edgar Z. *Coming of Age in America*. New York: Random House, 1968.

————. *The Vanishing Adolescent*. Boston: Beacon Press, 1960.

Fromm, Erich. *The Sane Society*. New York: Holt, Rinehart, and Winston, 1955.

Furnas, J. C. *Goodbye to Uncle Tom*. New York: William Sloane Associates, 1956.

Gable, Frank G. *The Third Force: The Psychology of Abraham Maslow.* New York: Grossman, 1970.

Gans, Herbert. *The Urban Villagers.* New York: Free Press, 1962.

Gardner, Hugh. "Some 'Real' Doctoring for Sick Societies," *Human Behavior* (September 1978), pp. 68–69.

Gelles, Richard. *The Violent Home: A Study of Physical Aggression between Husbands and Wives,* Sage Library of Social Research, 13. Beverly Hills, Calif.: Sage Publications, 1972.

Gergen, Kenneth J., and David Marlowe, eds. *Personality and Social Behavior.* Reading, Mass.: Addison-Wesley, 1970.

Gerth, Hans, and C. Wright Mills. *Character and Social Structure.* New York: Harcourt, Brace and World, 1953.

Glaser, Barney G., and Anselm L. Strauss. *The Discovery of Grounded Theory.* Chicago: Aldine, 1967.

Glaser, Daniel. "Criminality Theories and Behavioral Images," *American Journal of Sociology,* 61 (1956), 433–444.

Glass, John, and John Staude, eds. *Humanistic Society.* Pacific Palisades, Calif.: Goodyear, 1972.

Glasser, William. *The Identity Society.* New York: Harper and Row, 1972.

Glassner, Barry, and Jonathan A. Freedman. *Clinical Sociology.* New York: Longman, 1979.

Glueck, Sheldon, and Eleanor Glueck, eds. *Identification of Predelinquents.* New York: Intercontinental Medical Book Corporation, 1972.

Goethals, George, and Dennis S. Klos. *Experiencing Youth: First Person Accounts.* Boston: Little, Brown, 1970.

Goffman, Erving. *Encounters.* New York: Bobbs-Merrill, 1961.

———. *Interaction Ritual: Essays on Face-to-Face Behavior.* Garden City, N.Y.: Doubleday, Anchor, 1967.

———. "On Facework: An Analysis of Ritual Elements in Social Interaction," in Bennis, et al. (see above), *Interpersonal Dynamics,* pp. 226–249.

———. *The Presentation of Self in Everyday Life.* New York: Doubleday, 1959.

———. *Strategic Interaction.* Philadelphia: University of Pennsylvania Press, 1969.

Goldstein, Bernard. *Low Income Youth in Urban Areas.* New York: Holt, Rinehart and Winston, 1967.

Goode, William J. "A Theory of Role-Strain," *American Sociological Review,* 25 (1960), 483–496.

Goodenough, Ward. *Cooperation and Change.* New York: Russell Sage, 1963.

Goodman, Paul. *Growing Up Absurd.* New York: Random House, 1960.

Gordon, Chad, and Kenneth L. Gergen, eds. *The Self in Social Interaction.* New York: Wiley, 1968.

Gorman, Benjamin. *Social Themes.* Englewood Cliffs, N.J.: Prentice-Hall, 1971.

312   References

Gottlieb, David, and Charles E. Ramsay. *Understanding Children of Poverty*. Chicago: Science Research Associates, 1967.

Gould, Julius, and William L. Kolb. *A Dictionary of the Social Sciences*. Glencoe: Free Press, 1964.

Gouldner, Alvin W. "Reciprocity and Autonomy in Functional Theory," in Gross, ed. (see below), *Symposium on Sociological Theory*, pp. 241–270.

———, and S. M. Miller, eds. *Applied Sociology: Opportunities and Problems*. New York: Free Press, 1965.

Grier, William H., and Price M. Cobb. *Black Rage*. New York: Basic Books, 1968.

Grinder, R. E., ed. *Studies in Adolescence*. New York: Macmillan, 1963.

Groh, George W. *The Black Migration: The Journey to Urban America*. New York: Weybright and Talley, 1972.

Gross, Llewellyn, ed. *Symposium on Sociological Theory*. Evanston, Ill.: Harper and Row, 1958.

Gross, Neal. "The Sociology of Education," in Merton, et al., eds. (see below), *Sociology Today*, pp. 128–152.

———, Ward S. Mason, and Alexander W. McEachern. *Explorations in Role Analysis*. New York: Wiley, 1958.

———, Alexander W. McEachern, and Ward S. Mason. "Role Conflict and Its Resolutions," in Maccoby, et al. (see below), *Readings in Social Psychology*, pp. 247–258.

Guntrip, Henry J. S. *Personality Structure and Human Interaction: The Developing Synthesis of Psycho-Dynamic Theory*. New York: International Universities Press, 1969.

Guterman, Stanley S., ed. *Black Psyche: Modal Personality Patterns of Black Americans*. Berkeley, Calif.: Glendessary Press, 1972.

Haley, Jay. "Toward a Theory of Pathological Systems," in Watzlawick and Weakland, eds. (see below), *The Interactional View*, pp. 31–49.

Hall, Peter. "A Symbolic Interactionist Analysis of Politics," in Effrat, ed. (see above), *Perspectives in Political Sociology*, pp. 35–75.

Harris, Edward E. *Self-Attitude Critiques and Proposals*. New York: American Press, 1969.

Hartmann, H. *Ego Psychology and the Problem of Adaptation*. New York: International Universities Press, 1958.

Harvey, O. J., ed. *Motivation and Social Interaction*. New York: Ronald Press, 1963.

Hathaway, Starke R., and Elio D. Monachesi. *Adolescent Personality and Behavior: MMPI Patterns of Normal, Delinquent, Dropout, and Other Outcomes*. Minneapolis: University of Minnesota Press, 1963.

Hauser, Stuart T. *Black and White Identity Formation: Studies in the Psychosocial Development of Lower Socioeconomic Class Adolescent Boys*. New York: Wiley, 1971.

Havighurst, Robert J., and H. Taba. *Adolescent Character and Personality*. New York: Wiley, 1949.

————, et al., eds. *Society and Education: A Book of Readings*. Boston: Allyn and Bacon, 1967.

Hayakawa, S. I. *Symbol, Status and Personality*. New York: Harcourt, Brace and World, Harvest Books, 1963.

Heider, Fritz. *The Psychology of Interpersonal Relations*. New York: Wiley, 1958.

Henden, Herbert. *Black Suicide*. New York: Basic Books, 1969.

Hess, Robert O., and Gerald Handel. *Family Worlds*. Chicago: University of Chicago Press, 1959.

Hine, Frederick R. *Introduction to Psychodynamics: A Conflict-Adaptational Approach*. Durham, N.C.: Duke University Press, 1971.

Horrocks, John E., and Dorothy W. Jackson. *Self and Role: A Theory of Self-Process and Role Behavior*. Boston: Houghton Mifflin, 1971.

Horton, John. "Time and Cool People," in Feldman and Thielbar, eds. (see above), *Life Styles*, pp. 317–326.

Hughes, Everett C. "What Other?" in Rose, ed. (see below), *Human Behavior and Social Processes*, pp. 119–127.

Hundleby, John D., and Raymond B. Cattell. *Personality Structure in Middle Childhood and the Prediction of School Achievement and Adjustment*. Chicago: University of Chicago Press, 1968.

Hunt, Robert C., ed. *Personalities and Cultures: Readings in Psychological Anthropology*. Garden City, N.Y.: Natural History Press, 1967.

Hurlock, E. B. *Adolescent Development*. New York: McGraw-Hill, 1962.

Hyman, Herbert H., and Eleanor Singer, eds. *Readings in Reference Group Theory and Research*. New York: Free Press, 1968.

Inkeles, Alex. "Personality and Social Structure," in Merton, et al., eds. (see below), *Sociology Today*, pp. 249–275.

————. "Sociology and Psychology," in Koch, ed. (see below), *Psychology: The Study of a Science*, 6, pp. 317–387.

————, and Daniel J. Levinson. "National Character: The Study of Modal Personality and Sociocultural Systems," in Lindzey and Aronson, eds. (see below), *The Handbook of Social Psychology*, 2, pp. 977–1020.

Inselberg, Rachel M., Laura Searls, and Leocadia Burke. *Personality Attributes Associated with Various Mechanisms of Masculine Identification*. Pittsburgh: Carnegie Institute of Technology, 1964.

Iscoe, Ira, and H. W. Stevenson, eds. *Personality Development in Children*. Austin: University of Texas Press, 1960.

Jackson, Don D. "The Study of the Family," in Watzlawick and Weakland, eds. (see below), *The Interactional View*, pp. 2–21.

Jackson, George. *Soledad Brother: The Prison Letters of George Jackson*. New York: Bantam, 1970.

Jacobs, Paul. "Ethnic Pressures," in Ficker and Graves, eds. (see above), *Social Science and Urban Crisis*, pp. 95–98.

314   References

Jahoda, Maria. "Conformity and Independence: A Psychological Analysis," *Human Relations*, 12 (1959), 99–120.

——. *Current Concepts of Positive Mental Health: A Report to the Staff Director (Jack Ewalt) of the Joint Commission on Mental Illness and Health*, Monograph Series, 1. New York: Basic Books, 1958.

——. "Toward a Social Psychology of Mental Health," in M. J. E. Benn, ed., Symposium on the Healthy Personality, Supplement II: Problems of Infancy and Childhood, Transactions of Fourth Conference, Josiah Macy Jr. Foundation. New York: Josiah Macy Jr. Foundation, March, 1950.

James, William. *Principles of Psychology*. New York: Holt, 1890.

Jencks, Christopher. *Inequality*. New York: Basic Books, 1972.

Johnson, Charles S. *Growing Up in the Black Belt: Negro Youth in the Rural South*. Washington, D.C.: American Council on Education, 1941.

Johnson, Robert B. "Negro Reactions to Minority Status," in Barron, ed. (see above), *American Minorities*, pp. 192–214.

Jones, LeRoi. *Blues People*. New York: William Morrow, 1963.

Jones, Reginald L., ed. *Black Psychology*. New York: Harper and Row, 1972.

Joseph, Stephen. *The Me Nobody Knows: Children's Voices from the Ghetto*. New York: Avon, 1969.

Jung, Carl. *Psychological Types*. New York: Harcourt, Brace, 1923.

Kahn, Robert L., et al. *Organizational Stress: Studies in Role Conflict and Ambiguity*. New York: Wiley, 1964.

Kallen, D. J. "Inner Direction, Other Direction, and Social Integration Setting," *Human Relations*, 16 (1963), pp. 75–87.

Kaluger, George, and Charles M. Unkovic. *Psychology and Sociology: An Integrated Approach to Understanding Human Behavior*. St. Louis: Mosby, 1969.

Kandel, Denise B., and Gerald S. Lesser. "Parental and Peer Influences on Educational Plans of Adolescents," *American Sociological Review*, 34 (1969), 213–223.

Kantor, David, and William Lehr. *Inside the Family: Toward a Theory of Family Process*. San Francisco: Jossey-Bass, 1975.

Kardiner, Abraham, and Lionel Ovesey. *The Mark of Oppression*. New York: W. W. Norton, 1951.

Karon, Bertram P. *The Negro Personality: A Rigorous Investigation of the Effects of Culture*. New York: Springer, 1958.

Keil, Charles. *Urban Blues*. Chicago: University of Chicago Press, 1966.

Kelman, Herbert C. "Compliance, Identification, and Internalization: Three Processes of Attitude Change," *Journal of Conflict Resolution*, 2 (1958), 51–60.

Keller, Suzanne. "The Social World of the Urban Slum Child: Some Early Findings," *American Journal of Orthopsychiatry*, 33 (1963), 823–831.

Kelley, Harold H. "Two Functions of Reference Groups," in Swanson, et al., eds. (see below), *Readings in Social Psychology*, pp. 410–414.

Kemper, Theodore D. "Self-Conceptions and the Expectations of Significant Others," *Sociological Quarterly*, 7 (1966), 323–343.

Keniston, Kenneth. "Inburn: An American Ishmael," in White, ed. (see below), *The Study of Lives*, pp. 40–70.

———. *The Uncommitted: Alienated Youth in American Society*. New York: Dell, 1960.

———. *The Young Radicals: Notes on Committed Youth*. New York: Harcourt, Brace and World, 1968.

Kenyatta, Jomo. *Facing Mount Kenya*. New York: Vintage, 1962.

Kerckhoff, A. C., and T. C. McCormick. "Marginal Status and Marginal Personality," *Social Forces*, 34 (1955), 48–55.

Kerner, Otto. *Report of the National Advisory Commission on Civil Disorders*. New York: Bantam Books, 1968.

Killian, Lewis M., and Charles M. Grigg. "Urbanism, Race and Anomie," *American Journal of Sociology*, 67 (1962), 661–665.

Kinch, John W., ed. *Sociology in the World Today*. Reading, Mass.: Addison-Wesley, 1971.

Klapp, Orrin E. *Collective Search for Identity*. New York: Holt, Rinehart and Winston, 1969.

———. "The Fool As a Social Type," *American Journal of Sociology*, 55 (1949), 159–162.

Kluckhohn, Clyde. "The Study of Culture," in Coser and Rosenberg, eds. (see above), *Sociological Theory*, pp. 40–54.

———, and Henry A. Murray. "Personality Formation: The Determinants," in Kluckhohn, et al., eds (see below), *Personality in Nature, Society and Culture*, pp. 53–67.

———, et al., eds. *Personality in Nature, Society, and Culture*. New York: Knopf, 1955.

Koch, Sigmund, ed. *Psychology: The Study of a Science*, 1–6. New York: McGraw-Hill, 1963.

Kochman, Thomas. "'Rapping' in the Black Ghetto," in Feldman and Thielbar, eds. (see above), *Life Styles*, pp. 302–316.

Kovar, Lillian Cohen. *Faces of the Adolescent Girl*. Englewood Cliffs, N.J.: Prentice-Hall, 1968.

Kozol, Jonathan. *Death at an Early Age*. Boston: Houghton Mifflin, 1967.

Kramer, Judith R. *The American Minority Community*. New York: Thomas Y. Crowell, 1970.

Krieger, Alex D. "The Typological Concept," *American Antiquity*, 3 (1944), 271–288.

Kuhn, Manford H. "Major Trends in Symbolic Interaction Theory in the Past Twenty-five Years," *Sociological Quarterly*, 5 (1964), 61–84.

———. "Reference Group," in Gould and Kolb, eds. (see above), *A Dictionary of the Social Sciences*, pp. 580–581.

————. "Reference Group Reconsidered," *Sociological Quarterly*, 5 (1964), 5–21.

Kvaraceus, William C. *Negro Self-Concept: Implications for School and Citizenship*. Medford, Mass.: Lincoln Filene Center for Citizenship and Public Affairs, Tufts University, 1964.

————, and Walter B. Miller, et al. *Delinquent Behavior: Culture and the Individual*. Washington, D.C.: National Education Association, 1959.

Laing, R. D., and A. Esterson. *Sanity, Madness, and the Family*, 2nd ed. New York: Basic Books, 1971.

Leary, Timothy. *Interpersonal Diagnosis of Personality*. New York: Ronald Press, 1957.

Lee, Alfred McClung. "On Context and Relevance," in Glass and Staude, eds. (see above), *Humanistic Society*, pp. 247–257.

Lee, Dorothy. *Freedom and Culture*. Englewood Cliffs, N.J.: Prentice-Hall, 1968.

Lefcourt, Herbert M. "Internal vs. External Control of Reinforcements: A Review," *Psychological Bulletin*, 65 (1966), 206–220.

————, and Gordon W. Ladwig. "The American Negro: A Problem in Expectancies," *Journal of Personality and Social Psychology*, 1 (1965), 377–380.

Lefton, Mark. "Race, Expectations, and Anomie," *Social Forces*, 46 (1968), 347–352.

Leighton, Alexander H., John A. Clausen, and Robert N. Wilson. *Explorations in Social Psychiatry*. New York: Basic Books, 1957.

Lennard, Henry L., and Arnold Bernstein. *Patterns in Human Interaction: An Introduction to Clinical Sociology*. San Francisco: Jossey-Bass, 1969.

Levinson, Daniel J. "Role, Personality, and Social Structure," in Coser and Rosenberg, eds. (see above), *Sociological Theory*, pp. 284–297.

Levita, David. *The Concept of Identity*. New York: Basic Books, 1965.

Liebow, Elliot. *Tally's Corner*. Boston: Little, Brown, 1967.

Lindesmith, Alfred R., and Anselm L. Strauss. *Social Psychology*. New York: Holt, 1956.

Lindzey, Gardner, and Elliot Aronson, eds. *The Handbook of Social Psychology*, 2. Reading, Mass.: Addison-Wesley, 1969.

————, and Calvin S. Hall. *Theories of Personality: Primary Sources and Research*. New York: Wiley, 1965.

Lipman, Matthew. "Some Aspects of Simmel's Conception of the Individual," in Wolff, ed. (see below), *Essays on Sociology, Philosophy, and Aesthetics*, pp. 119–138.

Loomis, Charles P., and Zona K. Loomis, "Robert K. Merton as a Structural Analyst," in their *Modern Social Theories: Selected American Writers* (Princeton: D. Van Nostrand, 1961), pp. 246–326.

Lott, A. J., and Bernice E. Lott. *Negro and White Youth: A Psychological Study in a Border-State Community*. New York: Holt, Rinehart, and Winston, 1963.

Lowry, Ritchie P., and Robert P. Rankin. *Sociology: The Science of Society*. New York: Scribner's, 1969.

Lyman, Stanford M. *The Black American in Sociological Thought*. New York: Capricorn Books, 1972.

——, and Marvin B. Scott. "Coolness in Everyday Life," in Truzzi, ed. (see below), *Sociology and Everyday Life*, pp. 92–101.

Lynd, Helen M. "Clues to Identity," in Ruitenbeek, ed. (see below), *Varieties of Modern Social Theory*, pp. 3–54.

——. *On Shame and the Search for Identity*. New York: Harcourt, 1958.

Maccoby, Eleanor E., Theodore M. Newcomb, and Eugene L. Hartley, eds. *Readings in Social Psychology*. New York: Holt, Rinehart, and Winston, 1958.

MacIver, R. M. "Subjective Meaning in the Social Situation," in Coser and Rosenberg, eds. (see above), *Sociological Theory*, pp. 265–270.

Mack, Raymond, and John Pease. *Sociology and Social Life*. New York: Van Nostrand, 1973.

Malcolm X. *The Autobiography of Malcolm X*. New York: Grove Press, 1964.

Manis, Jerome G., and Bernard N. Meltzer, eds. *Symbolic Interaction: A Reader in Social Psychology*. Boston: Allyn and Bacon, 1967.

Mann, Thomas. *Confessions of Felix Krull, Confidence Man*. New York: Knopf, 1955.

Marcia, J. E. "Development and Validation of Ego Identity Status," *Journal of Abnormal and Social Psychology*, 3 (1966), 551–558.

——. "Ego Identity Status: Relationship to Change in Self-Esteem, General Maladjustment, and Authoritarianism," *Journal of Personality*, 35 (1967), 119–133.

Martin, D. G. "Consistency of Self-descriptions under Different Role Sets in Neurotic and Normal Adults and Adolescents," *Journal of Abnormal Psychology*, 74 (1969), 173–176.

Marx, Gary T. "The Psychological Context of Militancy," in Guterman, ed. (see above), *Black Psyche*, pp. 191–214.

Maslow, Abraham. *Motivation and Personality*. New York: Harper and Row, 1954.

——. *Toward A Psychology of Being*. Princeton: Van Nostrand, 1968.

Maas, Henry S., and Joseph A. Kuypers. *From Thirty to Seventy: A Forty-Year Longitudinal Study of Adults' Life Styles and Personality*. San Francisco: Jossey-Bass, 1974.

Masterson, James F. *The Psychiatric Dilemma of Adolescence*. London: Little, Brown, 1967.

Matza, David. *Becoming Deviant*. Englewood Cliffs, N.J.: Prentice-Hall, 1969.

——. *Delinquency and Drift*. New York: Wiley, 1964.

——, and Gresham M. Sykes. "Juvenile Delinquency and Subterranean Values," in Feldman and Thielbar, eds. (see above), *Life Styles*, pp. 374–383.

May, Rollo, E. Angell, and H. P. Ellenberger, eds. *Existence: A New Dimension in Psychiatry and Psychology*. New York: Basic Books, 1958.

McCall, George F., Michael J. McCall, Norman K. Denzin, Gerald D. Suttles, and Suzanne B. Kurth, eds. *Social Relationships*. Chicago: Aldine, 1970.

———, and J. L. Simmons. *Identities and Interactions: An Examination of Human Associations in Everyday Life*. New York: Free Press, 1966.

McCarthy, John D., and William L. Yancey. "Uncle Tom and Mr. Charlie: Metaphysical Pathos in the Study of Racism and Personal Disorganization," *American Journal of Sociology*, 76 (1971), 648–672.

McCord, William. "The Personality of Social Deviants," in Norbeck, et al., eds. (see below), *The Study of Personality*, pp. 311–325.

———, John Howard, Bernard Friedberg, and Edwin Harwood. *Life Styles in the Black Ghetto*. New York: W. W. Norton, 1969.

Mead, George Herbert. *Mind, Self and Society*. Chicago: University of Chicago Press, 1934.

———. *On Social Psychology*. Chicago: University of Chicago Press, 1964.

Melville, Herman. *The Confidence Man*. New York: W. W. Norton, 1971.

Meltzer, Bernard N. "Mead's Social Psychology," in Manis and Meltzer, eds. (see above), *Symbolic Interaction*, pp. 4–22.

Merrill, Francis E. "The Self and the Other: An Emerging Field of Social Problems," *Social Problems*, 4 (1957), 200–207.

Merton, Robert K. "The Role Set: Problems in Sociological Theory," *British Journal of Sociology*, 8 (1957), 106–120.

———. *Social Theory and Social Structure*. New York: Free Press, 1957.

———, et al., eds. *Sociology Today: Problems and Prospects*. New York: Basic Books, 1959.

———, and Paul F. Lazarsfeld, eds. *Continuities in Social Research: Studies in the Scope and Method of "The American Soldier,"* 2nd ed. New York: Arno, 1974.

———, and Robert Nisbet, eds. *Contemporary Social Problems*. New York: Harcourt Brace, Jovanovich, 1971.

Miller, Daniel R. "The Study of Social Relationships: Situation, Identity, and Social Interaction," in Koch, ed. (see above), *Psychology: The Study of a Science*, 5, pp. 639–737.

Miller, Elizabeth W. *The Negro in America: A Bibliography*. Cambridge, Mass.: Harvard University Press, 1966.

Miller, S. M. "The Outlook of Working-Class Youth," in Havighurst, et al., eds. (see above), *Society and Education*, pp. 232–240.

Miller, Walter B. *The Cool World*. Boston: Little, Brown, 1959.

———. "Lower Class Culture as a Generating Milieu of Gang Delinquency," *Journal of Social Issues*, 14 (1958), 5–19.

Mills, C. Wright. *The Sociological Imagination*. New York: Grove Press, 1959.

———, ed. *Images of Man*. New York: Braziller, 1960.

Minuchin, Salvador. *Families of the Slums: An Exploration of Their Structures and Their Treatment*. New York: Basic Books, 1967.

Mishler, Elliot G., and Nancy E. Waxler. *Interaction in Families: An Experimental Study of Family Processes and Schizophrenia*. New York: Wiley, 1968.

Mitchell, John. "Cons, Square-Johns, and Rehabilitation," in Biddle and Thomas, eds. (see above), *Role Theory*, pp. 207–12.

Miyamoto, S. Frank. "Self, Motivation, and Symbolic Interactionist Theory," in Shibutani, ed. (see below), *Human Nature and Collective Behavior*, pp. 271–285.

———, and Sanford M. Dornbusch. "A Test of Interactionist Hypotheses of Self-Conception," *American Journal of Sociology*, 61 (1956), 366–402.

Morris, Charles W. *Varieties of Human Value*. Chicago: University of Chicago Press, 1956.

Moynihan, Daniel P. *The Negro Family: The Case for National Action*. Washington, D.C.: Government Printing Office, 1967.

Murray, Henry A., and Clyde Kluckhohn. "Outline of a Conception of Personality," in Kluckhohn, et al., eds. (see above), *Personality in Nature, Society, and Culture*, pp. 3–49.

Mussen, P. H., and M. C. Jones. "Self Concepts and Motivations of Early and Late Developing Adolescents," *Child Development*, 28 (1965), 243–258.

———, J. J. Conger, and J. Kagan, eds. *Readings in Child Development and Personality*. New York: Harper and Row, 1965.

Muus, R. E. *Theories of Adolescence*. New York: Random House, 1962.

Natanson, Maurice, ed. *Philosophy of the Social Sciences*. New York: Random House, 1963.

National Commission for Children and Youth. *Social Dynamite*. Washington, D.C.: National Commission for Children and Youth, 1961.

Newcomb, Theodore M. *Social Psychology*. New York: Dryden Press, 1950.

Nisbet, Robert. *Sociology as An Art Form*. New York: Oxford University Press, 1976.

Norbeck, Edward, et al., eds. *The Study of Personality: An Interdisciplinary Appraisal*. New York: Holt, Rinehart, and Winston, 1968.

Olsen, Marvin E. *The Process of Social Organization*. New York: Holt, Rinehart, and Winston, 1968.

Pallister, Helen. *The Negative or Withdrawal Attitude: A Study in Personality Organization*. New York: Archives of Psychology, 1933.

Papajohn, John, and John Spiegel. *Transactions in Families: A Modern Approach for Resolving Cultural and Generational Conflicts*. San Francisco: Jossey-Bass, 1975.

Park, Robert E. *Society*. New York: Free Press, 1955.

———, and Ernest W. Burgess. *Introduction to the Science of Society*. Chicago: University of Chicago Press, 1937.

Parker, Beulah. *A Mingled Yarn: Chronicle of A Troubled Family*. New Haven: Yale University Press, 1972.

Parsons, Talcott. *The Social System*. New York: Free Press, 1951.

———, and Robert F. Bales. *Family, Socialization, and Interaction Process*. Glencoe: Free Press, 1955.

———, and Kenneth B. Clark, eds. *The Negro-American*. Boston: Beacon Press, 1965.

Pear, T. H. *Personality, Appearance, and Speech*. London: Allen and Unwin, 1957.

Pearson, Gerald H. *Adolescence and the Conflict of Generations*. New York: W. W. Norton, 1958.

Perlman, Helen H. *Persona: Social Role and Personality*. Chicago: University of Chicago Press, 1968.

Perry, Helen Swick, ed. *The Collected Works of Harry Stack Sullivan, M.D.*, Vol. 2. New York: W. W. Norton, 1964.

Perry, John A., and Murray P. Seidler, eds. *Contemporary Society*. San Francisco: Canfield Press, 1972.

Pettigrew, Thomas F. "Negro American Personality: Why Isn't More Known?" *Journal of Social Issues*, 20 (1964), 4–23.

———. *A Profile of the Negro American*. New York: Van Nostrand Reinhold, 1964.

Pfuetze, Paul E. *The Social Self*. New York: Bookman Associates, 1954.

Pollak, O. "Design of a Model of Healthy Family Relationships as a Basis for Evaluative Research," *Social Services Review*, 31 (1967), 369–376.

———. *Integrating Sociological and Psychological Concepts: An Exploration in Child Psychotherapy*. New York: Russell Sage Foundation, 1956.

Poussaint, Alvin. "Negro Self-Hate," *New York Times Sunday Magazine*, August 20, 1967, p. 52.

Proshansky, Harold, and Peggy Newton. "The Nature and Meaning of Negro Self-Identity," in Deutsch, et al., eds. (see above), *Social Class, Race, and Psychological Development*, pp. 178–218.

Quarantelli, E. L., and Joseph Cooper. "Self-Conceptions and Others: A Further Test of Meadian Hypotheses," *Sociological Quarterly*, 7 (1966), 281–297.

Rainwater, Lee. "The Crucible of Identity: The Negro Lower-Class Family," in Parsons and Clark, eds. (see above), *The Negro-American*, pp. 160–204.

———. "Work and Identity in the Lower Class," in Warner, ed., (see below), *Planning for a Nation of Cities*, pp. 105–133.

———, Richard P. Coleman, and Gerald Handel. *Workingman's Wife*. New York: Oceana, 1959.

————, and William L. Yancey. *The Moynihan Report and the Politics of Controversy*. Cambridge, Mass.: M.I.T. Press, 1967.

Ransford, H. Edward. "Isolation, Powerlessness, and Violence," *American Journal of Sociology*, 73 (1968), 581–591.

Redding, S. *On Being Negro in America*. Indianapolis: Bobbs-Merrill, 1951.

Reckless, Walter C., S. Dinitz, and E. Murray. "Self-Concept as an Insulator against Delinquency," *American Sociological Review*, 21 (1956), 744–746.

Redlich, Frederick C., and Daniel X. Freedman. *Theory and Practice of Psychiatry*. New York: Basic Books, 1966.

Reeder, Leo G., George A. Donahue, and Arturo Biblarz. "Conceptions of Self and Others," *American Journal of Sociology*, 66 (1960), 153–159.

Riesman, David, Nathan Glazer, and Reuel Denney. *The Lonely Crowd: A Study of the Changing American Character*. New Haven: Yale University Press, 1961.

Riessman, Frank. *The Culturally Deprived Child*. New York: Harper and Row, 1962.

Rodman, Hyman. "The Lower-Class Value Stretch," *Social Forces*, 42 (1963), 405–415.

Roebuck, J., and M. L. Cadwaller. "The Negro Armed Robber as a Criminal Type: The Construction and Application of a Typology," *Pacific Sociological Review*, 4 (1961), 21–26.

Rogers, Carl. "A Theory of Therapy, Personality, and Interpersonal Relationships, as Developed in the Client-Centered Framework," in Koch, ed. (see above), *Psychology: The Study of a Science*, 3, pp. 184–256.

Rohrer, J. J., and M. S. Edmonson. *The Eighth Generation*. New York: Harper, 1960.

Rose, Arnold M., ed. *Human Behavior and Social Processes: An Interactionist Approach*. Boston: Houghton Mifflin, 1962.

————. *The Negro in America*. Boston: Beacon Press, 1948.

Rose, Jerry D. "The Role of the Other in Self-Evaluation," *Sociological Quarterly*, 10 (1969), 470–479.

Rose, Peter I. "The Black Experience: Issues and Images," in his *Seeing Ourselves: Introductory Readings in Sociology*, New York: Knopf, 1972, pp. 257–269.

Rosen, Bernard C. "Conflicting Group Membership: A Study of Parent-Peer Group Cross-Pressures," *American Sociological Review*, 20 (1955), 155–161.

————. "The Reference Group Approach to the Parental Factor in Attitudes and Behavior Formation," *Social Forces*, 34 (1955), 137–144.

Rosenberg, Morris. *Society and the Adolescent Self Image*. Princeton: Princeton University Press, 1965.

Rosenman, Stanley. "The Similarity and the Coding of the Self-Concept and the Other-Concept," *Journal of General Psychology*, 56 (1957), 243–250.

Rosenthal, Robert A., Bernard E. Bruce, and Florence S. Ladd. *Pathways to Identity: Aspects of the Experience of Black Youth (Final Report)*. Harvard Graduate School of Education, 1971.

————, et al. *Different Strokes: Pathways to Maturity in the Boston Ghetto: A Report to the Ford Foundation*. Boulder, Colo.: Westview Press, 1976.

Rosenthal, Robert S., and Lenore Jacobsen. *Pygmalion in the Classroom: Teacher Expectation and Pupil's Intellectual Development*. New York: Holt, Rinehart, and Winston, 1968.

Ross, A. O. "Ego Identity and the Social Order," *Psychological Monographs*, 76 (1962), 1–33 (total no. 542).

Rotter, Julian B. "Generalized Expectancies for Internal versus External Control of Reinforcement," *Psychological Monographs*, 80 (1966), 1–28.

Rubin, Lillian. *Worlds of Pain*. New York: Basic Books, 1976.

Rubington, Earl, and Martin S. Weinberg. *Deviance: The Interactionist Perspective*. New York: Macmillan, 1973.

Ruitenbeek, Hendrik M. *Varieties of Modern Social Theory*. New York: E. P. Dutton, 1963.

Sanford, Nevitt. "Personality: Its Place in Psychology," in Koch, ed. (see above), *Psychology: The Study of a Science*, 5, pp. 488–592.

————. *Self and Society: Social Change and Individual Development*. New York: Atherton Press, 1966.

Sarbin, Theodore R. "Role Enactment," in Biddle and Thomas, eds. (see above), *Role Theory*, pp. 195–200.

————, and Norman L. Farberow. "Contributions to Role Taking Theory," in Dyal, ed. (see above), *Readings in Psychology*, pp. 361–372.

————, and Donal S. Jones, "An Experimental Analysis of Role Behavior," in Maccoby, et al., eds. (see above), *Readings in Social Psychology*, pp. 465–471.

Scanzoni, John. *The Black Family in Modern Society*. Boston: Allyn and Bacon, 1971.

Scarpitti, F. R., Ellen Murray, S. Dinitz, and Walter C. Reckless. "The 'Good' Boy in a High Delinquency Area: Four Years Later," *American Sociological Review*, 25 (1960), 555–558.

Schlesinger, Myron P. "Self-Perception, Identity, and Accommodation in the Ghetto and in the New York City Area," unpublished manuscript, Vocational Rehabilitation Center, Queens Hospital Center, Hicksville, New York.

Schmitt, Raymond L. *The Reference-Other Orientation: An Extension of the Reference Group Concept*. Carbondale, Ill.: Southern Illinois University Press, 1972.

Schon, A. L. *Poor Kids*. New York: Basic Books, 1966.

Schultz, David A. *Coming Up Black: Patterns of Ghetto Socialization.* Englewood Cliffs, N.J.: Prentice-Hall, 1969.

Schutz, Alfred. "Concept and Theory Formation in the Social Sciences," in Natanson, ed. (see above), *Philosophy of the Social Sciences,* pp. 231–249.

Schwartz, Charlotte Green. "Clinical Sociology—Qualitative Sociology as Practice in Everyday Life," *New England Sociologist* (Fall 1978), 4–9.

Sears, Robert R., Lucy Rau, and Richard Alpert. *Identification and Child Rearing.* Stanford: Stanford University Press, 1965.

Secord, Paul F., and Carl W. Backman. "Personality Theory and the Problem of Stability and Change in Individual Behavior: An Interpersonal Approach," *Psychological Review,* 68 (1961), 21–33.

Seeman, Melvin. "On the Meaning of Alienation," in Coser and Rosenberg, eds. (see above), *Sociological Theory,* pp. 524–538.

Seidman, Jerome S., ed. *The Adolescent: A Book of Readings.* New York: Holt, Rinehart, and Winston, 1960.

Shaw, Clifford R. *The Jack-Roller: A Delinquent Boy's Own Story.* Chicago: University of Chicago Press, 1930.

Sherif, Muzafer. *Social Interaction: Processes and Products.* Chicago: Aldine, 1967.

Sherwood, John. "Self-Identity and Referent Others," *Sociometry,* 28 (1965), 66–81.

Shibutani, Tamotsu, "Reference Groups as Perspectives," *American Journal of Sociology,* 60 (1955), 562–569.

———. *Society and Personality: An Interactionist Approach to Social Psychology.* Englewood Cliffs, N.J.: Prentice-Hall, 1961.

———, ed. *Human Nature and Collective Behavior: Papers in Honor of Herbert Blumer.* Englewood Cliffs, N.J.: Prentice-Hall, 1970.

Shils, Edward A., and H. A. Finch. *Max Weber on the Methodology of the Social Sciences.* New York: Free Press, 1949.

Shoemaker, Sydney. *Self-Knowledge and Self-Identity.* Ithaca, N.Y.: Cornell University Press, 1963.

Short, James F., Jr., and Fred L. Strodtbeck. *Group Process and Gang Delinquency.* Chicago: University of Chicago Press, 1965.

Shostak, Arthur B., and William Gomberg, eds. *Blue Color World.* Englewood Cliffs, N.J.: Prentice-Hall, 1964.

Silberman, Charles E. *Crisis in Black and White.* New York: Random House, 1964.

Simmel, Georg. *Conflict and the Web of Group Affiliations.* Glencoe: Free Press, 1955.

———. *Essays on Sociology, Philosophy, and Aesthetics by Georg Simmel et al.,* ed., Kurt H. Wolff. New York: Harper Torchbooks, 1965.

———. "Types of Social Relationships by Degree of Reciprocal Knowledge of Their Participants," in Kurt H. Wolff, ed., trans., *The Sociology of Georg Simmel,* (New York: Free Press, 1950).

Sites, Paul. *Control: The Basis of Social Order*. Port Washington, N.Y.: Dunellen, 1973.

Sorokin, Pitirim. *Contemporary Social Theories*. New York: Harper and Row, 1928.

Sowell, Thomas. *Black Education: Myths and Tragedies*. New York: McKay, 1972.

Spear, Allen H. *Black Chicago: The Making of a Negro Ghetto, 1890–1920*. Chicago: University of Chicago Press, 1967.

Spiegel, John P. "The Resolution of Role Conflict within the Family," in Bell and Vogel, eds. (see above), *A Modern Introduction to the Family*, pp. 361–381.

Spitzer, Stephan P., ed. *The Sociology of Personality: An Enduring Problem in Psychology*. New York: Van Nostrand Reinhold, 1969.

———, Carl Couch, and John Stratton. *The Assessment of the Self*. Iowa City, Iowa: Sernoll, 1971.

———, and Robert M. Swanson. "Sociological Perspectives on the Person," in Spitzer, ed. (see above), *The Sociology of Personality*, pp. 189–207.

Spranger, Edouard. *Types of Man*. Halle: Niemeyer, 1928.

Staples, Robert, ed. *The Black Family: Essays and Studies*. Belmont, Calif.: Wadsworth, 1971.

Stein, Morris I. "Explorations in Typology," in White, ed. (see below), *The Study of Lives*. New York: Atherton, 1963.

Stone, Gregory P., and Harvey A. Farberman. *Social Psychology through Symbolic Interaction*. Waltham, Mass.: Ginn-Blaisdell, 1970.

Stonequist, Everett V. *The Marginal Man*. New York: Scribner's, 1937.

Strauss, Anselm L., ed. *George Herbert Mead on Social Psychology*. Chicago: University of Chicago Press, 1964.

———. *Mirrors and Masks: The Search for Identity*. New York: Macmillan, 1959.

———. *Negotiations: Varieties, Contexts, Processes, and Social Order*. San Francisco: Jossey-Bass, 1978.

———, ed. *The Social Psychology of George Herbert Mead*. Chicago: University of Chicago Press, 1956.

Stryker, Sheldon. "Identity Salience and Role Performance: The Relevance of Symbolic Interaction Theory for Family Research," *Journal of Marriage and the Family*, 30 (1968), 558–564.

Sullivan, Harry Stack. *The Interpersonal Theory of Psychiatry*. New York: W. W. Norton, 1953.

Sutherland, E. H. *Principles of Criminology*, 5th ed., rev. ed., Donald R. Cressey. New York: Lippincott, 1955.

Sutherland, Robert L. *Color, Class, and Personality*. Washington, D.C.: American Council on Education, 1942.

Suttles, Gerald D. *The Social Order of the Slum: Ethnicity and Territory in the Inner City*. Chicago: University of Chicago Press, 1968.

Swanson, Guy, et al., eds. *Readings in Social Psychology*. New York: Holt, 1952.

Symonds, P. N., and A. R. Jensen. *From Adolescent to Adult*. New York: Columbia University Press, 1961.

Szasz, Thomas. *The Myth of Mental Illness: Foundations of a Theory of Personal Conduct*, rev. ed. New York: Harper and Row, 1974.

Terkel, Studs. *Hard Times*. New York: Pantheon, 1970.

———. *Working*. New York: Avon, 1975.

Thomas, Piri. *Down These Mean Streets*. New York: Knopf, 1967.

———. *Savior, Savior, Hold My Hand*. New York: Knopf, 1972.

Thomas, W. I. "Three Types of Personality," in Mills, ed. (see above), *Images of Man*, pp. 406–409.

Thompson, James D., and Donald R. Van Houten. *The Behavioral Sciences: An Interpretation*. Reading, Mass.: Addison-Wesley, 1970.

Truzzi, Marcello, ed. *Sociology and Everyday Life*. Englewood Cliffs, N.J.: Prentice-Hall, 1968.

Turner, Ralph H. "Role-Taking, Role Standpoint, and Reference Group Behavior," in Biddle and Thomas, eds. (see above), *Role Theory*, pp. 151–159.

Valentine, Bettylou. *Hustling and Other Hard Work*. New York: Free Press, 1978.

Valentine, C. W. *The Normal Child*. Baltimore: Penguin, 1956.

Videbeck, Richard. "Self-Conception and the Reactions of Others," *Sociometry*, 23 (1960), 351–359.

Warner, Sam Bass, Jr., ed. *Planning for a Nation of Cities*. Cambridge, Mass.: M.I.T. Press, 1966.

Warner, W. Lloyd. *Color and Human Nature: Negro Personality Development in a Northern City*. Washington, D.C.: American Council on Education, 1941.

Watzlawick, Paul, and John H. Weakland, eds. *The Interactional View*. New York: W. W. Norton, 1977.

Weber, Max. "Social Action and Social Interaction," in Coser and Rosenberg, eds. (see above), *Sociological Theory*, pp. 66–71.

———. "Subjective Meaning in the Social Situation," in Coser and Rosenberg, eds. (see above), *Sociological Theory*, pp. 235–246.

Weinstein, Deena, and Michael Weinstein. *Roles of Man: An Introduction to the Social Sciences*. Hinsdale, Ill.: The Dryden Press, 1972.

Weinstein, Eugene A., and Paul Deutschberger. "Tasks, Bargains, and Identities in Social Interaction," *Social Forces*, 42 (1964), 451–456.

Weiss, Robert S. "The Fund of Sociability," in Kinch, ed. (see above), *Sociology in the World Today*, pp. 29–37.

Weissberg, Charlotte. "Self-Evaluations and School Withdrawal: The Subjective Views of Lower-Income Black Adolescents," unpublished doctoral dissertation, University of Chicago, 1973.

Wheelis, A. *The Quest for Identity*. New York: W. W. Norton, 1958.

White, Robert W. *The Abnormal Personality.* New York: Ronald Press, 1956.

————. *The Enterprise of Living: A View of Personal Growth.* New York: Holt, Rinehart, and Winston, 1977.

————. *Lives in Progress.* New York: Dryden Press, 1952.

————. "Motivation Reconsidered: The Concept of Competence," *Psychological Review,* 66 (1959), 297–333.

————, ed., *The Study of Lives: Essays on Personality in Honor of Henry A. Murray.* New York: Atherton, 1963.

Whyte, William Foote. *Street Corner Society.* Chicago: University of Chicago Press, 1953.

Wilson, Everett K. *Sociology: Rules, Roles, and Relationships.* Homewood, Ill.: Dorsey Press.

Wilson, Robert N. "Personality as Creative Struggle," in White, ed. (see above), *The Study of Lives,* pp. 348–363.

Winter, David, et al. "The Classic Personal Style," *Journal of Abnormal and Social Psychology,* 67 (1963), 254–265.

Wirth, Louis. "Clinical Sociology," *American Journal of Sociology,* 371 (1931), 49–66.

Witenberg, Earl G., ed. *Interpersonal Explorations in Psychoanalysis.* New York: Basic Books, 1973.

Woelfel, Joseph, and Archibald O. Haller. "Significant Others, The Self-Reflexive Act and the Attitude Formation Process," *American Sociological Review,* 36 (1971), 74–87.

Wolfe, Bernard. *The Late Risers.* New York: Random House, 1954.

Wolff, Kurt H., ed. *Essays on Sociology, Philosophy, and Aesthetics, by Georg Simmel.* New York: Harper Torchbooks, 1965.

————. *The Sociology of Georg Simmel.* New York: Free Press, 1950.

Wright, Richard. *Black Boy.* New York: Harper, 1945.

————. "The Psychological Reactions of Oppressed Peoples," in his *White Man, Listen!* Garden City, N.Y.: Doubleday, Anchor, 1957.

Wrong, Dennis. "The Oversocialized Conception of Man in Modern Sociology," in Coser and Rosenberg, eds. (see above), *Sociological Theory,* pp. 112–122.

Wylie, R. C. *The Self Concept: A Critical Survey of Pertinent Research.* Lincoln: University of Nebraska Press, 1961.

Witmer, H., et al., eds. *New Perspectives on Delinquency.* Washington, D.C.: Government Printing Office, 1956.

Yarrow, Marian R., and B. Lande. "Personality Correlates of Differential Reactions to Minority Group-Belonging," *Journal of Social Psychology,* 38 (1953), 253–272.

Zinn, Howard. "The Battle-Scarred Youngsters," *Nation,* 197 (1963), 193–197.

Znaniecki, Florian. "Subjective Meaning in the Social Situation, II," in Coser and Rosenberg, eds. (see above), *Sociological Theory,* pp. 223–228.

Index

LIBRARY OF CONGRESS CATALOGING IN PUBLICATION DATA

Mancini, Janet K.
  Strategic styles.

  Bibliography: p.
  Includes index.
  1. Afro-American youth—Massachusetts—Boston—
Case studies. 2. Roxbury, Mass.—Social conditions. 3. Boston—Social conditions—Case studies.
4. Afro-American youth—Case studies. 5. Adjustment (Psychology)—Case studies. I. Title.
F74.R9M36   302   79-56773
ISBN 0-87451-179-8